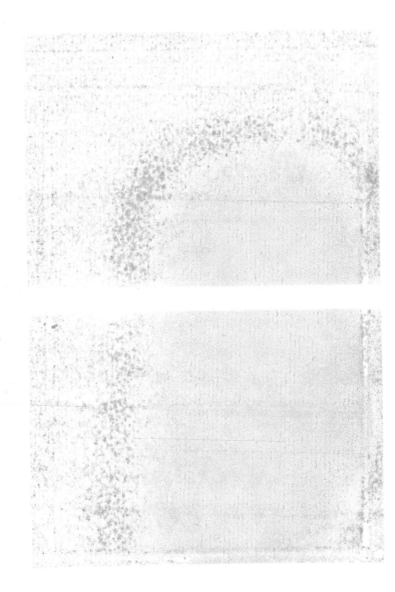

ENGLISH RECUSANT LITERATURE
1558–1640

Selected and Edited by
D. M. ROGERS

Volume 276

WILLIAM WARMINGTON
A Moderate Defence
1612

ST. JEROME
Certaine Selected Epistles
1630

WILLIAM WARMINGTON

A Moderate Defence of the
Oath of Allegiance
1612

The Scolar Press
1975

ISBN 0 85967 277 8

Published and printed in Great Britain by
The Scolar Press Limited, 59-61 East Parade,
Ilkley, Yorkshire and
39 Great Russell Street,
London WC1

NOTE

The following works are reproduced (original size) with permission:

1) William Warmington, *A moderate defence*, 1612, from a copy in the Bodleian Library, by permission of the Curators.
References: Allison and Rogers 882; STC 25076.

2) St. Jerome, *Certaine selected epistles*, 1630, from a copy in Cambridge University Library, by permission of the Syndics.
References: Allison and Rogers 412; STC 14502.

A MODERATE

DEFENCE OF THE

OATH OF ALLEGIANCE:

Wherein the Author proueth the
said Oath to be most lawful, notwithstanding
the Popes Breues prohibiting the same; and solueth the
chiefest obiections that are vsually made against it; perswading
the Catholickes not to resist souerzigne Authoritie
in refusing it.

Together with the Oration of *Sixtus* 5. in the Consistory
at Rome, vpon the murther of *Henrie* 3. the
French King by a Friar.

Whereunto also is annexed strange Reports or
newes from Rome.

By WILLIAM WARMINGTON Catholicke Priest,
and Oblate of the holy congregation of S. Ambrose.

IEREM. 4.
Iurabis, Viuit Dominus, in veritate, in iudicio, & in iustitia.
Thou shalt sweare, Our Lord liueth, in truth, in iudgement,
and in iustice.

Permissu Superiorum.
An. Dom. 1 6 1 2.

An Admonition to the Reader.

THe purpose of the Author in this Treatise is to manifest vnto such as imbrace the Romaine faith, that they may take the Oath of allegiance vnto his Maiestie without any preiudice vnto the same. And therefore if in this his ensuing discourse he hath inserted any peculiar doctrines of the Church of Rome, those that are of an aduerse perswasion ought not to take offence, but rather make true vse thereof; and haue iust cause to acknowledge the clement and moderate proceeding of the State herein.

THE PREFACE OF
THE AVTHOR TO THE
READER.

HEN by the prouidence of Almightie God, (courteous Reader) who sweetly disposeth all things, I was by two Pursuiuants apprehended the 24. of March 1607. after our English accompt, and committed to the Clinke by the Lord Bishop of London on the 26. of the same moneth, 1608; I entred somewhat more deepely into the consideration of the controuersie of the Oath of allegiance, then before, whilest I was at libertie, I had done. And presently consulting with some of my brethren whom I found there prisoners before my comming, I thought it very expedient to informe the Popes Holinesse of the lamentable estate of our countrie, what miseries and imminent dangers such Catholikes, as should refuse the Oath of allegiance, were like to fall into by reason of his Breues prohibiting them to take it; what diuision among Catholickes, what perturbation they were vndoubtedly to breed in the Church of England, (our dread Soueraigne being thereby not without iust cause exasperated) hoping by such meanes to procure a remedy before the malady

¶ 2   grew

grew too desperate. But they more prudent, and better experienced in such like Romane informations then my selfe, thought it better in their iudgements, and more expedient, with patience to expect future euents from Rome, and not so to proceed, as being to small or no purpose at all.

Hereupon I rested satisfied, though sorie in mind to consider the manifold euils that were like to ensue, as long as these two principall powers, Ecclesiasticall and ciuill, the Pope and our King, were at variance; and did not intend to set pen to paper of this matter; for that I knew my selfe the meanest among the rest of my brethren that had taken the Oath, and because I had (as I thought) in discharge of my particular duty, made sufficient proofe of my loyaltie towards his Maiestie, by accepting the Oath when it was required at my hands. In the end, aduised by a friend one of my brethren, to premeditate and prouide reasons for our taking it, to be sent to Rome; for it was to him more then probable he said, that in short space after we should receiue a commandement from his Holinesse so to do: and desirous withall to yeeld some satisfaction to the State, for the great scandall certaine of our brethren had giuen, by their perfidious inconstancie in taking the Oath, & anon after (being freed from troubles) relented and impugned (as hath bene reported) that which they seemed by their act to haue iudged lawfull: I resolued vpon mature consideration, to reduce into some method for helpe of my memorie, and satisfaction of a friend, certaine notes which in scattered papers I had collected cōcerning this matter: not intending yet to publish them for feare first of

offending

offending fome Catholikes, who pretending the Oath
to be vnlawfull (though they know not well wherein,
are ready with rafh cenfures to iudge and condemne,
before fentence of condemnation from the chiefe
Iudge be giuen: but efpecially I feared leſt I ſhould offend the Popes Holineſſe, who in his Breues hath either admoniſhed or prohibited all Catholikes to take
it, or to teach the lawfulneſſe thereof. At length knowing my intention to be, not to offend any one , nor to
contemne his Holineſſe commandement; but to aduance, what in me lyeth, the glory of God, by ſetting
downe ſincerely what in my iudgement is truth , and
perſwading euery Catholike ſubiect to render to *Cæſar*
thoſe things which are *Caſars*, to performe his dutie to
his Maieſtie in taking the Oath of allegiance, & to ſeeke
thereby to remoue the imputation of treachery and
treaſon : I held it my dutie both to God and man, to
breake ſilence, to caſt away this humane feare, and to
put on the mantle of charitie, *quæ foras mittit timorem.* 1. Ioh. 4
Howbeit (gentle reader) whileſt I meditated to go forward in theſe my labours, for the benefite of my brethren in Chriſt the Catholikes of England , ſodainly
that queſtiõ of our B. Sauiour, as it were to deterre me
from thẽ, came into my mind: *Quis ex vobis volens tur-*
rim ædificare: Which of you minding to build a tower,
doth not firſt ſit downe and recken the charges that
are neceſſarie, whether he haue to finiſh it: leſt, after he
hath laied the foundation, and is not able to finiſh it, all
that ſee it, begin to mocke him, ſaying , That this man
began to build , and he could not finiſh it? I forthwith
ſtayed, and caſt my accompts, that is , I weighed the
ſmall meanes I had to relieue me taking paines, my

A   infirme

infirme and feeble body, flender furniture of bookes, and many interrupted diftractions which my pouerty in prifon miniftred vnto me, and confidered whether I might be able to bring this fhort treatife to an end, & fo auoide that illufion : *This man beganne to build, and he could not finifh it* . Then though my meanes and abilitie euery way I knew to be fmall , yet trufting in the affiftance of almightie God, whofe glorie hereby I principally feeke, and is the chiefeft reafon of this my proceffe , I was by and by encouraged to attempt the defending of this Oath, (which I iudged farre beyond my talent) calling to remembrance that of the Prophet:

Pfal. 17. *In Deo meo tranfgrediar murum*: In my God I will paffe

Philip 4. ouer a wall. And the faying of S. *Paule*: *Omnia poffum in eo qui me confortat* . I can do all things in him (that is, through his helpe) that ftrengtheneth me: nothing

Phil. 2. v. 13. doubting alfo but, *Qui operatus eft in me velle, operaretur & perficere pro bona voluntate.* He that wrought in me to will, would likewife worke to accomplifh according to his good will . Vpon this confidence then of Gods affiftance, and for the inftruction of certaine Catholikes, who fimply beleeue the inconfiderat affertions of fome of their teachers; that fuch as take the Oath, do, and muft renounce the Popes fpirituall auctoritie of excommunication; and abiure or condemne for herefie a difputable pofition, to wit, that the Pope may depofe for herefie or apoftacie; which is moft vntrue, as will eafily appeare to him that without paffion and with iudgement fhall reade the Oath, or this my booke. Thefe and fuch like I exhort not to be too credulous in a matter of fo great moment as this is, giuing eare to euery one that will fay, it may not be taken, and can fhew

them

them no true reason why, nor in what point it is vnlawfull. If any list wilfully to reiect this my wholsome
counsaile, and will rather still giue eare to such as worke
their ouerthrow, what else can they in reason expect
but losse of lands and goods, perpetuall imprisonment
by the law, finall destruction to them and theirs, and
haply get no merite to benefite their soules, if his Maiestie (in clemencie excelling) be much exasperated?
which with carefull regard ought to be looked vnto,
because, *Qui nimium emungit, elicet sanguinem*: He that
straineth too much, draweth bloud. And may not his
Princely Maiestie be well sayd to excell in mercie and
clemencie, who first with speede vpon the discouery of
the Gun-powder treason, set forth his Proclamation
worthy neuer to be forgotte, therby to stay the furie of
the people, readie doubtlesse at that time to haue murthered all that should beare the name of Catholike,
without respecting who were innocet or who were nocent? & after, himselfe, as *Augustus Cæsar* in person pleaded for the life of a souldier, by his pen interpreting the
Oath of allegiace, pleaded as it were (to giue satisfactiõ
of his Royall meaning & intent of the law) for such as
he needed not so farre to condescend vnto? This rare &
worthy example of our most learned & most prudent
Prince, I must needes say, was to me, (the least among
many others) a very vrgent motiue to aduenture this
spirituall combat of defending according to my power
the Oath of allegiance. *Studiosè* (saith *Cicero*) *plerique*
facta Principum imitantur. Many follow diligently the
facts (or examples) of Princes. And if you reade the
booke of the Iudges, you shal see what encouragement
the example of *Gedeon* then Iudge of the Israelites

Suetonius in Augusto.

Cic. lib.1. Offic.

gaue

gaue vnto his fmall armie confifting but of 300 fouldiers, againft the Madianites their enemies in number almoft infinite . *Quod me videritis facere* (faid this great Captaine) *hoc facite:ingrediar partem caftrorum,& quod fecero fectamini*. What you fhall fee me do,do you the fame: I will enter into a part of the army , and what I fhall do , that do you follow: which they did, and obtained a happie victory . To whom can I better liken our mightie Monarch king *Iames* then to that worthy *Gedeon*? To me he feemeth likewife in effect to fay vnto his fubiects,What you fee me do,do ye the fame, as I haue begun to write , fo follow my example , endeuoring by pen to defend my right, which is all I require by the Oath. Who admireth not the profound wifdome and great pietie of his Maieftie, that he forefeeing the fatall and wilfull fall of diuers of his beloued fubiects,by reafon of the Popes Breues prohibiting the Oath of allegiance,would be pleafed for them & their good, to retire himfelfe from his princely recreations, to painefull labor both with mind and body,and to be the firft that with his pen writ a learned Apologie for the Oath? Wherein for fatisfaction of the perplexed confciences of fome of his fubiects, his Highneffe imitating our Bleffed Sauiour, *qui vult omnes faluos fieri,& neminem vult perire*,who is willing all fhould be fafe,& will haue none to perifh, interpreted his meaning to be,not to derogate from the Popes fpiritual authoritie, but to require his fubiects to performe their loyalty & naturall obedience onely in temporals,which is due by the law of God & nature;therby to draw all to his loue and their owne fafety.Vouchfafe then,beloued reader, to fpend fome idle and vacant time to perufe this fhort

Treatife,

Iudic.7.

1.Tim.4.

Treatife, written by thy welwiller for thy behoofe, to
confirme thee if thou take the Oath, or to perſwade
thee if thou feareſt it to be vnlawfull; the time thou
ſpendeſt herein may counteruaile thy paines. Doubt
nothing; if thou be Catholike, he is a Catholike prieſt
that writeth, and teacheth thee herein Catholike doctrine: if thou be none, yet giue this booke the reading,
aſſuring thy ſelfe this Author to be likewiſe a good &
loyall ſubieƈt, and as ſuch he purpoſeth to liue and die.
Feare God, honor the King, and in charitie pray for
me thy hearty welwiller.

Thine euer in Chriſt Ieſus

WILLIAM WARMINGTON
Prieſt.

A 3   A

A Table of the principall points contained in this Treatise.

Whe-

The

TO

TO THE CATHO-
LICKES OF ENGLAND.

Eloued brethren in Chriſt Ieſus: Whereas the Kings moſt excellent Maieſtie, being the true, lawful, and right inheritour to the Crowne and Realme of England, by the proui-dence of almightie God entred and poſſeſſed the ſame with tranquillity and peace, and the great applauſe of all his ſubieſts, as well Catholickes as Proteſtants, or others of different ſeſts and opinions: his Highneſſe, as it were to requite their dutifull affeſtion, forthwith gaue great hope of a moſt happie and proſperous regiment; and out of his bountie and clemencie extended many his moſt royall fa-uours indifferently vpon all, till ſuch time as ſome of the one ſort (to wit, a few giddie headed, deſperate, and diſloyall Catholicks aſſociated with certaine of the *Societie*) prouo-ked his wrath and indignation againſt them, yea and all the profeſſors of the ſame religion for their faſt. Who was not moued (as all men will confeſſe) without iuſt cauſe, for that they (viz. Catholickes) onely either concealed, or moſt bar-barouſly attempted in that helliſh-like manner of gunpow-der fire (the memorie whereof muſt needs remaine for euer moſt grieuous to all true hearted Catholike ſubieſts) the cruell murther of ſo many worthie Commons, and Noble perſonages, in Parliament aſſembled; yea of the moſt to-wardly and innocent yong Prince, the Queene, and King himſelfe: and then ſoone after alſo had followed vndoub-tedly the deſolation, ruine, and deſtruſtion of the whole

B   realme

realme of England.

Hereupon by the generall confent of all three eftates and the Kings Maieftie, it was thought neceffarie, an Oath of allegeance in fuch forme fhould be framed and enacted, as Catholikes (for whom chiefly it was made) fhould haue no caufe fcrupuloufly to refufe to take the fame; and the Kings Highneffe with his whole eftate might be better fecured, and freed from all feares and dangers: imitating herein other Kings and Princes as occafions fhall be offered them.

If euer the Kings of France or Spaine, or other Princes whatfoeuer had caufe to exact an Oath of fealtie of their fubiects for fafetie of their perfons or ftate; then certes no man that hath but common fenfe will denie but our King hath more then iuft, vpon fo horrible and monftrous caufe giuen, as the like haply was neuer heard of from the beginning of the world.

Could any man haue thought it ftrange, or held it crueltie, if, being in fuch wife, and by fuch perfons prouoked, he had in his wrath and indignation rigoroufly proceeded againft all others of the Romane religion, as fufpecting them to beare no better mind towards him? though manie thoufands doubtleffe no way confented, nor were euer priuie to that horrible fact.

And if he had, what ruine of Catholike families, what hauocke of Chriftian bloud, with the deftruction of foules, and other infinite miferies fhould we haue feene? But the omnipotent God (whofe name be bleffed for euer) who hath the rule and gouernment of the hearts of Kings, inclined his royall heart to mercie and compaffion of his fubiects, knowing right well the faith and loyaltie of many of the fame religion, as his Maieftie moft benignely expreffed in his Proclamation; and that he fhould haue punifhed the innocent with the nocent, as well his friends as his foes. Oh what follie were it for a man to wake a fleeping Lion, or ftirre a neft of wafpes or hornets, whereby he might endanger himfelfe to be bitten or ftong moft grieuoufly? Then how much greater is the follie of fuch, as feare not to irritate or incenfe

a King,

a King, who naturally defireth nothing more then peace and quietneffe to himfelfe and his people? We learne in holy writ how dreadfull is the terror of a King, in that it is compared to the roaring of a Lion: *Sicut rugitus Leonis, ita & terror Regis : qui prouocat eum, peccat in animam fuam.* As the roaring of a Lion, fo is the terrour of a King : he that prouoketh him offendeth againft his owne life. Prou.20.

Example we haue of King *Dauid*, who was ftirred to wrath by *Hanon* King of Ammonites vpon ingratitude for his loue and kindneffe. For, *Dauid* hearing of his fathers death, fent fome of his feruants to comfort him : *Hanon* following euill counfell, forfooth, that Dauid did not fend to condole with him and comfort him, but to efpie the Citie and ouerthrow it. Whereupon moft vngratefully he euill intreated the embaffadours, fhauing halfe their beards, and ignominioufly cutting their garments vnto the buttockes. King *Dauid* herewith moued to anger, prouided an armie to reuenge this iniurie ; ouerthrew of the Syrians that affifted the Ammonites feuen thoufand chariots, and flue forty thoufand footmen, made hauock of the Ammonites bloud, and wafted the cities of King *Hanon*, deftroying the people in moft rufull maner : as you may reade in the fecond booke of the Kings and Paralipomenon. Confider the imprudence and wickedneffe of this king; imprudence, in not forefeeing what dangers he might caft himfelfe into, by making his friend his foe, and ftirring him to ire that fought to liue in peace. Wickedneffe, in rendring euill for good, and procuring warres (the euent whereof is various) which was caufe that many innocent perfons, who were not confenting to *Hanons* fact, nor euer haply wifhed *Dauid* hurt, were in that fury flaine. 2.Reg.10. 1.Paralip.19. 20.

We reade likewife how this holy king *Dauid*, being in the defert perfecuted by *Saul*, purpofed and prepared to reuenge himfelfe on malicious *Nabal*, for contemning him and his feruants (whom in his diftreffe he had fent in peaceable and friendly fort for victuals and reliefe) faying, Who is *Dauid?* and what is the fonne of *Ifai?* There are feruants multiplied 1.Reg.25.

B 2

tiplied now a dayes, which flie from their maifters. Shall I
then take my breads, and my waters, and the flefh of my
cattell which I haue killed for my fhearers, and giue it to
men whom I know not whence they are? Hereupon *Dauid*
in wrath fet forward to be reuenged, and purpofed not to
haue left nor *Nabal*, nor any belonging to him, to piffe a-
gainft a wall, had not his wife *Abigail* by her wifedome pre-
uented the fhedding of innocent blood, meeting with *Dauid* and pacifying him with gifts, prudent fpeeches, and difcreete behauiour.

Theod. lib. 5.
cap. 17.
    In the Ecclefiafticall hiftorie is likewife noted, how that
renowmed Emperour *Theodofius* vpon rage caufed many
innocents in Theffalonica to be put to death, for the murther of one Noble man of his court. Many moe examples
both facred and prophane might be here alledged to this
purpofe, but thefe may fuffife to giue vs a tafte of the miferies that fal on many, yea on fuch as neuer offended, when a
Prou. 16.
Prince is iniured and prouoked to anger. *Indignatio Regis,
nuncij mortis: & vir fapiens placabit eam.* The indignation of
a king, is meffengers of death: and a wife man will appeafe
it.

    If king *Dauid* or *Theodofius* might pretend iuft caufe to
reuenge their wrongs in fuch fort by feuere punifhment not
onely of the offenders, but alfo of the guiltleffe: then furely
none can deny but king *Iames* our dread Soueraigne had
much more againft the confpirators in the notorious gun-
powder-treafon, and many others of the fame religion, whó
he might well fufpect to be of the fame confederation. In
this, there was not a contempt onely of his feruants, nor a
fhauing of beards, or paring their garments to the buttocks,
nor yet the murthering of one of his Nobles: but (out alas)
here was intended a moft pitifull flaughter of the Kings
owne perfon, the Queene his wife, the yong Prince his
fonne, the Nobilitie, and people in great numbers: and then
eftfoones had followed a finall deftruction of infinite foules
and bodies, and of this whole florifhing kingdome; as euery
one that is but meanely wife muft needes know. In that his
Higneffe

Highneſſe then proceeded no further in furie and indignation againſt Catholickes, (being by them ſo incenſed) but
ſtaied his hands by the execution only of a few principals in
that aⒸiõ, muſt needs be imputed, firſt to the prouidence of
Almightie God, (who guideth the hearts of kings) and next
to his rare and ſingular clemency, who ſeemed ready to pardon, loath to puniſh by bloud ſo many as in that conſpiracy
offended, or to vſe ſuch ſeueritie as the crime deſerued. In
puniſhing ſome, he praⒸtiſed iuſtice; in pardoning others he
extended his mercie: which two vertues make a Prince renowmed, and by which, eſpecially mercie or clemency, a
king is moſt ſtrongly fortified and preſerued, according to
that of *Salomon* : *Miſericordia & veritas cuſtodiunt regem* , &
roboratur clementia thronus eius. Mercie and Truth keepe the
king, and with Clemencie his throne is ſtrengthned.

See his Maie-
ſties procla-
mation.

Prou. 20.

  Greatly were it to be wiſhed that this his mercy might not,
but it is to be feared, that through the default of ſome it may
be turned into furie, as ſometime it happeneth when the clemencie of a Prince is not regarded, or abuſed: that no *Nabal*
were to be found ſo preſumptuous hardie as to contemne,
not the Kings ſeruants, but himſelfe, in withſtanding his will
by vndiſcreete, if not obſtinate, refuſing to take the Oath of
allegeance ſo iuſt and reaſonable, made onely for the ſafety
of the King and kingdome, and exaⒸted as a note to diſtin-
guiſh friends from foes, good ſubieⒸts from euill affeⒸted;
and to take from Catholicks the heauie imputation of treaſon and treacherie, which hath lien long on their necks. A
child if he ſee his father in anger chaſtiſing his brother, fea-
reth, though he offended him not: and ſo doth the ſcholler
in the ſchoole dread the rod when the maiſter in rage cor-
reⒸteth one of his fellowes. The L ion roareth in the deſert,
and all feare that here the noyſe. *Leo rugiet, quis non timebit?*
How much more then is a king to be feared, who vnder God
hath power of life and death, as *Pilate* ſaid to our Sauiour:
*Neſcis quia poteſtatem habeo crucifigere te , & poteſtatem habeo
dimittere?* Doeſt thou not know that I haue power to cruci-
fie thee, and haue power to let thee go? ᵃWhich power was

Amos. 3.

a Aug. Trac.
116. parum à
medio Tom.
9.

B 3

giuen

giuen him from aboue , as is plaine. Confider in what cafe rich *Nabal* was, when he heard his wife *Abigail* recount vnto him (who by her prudence had appeafed and pacified *Dauid* coming in furie and rage to reuenge)what *Dauid* had intended againft him ; he feared and trembled in fuch wife, as with the newes he became euen fenfleffe : *Et emortuum* *eft cor eius intrinfecus, & factus eft quafi lapis* : that is , And his heart was dead inwardly , and he became as a ftone ; and thereupon within ten daies after , ftriken by God , gaue vp the ghoft. Had *Nabal* caufe to feare *Dauid*, not then accepted of the people for king, *Saul* being yet aliue : and haue not we iuft caufe to feare how we offend and ftirre to ire our dread Soueraigne, fo mightie a Monarch? Was the occafion that *Nabal* gaue, in comparifon of that of our Catholickes alike? Conferre the crime of the one and the other, and you fhall find great inequalitie , as great, as betweene a word and a blow; yea fuch a blow, as pofterity will hardly beleeue could be offered, when they fhal reade it in Chronicles. Meane while, we that by Gods goodnes are yet liuing, and be eye witneffes thereof, haue caufe to lament and teftifie with *Habacuc* the Prophet, *Quia opus factum eft in diebus noftris, quod nemo credet cum narrabitur.* That a worke hath bene done in our daies, which no man will beleeue when it fhall be told : and to wifh that fome difcreete *Abigail* may be found to ftep forth and meete with our liege Lord comming in great ire to reuenge, and with prudence to pacifie and perfwade him to furceafe, for the loialtie and true affection of many other his innocent Catholicke fubiects, who lie proftate at his royall feete lamenting their brethrens follie, and humbly befeeching pardon, with offer for, and in his defence of both life and limme.

But (woe is me) whileft fome endeuour to quench a flaming fire, by taking away the wood, knowing that, *Cum defecerint ligna, extingnetur ignis;* When the wood faileth , or is taken away , the fire will be quenched : others put more wood to the fire, and fo increafe the flame. Whileft his Maieftie meditateth mercie, and requireth that which iuftly he

may,

1.Reg.25.

Habac.1.

Prou.26.

may, and we in confcience are bound to performe; *Nabal,* yea many *Nabals* arife, and do adde matter to kindle his wrath, in refifting his will, and denying his iuft demand: which is, only to difcharge their duties, in rendering to *Cæ-far* that is *Cæfars,* to fweare fealtie and true obedience vnto him in temporals, according to the tenure of the Oath, framed and enacted the third yeare of his reigne, without derogation to any fpirituall authoritie of the Pope, or infringement of any point of the Catholicke faith. The caufe then wherefore this Oath of allegeance was made, no man can doubt but the moft barbarous Gun-powder confpiracy was the onely vrgent motiue, it neuer being (in common knowledge) fo much as thought of before. The fcope and end thereof was, that by taking or refufing the fame, the King and State might diftinguifh betweene true and faith- *Regis Præmo.* full, and hollow-hearted Catholicke fubiects: and his Ma- *Pag.12.* ieftie might be more fully affured of their conftancie and fidelitie in time of need, vpon any caufe to be offered what-foeuer; or by Prince, people, Pope, or whofoeuer.

And can any man maruell, that the Pope is therein named? Doth this fcandalize any? Confider but what they were that inferted it; the time, and place, and pretence of reafon they had or might haue to imagine (being fo ad-uerfe or oppofite to him in religion, and the Treafon fo frefh in memorie) that his Holineffe might giue leaue or encouragement, or at leaft be priuie, and fo to winke at fuch an attempt; prefuming that no Catholicke durft en-terprife fuch a fact, without conniuence at leaft of fupreme authoritie. And had they not caufe to feare or doubt him more then any other, none being therein culpable but only Iefuites and Catholickes; of whom, fome haply thinke themfelues bound to obey him whatfoeuer he command, for that in their opinion he cannot erre in commanding? Howbeit we that are by Gods grace Catholicks alfo, agree-ing in all points with Chrift his Vicar the Pope of Rome, in vnitie of faith, do no way fufpect that euer he was confen-ting, much leffe gaue way to authorize fuch enormous and wicked

wicked defignements: though withall we diffent from them that thinke he cannot erre, no not in a matter of fact. The State there affembled, were not fuch babes, as that they needed be taught of the Pope his proceedings with Princes about their depriuations or depofitions for diuers crimes, when he hath hope to preuaile, but efpecially for herefie or apoftafie. They knew right well likewife, that if his Highnes fhould be by his Holineffe denounced and declared an he-reticke, what dangers might foone after enfue : therefore was it thought wifedome to preuent a mifchiefe ere it hap-pen, in exacting an Oath of allegeance at Catholicks hands, in that maner and forme as it is fet downe, thereby more firmly to binde them to the performance of their dutie, whereto otherwife by the law of God and nature they reft obliged. For it is to be prefumed, that a Chriftian, an honeft man, that hath feare of Gods iudgements, wil not become perfidious, nor rafhly or vniuftly breake that oath, which difcreetly and iuftly he confented to take. *Iurabit proximo* *fuo, & non decipiet*: He will fweare to his neighbour, and wil not deceiue him. By this now I truft *(deare Catholicke* brethren) you are fatisfied, that an Oath of allegeance may be iuftly exacted at our hands, and that we are bound to fweare fealtie to our Prince, when it fhall be required of vs. But you make doubt, left more be contained in this Oath, then fealtie or ciuill obedience to his Maieftie ; viz. fome points againft the fpirituall authoritie of the Pope, which you being Catholickes may not gainfay, but are bound in confcience to maintaine. If you could fatisfie vs (fay you) that nothing is therein contained againft any ar-ticle of faith; and that we may difobey his Holineffe (who prohibiteth the taking thereof) without danger of mortall finne, you fhall do vs a fingular pleafure: therfore I pray you refolue vs herein that are much perplexed about it, by rea-fon of the great corporall troubles we are like to fall into, if by difobeying the King we refufe it ; or for the hazard of our foules (as we thinke) if in difobeying the Pope, and fcandalizing our brethren the Catholickes, we take it.

Beloued

Pfal. 14.

Beloued brethren, I truſt you expeƈt not at my hands that I ſhould fully and exaƈtly diſcuſſe euery point of the Oath, and anſwer euery ſcrupulous difficultie that ſome vſe to make (albeit it might be eaſie to effeƈt:) for it would require a better librarie then mine is at this preſent, more labour then I can well affoord, by reaſon of my feeble bodie, and a larger treatiſe then I meane to make. Your deſire is (as I preſume) onely to know whether the principall points thereof, as depoſing the Kings Maieſtie, diſcharging his ſubieƈts of their obedience, diſpenſing and abſoluing in this Oath, and ſuch like, be matter of faith, which bind euery Chriſtian man ſtedfaſtly to beleeue the ſame, vnder paine of damnation; or elſe but matter of opinion. And ſecondly, what you ought to doe concerning the Popes Breues, whether you may lawfully diſobey them or no. Theſe points indeed are the chiefeſt, whereon the reſt haue their dependãce, which with Gods aſſiſtance I ſhal endeuor ſo to handle, as you ſhall not need to doubt of the lawfulnes of the Oath, nor hazard all your eſtates for refuſing the ſame; yet ſo, as whatſoeuer ſhall be here in this my treatiſe written, I humbly ſubmit to the cenſure of the holy Catholicke and Apoſtolicke Church. *Errare quidem poſſum, homo enim ſum, hæreticus eſſe nolo:* Well I may erre, for a man I am, but hereticke will I neuer be.

In the dayes of *Samuel* the Prophet, after the people of *Iſrael* had bene foure hundred yeares ruled and gouerned by certaine rulers called Iudges, vpon occaſion of *Samuels* ſonnes miſdemeanour in their gouernment, all the elders of *Iſrael* câme to *Samuel* in Ramatha, and they ſaid vnto him: *Behold thou art old, and thy ſonnes walke not in thy wayes; appoint vs a King, like as all nations haue.* Whereupon, though this word highly diſpleaſed *Samuel*, God commanded him to heare them; howbeit he ſhould witneſſe and foretell them the authoritie or right of a King: which he did, ſaying, *This will be the right of a King that is to gouerne ouer you, &c.* All which things in the text of Scripture expreſſed by *Samuel*, are a Kings right (as ſaith the Gloſſe) in time of need,

1.Reg.8.

Gloſſ.ordin. in hunc locũ

C

Tho.1. 2. q.
105.ar.1.ad 5

neede, for the good of the weale publike; though it were to
be wiſhed that many of thē were moderatly vſed, eſpecially
all thoſe things which ſeeme to make the people that is ſubiect, to be ſeruile or ſlauiſh: and which reſpect not the common good , but rather the will of the man exalted in the
kingdome. Theſe or ſuch like did *Samuel* foretell them , to
withdraw them from asking a king, becauſe it was not expedient for them: and becauſe , that gouernment for the
greatneſſe or excellencie of power , is eaſily conuerted into
tyrannie.

    After this, God ſent *Saul*, and then reuealed vnto *Sa-
muel*, that he was the king that ſhould gouerne his people
Iſrael, and commanded to annoint him. Which he did, ſay-
1.Reg.10. ing : *Ecce vnxit te Dominus ſuper hæreditatem ſuam in Principem , & liberabis populum ſuum de manibus inimicorū eius qui
in circuitu eius ſunt.*Behold our Lord hath annointed thee to
be Prince ouer his inheritance , and thou ſhalt deliuer his
people from the hands of their enemies which are round a-
bout them. Not long after , king *Saul* for diſobeying the
precept of God giuen him by *Samuel*, was by God depriued of his kingdome, as the Scripture ſaith, and not by *Samuel*, as ſome would haue it. *Quia proieciſti ſermonem Domi-
1.Reg.15. ni, & proiecit te Dominus ne ſis Rex ſuper Iſrael.*Becauſe thou
haſt reiected the word of our Lord , our Lord alſo hath reiected thee, that thou maieſt not be king ouer Iſrael.

    By this example ſome gather (as they thinke) a ſtrong ar-
gument, *viz. à fortiori*, that the Church of God, and the
Pope, Chriſts vicar in earth, may iuſtly depriue or diſpoſſeſſe
kings of their ſcepters and dominions vpon cauſe giuen, as
for hereſie or apoſtaſie, &c. when as the Synagogue and *Samuel* had this authoritie, who *de facto* depoſed *Saul* for diſobedience onely.

    If this were true , then indeede were the argument of
ſome force ; for it cannot be denied , but that the ſpirituall
power of the Church of Chriſt , is much greater then was
that of the Synagogue of the Iewes, and the Pope hath
* more ample * ordinarie authoritie then *Samuel* had : yet it
                                               followeth

followeth not hereof, that either the Pope, or Church, by any power receiued from Chriſt Ieſus, can depriue, depoſe, or diſpoſſes any lawfull Prince or priuate man, that is not a vaſſall, feudatarie or ſubiect vnto him, of his goods temporall, ſtate, crowne, or dignitie : becauſe neither the Synagogue, nor *Samuel* were euer endued with this power. It is not any where to be found in all the old Teſtament that the Synagogue of the Iewes (the figure of Chriſts Church) or high Prieſt or Biſhop for the time being, could, or *de facto* euer did depoſe any lawfull king of Iſrael or Iuda from their Empire, were he neuer ſo wicked, neuer ſo peruerſe or cruell, and in his place did ſubſtitute an other. Whereby then is euident, that no good argument can be gathered by this example, to proue ſuch power to be in the new law, and in the Church or gouernours thereof.

That *Samuel* depoſed not king *Saul* by any authoritie in him exiſting, but Almightie God himſelfe, may eaſily be proued thus: for either he muſt depoſe him by temporall authoritie as he was a Iudge, which could not be, he being depriued thereof when *Saul* was made king, and was no more a gouernour but a ſubiect; or elſe by ſome ordinarie power of ſpirituall iuriſdiction ouer him, which he had not, for that he was nor Biſhop nor Prieſt (though a great Prophet) but only a Leuite, as *Genebrard*, Saint *Hierome*, Cardinall *Bellarmine*, *Hector Pintus* and others affirme; to whom ſuch iuriſdiction did no way appertaine. Therefore *Samuel* depoſed him not, but onely as an extraordinarie Embaſſador executed the will and iudgement of God in his depoſition, who had giuen him a ſpeciall warrant or commandement as touching the ſame, which will appeare manifeſtly to him that readeth the Scripture: *Sine me, & indicabo tibi qua locutus eſt Dominus ad me nocte.* Suffer me (ſaid *Samuel* to the king when he came to him) and I will declare vnto you what our Lord hath ſpoken to me in the night. And then forthwith deliuered his meſſage, that which God had reuealed vnto him, to wit, that our Lord had ſo reiected him and his progenie, as (albeit he were in perſon to enioy the kingdome

Geneb. in PC 98.

Hierom. lib. 1. in Iouin

Bellar. in Pſal. 98.

Pintus in E-zech. c. 45. p. 549.

1. Reg. 15.

dome

dome to his liues end , as he did fortie yeares) that none of
his ſtocke or ſeed ſhould ſucceſſiuely reigne after him, and
be of that line of whom Chriſt the Meſſias was to be incar-
nate.

If then neither the Synagogue nor *Samuel* did , or could
by any ordinarie power depoſe *Saul*, elected by God , I do
not ſee how by this example any good argument can be
drawne in conſequence for the Churches , or the Popes ordinarie power of depoſing Princes. Had ſuch authoritie bin
graunted to the Synagogue or high Prieſts in the old law,
why I pray you had it not bene practiſed on the perſons of
Achaz, Manaſſes, Amon, Ioachaz and other kings of Iuda,
who were much more wicked then *Saul* was? and on impious *Ieroboam* that led with him all Iſrael to Idolatrie? *A-
chab, Ochozias, Ioachaz*, and the reſt of the kings of Iſrael,
who exceeded in all kind of impietie? in whoſe dayes flori-
ſhed *Ahias, Semeias, Elias , Eliſeus, Iſaias, Ieremy*, and other
great Prophets, indued with maruellous courage, zeale, authoritie, and ſanctitie of life ; yet none went about to depoſe or take the crowne from the head of any Prince lawfully inueſted , though he were neuer ſo wicked: knowing
right well, that whatſoeuer they wrought with Princes a-
bout the ouerthrow of ſome, or ſetting vp of others, or foretold what was to happen vnto them; it was not by any ordinarie power that they had , but extraordinary, by ſpeciall
commandement and reuelation from Almightie God. Now
by this fact of *Samuel* it may well be deduced, that whenſoeuer the Pope, gouernour of Gods houſe, ſhall haue ſpeciall
reuelation from aboue, as *Samuel* had, that ſuch a particular
king is to be depoſed, and another placed in his roome; thē
it cannot be denied but he may do as *Samuel* did, that is, as I
haue ſaid , he may and ought to declare the will of God reuealed vnto him without any concurrence to the execution
thereof, onely denouncing Gods ſentence of deiection or
depoſition of ſuch a Prince , when he knoweth certainly,
that ſo is the will and pleaſure of our Lord, whoſe will none
may contradict . *Voluntati eius quis reſiſtit?* Who is able to
refiſt

refift his will? nor is any to expoftulate why he doth fo. And if fuch a thing fhould euer happen, then were the argument good and found, otherwife, weake, and of no force.

If any man after this, obiect vnto me, that *Athalia* was depofed, and flaine by the commandement of *Ioiada* the high Prieft, when fhe had reigned feuen yeares : therefore it feemeth he had authoritie frō God fo to do; and if he had, why fhould not the Pope haue the like ouer exorbitant Princes?

For folution hereof, I referre him to the place of holy Scripture, where he may fee with halfe an eye, that *Athalia* 4.Reg. 11. was no lawfull Queene, but an vfurping tyrant; who had murthered all the kingly race, and fo intruded her felfe moft vniuftly. Whereupon *Ioiada*, high Prieft, brought forth, and prefented to the people *Ioas*, fonne to *Ochozias*, who was ftrangely preferued, by meanes of his Aunt *Iofaba*, when he was but an infant, from that tyrannous flaughter made by his Grandmother *Athalia*; and together with their full confents, performing the dutie of a good fubiect, reftored the true heire to the right of his kingdome; which could hardly haue bene effected without the high Priefts affiftance, who was the chiefeft in matters of religion ; and therefore much honoured and refpected of the people. So this fact of *Ioiada* proueth nothing, but that it is lawfull for a ftate or commonwealth to depofe an vfurper, and reftore the true heire to his right; and not that he had any authoritie to depofe any lawfull Prince, were he otherwife neuer fo exorbitant in life, manners and beleefe, or cruell in his gouernment.

Well Sir, though this be granted, that neither the Synagogue of the Iewes, nor *Samuel* the Prophet, nor *Ioiada* the high Prieft, had authoritie to depofe Princes and difpofe of their temporals; yet can we not be perfwaded but that the Church of Chrift, and his Vicar in earth the Pope (whofe power is not limited to one fort of people, as it was in the old law, but is extended ouer all Chriftians, as well Princes as people, throughout the world) may iuftly depofe kings and difpofe of their kingdomes, when he fhall iudge it expedient to the glory of God, and vtilitie of the Church. And

C 3   the

the rather becaufe this hath bene practifed by diuerfe precedent Popes vpon certaine Princes in thefe latter ages, for crimes adiudged by them to deferue the fame: which we fuppofe they would neuer haue enterprifed, had they not fufficient warrant out of holy Scriptures, or examples of the Apoftles and ancient Bifhops of Gods Church, or elfe authoritie from the holy Ghoft by a definitiue fentence in fome generall Councell. We pray you touch this point fo as you may refolue vs throughly, whether they haue all, or fome of thefe proofes for that authoritie: if they haue not, then is it cleare in our opinions not to be *de fide*; and if it be not a point of faith, binding all to beleeue that his Holines hath fuch authoritie, we fee no reafon why (vpon his bare commandement) we fhould fo deepely plunge our felues into a fea of calamities, as of neceffitie we muft, by lofing all lands and goods whatfoeuer we haue, to the vtter vndoing of our felues, wiues and children, and hazarding our liues by perpetuall imprifonment, for refufing to performe our dutie to our Soueraigne, by taking the Oath of allegiance, wherein we fweare fealtie and ciuill obedience, which is due by the law of God and nature. *Reddite quæ funt Cæfaris Cæfari, & quæ Dei Deo.* Render (faith our Sauiour) *to Cæfar that which is Cæfars, and to God that which is Gods.* Befides, if we refufe it, we fhall not take away, but greatly increafe the heauie imputation of treafon and treacherie, which our aduerfaries haue this long time layd on Catholickes, and confirme them in this their wrong opinion, that to be a true Catholicke of the Romane Church, and a good fubiect, cannot ftand and agree together.

Beloued brethren, left any man be fcandalized at this my writing, iudging it not to fauour of a true Catholick heart, nor of an obedient child of the Apoftolicke Church, but rather to proceed from an euill affected minde fraught with paffion; accept for a premunition, and I wifh I may not be miftaken; *that fincerely and without fpleene or paffion, I intend, to fet downe nothing, but what I fhall thinke in my opinion to be truth; and that I honour and reuerence with

heart

heart and mind the holy Catholicke Church of Rome, acknowledging and ſtedfaſtly beleeuing with the holy Fathers,that to be the mother of Churches, the Sea of *Peter,*
the rocke againſt which hell gates ſhall not preuaile; the
houſe of God,out of which who eateth the Lambe,is profane, and out of which no ſaluation is to be hoped for, as
the great D. *S.Auguſtine* and others do teach vs ; and that
the Pope is the chiefe Biſhop and Paſtor thereof, Chriſts
Vicar in earth, and ſucceſſor to *S.Peter* prince of the Apoſtles,who by his ſpirituall power giuen by Chriſt our Lord,
hath iuriſdiction ouer all Chriſtian Princes and monarchs
as well as poore men, ſo farre as is requiſite to the conuerſion and feeding of ſoules.

In ſerm. ſuper
geſtis Emer.
Donat. and
elſewhere.
Hieron. ep.ad
Dam.
Amb. 1.Tim.
3.
Aſhan ep.ad
Felicem.

But I cannot eaſily be induced to beleeue, that this power giuen him by Chriſt in *S.Peter*, extendeth it ſelfe to the
depriuation or depoſition of ſecular Princes of their dominions; or to the depoſing of any lay-mans temporall goods
and patrimonie, for any cauſe whatſoeuer, yea for hereſie
it ſelfe, who is not temporally a vaſſall and ſubiect to his
Holineſſe. And if his ſpirituall authoritie giuen him by our
Sauiour,can worke no ſuch effect,much leſſe his temporall,
which was neuer granted by Chriſt (by whom he ought to
haue whatſoeuer he hath for the good gouernment of his
Church) but by holy ſecular Princes, whereof Cardinall
Allen writeth thus : *The chiefe Biſhops of Chriſts Church, our*
ſupreme Paſtors in earth,by Gods prouidence,and by the graunts
of our firſt moſt Chriſtian Emperours and Kings, and by the
humble and zealous deuotion of the faithfull Princes and people
afterwards,haue their temporall ſtates, dominions and patrimo-
nies,whereby they moſt iuſtly hold and poſſeſſe the ſame, and are
thereby lawfull Princes temporall, and may moſt rightfully by
their ſoueraigntie make warres in their owne and other mens iuſt
*quarell, as occaſion ſhall vrge them thereunto.*This he.The like
in effect writeth the moſt excellent lawyer D.*Barclai*, that
the Pope himſelfe is no otherwiſe excluded from temporall
ſubiection to ſecular Princes,then that by the benefite or liberalitie of Kings he was made a King,forſooth a politicall
Prince,

In his anſwer
to the Eng.
inſt.pag.144.

Lib.de pote-
ſtate Papæ,c.
15.

Prince, acknowledging none for his ſuperiour in temporals.
And the ſame doth the moſt earneſt maintainer of the Eccleſiaſticall Iuriſdiction confeſſe, whom many thinke to be

Sub nomine
Franciſci Ro-
muli.
pag. 114.

Cardinall *Bellarmine*, in his anſwer to the principall chapters of an Apologie, &c. *Generalis (inquit) & veriſſima eſt
illa ſententia, debere omnes omnino ſuperiori poteſtati obtempera-
re. Sed quia, &c.* It is a generall and moſt true ſentence, that
all ought to obey higher power: but becauſe power is of
two ſorts, ſpirituall and temporall, eccleſiaſticall and politicall, whereof the one belongeth to Biſhops, the other to
Kings; Biſhops ought to be ſubiect to Kings in temporall
things, and Kings vnto Biſhops in ſpirituals: as copiouſly

Gelaſius.
Nicolaus.

do diſpute *Gelaſius* the firſt, in his Epiſtle to *Anaſtaſius*, and
Nicolas the firſt, in his Epiſtle to *Michael.* But becauſe the
Biſhop of Rome is not only the chiefe Eccleſiaſtical Prince,
to whom all Chriſtians by the law of God are ſubiect, but
is alſo in his owne Prouinces a temporall Prince; neither
doth he acknowledge any ſuperiour in temporals, as nor o-
ther abſolute and ſoueraigne Princes do in their kingdoms
and dominions, thence it proceedeth that he hath no power
aboue him in earth. Not then becauſe he is chiefe Biſhop,
and ſpirituall father of all Chriſtians, therefore he is deliuered from temporall ſubiection, but becauſe he enioyeth a
temporall principalitie ſubiect to none. In thoſe things
therefore which appertaine to the good of the commonwealth, and ciuill ſocietie, and are not repugnant to the diuine ordinance, Clerkes are no leſſe bound to obey the ſoueraigne temporall Prince, then other citizens or ſubiects;
as Cardinall *Bellarmine* himſelfe verie notably ſheweth:

In lib. de Cle-
ricis, c. 28.

*Quia clerici, præterquã quod clerici ſunt, ſunt etiã ciues, & par-
tes quædam Reipub. politicæ. Non ſunt exempti clerici vllo modo,
inquit, ab obligatione legum ciuilium, quæ non repugnant ſacris
canonibus vel officio clericali:* That clergie men, beſides that
they are clergie men, are alſo citizens and certaine parts of
the politicall commonwealth. Clerkes (ſaith he) are not exempted by any meanes from the bond of the ciuill lawes,
which are not repugnant to the ſacred canons, or their cle-
ricall

ricall office. By this you may see, that the Pope hath his temporalities and temporall power, not from Christ, but from *Constantine* and other Christian Princes and people, and was euer subiect to ciuill gouernment of Emperours, till such time as by their graunts he was made a King and temporall Prince, and so had no superiour; and that Clerks (as parts of the political cōmonwealth) are bound to obey al iust lawes of the same cōmonwealth no lesse then the Laitie: but more of this in another place, as occasion shall serue. Now to come somewhat nearer the question that I promised, and you desire to be resolued on, as touching the Popes authoritie to depose Princes of their temporall dominions: First you are to note, that of this matter there are two opinions much different the one from the other, one of the Canonists, another of Diuines. The Canonists hold it for true doctrine to be maintained, that all power whatsoeuer is in this world, either temporall and ciuill, or spirituall and ecclesiasticall, was giuen directly by Christ to *Peter* and his successors; and what power any Kings or Princes in the whole world, either Christians or Infidels haue, it all dependeth of the Pope, and is deriued from him to them, as touching the temporall execution: so that as Lord of the world, he may depose Princes, take away their kingdomes and principalities, and giue or dispose them to whom he list, though no man know the cause why he doth so; if he shall iudge there is sufficient cause to do it. If this were true doctrine, then woe to all Princes that should at any time yea but breake amitie and friendship with him that sitteth in *Peters* seate: what securitie could they haue of their estates? Then might they expect, of Princes and rulers to be made priuate men and subiects; then may it be granted that our Soueraigne were not vnlike to be depriued of his temporals, his subiects to be discharged of their obedience, and his territories giuen in prey to his enemies. But this opinion is held to be most false by many Diuines, because it cannot be proued either by authoritie of Scripture, or by

Tho. Bozius, Carerius. D. Marta. and others.

D   tra-

tradition of the Apostles, or practife of the ancient Church, or by the doctrine and teftimonies of the ancient Fathers. Lib.2.cap.11 Howbeit *Bozius* a late writer moft ftoutly defendeth the fame, and greatly blameth many excellent Diuines (among whom is renowned Cardinall *Bellarmine*) and calleth them Lib.5.cap.vlt. new Diuines, faying moreouer, that they teach moft manifeftly falfe doctrine, and repugnant to all truth, becaufe they fay that Chrift as man, was neuer a temporall king, nor had any temporall dominion on earth, nor did exercife or practife any regall power, (for by thefe affertions, the principall foundations of *Bozius* friuolous arguments are ouerthrowne) which as moft true they confirme by the teftimo-Math.8.
Luc.9. ny of our Sauiour himfelfe. Foxes (faith he) haue holes, and the foules of the aire nefts, but the Sonne of man hath not where to put his head. If Chrift Iefus as he was the fon of mā had not fo much in this world as a cottage to reft himfelf in: where I pray you is his kingdome? where is his temporall dominion? who can conceiue that one can be king and Lord, who hath no kingdome or Lordfhip in the vniuerfall world? We know well that as he is the Sonne of God, he is the King of glory, King of kings, Lord of heauen and earth, Pfal.23. and of all things, (*Domini enim eft terra & plenitudo eius*) and reigneth with the Father and the holy Ghoft for euer: but what is this to a temporall kingdome? what is this to the imperiall dignitie of fecular maieftie? Therefore I meane not to ftand to confute this opinion of Canonifts, which hath Lib.5.de fum
Pont.c.2.& 3 bene moft learnedly confuted by Cardinall *Bellarmine*, but to let it paffe as moft abfurd, that cannot be proued by any found reafon, nor ancient authorities either of Scriptures, Fathers, or Councels; but maintained by captious fallacies, vnapt fimilitudes, and corrupt interpretations.

An other opinion there is of Diuines, who diflike, and with moft ftrong reafons do confute the Canonifts pofitiōs, but yet fo as they vphold and labour to maintain the Popes temporall power, though in other fort then the former, that De Ro.Pont.
lib.5.c.6. is, indirectly, or cafually and by confequence. This then they write, and namely Cardinall *Bellarmine*: *Afferimus, Pontificem,*

tificem, vt Pontificem, et ſi non habeat vllam merè temporalem po-
teſtatem, tamen habere in ordine ad bonum ſpirituale ſummam po-
teſtatem diſponendi de temporalibus rebus omnium Chriſtiano-
rum. We affirme that the Pope, as Pope, although he hath
not any meerly temporal power, yet in order to the ſpiritual
good, he hath a ſupereminent power to diſpoſe of the tēpo-
rall goods of all Chriſtians. And againe in the ſame chapter:
Quantum ad perſonas, non poteſt Papa, vt Papa, ordinariè tem-
porales Principes deponere, etiam iuſta de cauſa, eo modo quo de-
ponit Epiſcopos, id eſt, tanquam ordinarius iudex, &c. As touching the perſons, the Pope as Pope cannot ordinarily depoſe temporall Princes, yea for a iuſt cauſe, after that ſort as
he depoſeth Biſhops, that is, as an ordinary iudge : yet he
may change kingdomes, and take from one, and giue to an
other as the chiefe ſpirituall Prince, if that be neceſſarie to
the health or ſauing of ſoules. And in the ſame booke the
firſt chapter, where he putteth downe the Catholicke opinion (as he ſaith) he altereth it ſomewhat in this manner.
Pontificem vt Pontificem, &c. That the Pope as Pope, hath Lib.5.cap.1.
not directly and immediatly any temporall power, but only
ſpirituall; yet by reaſon of the ſpirituall, he hath at leaſt indirectly a certaine power, & that chiefe or higheſt in tēporals.

You haue here ſet downe by Cardinall *Bellarmine*, the
opinion of Diuines, that the Pope as Pope, or chiefe Biſhop
as chiefe Biſhop, hath not directly and immediatly any temporall power to depoſe Chriſtian Princes, but that indirectly, I wot not how, he may depoſe them, and diſpoſe of their
temporals: and ſo in effect, and after a ſort, agreeth with
the Canoniſts, that indeed ſuch power is rightly in him; only he differeth about the manner, with a reſtraint, from infidels to Chriſtian Princes. But I truſt, as he in improuing the
Canoniſts aſſertiō of direct power ouer al the world, driueth
them to Scriptures, or tradition of the Apoſtles; ſo likewiſe
we may require that he proue his indirect power by one of
theſe two wayes. If he cannot, as moſt certainely he cannot,
then why ſhould men giue more credite to him then to
the other, they being as Catholike, and haply no leſſe lear-

ned

ned then he? Why fhould his opinion be thought more true
then the former? To difproue the Canonifts thus he writeth:

*Ex Scripturis nihil habemus, nifi datas Pontifici claues regni cœ-
lorum, de clauibus regni terrarum nulla mentio fit. Traditionem
Apoftolicam nullam aduerfarij proferunt.*Out of Scriptures we
haue nothing, but that the keyes of the kingdome of heauen were giuen to the Pope, of the keyes of the kingdome
of the earth no mention is made at all. Apoftolical tradition
our aduerfaries produce none. hereby it feemeth the Cardinall goeth about to proue againft his aduerfaries, that becaufe the keyes of the kingdome of the earth are no where
mentioned in the Scripture to be giuen to *Peter* and his fuc-
feffors, therefore the Pope hath not any direct authoritie to
depofe the Princes of the world, nor difpofe of their temporals: infinuating that the keyes of the kingdome of heauen
promifed and granted to *Peter* (or to the Church in the perfon of *Peter*) can worke no fuch effect, nor were granted to
depriue Chriftian Princes or others of their fcepters and regall dignities; but onely by cenfures and fpirituall authority
to exclude vnworthy finners from eternall felicitie, and admit fuch as are truly penitent to the kingdome of heauen. If
this argument be good againft the Canonifts, then why
is it not alfo good againft Cardinall *Bellarmine* himfelfe,
when as he can no more produce Apoftolicall tradition to
confirme his indirect authoritie, then the other their direct? And of the keyes of the kingdome of the earth, required for depofing Princes and difpofing of temporals, no
mention is made in all the Scriptures, no not for his indirect
or cafuall authoritie.

Confider befides I pray you (for it is worth the noting)
how obfcurely and ambiguoufly, he writeth of the Popes
power to depofe, thereby haply intending to feeke fome
ftarting hole of equiuocation if occafion ferue; and meane
while leaue his reader doubtfull, and ftill to feeke of his
meaning, which in my fimple iudgement is fuch as the iu-
dicious wit can hardly conceiue, nor tell what he would
fay. As for example, that the chiefe Bifhop as chiefe Bifhop
                                                    hath

hath not any power meerly temporall,&c. as is noted before lib.5. cap.6. and in the same chapter: The Pope as Pope cannot ordinarily (note) depose,&c. no not for a iust cause: mary as he is the chiefe spirituall Prince he may depose and dispose,&c. Helpe me good Reader to vnderstand this riddle, how these two differ in some essentiall point, Pope, and chiefe spirituall Prince. I must confesse that I vnderstand not how he is the chiefe spirituall Prince, but as he is Pope, that is, the Father of Fathers, or chiefe Pastor of soules in the Church of God. It is wel knowne that this title Pope, or *Papa* in Latin, hath bene attributed to many ancient Patriarchs and Bishops; as well as to the Bishop of Rome (though principally to him, and now is appropriated to him alone) and for nought else, but for being Bishops and Ecclesiasticall Princes of the Church: and for that cause only, & not for being a temporal Prince, *Peters* successor, hath his denomination. Which in effect D. *Kellison* affirmeth, saying: I grant with S. *Bernard*, that the Pope as Pope hath no temporall iurisdiction, his power, as he is Pope, being onely spirituall. If then it be so, that the Pope as Pope hath no temporall power ouer Princes, nor can depose them, *etiam iusta de causa*, as the Cardinall saith, surely I cannot with cristall spectacles see how he can depose as a spiritual Prince, there being no perceptible difference betweene them.

D. Kellisons Reply to M. Sutcl. ca. 1. f. 9. Bern. lib. 2. de consid.

If I should stand to note vnto you the rest of his obscurities and ambiguities, I feare I should be too tedious, therefore I purpose to surceasse, and leaue them to your prudent consideration : as, The Pope hath not any power meerely temporall; he cannot as Pope ordinarily depose temporall Princes, as an ordinarie iudge; he hath at least indirectly a certaine power, and that chiefest or highest in temporals: and such like, which seeme no lesse fearfully then obscurely written and taught.

This doubtful doctrine of most learned Cardinal *Bellarmine*, and the varietie or contrarietie of opinions betweene him and other very learned Clerkes in Gods church about this matter of deposition, is to me a most strong argument,

that

that it is not *de fide* : for if it were, then would there be an vniforme confent and perfect agreement among them, not onely of the thing controuerted, but alfo of the manner, and caufes thereof, no leffe then is of Purgatorie, prayer to Saints, of the reall prefence of Chrifts bodie and bloud in the B. Sacrament, of the virginitie of our B. Ladie, incarnation of Chrift, feuen Sacraments, and fo of all other points of faith. Then would a matter of fuch moment haue bene found in the writings of fome ancient Father, as well as other of leffe importance; but for wel neare a thoufand yeares continuance, till the time of *Gregorie* the 7. it was neuer chalenged, mentioned or defended by any writer: or elfe it would haue bene defined in fome generall Councell, whofe authoritie bindeth all Chriftians to beleeue whatfoeuer is there decreed, to be *de fide*, without controuerfie; which to this day neuer was, no not in the third Councell of Lateran vnder *Innocentius* 3. as fome ignorantly thinke, and build them ftrong caftles in the aire; and others inconfiderately auerre, howbeit not fimply and plainly, but fomewhat timoroufly, which they need not do if it were fo, but

Prou. 10. fhould confidently auouch it fo to be. *Qui ambulat fimpliciter, ambulat confidenter*. He that goeth fimply and plainly to worke, goeth confidently. A matter of faith is to be taught fincerely and perfpicuoufly, not doubtfully or guilefully, as it were to deceiue his readers, or thereby to hold them in fufpence in fuch wife, as they fhall euer remaine perplexed and to feeke of the true meaning of what is written.

O fir, if you reade that Councell of Lateran, cap. 3. you fhall finde it plainly decreed, that Princes which be negligent in purging out of their territories the filth of herefie, are to be depofed.

This indeed were fomewhat to the purpofe, if it were true as you fay; but if you beleeue fo, you are in an errour: for who readeth that chapter, fhall well perceiue it was not there decreed or defined, but treated of the manner how certaine fecular powers or temporall Lords (without fpecifying Kings) might be proceeded withall; and nothing de-

decreed *de fide* concerning depofition of Princes: if it had bene defined matter of faith, it muft of neceffity haue bound all Catholickes, as well Princes as people, to beleeue it, and accept thereof. Moreouer, fuch a decree muft alwayes haue continued immutable, and could not be abrogated, as Cardinall *Bellarmine* writeth : *Decreta de fide immutabilia funt, nec poffunt vllo modo abrogari poftquam femel ftatuta funt.* The decrees of faith are immutable, neither can they be abrogated by any meanes after they are once decreed. And if it be no decree of faith (as it is not) but onely of reformation, who I pray you will fay it doth bind, till it be accepted and receiued? Famous Cardinall *Tolet* faith no; and for his affertion citeth the Canon law, *Can. In iftis, dift. 4. Vt lex vim habeat, debet effe recepta ab his quibus lex datur; fi enim lex promulgata eft, fed non recepta, non obligat.* For a law to be of force, it ought to be receiued of thofe to whom the law is giuen; for if a law (to wit Ecclefiafticke) be promulgated, but not receiued, it bindeth not. Do we not fee that the wholefome lawes or decrees of the Councell of Trent touching reformation, binde not where they are not yet receiued, as in France and other places? And is any man fo vnwife to thinke, that Princes will euer receiue fuch decrees as may bereaue them of their fcepters and temporall ftates, and turne to their vtter ruine? Neuer was it hitherto feene, nor euer will it be by all likelihood in Great Brittaine, or any other kingdome.

Furthermore, in that chapter is no mention made of excommunicating Emperour or Kings, nor depofing them, nor abfoluing their fubiects from their naturall obedience, but of excommunicating herefie, giuing ouer fuch as are condemned for that crime, to the fecular magiftrate to be punifhed; and ordering withall, that certaine other fecular powers or principall Lords inferiour to Kings, as may be Poteftates, Confuls, Rectors, or fuch like (which by the conftitution of Fredericke 2. Emperour is euident) fhould be compelled (if neede were) to take an oath to do their endeuour for the extirpation of heretickes out of fuch pla-

ces

Bellar. lib. 2. Conc c. 17.

Tolet. de 7. pec. mor. c. 18

pag. 64

ces as fhould be vnder their gouernment;when ofneceffitie
both Emperour and kings ought to haue bene fpecified , if
the Councell had meant to haue included them in that law.

In pœnalibus (faith *Samuel Sa*) *& reftrictione vtendum , & pia
interpretatione.*In penals we are to vfe both a reftriction,and
a pious interpretation. Likewife, *Pœnæ non extendendæ vltra
cafus iure expreffos* : Punifhments are not to be extended beyond the cafes expreffed in the law. Then why fhall this be
enlarged , and extended to kings , who are not expreffed in
the decree of the Councell? Therefore this chapter maketh
nothing for the Popes authoritie to depriue kings of their
crownes and dignities:and fo confequently is of no validitie
againft the Oath of Allegiance made *anno tertio Iacobi Regis
fereniffimi.*

But for better clearing this point, it fhall not be amiffe to
fet downe the decree of the Councell as it is, leauing it to
the confiderations of the learned, to iudge whether it be of
faith or no, which beginneth thus:

Excommunicamus & anathematizamus omnem hærefim,&c.
We excomunicate and anathematize all herefie that exal-
teth it felfe againft this holy, orthodoxe,Catholicke faith,
which aboue we haue declared,&c.And let fuch as are condemned , be left vnto fecular powers if they be'prefent, or
vnto their Bailiffes (or Prefidents) to be punifhed with due
punifhment, Clearkes being firft degraded from their orders. And fuch as fhall be found noted with fufpition onely , vnleffe according to the confideration of the fufpition
and the qualitie of the perfon, they fhew their owne inno-
cencie by a meete purging, let them be excommunicated,
and auoyded of all , till they haue made condigne fatisfaction, fo that if for the fpace of a yeare they ftand excommunicate, from that time forward let them be condemned as
heretikes. All which feemeth not to ferue the Cardinals
turne to proue the Pope to haue power to depofe,and therfore in his anfwer to D.*Barclai* page 30.he omitted it fauing
the firft fentence *Excommunicamus*. It followeth in the
Councell:

Moueantur

Moneantur autem & inducantur, &c. And let the secular powers, yea of what office soeuer, be admonished and induced, and if need be, compelled; as they desire to be reputed and accompted faithfull, so for the defence of faith, let them take publikely an Oath , that they will endeuour *bona fide,* to their power , to roote out of the lands subiect to their iurisdiction all heretikes marked out by the Church , so that henceforward, whensoeuer any shall be assumed into either spirituall or temporall potestacie, he be bound to confirme this chapter. This part also the Cardinall left out, as not being any thing for his purpose, and taketh hold of this clause ensuing.

Si vero Dominus temporalis. And if the temporall Lord being required and admonished by the Church, shall neglect to purge his land from this hereticall filth ; let him be excommunicated by the Metropolitan and comprouinciall Bishops. And if he shall contemn to make satisfaction within a yeare, let this be signified to the Pope, that he may from that time denounce his vassals absolued from his fealtie, and may expose his land to be occupied by Catholikes, who hauing rooted out the heretickes , may possesse it without any contradiction , and conserue it in the puritie of faith , the right of the principall Lord reserued , so that to this he be no hinderance , nor oppose any impediment , the same law notwithstanding being kept about those who haue not principall Lords.

How greatly might it haue bene wished, that the most illustrous Cardinall *Bellarmine,* either in *Tortus* , or in his answer to D. *Barclai,* or in some other of his learned workes, had so clearely explicated this latter part of the Councell, esteemed of him the greatest and most famous (howbeit the Councell of Chalcedon for number of Bishops was much greater)that all might haue rested satisfied of the irrefragable decree of the Popes power to depose Princes?May it not be said vnto him; *Quousq, animam nostram tollis?* if this be of faith,*dic nobis palam.*But this,his Gr.(with his good leaue be it spoken) hath not yet performed , no not in his last against

See Tortus p.73.Colon.

E   D.*Barclai*

D. *Barclai*; howsoeuer he laboureth to beate downe a simple reader with words full of terror , to wit: That it is the
voice of the Catholicke Church, and he that contemneth to
heare her as (he saith) *Barclai* hath done, is no way to be accompted a Chriſtian, but as a Heathen and Publican. And, if
the Pope hath not power in earth , to diſpoſe of temporals,
euen to the depoſition of thoſe Princes, who are either thē-
ſelues heretikes , or in any ſort do fauour heretikes ; why at
the edition of this Canon, did none of ſo great a number,
reclame againſt it? Why durſt not, no not one, among ſo many Embaſſadors of Emperours and kings, once mutter at it?

This lo, is all the Cardinall bringeth for proofe of the ſuppoſed decree of faith , in the third Councell of Lateran,
(which is little to the purpoſe , and not ſo dreadfull as the
words import, if it be well conſidered) ſaying: It is the voice
of the Catholicke Church. What? that it is a point of faith
there concluded, binding all Chriſtians to beleeue , that the
Pope hath power to depoſe kings, and diſpoſe of temporals?
Was there *Anathema* thundred againſt any that ſhould not
beleeue it? Nothing leſſe ; as you may ſee if ye note the
words. And therfore *Barclai* hath not contēned the Church
(nor others that agree with him in opinion) who did alway
highly reuerence whatſoeuer ſhe decreed, *tanquam de fide*, in
any general Councell; whoſe ſoule I truſt doth reſt in peace,
and whoſe defence I make no doubt but ſome will take in
hand.

Then his Grace demandeth , why none reclamed againſt
this Canon, nor any Embaſſadour once muttered at it? This
why, in my iudgement, may be anſwered with a, Wherfore
haue Metropolitans and Biſhops all this time, being almoſt
400. yeares agone, bin ſo negligent in performing their dutie, by admoniſhing and excommunicating their Princes, if
this decree did bind them? And wherefore haue not Biſhops
that were remiſſe and negligent in purging hereſie out of
their Dioceſſes, bene depoſed according to the Councels
order, as appeareth in the end of this Canon? The words are,
*Volumus igitur & mandamus , & in virtute obedientia diſtrictè
præcipi-*

*præcipimus,&c.*We will therefore and cōmand,& in the vertue of obedience do ſtraightly charge,that for the effe&uall execution of theſe things, Biſhops watch diligently ouer thei Dioceſſes, as they will auoide the Canonicall reuenge. For if any Biſhop ſhall be negligent or remiſſe in purging out of his dioceſſe the leauen of hereticall deformitie, when that ſhall appeare by euident ſignes, let him be depoſed frō Epiſcopall office, and into his roome let another that is fit be ſubſtituted, who will, and is able to confound hereticall prauitie,This out of the Councell. Are theſe to be reputed as Heathens and publicans for not obeying the voice of the Church in this point? I know the Cardinall will not be ſo ſeuere a iudge,in ſuch wiſe to cenſure them, albeit they obey not the ſtraight commandement of this great and famous Councell,whoſe decrees of reformation, as alſo of all other general Councels,they are more bound to accept and put in execution, then kings and ſecular potentates.

Conc. Trid.
Seff.25.c.22.
& de reform.
cap.20.

And is it not more then probable that ſome there reclamed,ſome muttered, though the Cardinall haply find it not regiſtred,when according to the order of the Councell, and by vertue of this decree it was neuer executed? Then,*Nonne fruſtra eſt illa potentia quæ nunquam redigitur in a&um?*Yes ſaith Cardinal *Bellarmine,*ſpeaking in a like caſe,of Chriſts regall power in earth, vpon thoſe words of our Sauiour: *Regnum meum non eſt de hoc mundo.*Chriſt neuer exerciſed regal power in this world:for he came to miniſter,notto be miniſtred vnto. Therefore in vaine (ſaith he) had he receiued regall authoritie; *fruſtra eſt enim potentia quæ nunquam redigitur in a&um.*

Ioan.18.

But ſuppoſing with the Cardinall there were not then any reclamation nor any muttering againſt it , yet may ſuch a conſtitution being neuer receiued, or vpon diſuſe of ſo long time, be iuſtly ſaid to be abrogated , as many Canons and Decrees of this, and other Councels haue bene. And namely,that in this Councell which forbiddeth new religions to ariſe, Can.13.ſince which time, notwithſtanding, haue riſen the Minims of *S.Francis de Paula,*the religiō of the Ieſuites,

Panormitan.
Io.Andr.

Conc.Trid.
Seſſ.25.c.16.

E 2   and

and others. That Metropolitans should celebrate prouinciall Councels euery yeare, was appointed ca. 6. which is not

Can. 3. obferued. And in the Councell of Lateran vnder *Leo* 10. was decreed, that Monafteries after the deceaffe of the Abbots fhould not be giuen away to any in *commenda*, or cómended to any who were not religious: but how this like-

Conftantino.
Conc. can. 50
& 59. wife is obferued, the Monkes and religious of Italie, France, and other countries can teftifie. In the fixth generall Councell, clergie men were forbidden to play at dice; and it was ordered that Baptifme fhould be adminiftred onely in Churches: which are not kept. Many mo inftances out of other Councels might be to this purpofe produced, but to auoide tedioufneffe thefe few may fuffife.

Now for a further anfwer, I wifh you to note, that this Councell indeed (as by the words in the chapter is cleare) did firft excommunicate all herefie that lifted vp it felfe againft that faith which the Fathers had fet down in the two precedent chapters: and ordained that fuch as were therefore condemned, as alfo all other heretickes, fhould be left vnto the fecular powers to be condignly punifhed. Secondly, this holy Synode decreed, that fuch as were onely fufpected of herefie fhould cleare themfelues of that note within a yeare after admonition; otherwife they were to be excommunicated and auoyded till they had made condigne fatiffaction. Which was but the right practife and true proceeding of the Church, to inflict fpirituall cenfures, that the foules of the offendors might be faued in the day of our Lord, leauing them to the fecular Magiftrates to be further punifhed temporally.

Thirdly, it was fet downe in this Synode, as meete and conuenient, that fecular powers fhould be admonifhed, and if need were, compelled to take a publike oath for defence of faith, and to do their beft endeuours to roote out of their territories, all fuch heretikes as fhould be denounced by the Church: & none to be affumed into office which fhould not by oath confirme this chapter. By fecular powers and fuch as fhall be affumed into poteftacie or office, either fpirituall

or

or temporal, was not nor could be meant Emperor or King, but rather Prefidents or Gouerners of Prouinces fubiect vnto Kings, and abfolute Princes; who being Catholickes, may by their excelling power affifting the Church, compell them to confirme this chapter by taking fuch an Oath : but themfelues cannot be compelled by any, hauing no fuperior on earth in temporals to force them thereunto. Neither may it be faid properly, that a King, coming to his crowne by lawfull fucceffion and inheritance, or election, is affumed into office by any, his fubiects or others; for then it would follow, that he were not *fupremus Dominus*, a Soueraigne, but in fome fort inferiour to thofe that do affume him; becaufe he that is affumed or taken into office, receiueth authoritie from him that affumeth. As, the Pope creating a Cardinall, and faying, *Affumimus te in fancta Romana Ecclefia Cardinalem*, We affume thee to be a Cardinall of the holy Romane Church, giueth him by his fupreme authoritie that fpirituall office and dignitie of affifting him in the gouernment of the Church, and his temporall ftate, and to haue *vocem actiuam & paffiuam* in the election of the Pope, &c. But his Holineffe, though elected by the Cardinals, cannot properly be faid to be affumed by them to the Popedome, becaufe he receiueth no power or authoritie from them, but immediatly from God.

Finally, to the latter part, *Si vero dominus temporalis* : on which Cardinall *Bellarmine* fortifieth his affertion of the Popes authoritie to depofe Princes, faying, It is the voice of the Church: it may be anfwered, that the Church here defined it not, as he well knoweth; if fhe had, no doubt but his Grace would haue fpoken it plainly to put all out of doubt. By temporall Lords in this place, ought not to be vnderftood Kings, but rather fuch as are explicated in the Emperours conftitution, to wit, Poteftates, Confuls, Rectors, as hereafter followeth pag. 34. or fuch feudatarie Princes as haue principall Lords ouer them, like to certaine in Italy, where this Councell was held : which is manifeft by this Canon, that referueth the right of the principall

Lord,

Lord, *Saluo iure Domini principalis*. But I know some will say, that Kings and absolute Princes are to be also included, for that the words in the latter end seem to import so much, *The same law being kept about those who haue not principall Lords*: which ought to be vnderstood of absolute Princes. *Lord*, being a generall word, signifying sometime Kings. May it not be admired, that out of this obscuritie of the law, men will enforce Kings to be vnderstood, and to be subiect to temporall punishments, who acknowledge no superiour on earth to punish them in temporals, especially when as no mention is made of them at all in the law? In penals (as I haue said before pag. 51.) a restriction is to be v-sed, not an ampliation; and Kings are no lesse to be named or specified by the orderly proceeding of the Church, then

Conc. Trid.
seff. 24. de re-
form. cap. 1.

Cardinals, who are alwayes named in *pœnis*, or else not in-cluded, though the Pope command *sub pœna excommunicati-onis* all Patriarchs, Archbishops or Bishops, of what digni-tie soeuer. If yet any will enforce, that *By those who haue not principall Lords*, Kings are or may be vnderstood, it helpeth them nothing at all, for that such a law, first neuer receiued, and againe *per desuetudinem*, being neuer by the Church put in practise, is abrogated and of no validitie.

Neither was it defined in this Councell (as all men of meane iudgement may see) that the Pope hath authoritie to absolue subiects from their loyaltie or naturall obedi-ence due to their Princes; but onely signified, that he might denounce the vassals of certaine temporall Lords, absolued (as it were by vertue of some former law, to wit, that of

15. q. 6. ca:
Nos sanctorū

Gregorie 7, Nos sanctorum, or some other) from their fealtie, who being admonished and excommunicated by the Me-tropolitane, shall contemne to make satisfaction within a yeare: which is not to absolue them by any authoritie giuen by this Councell, and so it maketh nothing against the Oath of allegiance: *That the Pope cannot absolue me from this Oath*.

Then lastly it followeth: *And may expose his land to be occu-pied by Catholickes*. Is not this (trow ye) the groundworke of the Cardinals bulwarke for the Apostolicall authoritie

of

of depoſing Princes, and diſpoſing of their temporals? It ſeemeth yes, in his anſwer to D. *Barclai*; howbeit his Grace
bringeth nothing to proue ſuch power to be in the Pope, Supra pag. 54
but onely ſaith that, you wote not what, is the *voice of the*
Catholicke Church , and he that contemneth to heare her, is no
way to be accounted a Chriſtian, but as a heathen and Publican.
What words here in the name of God import a definition?
The Councell, as you may ſee, vſeth none of theſe words to
make a decree *de fide, ordinamus, ſtatuimus, definimus*, we ordaine, decree, define the Pope to haue authoritie to depoſe,
nor *anathema qui hoc non credit, anathema* to him that beleeueth not this, nor yet, *Hæc eſt fides Catholica*, This is the Catholicke faith : but onely ſaith, That if the temporall Lord
admoniſhed by the Church, ſhal neglect to purge his countrey from hereſie, he is to be excommunicated by the Metropolitan; and if he contemne to make ſatisfaction within
a yeare, it is to be ſignified to the Pope, that he may expoſe
his land (which is not to depoſe *authoritatiuè*) to be occu-
pied by Catholickes, *crucem prædicando* , that is, to giue
indulgences or pardons to ſuch as ſhall voluntarily take
armes, and aduenture their liues to fight againſt heretickes;
and as he is accuſtomed in like ſort to grant to all Chriſtians that ſhall arme themſelues and labour to expell the
Turks or Saracens out of the countries they vſurpe vpon, or
the holy land : as will appeare plainly to him that readeth
this Canon of the Councell. For, it followeth immediatly:
Catholici vero, qui crucis aſſumpto charactere ad hæreticorum
exterminium ſe accinxerint, illa gaudeant indulgentia, illoǵ, pri-
uilegio ſint muniti, quod accedentibus in terræ ſanctæ ſubſidium
conceditur. And let the Catholickes, who hauing taken the
ſigne of the croſſe, ſhall addreſſe themſelues to the rooting
out of heretickes, enioy the ſame indulgence, and be armed
with the ſame priuiledge which is granted to ſuch as prepare themſelues to the recouery of the holy land. Hereby
euery man may ſee, that in this wiſe to expoſe a country by
ſuch priuiledges and pardons to Prince or people, who either vpon zeale of dying Martyrs, as they thinke, or rather
coue-

couetous defire to enlarge their dominions, and to entich themfelues with others fpoiles, are ready to take fuch an occafion, and to runne before they be fent; is nothing to this purpofe,for depofing a lawfull Prince by any authority giuen the Pope by our Sauiour Chrift in S.*Peter*, or by the holy Ghoft in a generall Councell. You will fay vnto me, Are not heretickes being obftinate,vpon contempt of the Churches fword of excommunication,to be punifhed temporally by depriuation and confifcation of their goods,yea and by death too? Yes. But by whom? Not by any decree of Pope or Councell,but by the wholefome lawes of Emperors and Kings:for the Church,that is, the Paftors therof, after excommunication, *quia non habet vltra quod agat*, becaufe fhe can proceed no further, is accuftomed to deliuer ouer obftinate heretickes and fuch as fhe condemneth, to the fecular magiftrate to be punifhed temporally, whofe right it is,as *Cofterus* writeth; which is alfo manifeft in the Councell of Conftance, in the punifhment of *Hierome* of Prage and *Iohn Huffe*,who being declared to be heretickes, excommunicated and condemned, were forthwith deliuered ouer to the fecular power to be punifhed by death. *Romanæ Ecclefiæ confuetudo* (faith *Cofterus loco citato*) *in puniendis hæreticis talis eft,&c.*The cuftome of the Church of Rome in punifhing heretickes,is after this manner: After they are apprehended by the ciuill or ecclefiafticall magiftrate, firft they are examined by learned & ecclefiaftical men whether they be indeed heretickes : which being found,they are inftructed in the right faith,&c.Then(faith he) if they remain obftinate,*ab Ecclefiæ gremio vt putrida mēbra excōmunicationis gladio refecantur : qui fecundùm legum Regumq́ decreta, prout fas eft, in eos animaduertant. Nulli enim competit Ecclefiaftico, vel fanguinem fundere,vel capitis quenquam condemnare.* They are cut off with the fword of excommunication as rotten members from the lap of the Church, and are deliuered to the ciuill magiftrate to be punifhed, who according to the decrees of lawes and Kings may punifh them, as reafon is. For it is not meete for any Ecclefiafticall perfon either to

fhed

[margin: Tho.2.2,q.11. ar.3.]

[margin: Cofterus in fidei demonft propo.3.c.12. Con.Conftan feff.21]

ſhed blood, or to condemne any to death.

In the generall Councell of *Conſtance* was pronounced a definitiue ſentence againſt *Iohn Huſſe*, wherein for his pertinacie in hereſie, as that Councell tooke it, his degradation was committed to ſixe Biſhops, as writeth *Molanus* out of *Cochlæus*, and his execution to the ſecular power. *Hæc ſanɕta Synodus Ioannem Huſſe, attento quòd Eccleſia Dei non habeat vltra quod agere valeat, iudicio ſæculari relinquere, & ipſum curiæ ſæculari relinquendum fore decernit.* This holy Synode decreeth, conſidering that the Church of God can proceed no further, (to wit, then to excommunicate, and other ſpirituall puniſhments) to leaue *Iohn Huſſe* to ſecular iudgement, and that he ought to be left to the ſecular Court. Hence (ſaith *Molanus*) it is euident, with what ſmall conſideration ſome write, that *Iohn Huſſe* was burnt vpon the ſentence of the Councell of Conſtance, when as it was left to ſecular iudgement. Taken out of *Cochlæus lib. 2. ex Huſſita.* Now let it be demanded why heretikes, noble or ignoble, haue not bene, and yet are to be depriued of their temporals, and puniſhed by death, by vertue of that decree of Pope *Innocentius* in the Councell of Lateran, but rather by the decree of *Fredericke* the ſecond, Emperour, which he made (being ſolicited thereto by the Pope) anone after that Councell at Padua 22. Februarij, indiɕt. 12. againſt certaine heretikes called Patareni, if that of the Pope or Councell were to bind and be of force? If the firſt were obligatorie, what needed the ſecód of like forme to be made? The Emperor might wel haue ſpared his labour, if that former had bene deemed ſufficient. And this is certaine, and a ſufficient proofe of the inſufficiencie thereof, that the ſubſequent Popes, *Innocentius* 4. *Alexander* 4. and *Clemens* 4. would haue their Iudges to puniſh and proceed againſt heretikes, by vertue of that conſtitution of *Fredericke*, and not by the chapter of Lateran: which they would neuer haue done by *Cæſars* law, and not their owne, had they not knowne that *Cæſars* law in that behalfe was of greater force, and much more moment then their owne.

F   And

Molanus de fide hæret. ſer. l. 2. c. 2.

Can. corripiantur. 24. q. 3.

Direɕt. inquiſit. lit. A poſt. p. 13. 17. 51.

And left you fhould, hauing perchance neuer feene this imperiall Decree, doubt thereof, I haue thought good to fet it downe at large, which is this. *Statuimus etiam hoc edicto in perpetuum valituro, vt Poteftates & Confules, feu Rectores, quibufcunq; fungantur officijs, defenfione fidei praftent publicũ iuramentum, quòd de terris fua ditioni fubiectis vniuerfos hæreticos ab Ecclefia denotatos bona fide pro viribus exterminare ftudebunt, ita quod amodo quandocunq; quis fuerit in perpetuam poteftatem, vel temporalem affumptus, hoc teneatur capitulum iuramento firmare, alioquin neque pro Poteftatibus, neque pro Confulibus, feu confimilibus habeantur: eorumq; fententias ex tunc decernimus inutiles & inanes. Si vero Dominus tẽporalis requifitus & monitus ab Ecclefia terram fuam purgare neglexerit ab hæretica prauitate, poft annum à tempore monitionis elapfum, terram ipfius exponimus Catholicis occupandum: qui eam exterminatis hæreticis abfq; vlla contradictione poffideant, & in fidei puritate conferuent: faluo iure Domini temporalis: dummodo fuper hoc nullum praftet obftaculum, nec aliquod impedimentum apponat: eadẽ nihilominus lege feruata contra eos qui non habent Dominos temporales &c. Datum Padua. 22. Februarij, indictione 12.*

In Englifh thus : We decree alfo by this edict, for euer to be of force, that Poteftates, and Confuls, or Rectors, what offices foeuer they beare, for defence of faith, take a publike oath, that they fhall ferioufly endeuour what in them lieth, to roote out all heretikes noted by the Church, out of the countries fubiect to their gouernment, fo that from hencefoorth, whenfoeuer any fhall be affumpted to a Poteftacie for euer, or for a time, let him be bound to confirme this chapter by oath, otherwife let them not be efteemed for Poteftates, or for Confuls, or fuch like : and their fentences we decree forthwith to be vnprofitable and of no force. And if the temporall Lord, required and admonifhed by the Church, fhall neglect to purge his countrie from hereticall prauitie, after a yeare expired from the time of the admonition, we expofe his countrie to be occupied by Catholikes: who, when the heretikes are rooted out, may poffeffe it without any contradiction, and maintaine it in the puritie
of

of faith : the right of the principall Lord being referued : fo
that vpon this he bring no obſtacle , nor procure any impediment : the ſame law notwithſtanding being obſerued a-
gainſt them that haue not principall Lords, &c. Giuen at
Padua 22. of Februarie, indiction 12.

Now can any man perceiue by this imperiall law (procured, and vſed by the Church in the puniſhment of heretikes)
that kings are bound to take the oath therein ſpecified? or
that it is meant, their countries ſhould be giuen from them,
if after the Churches admonition they yet remaine negligent in extirpating heretikes? Nothing leſſe. Firſt, becauſe
kings are not named or mentioned , which is requiſite; but
Poteſtates (as are in Italie) Conſuls, and Rectors, or Gouernours of prouinces , ſuch as are inferiors , or ſubiect to the
Emperour or kings; therefore they are not compriſed in
the law. Nor ſecondly , can they be compriſed therein
(though perchance you will ſay, that by the latter clauſe, it
is meant alſo by kings ; and all other abſolute Princes, who
haue no dependance of the Emperour) for that they are
not bound to the keeping of the law being penall. *Princeps*   L. Princeps D
enim ſolutus eſt legibus. For the Prince is freed from lawes.   de legibus.
That is, as the Grecians vnderſtand, frō the penalty of lawes.

Thirdly, the Emperor being no ſuperior to abſolute kings,
cannot conſtraine them by any law ciuill , nor puniſh them.   L. non magi-
For, *Par in parem non habet imperium , multo minus inferior in*   ſtratus D. de
ſuperiorem. A peere or equall hath not dominion ouer his   recep. qui
equall, much leſſe an inferiour ouer his ſuperiour ; as ſub-   arbi.
iects ouer their lawfull Prince. Now if the Emperour, or a-
ny other Peere, may by vertue of that law, depriue an abſolute king of his kingdome , and confiſcate whatſoeuer he
hath (which are grieuous puniſhments) then is he ſubiect
to penall lawes, and to be corrected not onely by his peeres   Tert. ad Sca-
but alſo by inferiors, and his owne ſubiects: which is abſurd,   pulā Præſid.
and againſt the authorities aboueſaid , and iudgement of   Carthag.
ancient Fathers, *Tertullian, Ambroſe , Gregorius Turonenſis,*   Amb. in li. qui
and others; who write, that a king is inferiour but to God a-   inſcrib. Apol.
lone, that is, in temporals : that they are not to be puniſhed   Dauid.

by

by penall lawes, being defended with the power of their em-

Greg.l.5.hist.
c 7.

pire:&, if thou (speaking of a king) dost offēd, who shall correct thee, who shal cōdemn thee, but he that hath pronoūced
himselfe to be Iustice? This being so, then cannot that law, of
the Emperor take hold on kings, nor punish thē temporally.

But supposing that chapter of the Councell, whereof we
spake before, or rather of *Innocentius* in the Councell, were
a decree, what then? doth it follow infallibly that it is *de
fide*? No. The most reuerend Cardinall *Bellarmine* will tell

Bella l.2.Con
cap.12.

you, that in Councels the greatest part of the acts appertaine
not to faith, as disputations, reasons, explications, &c. *Sed
tantum ipsa nuda decreta, & ea non omnia, sed tantùm quæ proponuntur tanquam de fide.* That is, But onely the verie bare
decrees, and not all those neither, but onely such as are proposed as of faith. For sometime (saith he) Councels do define somewhat, not as certaine, but as probable, as the
Councell of Vienna, which decreed to be holden as the
more probable, that grace and vertues are infused to infants
in Baptisme, as is, *Clement. vnica de summa Trinit. & fide Cath.*

Why then Sir, how shal I know when a decree is of faith,
and when it is not? Cardinall *Bellarmine* in the place aboue
noted will put you out of doubt thereof. *Quando autem de-
cretum proponatur tanquam de fide, facilè cognoscitur ex verbis
Concilij; semper enim dicere solent, se explicare fidem Catholicam
vel hæreticos habendos qui contrariū sentiunt, &c.* Whē a decree
is proposed as of faith, it is easily knowne by the words of
the Councel; for they are alway accustomed to say, that they
explicate the Catholike faith, or, they are to be held for heretikes that think the contrarie; or which is most vsuall, they
say Anathema, and exclude out of the Church, those that
are of contrary opinion. And when they haue none of these,
it is not certaine that the matter is of faith. This he. By which
you learne, & may secure your conscience, that the doctrine
of depositiō of Princes, either directly or indirectly, ordinarily, or extraordinarily, casually or by consequence, was neuer in such sort decreed in the Councell of Lateran, or any
other Councell to this day : nor euer defined by any Pope

ex

ex cathedra (as fome take it) in Confiſtorie,*tanquam res fidei formaliter*, as a matter of faith formally.

If yet further you defire to know what Authors write, that the Popes authoritie in things temporall (as depofing Princes, and difpofing kingdomes you take to be) was ne-uer defined; you may reade Cardinall *Allen* againſt the En- Alanus. glifh Iuſtice,c.4.f.326. who faith, that it is a meere matter of Diuinitie difputable in fchoole, and no certaintie as yet defined by the Church, touching the Popes authoritie in things temporall.The fame affirme *Couarruuias*, p.2. pag. Couarruuias. 504.*Nauarrus*,as is there noted by *Couar.*& in *cap.Nouit de* Nauarrus. *iudicio notab. Bensfildius de iure & damno lato,c.*7.and others. Bensfildius.

Here it may be you will obieƈt vnto me, and fay, that *Paulus* 5. in prohibiting by his Breues the Oath of allegi-ance, feemeth there to define *ex cathedra* the Popes autho-ritie in temporals, as fome of our Paſtors fince this contro-uerfie teach vs; I pray you let me know your opinion,whe-ther they be definitiue fentences or no.

Beloued brethren, aſſure your felues they deceiue you, that fo ignorantly inſtruƈt you; and while they leade you into an errour, they hazard your ouerthrow. Thofe Breues are no definitions, but rather admonitions or aduertife-ments, as the firſt, dated 10.*Kalendas Octobris*,1606.which hath: *Propterea admonemus vos,vt ab hoc atque fimilibus iura-mentis præſtandis omnino caueatis,&c.*Therefore we admonifh you to beware of taking this and the like Oaths; affirming it withall to be vnlawfull.Or elfe precepts, (though not obli-gatorie *ad mortale peccatum*) as the fecond feemed to be, dated 10.*Kalend. Septembris*,1607. prohibiting the taking thereof. All which make not a definition *ex cathedra*; and it may wel be prefumed,that his Holineſſe neuer had any fuch intention to fet forth fuch a decree.To know when a decree is *de fide*, you may learne by that I told you a little before out of Cardinall *Bellarmine*, whofe rule is well to be confi-dered. If thefe Breues were definitions *de fide ex cathedra* (as fome moſt fondly and ignorantly ſticke not to auouch)fome of thofe claufes and interminations mentioned by Cardinal

F 3 *Bel-*

Bellarmine had bene inserted; they must haue bene generall, and ought to bind all Christian people as well as English Catholickes: for what is faith in one countrey, ought to be such through the world, and to be agreed vpon among learned men without controuersie. But these, being directed to one particular nation, and for this one particular cause of the Oath of allegiance, can be no decree *ex cathedra*, but rather priuate exhortatory letters, no precepts, as a late writer affirmeth them to be : *Priuatis literis Catholicos monuit Pontifex* (saith *Eudæmon*) *iuramentum id suscipi per diuinam legem non licere, proinde quiduis potius paterentur*. The Pope admonished Catholickes in his priuate letters (saith *Eudæmon* a Iesuite) that it was not lawful by the law of God to take that Oath, therefore they should rather suffer any thing. Which may be of little force, and not bind, specially if they were procured by sinister meanes, as by surreption, wrong information, and so forth, as with great reason it may be presumed these were, by a person more turbulent then was fitting for one of his function and vocation, whose merit haply might haue bene greater by deuout saying one paire of beades, then was by his labours and trauailes with his Holinesse to kindle quenched coales, as most probably he did in playing the soliciter, and procuring those Breues; whereby he hath brought all in brandlement, set no small contention and diuision among brethren and friends, and raised a tempestuous sea of calamities and troubles, where a happie calme of peace and quietnesse was not vnlike to be: for which God pardon his soule.

Andræas Eudæmon societatis Iesf. in præfat. ad Tortur Torti.

Moreouer, some good Authors not only doubt whether the Pope alone may determine or define matters of faith, but plainely seeme to say, such a determination doth not bind; and so he cannot without a generall Councell. *Determinatio solius Papæ* (saith *Gerson*) *in his quæ sunt fidei, non obligat, vt præcise est talis ad credendum*. The determination of the Pope alone, in matters of faith, as it is precisely such, bindeth not to beleeue. And *Petrus de Alliaco* sometime Cardinall of Cambray, in his treatise of the reformation of the

Io. Gerson. tract. de examinatione doctrinarum, consid. 2.

the Church of Rome, offered to the Councell of Conftance
begun *an.*1414. writeth in this fort, as appeareth in M.
Blackwels large examination. *In hoc non debet Papa aut eius* Petrus de Al-
Curia,&c. Herein (as touching the reformation of the bo- liaco.
die of the whole Church of Rome) the Pope or his Confiftorie ought not to reiect the deliberation of a generall
Councell, becaufe, as the Gloffe, 19.*dift.fuper cap. Anafta-* 19.dift.fuper
*fius,*faith, The Pope is bound to require a Councell of Bi- cap.Anaftaf.
fhops,when any point of faith is to be handled: which I do
not vnderftand of the articles of faith, but of difficult matters, that touch the vniuerfall ftate of the faithfull Church:
which *Archidiaconus* noteth, where approuing the faid 15.dift.c Sicut
Gloffe, he addeth, That it were too dangerous a matter to
commit our faith to the arbitrement of one man, and that
therefore the Pope in new and hard cafes, was accuftomed
to haue recourfe to the deliberation of a Councell. Now
let your learned inftructors perufe and confider well the
forefaid Authors (Catholicke) and the Gloffe, with the approbation thereof,alfo Catholicke; and then I perfwade my
felfe,they wil with more aduifement giue you better inftru-
ctions, and confeffe that thofe Breues are farre from definitiue fentences; if not,I wifh for your good, you may light
on better, and better experienced, left the blind leading
the blind,both fall into the pit: *Si enim cœcus cœcum ducit,*
ambo in foueam cadent.

Well, grant they are no definitions, yet it cannot be denied, but that therein his Holineffe hath declared, many
things to be contained in the Oath againft faith, and the
health of foules, and thereupon prohibited all Catholickes
to take the fame; whofe commandement (if any other) is to
be obeyed,by S.*Pauls* doctrine: *Obedite Prapofitis veftris, &* Heb.13.
fubiacete eis : ipfi enim peruigilant quafi rationem pro animabus
veftris reddituri. Obey your Prelates, and be fubiect vnto
them; for they watch, as to render account for your foules.
How can this be anfwered? or how can they free themfelues
from mortall finne, that by taking the Oath,feeme to contemne foueraigne authoritie? Very well. If indeede there
were

were contempt (as some either caried away with passion, or through ignorance and small consideration beare you in hand) then a hainous sinne would it be to transgresse the precept of the supreme Prelate Christs Vicar; for, contempt of any superiour, though in *re leuissima*, is alway a mortall sinne. But it is not so in this our case, it is not all one we know, *nolle obedire*, and *non obedire* : conscience setled on good grounds, is the onely motiue to such as take it, not to obey, beleeuing it to be most lawfull.

That his Holinesse hath affirmed in *genere*, as his opinion, many things to be contained in the Oath repugnant to faith and health of soules, is manifest in the Breues ; yet because he hath not specified any one particular clause (which was much desired) nor Father *Parsons* in his Catholicke letter, nor Cardinall *Bellarmine* in Tortus, or other booke of his, haue explicated or cleared the Popes meaning, what they be, nor any other writers that haue handled this matter, and written in defence of them (as doubtlesse they would haue done, if they could tell which were against faith) his Holinesse (in my iudgement) cannot iustly condemne such of a contempt, as with reason and vpon good grounds hold the contrary: who are not bound to alter their opinions vpon any such assertion of any priuate Doctor, vnlesse their vnderstanding be first conuinced, either by good reason, or authorities of Scriptures, Fathers, or some generall Councell. If any man be scandalized, and please to carpe hereat as at strange doctrine, let him reade the famous and learned S.*Tho.More* in his Epistle to D.*Wilson*, where he shall see the very same taught in this manner. Many things (euerie man learned woteth well) there are, in which euery man is at libertie, without perill of damnation, to thinke which way he list, till the one part be determined for necessarie to be belieued by a generall Councell. And in another place of his workes, thus he writeth: If it so hap, that in any particular part of Christendome, there be a law made, that be such, as for some part thereof some men thinke that the law of God cannot beare it, and some other thinke yes; the thing being

Tho.More in his epist. to D. Will. p. 1445.

In epist. ad filiam, pa. 1439.

being in fuch manner in queftion, that through diuers parts of Chriftendome, fome that are good men and cunning, both of our owne dayes and before our dayes, thinke fome one way; and fome other of like learning and goodneffe, thinke the contrary. In this cafe he that thinketh againft the law, neither may fweare that law lawfully was made, ftanding his own confcience to the contrary; nor is bound vpon Gods difpleafure to change his own confcience therein, for any particular law made any where, other then by the generall Councell, and by a generall faith growne by the working of God vniuerfally through all Chriftian nations : nor other authoritie then one of thefe twaine (except fpeciall reuelation, and expreffe commandement of God:) fith the contrary opinions of good men and well learned, as I put you the cafe, made the vnderftanding of the Scriptures doubtfull, I can fee none that lawfully may command and compell any man to change his own opinion, & tranflate his owne confcience from the one fide to the other. This he. And in another Epiftle to his daughter *Margaret*, pag. 1440 If it be not fo fully plaine and euident (as appearing by the common faith of Chriftendome) yet if he fee but himfelfe with farre the fewer part thinke the one way, againft far the more part of as learned and as good as thofe are that affirme the thing that he thinketh, thinking and affirming the contrarie, and that of fuch folke as he hath no reafonable caufe, wherefore he fhould not in that matter fuppofe, that thofe which fay they thinke againft his mind, affirme the thing that they fay, for none other caufe, but for that they fo think indeed : this is of very truth, a very good occafion to moue him, and yet not to compell him to conforme his mind and confcience vnto theirs. By this doctrine of Sir *Thomas More* it is cleare, that the Popes opinion of the Oath, though it may feeme to fome, to be a verie good occafion to moue men not to take it, yet it is not fufficient to compell them to conforme their mind and confcience vnto his; when as they that haue taken it, and alfo many others both vertuous and learned, are of contrarie opinion, nothing to be contained in that Oath againſt or repugnant to faith; nor neuer hath this point in controuerſie bene yet defined.

Will you ſay then that the Pope hath erred in ſetting forth this his opinion and prohibition? No, I dare not preſume to affirme that therein he hath erred, for the reuerence and honor I beare to the Sea Apoſtolick, nor take vpon me to be iudge ouer him, *Qui parem ſuper terram non habet,*to vſe Saint *Bernards* words; leſt I be thought to neglect the doctrine of the holy Ghoſt taught by S. *Paul: Tu quis es qui iudicas alienum ſeruum?* and, *Tu autem quid iudicas fratrem tuum? aut tu quare ſpernis fratrem tuum?* Who art thou that iudgeſt anothers ſeruant? and why doeſt thou iudge thy brother? If I be taught and forbiddē to iudge or deſpiſe my brother, my equall; then much more ought I not to iudge or contemne him, *qui à nemine iudicatur,* that is not to be iudged by any man: *abſit hoc à me,* let ſuch temeritie be farre from me, the leaſt in Gods houſe. But when in matters of fact, he proceedeth by information of others,(as in this our caſe of the Oath he hath) I truſt it is no temeritie, or any ſin at all, to ſay that he may erre; yea and ſometimes by falſe ſuggeſtions, or wrong informations, he hath erred in Rome it ſelfe. And which is more, Councels alſo in facts, or particular iudgements may erre, as Cardinall *Bellarmine* noteth. *In Scriptura* (ſaith he) *nullus poteſt eſſe error, ſiue agatur de fide, ſiue de moribus, &c. At Concilia in iudicijs particularibus errare poſſent. Nec non in præceptis morum, quæ non toti Eccleſiæ, ſed vni tantum aut alteri populo proponuntur.* In the Scripture can be no error, whether it treate of faith, or of manners, &c. but Councels in particular iudgements may erre. And alſo in precepts of manners, which are not propoſed to the whole Church, but to one or other people onely.

It ſeemeth alſo not to be any hereticall doctrine to hold, that not onely in matters of fact, but likewiſe in faith the Pope alone without a Councell may erre, for that he is no God, but a man ſubiect to errors; to whom as he is *Peters* ſucceſſor, Chriſt neuer ſo promiſed the aſſiſtance of the holy Ghoſt, that he in perſon ſhould not erre, but to *Peter* together

L.2. de conſid
c.2.
Rom.14.

Li.2. Concil.
cap.12.

ther with the Apoſtles, aſſembled at his ſermon before his paſſion, who repreſented the whole body of the Church, as appeareth by the words of our Sauiour in Saint *Iohns* Goſpell: *Paraclitus autem Spiritus ſanctus, quem mittet Pater in* Iohn. 14.c. *nomine meo, ille vos docebit omnia, & ſuggeret vobis omnia, quæcunque dixero vobis.* You may note how the holy Ghoſt then promiſed, and afterward ſent on the day of Pentecoſt, was promiſed to all, and ſent vnto all, not to *Peter* alone. And in the ſame chapter, that this holy Ghoſt was to remain with them, and be in them. *Apud vos manebit, & in vobis erit.* Ioh. 16. And in another place. *Cū autem venerit ille Spiritus veritatis, docebit vos omnem veritatem.* And when he ſhall come, the Spirit of truth, he will teach you all truth. In all theſe places is manifeſt that Chriſt ſpake alway in the plurall number, that the holy Ghoſt the Comforter, ſhould remaine and be in his Church, and ſhould teach his Church all truth, and not any one of his Apoſtles ſucceſſors in particular. This ſpecial priuiledge of not erring in matters of faith, was reſerued for his deare ſpouſe the Catholike Church alone, as appeareth euident likewiſe in Saint *Matthewes* Goſpell: *Tu es Petrus,* Math. 16. *& ſuper hanc petram ædificabo Eccleſiam meam, & portæ inferi non præualebunt aduerſus eam.* Thou art *Peter*, and vpon this rocke I will build my Church, and the gates of hell ſhall not preuaile againſt her. That is, the Church (as *Ianſenius* and others vnderſtand it) repreſented in a generall Councell, which Church is called by Saint *Paul, Columna & firmamen-* 1. Tim. 3. *tum veritatis:* The pillar and groundworke of truth. Not any one man in the houſe of God was euer ſuch. And *Alphonſus de Caſtro*, a great learned man, and an earneſt defender of this Church againſt hereſies and heretikes, bluſheth not to write plainely that, *Omnis homo errare poteſt in fide, etſi Papa* Contr. hæreſ. *ſit:* Euerie man may erre in faith, yea the Pope himſelfe, l.1.c.4. without exception. Yet I neuer heard that he was condemned of hereſie, or ſinne, for ſaying ſo. This then being ſo, no man of vpright iudgement, can with reaſon cenſure him of hereſie, that ſhall affirme, The Pope may erre in his opinion of the Oath; for, *Hæreſis eſt circa ea quæ ſunt fidei, ſicut circa* 2.2.q.11.ar.2

propriam

2.2.q.11. ar.2. *propriam materiam* : as S.*Thomas* faith. Nor of mortall fin, ifhe refufe to obey his prohibition for taking thereof, the Tho.22.q. taker not intending to contemne his commandement, *(ad* 104.a.2.ad 1. *inobedientiam enim requiritur quòd actualiter contemnat præceptum)* nor to tranfgreffe againft the law ofGod; but onely to render to *Cæfar* that which is *Cæfars,* that is, ciuill obedience, due vnto him both by the law of God and nature; without denying or derogating anie authoritie fpirituall of the Sea Apoftolicke,according to his Maiefties declaration and interpretation ofhis owne meaning,fet downe at large in his Apologie and Præmonition. The intention then being good, the end good and iuft, the act offuch as take it cannot be but good and lawfull, and no fin at all. For *fe-* Tho.2.2.q 89 *cundum finem morales actus fpecies fortiuntur*. And as true it is, ar. 5.ad 1.& q. that, *Actus agentium non operantur vltra ipforum voluntatem* 105 a.1. *feu intentionem*. And this much as touching the Popes opinion or affertion in his Breues.Now it remaineth to refolue the difficultie of his precept, or prohibition of the Oath; whether Priefts and Catholickes in England be bound vnder paine of deadly finne to obey it, and fo to difobey the Kings Highneffe, who for his more fecuritie,vpon fo iuft a caufe,requireth the fame.

The caufe why the Pope prohibited Catholickes to take the Oath of allegiance as it lieth, may feeme to haue bene, for that in his opinion he was perfwaded many things to be contained therein repugnant to faith. Which opinion fuppofed true, no man indeede can take it without perill of damnation; becaufe euery Chriftian is bound *vfque ad effufionem fanguinis inclufiue,* to profeffe and maintaine all points of faith, when occafion of perfecution fhall be offered, againft heretickes, Iewes, Turkes, or what infidels foeuer, Math.10. according to the doctrine of our Sauiour: *Qui autem nega-* Luk.9. *uerit me coram hominibus, negabo & ego eum coram Patre meo:* And he that fhall denie me before men, I will alfo denie Luk.14. him before my Father. Likewife in another place: *Qui non renunciat omnibus quæ poffidet, non poteft meus effe difcipulus.* And then were it *malum, non quia prohibitum, verùm ex fe,*

to

to take fuch an oath. But till it appeare more cleare, and be more fubftantially proued then hitherto hath bene by any, that fome point therein contained, is manifeftly againft faith,& what that point is; I cannot fee why any man fhould forthwith vpon a bare commandement, though of the fupreme Paftor, hazard his life in perpetuall bonds, with loffe of all that he hath, and vtter ruine of his deareft wife and children. For his priuate will, fubiect to error, can be no infallible rule of mans actions, but the will of God, which is alway right: and hereupon a man may in cafe be difobeied, be he Prince or Prelate, but the moft righteous God neuer. For that the commandement of God is alway iuft, wherein can be no error, no not in willing *Abraham* to kill his fonne Gen.22. *Ifaac* : nor in commanding the Iewes to fpoile the Ægyp- Exod.12. tians of their goods: nor alfo in bidding the Prophet *Ofea* Ofe.1. to commit fornication. The reafon hereof you may reade in *S. Thomas.* But an earthly King, Prince or Prelate, yea See S.Tho.22 the Prince of Prelates may, and doe fometimes command q.104.ar.4. iniuft things, or may vfurpe dominion iniuftly: in which cafes, fubiects are not bound to obey them, *nifi forte per acci-* 22.q.104.ar.6. *dens* (as *S. Thomas* noteth) *propter vitandum fcandalum vel periculum* : vnleffe haply accidentally, for auoiding fcandall or danger. That fome Kings and fecular Princes haue vfurped domination, and commanded iniuftly, no man I thinke will doubt, and our domefticke aduerfaries will eafily grant: but to fay that the Prince of Prelates, the Pope, *Peters* fucceffor fhould erre in commanding, or command that which is iniuft (*guarda la gamba*, take heed) fome nicely precife, pure and rigid, if not fimple and foolifh people, *audito verbo hoc fcandalizabuntur*, no leffe then the Pharifees were fcandalized at the doctrine of our bleffed Sauiour, as we reade in *S. Mathewes* Gofpell : for that they thinke of Math.15. like, the Pope fo to be confirmed in grace, that he cannot once commit a mortall fin. If they will fo eafily be fcanda- Greg. hom.7. lized for fpeaking the truth, I truft I may be bold, without in Ezech. fin, to fay with *S. Gregorie* : *Si de veritate fcandalum fumitur,* Haimo in *vtilius nafci permittitur fcandalum, quàm quòd veritas relinqua-* Math.c,18.

tur.

*tur.*If ſcandall be taken for ſpeaking truth,it is better a ſcandall ſhould be permitted to ariſe, then truth left vntold . I will relate therefore certaine true faƈts, but not cenſure them,which without this,or ſuch like occaſion offered,I euer purpoſed to haue concealed; and referre to the readers iudgements whether they were errors in gouernment,and ſinnes, or no.

When *Sixtus Quintus*, otherwiſe a prudent Prince and learned Paſtor, commanded a boy of fourteene yeares of age to be hanged in Rome, for a fault which in many mens iudgements deſerued not death , but rather whipping, or ſome ſuch puniſhment;and being in all humility told by the Iudge, that by the ciuill lawes he was not to be executed till he came to the age of 16: he anſwered,Then I will giue him two of my yeares.Whereupon the poore lad,contrarie to law, ended his life in poſt haſt in a halter. Whether this were a iuſt ſentence or iniuſt, I will not ſay; it ſeemed at his departure out of this life,to be ſcored among his miſdeeds: for being in *extremis,* one like in habit to *S.Francis* appeared to him,who had appeared long before,& foretold al his fortunate riſings to honor,and now warned him to prepare to die,for his time was come . Hereat *Sixtus* appalled,ſaid: Diddeſt thou not promiſe me that I ſhould reigne one luſtre and halfe? (a luſtre is the ſpace of fiue yeares.)Yes; and now it is in maner expired (he had then reigned fiue yeares,foure moneths,and three daies); for if you remember, you gaue a boy two yeares,to hang him.This I heard conſtantly reported by manie in Rome preſently vpon his death . But who this was that appeared, *S. Francis,* or ſome other transfigured in his habite,it was not knowne,and I leaue to the conſideration of men to thinke what they liſt.

Likewiſe it happened,that in his time a Clergie man,nephew vnto old *Martinus Nauarrus* the great Canoniſt, coming into *S.Peters* Church(doubtleſſe with intent to pray) found ſtanding againſt a pillar by our Ladies altar a pilgrims ſtaffe, wherewith he ſtrake the Iudge of the Suitzers, being on his knees at his praiers before the crucifixe altar,

and

and brake his head fo,as the bloud ran about his eares, and
fell on the pauement; whereby the Church being profaned,
forthwith all Maffes and other diuine feruice ceaffed for a
time, (I fpeake what I know,being then *oculatus teftis:*) incontinently the partie fled toward the new Church,but pur-
fued by certaine Suitzers attending on the faid Iudge, was
apprehended ; and the Pope then fitting in Confiftorie,ad-
uertifed of the fact,who commanded a ghoftly father to be
prouided for him, (religioufly and well done for fafetie of
his foule) and that he fhould not hope for life, but prepare
to die out of hand, (*fummum ius*) for he would not dine till
the offender were hanged. A hard fentence of the fupreme
Paftor.Hafte here made wafte of bloud.Would God he had
well confidered *S.Ambrofe* his penance enioyned *Theodofius*
the Emperour,and his humble acceptation thereof,viz. not
to punifh any malefactor to death for a moneths fpace after
the crime committed; then haply his wrath and indignation might haue bene pacified, and the offenders life faued.
Incontinently a gallowes was fet vp before the Suitzers
gate, and the Spanifh gentleman brought to execution
within three houres after the blow giuen, the Pope ftanding in a gallerie of his pallace (Confiftorie being ended)to
fee him coming, as was moft certainly reported vnto me
then lying in the pallace, by fuch as had reafon to know it :
and would not be pacified or intreated for his life, neither
by the Spanifh Ambaffadour, who pofted to the Court to
that end,though in vaine, for audience would not be granted, nor by any other; howbeit his feruant the Suitzer, in
fhort fpace after recouered, and liued diuers yeares after
that to my knowledge. How iuft thefe commandements
were,I referre to the readers iudgement; and whether they
fauoured not more of a paffionate fecular Prince, then of a
milde fpirituall Paftor.

　　Moreouer, the faid Pope hauing created Cardinall the
Deane of Toledo, *Mendoza* by name, a verie noble and
worthie gentleman, a comely and courteous Prelate, and
well beloued of many; dealt often with the faid Cardinall

to refigne his Deanrie into his hands, by reafon of the in-
dignitie he fhould be driuen into, if at any time after, he
were to refide in his Deanrie accoŕding to order, by taking
inferior place in the Church to the Biſhop of the Dioceſſe,
being no Cardinall; which was a thing he would not confent vnto, faying, they were *incompatibilia*, Deane and Cardinall in one perfon. The Cardinall vnwilling to lofe fo
great reuenewes by making fuch a refignation, thought it
no finne therein not to yeeld to his Holineſſe. Pope *Sixtus*
notwithſtanding out of his abfolute authoritie *volens nolens*
depriued him of his Deanry, & beſtowed it on another Spa-
niard, who after *Sixtus* death, plaied leaſt in fight, for feare
what might befall him by fome of the Cardinall his friends
for accepting or feeking it. And the Pope to make his dona-
tiō valid, fent *Monſignore Burgheſius Auditor di camera*, (who
fitteth now in *Peters* chaire) with ſtraight commandement
vnto Cardinall *Mendoza*, either forthwith to fend the writings of his Deanrie, or elfe to go immediatly with the faid
Prelate to the Caſtle. The Cardinall hereat fore perplexed
and ſtraightned on euerie fide, making choice of the leſſe e-
uill, chofe rather quietly, though much againſt his liking,
to fend his writings, and be depriued of his Ecclefiaſticall
liuing, then bereaued of his temporall life in the caſtle of S.
Angelo; whence is hard getting foorth for any that ſhall enter therein. Many hereat muttered and murmured, iudging
the commandement to fauour of great iniuſtice.

　After this, Pope *Clement* in the beginning of his reigne,
with more haſte thē good ſpeed, refembling likewife rather
a paſſionate Prince then a meek Paſtor, gaue order or commandement that a certaine gentleman of Cardinall *Farneſius* apprehended on Saturday before Palmfunday, ſhould
be executed the wednefday following, being the feaſt of the
Annunciation of the bleſſed virgine *Marie*, and in the holy
weeke, againſt all clement Chriſtian cuſtomes and good order, which fpare to execute any malefaĉtor on fuch times:
& would not hearken to any other information then that of
the Gouernour, the gentlemans knowne aduerfarie, no not
　　　　　　　　　　　　　　　　　　　　　　　　of

of the Cardinall, who hearing thereof, with all ſpeed poſted from Grotta ferrata toward his Holineſſe at Rome, for
his ſeruants life: albeit in vaine, for he was inexorable, and
audience would not be granted him, till the poore gentleman had loſt his head; whereupon the Cardinall being offended, departed, and refuſed to come to the Court for the
ſpace of a moneth after. Was this apprehenſion and execution for any hainous crime trow ye? Thus ſtood the caſe. Certaine Sbirri or Sergeants, were ſent from the Gouernour
to the pallace of Cardinall *Farneſius* (he being abſent twelue
miles off, at Grotta ferrata) to apprehend ſome other of
his familie of baſer condition, who finding the partie in the
open Court together with one of his fellowes, they laide
hands on him: the partie and his fellow, and the two Sbirri
ſtriuing and ſtrugling each with other, an Engliſh maſtife
dogge, whereof the Cardinall made great reckoning, fell on
the Catchpols of himſelfe, and the meane while they
gat out of their hands. The ſayd gentleman ſeing this ſtir,
came to them, and demanded how they durſt be ſo bold
to make ſuch an attempt in that place, and whether they
knew where they were, and in whoſe houſe, which (being
priuiledged as a ſanctuarie) ought better to be reſpected
of ſuch as they were, and ſuch like words. The Sbirri departed with complaint to the Gouernour, who haſteneth
to the Pope, and informeth him in ſuch ſort, as the gentleman by his commandement was preſently taken, and executed as is aboue ſaid: and ſo ſhould the dog bene hanged
too if he could haue bene found, but he was ſecretly conueyed away. And this loe was the crime for which he loſt
his life, as was bruited and knowne through all the citie,
and was beſides told me by ſuch of the family as had reaſon
not to be ignorant of the buſineſſe: at which fact many
grudging ſaid, The Pope might more fitlie haue bin called
Leo then *Clement*.

Well, if for relating theſe truths any man be offended, let
him blame certaine ſilie ſoules whoſe fond importunitie
hath vrged me thereto, for that they thinke, and will ſome-

time

time fay, that the Pope his actions are irreprehenfible,he cannot commit a mortall finne, nor command vniuftly; as if he were more then a mortall man,halfe a God, or fo confirmed in grace that he could no way erre, as was the Mother of God. But the more prudent fort will eafily grant that he is a man, fubiect to humane infirmities, and not fo confirmed in grace as that he cannot erre in his morall actions; that is a priuiledge they know rather proper to the Mother of God,then common to Chrifts Vicars, which (if I be not deceiued) was neuer yet granted to any of them. Marie fome of thefe, *prudentes apud femetipfos*, dare boldlie auouch,that if *Peters* fucceffour fhal at any time excommunicate a Prince fallen into fchifme, herefie or apoftacie, or other crime adiudged by him to deferue fo to be cenfured, and thereupon depriueth him of his Regall fcepter, depofeth him of all temporall dominion,and difpofeth of his territories to fome other whom he fhall iudge better to deferue the fame; or authorifeth fubiects to raife tumults and take armes againft fuch a one, and abfolueth them of their fidelitie and natural allegiance,or inciteth other neighbour Kings and Princes by mightie power, to inuade his dominions, or finallie whatfoeuer he command in this or the like fort, they are bound forthwith to obey him and his fentence, what perill foeuer may fall vnto them for it; though by fo doing they are to lofe their liues who (as they imprudently thinke) hath in fuch a cafe fo fupreme authoritie ouer him as exceedeth all limits,& is fo directed by the holy Ghoft that he cannot command iniuftly : fo *omne nimium vertitur in vitium*,this loe is the prudence of fome imprudent Catholickes, who headlonglie without due confideration runne on themfelues, and animate others to run through ouer blind obedience to their vtter deftruction; but this point of obedience refteth now to be more largely difcuffed.

It cannot be denied but that obedience is a morall vertue(whereas it is a part of iuftice, whofe office is to render to euery one that which is his:)the fpeciall obiect of which

is

is the secret or expresse precept of the superiour, to whom e-
uery inferiour, both by the law and ordinance of God and
nature, ought in all things lawfull, not to be refractarie, but
subiect & obedient. Yet it may so happen againe, that for
two respects a subiect or inferiour may not be bound alway to obey his superiour: the one is by reason of the precept of a higher power commanding contrary, as vpon that
of *S. Paul, Qui potestati resistunt, ipsi sibi damnationem acqui-* Rom.13.
runt: They that resist power, the same get to themselues
damnation. The Glosse saith, *Si quid iusserit Curator, &c.* If Ang.in ser.6.
de verbis Do-
the Curator, or gouernour, command any thing against the mini, to. 10.
Proconsul, art thou to do it? Againe if the Proconsul command thee one thing, and the Emperour an other thing, is it
to be doubted that contemning the one, thou art to serue
and obey the other? Then if the Emperour one thing, and
God command an other, thou art bound to obey God and
not the Emperour. So semblably if the Pope command one
thing, and the holy Ghost in Scriptures an other, who
doubteth which is to be obeyed or disobeyed? The other is,
when the superiour commandeth any thing wherein the
inferiour is not subiect vnto him, exceeding the limits of
his power: all power whatsoeuer vnder the cope of heauen
being contained within certaine limits, which no power-
able person is to exceede.

Here if any obiect *S. Paul*, teaching children and seruants
to obey their parents and maisters in all they command: *Filij* Coloss.3.
obedite parentibus per omnia: and, *Serui obedite per omnia do-*
minis carnalibus: children, obey your parents in all things: &,
seruants, obey in all things your carnall maisters: therefore
the Pope is to be obeyed in all things. I answer them, that it
is to be vnderstood, in all things that appertaine to the
right of parents & maisters, and as farre as they haue power
to command; as maisters their seruants in seruile things, and Tho 2.2.q.
parents their children in domesticall affaires belonging to 104.c.5.
their paternall care: for neither can they command such as
are vnder them to keepe virginitie, or to marry, or to enter
into religion, to go in pilgrimage, or such like; if they

should, the inferiour is not bound to obey. No more can the Pope, albeit he hath *plenitudinem potestatis in Ecclesia*, iustly command any thing wherein he hath no power, nor any persons which are not subiect vnto him: for that none is to be reputed a superior, but in respect of them, ouer whom as ouer subiects he receiueth power, whether he hath it ordinary, or by commission. Neither are Religious men, who vow obedience to their superious, bound of necessity to obey them in all whatsoeuer lawfull things they command, (albeit in way of perfection they may) but onely in such as appertaine to their regular conuersation, or according to their rule which they professe. And if their superiours shold by indiscretion or otherwise command any thing against the law of God, (yea were he the Pope himselfe) or against the profession of their rule, such obedience, I deeme, nor they nor any will doubt to be vnlawfull; and they were not bound to obey, as *Innocentius* & others affirme. So then we may distinguish obedience to be of three sorts: one sufficiēt to saluation, which obeyeth in all matters wherein he is bound: another perfect, which obeyeth in all things lawfull: and the third indiscreet, which is ready to render obedience yea in vnlawfull or iniust things.

And this is the obedience wherewith many (alas) in these our dangerous dayes seeme so deeply possessed, (dangerous I say) for that within such obedience (*latet anguis in herba*) lyeth hidden a mystery of mischiefe, and which is so highly by diuerse recommended to their auditours, who sticke not boldly to say, that by obeying Pastors and Prælats, and the supreme Pastor among the rest, he cannot sin, but by refusing to obey, he may sinne; therefore it is best and securest alway to obey whatsoeuer is by them commanded, alledging S. *Paul: Obedite Præpositis vestris:* Obey your Prelats, without distinction: not attending that the same holy Ghost who taught vs this doctrine by the vessell of election, hath likewise taught vs by the mouth of the Prince of Apostles, and cannot be contrary to himselfe, that we are no lesse bound to obey and be subiect to kings

and

Marginal notes:

Tho. 2.2.q. 67. ar. 1.

Tolet. de 7. pec. mort. c. 16. n. 3.
Tho. 2.2 q. 104. a. 5. ad 3.
Innocen. in c. ne Dei. 43. de Simon.
Martin. de Carazijs in tract. de principibus q. 48.
Felin. in cap. Accepimus de fide instrum.

Hebr. vlt.

and their officers, to wit: *Subiecti estote omni humanæ crea-* 1.Pet.2.
tura propter Deum: siue Regi quasi præcellenti: siue ducibus tan-
quam ab eo missis, ad vindictam malefactorum, &c. Be ye fubiect to euery humane creature for God: whether to the
King as to the precellent, or to his Captaines as fent from
him, for the punifhment of malefactors, &c. For that the
politicall or ciuill power, yea of heathen or perfecuting
Neros (as in the Apoftles times were no other) is no leffe
from God, and immediate from him, then is the Ecclefia-
fticall or fpirituall. *Non est enim potestas nisi à Deo*: for there Rom. 13.
is no power but of God. When he faith, No power, is there
any excepted? Is it not meant as well of the temporall, as
of the fpirituall? *Chrysostome* vpon this place hath thefe
words: *Deus ita exigit, vt creatus ab eo Princeps vires suas ha-*
beat; God fo requireth, that a Prince created haue his
power from him; then not from the people. If you
reade *Salomon* in the booke of Wifedome. you fhall find it
moft cleare, that the power of Kings and Rulers is imme-
diat, not from men, but from God. *Præbete aures vos, qui* Sap.6.
continetis multitudines, &c: quoniam data est à Domino pote-
stas vobis, & virtus ab Altissimo, &c. Giue eare you, that
conteine multitudes: (who are they but temporal Princes?)
becaufe power is giuen to you from our Lord, and vertue
from the Higheft, without any diftinction of *mediate*, &c.
It followeth a little after who are meant: *Ad vos ergo Re-* ver.10.
ges sunt hi sermones mei, vt discatis sapientiam, &c. To you
therefore ô kings are thefe my words, that you may learne
wifedome, &c. Thefe two powers then, Ecclefiafticall and
ciuill, as they are both from God, fo are they both diftinct
and feparate from other, and independent of each other, as
after fhall be proued.

And euen as God hath ordeined and concluded the waters and maine fea within certaine limits, which they may
not paffe, but muft breake their raging waues where they
are appointed, as is in holy Writ: *Legem ponebat aquis, ne* Prou.8.
transirent fines suos. He made a law for waters, that they
fhould not paffe their bounds: and in *Iob*: *Et Dixi, vsque* Iob.38.
huc

huc venies, & non procedes amplius, & hic confringes tumentes fluctus tuos. And I said (saith God) hitherto thou shalt come, & thou shalt proceed no further, and here thou shalt breake thy swelling sources. So likewise his omnipotent wisdome, haply to auoide all confusion and other mischiefes, which might arise by intermedling with each others power, hath appointed the their seuerall and distinct ends, their limits & bounds, which they may not passe, nor inuade each others empire : as mellifluous S. *Bernard* writing to Pope *Eugenius* 3. doth more then insinuate. *Habent hæc infima & terrena Iudices suos, Reges & Principes terræ. Quid fines alienos inuaditis? quid falcem vestram in alienam messem extenditis?* These base and terrene things haue their Iudges, Kings and Princes of the earth. Why do you inuade other mēs boūds? why do you thrust your sythe into others haruest? By which is euident that Popes may, and do sometimes exceede their limits, to wit, spirituall authority, when by vsurpation they intermeddle in terrene things or temporall authority, being the proper bounds of Kings and secular Princes, which ought not to be inuaded by Ecclesiasticall persons. And to this effect writeth most excellently amongst latter Diuines *Ioannes Driedo*, affirming this distinction to be *de iure diuino. Christus* (saith he) *vtriusque potestatis officia discreuit, vt vna diuinis & spiritualibus rebus atque personis, altera profanis ac mundanis præsideret.* Christ hath so parted the offices of both powers, as the one might gouerne ouer diuine and spirituall things and persons, the other ouer profane and mundane. And a little after: The distinction therefore of Ecclesiasticall Papall power from the secular and Imperiall power is made by the law of God. And in the same chapter; Whereupon the Pope and the Emperour are in the Church not as two chiefe gouernours deuided among themselues, (neither of which do acknowledge or honour the other as superiour) because a kingdome deuided against it selfe will be desolate. Neither are they as two Iudges subordinate, so as the one receiueth his iurisdiction from the other : but they are as two gouernours, which are the Ministers of one God

Lib.1.de consid.cap.5.

Lib.2.de liber.Eccle.c.2.

God, deputed to diuers offices, in such wise as the Emperour is to rule ouer secular causes & persons, for the peaceable liuing together in this world : and the Pope may rule
ouer spirituals to the gaine of Christian faith and charitie.
This *Driedo*. That these two dignities are distinct, hauing
no dependance of each other, Cardinall *Bellarmine* himselfe
proueth, cōparing them to the two great lights or planets,
the Sunne and Moone. *Nota(saith he)quemadmodum non est*
idem sydus Sol & luna, & sicut lunā non instituit Sol, sed Deus: Bellar.l.5.de
ita quoque non esse idem Pontificatum & Imperium, nec vnum Ro.Pont.c.3.
ab alio absolute pendere. Note that euen as the Sunne and
Moone are not one and the same planet, and as the Sunne
did not institute or appoint the Moone, but God : so likewise the Papacy and Impery are not one and the same, nor
the one do absolutely depend of the other. By these two
great lights Sun and Moone , Pope *Inocentius* interpreteth Cap.Solite de
to be meant two dignities, which are Pontificall authority, maiorit. &
and Regall power. obedien.

Moreouer this distinction of these two great powers,
that ancient and renowmed *Hosius* Bishop of Corduba
writing to *Constantius* the Arrian Emperour most mani- L.2.de liber.
festly sheweth: whose sentence is related in an Epistle of ho- Christ.c.2.
ly *Athanasius* in this manner: *Tibi Deus imperium commisit,* Atha. ep. ad
nobis quæ sunt Ecclesiæ concredidit: & quemadmodū, &c. To you solit.vitam
God hath committed the Empire , to vs he hath deliuered agentes.
those things which belong to the Church : and euen as he
that with malignant eyes carpeth your Empire, contradicteth the ordinance of God, so do you also beware, left, if
you draw to you such things as belong to the Church , you Math.22.
be made guiltie of a great crime. Giue, it is written, to Cæ- Mar.12.
sar those things which are *Cæsars* , and to God those which
belong to God. Therefore neither is it lawfull for vs in earth
to hold the Empire ; nor you ô Emperour, haue power o-
uer incense and sacred things. Thus this learned Bishop, and In cap.Inqui-
renowmed in the first Councell of Nice. Hereupon *Innocen-* sitioni de sen.
tius the third, and *Panormitan* conclude, that laickes are not excom.
bound to obey the Pope in those things that are not spirituall

tuall, or which concerne not the foule, as they fpeake: but
onely in thofe places which are fubiect to his temporall iu-
rifdiction. That thefe two powers are independent of each
other, and the temporall not fubordinate to the fpirituall,
but, fince the comming of Chrift, feparate, and fo diftinguifhed by their proper acts, offices and dignities, that the one
may not vfurpe the right and power of the other without
iniurie to each other, Pope *Nicolas* the firft, plainly witnef-
feth in his Epiftle to *Michael* the Emperour; as appeareth
alfo in the Canon law; which you may reade in D. *Barclai*
of worthie memorie, in cafe you can get it. Which place I
may not pretermit to note vnto you as it is fet downe in
Cardinall *Bellarmine* : *Idem mediator Dei & hominum, homo*
Chriftus Iefus, fic actibus proprijs, & dignitatibus diftinctis of-
ficia poteftatis vtriufq; difcreuit, &c. The fame Mediator of
God and men, the man Chrift Iefus, hath fo feuered the
offices of both powers, by proper acts and diftinct dignities, that both Chriftan Emperours for eternall life, fhould
haue neede of the chiefe Bifhops, and the chiefe Bifhops for
the courfe of temporall things onely, fhould vfe Imperiall
lawes. Here (faith the Cardinall) the Pope fpeaketh not of
the onely execution, but of power and dignitie, &c. For
whatfoeuer Emperours haue, Pope *Nicholas* faith, they haue
it from Chrift. I aske then, either the chiefe Bifhop can take
from Kings and Emperours this execution, as being himfelfe chiefe King and Emperour, or elfe he cannot? If he can,
then is he greater then Chrift: if he cannot, then hath he not
in deed Regall power. This he: Who in the fame chapter
bringeth Pope *Gelafius* to this purpofe. *Duo funt (inquit)*
Imperator Augufte, quibus principaliter mundus hic regitur, Au-
thoritas facra Pontificum, & Regalis poteftas, &c. There are
two things O noble Emperour, whereby principally this
world is gouerned, the facred authoritie of Bifhops, and
Regall power, &c. Where it is to be noted (faith *Bellarmine*)
that *Gelafius* fpeaketh not onely of the excution, but of the
verie power and authoritie, left our aduerfaries fay (as they
are accuftomed) that the Pope hath indeed both powers, but
com-

Can. cum ad
verum. ventū
eft, dift. 9 6.
Barcl. de po-
teft. Pap. c. 13.
L. 5. de Rom.
Pont. c. 3.

Gelaf. ep. ad
Anaft. Imp.
Decret. dift.
96. Can. Duo
funt.

committeth the execution to others. That the ends likewife
of thefe two powers are different, the Cardinall confeffeth,
faying, that the politicall hath for her end temporall peace,
and the Ecclefiafticall eternall faluation. And hereto agree-
eth *Nauarre in Relect. cap. Nouit de iudic. nu. 90.* By this now is Nauar.
apparent that thefe two powers, their ends, offices, and
dignities are diftinct and feparate from each other.

If then the one command any thing which appertaineth
not to his power, or wherein he is not fuperiour, it is a generall rule (as Cardinall *Tolet* noteth) that fuch a one is not Tolet. de 7.
of dutie to be obeyed: *Unicuique fuperiori* (faith he) *obedi-* peccatis
endum eft ex obligatione, in his tantum in quibus eft fuperior. And mort. c. 15.
the inferior difchargeth well his dutie, if he promptly obey
in thofe things wherein he is inferior; as a feruant in *feruili-*
bus, fuch as appertaine to a feruant: and for this citeth Pope
Innocentius cap. Inquifitioni de fent. excom. Whereupon, if the
Pope fhould (*in virtute obedientiæ*) command any man to
giue away his vineyard or houfe, or fell his patrimonie (as
Bellocchio cupbearer to *Sixtus* 5. would haue had the Pope
by his Breue to command a fubiect of his to do, becaufe the
poore mans land lay commodioufly for him, and pleafed
him (*Naboths* cafe:) which his Holineffe refufed to do, anfwering, he could not, he might do no mã wróg,) or a cleargie man to refigne his benefice with cure to fome vnworthy
perfon, which is againft a diuine precept, he is not to be o-
beyed, as the fame author affirmeth in the chapter aforefaid.
And alledgeth *Panorm. in cap. Inquifitioni de fent. excom.* and
Io. Andr. c. Cum à Deo. de refcript. Much leffe is any[a] fuperior, a Cap. litteras
yea the Pope himfelfe to be obeyed (according to [b] *Panor-* de reft. fpoliat
mitan) commanding any finne, though but [c] veniall. And b Cap. Inqui-
[d] *Syluefter: Intellige etiam fi Papa credit mãdatum iuftum, & ta-* fit. &c.
men fubdito conftat illud in fe continere peccatum: Vnderftand, c 11. q. 3. can.
although the Pope beleeueth his mandate to be iuft, but yet Quid ergo.
the fubiect knoweth it contains a fin. *de reftit. fpol. lit.* Here d Verbo o-
bedientia, nu.
may be noted, that the Pope may hold one opinion, and an 5.
inferiour may hold the contrarie, and more true, without
finne. Yea and a Bifhop, in cafe the Pope fhould command
I   him

him to be abfent from his refidence without fome neceffitie,

Inftruct.facer l.5.c.4.nu.3.
he is not bound to obey; becaufe(faith *Tolet*)*cum abſq̃ cauſa rationabili aliquid præcipitur, non debemus audire.* When any thing is commanded without reafonable caufe, we ought not to obey, for it were more then is due. And the fame Car-

Li.de 7.pec. mort.c.15.
dinall in another place faith thus : *Nullus obligatur obedire ſuo ſuperiori in actibus interioribus puris, puta intellectus & volun-tatis.* No man is bound to obey his fuperior in pure interior acts, to wit, of the vnderftanding and will. Who explica-teth himfelfe; If a fuperior fay vnto his inferior, Loue thine

See. S.Tho. More epift. ad filiam.
enemie, or this man in particular; or elfe, beleeue this or that opinion, the inferior is not bound to beleeue it, nor to obey: becaufe(faith he)the foule is fubiect only to God. And

2.2.q.104 art.5.
for proofe alledgeth Saint *Thomas*, whofe words are : *In his quæpertinent ad interiorem motum voluntatis, homo non tenetur homini obedire, ſed ſolum Deo.* In fuch things as appertaine to the inward motion of the will , a man is not bound to obey another man, but onely God. And this he affirmeth to be the common doctrine. Out of thefe cafes you may gather, and fecure your confcience, that a fuperiour, yea Chrifts Vi-car the Popes Holineffe, may be difobeyed without fcruple of finne, *(modo abſit contemptus)* notwithftanding his com-mandement prohibiting the Oath of allegiance : becaufe no man can force any to beleeue that which is matter onely of opinion, not of faith formally, vnleffe his vnderftanding be firft conuinced, that it is an infallible truth which is com-manded. And this of the Oath being an inward act of the vn-derftanding , is not fubiect in that cafe to the commande-ment of any man, according to the doctrine of the Authors aforefaid. And furthermore , by obeying his Holineffes Breues, and difobeying his Highneffe law in a matter as yet vndetermined ; great damage to many is more then likely to enfue , and infinite fcandals, to the loffe of foules, to arife in the Church; which euerie Chriftian man and good fub-iect is bound to auoide. *Qui amat periculum, peribit in illo.* He that loueth danger fhall perifh in it. And, *Qui cauſam damni dat, damnum dediſſe videtur.* It feemeth he doth the hurt, that giueth

giueth caufe thereof. If this fatisfie you not, lend me a patient and diligent eare, and you fhall heare more.

If I fhew you by the authoritie of the Sea Apoftolicke,
that his Holines, who fitteth now at the fterne, *Paulus Quintus*, forbidding all Catholickes to take the Oath of allegiance, is not therein to be obeyed, I truft you will require no
other teftimonie, but beleeue it to be lawfull, and refolue
not to hazard your eftates for refufing it hereafter. Marke
then what a learned Cardinal writeth of *Innocentius 3.*Pope:
Eleganter dicit Innocentius de fent.excom.cap.Inquifitioni, quòd Francifcus de
Papa non eft obediendum quando vehementer præfumitur ftatum Zabarel.de
Ecclefiæ perturbari, vel alia mala ventura. Et peccaret obedien- fchifmat.
do, cùm deberet futura mala præcauere. Elegantly faith *Innocentius*, that we are not to obey the Pope when there is ve-
hement prefumption that the ftate of the Church is to be
perturbed, or other euils are like to enfue. And in obeying,
a man fhould fin, when as he ought to preuent future euils.

Now tell me, I pray you, or let our domefticke aduerfaries, or fuch as are inwardly perfwaded, that the Pope cannot, by any authoritie deriued from Chrift, dethrone Kings
directly or indirectly (howbeit forfooth in policie refufe to
take the Oath, and difcharge their dutie to *Cæfar*, for feare
of lofing friends and commodities) nor difpoffeffe any priuate man of his temporals, who is not his fubiect (of which
fort there are many:) let them I fay, or any one of them tell
me, whether by difobeying the Kings highneffe, and obeying the Pope in this cafe of the Oath, the Catholick Church
in England is not like to be greatly afflicted, the memorie
of the Gun-powder treafon reuiued, the Catholickes miferies aggrauated, the heate of perfecution continued and
increafed, whole families vtterly ruined, propagation of
faith hindered, many foules loft, and a thoufand euils like
to follow, with manie fcandals to the State and all the
Realme, by reafon of obeying his Holineffe Breues, if our
moft clement Prince with rigour vpon this their indifcreete
obedience, profecute his law, made for the fecuritie of him
and his pofteritie? The authoritie aforefaid being of a Pope

(as that Author affirmeth) cenfureth fuch a one to offend (note well) in obeying; whom? the Pope: when as he is bound to beware before hand, or preuent fuch future euils or dangers. Then ought not all Catholickes and good fubiects doe what in them lieth to preuent the manifold euils that hang ouer their heads, by fatisfying the Magiftrate, and refufing to obey fuch a precept as is the only caufe thereof, (for had no prohibion come from Rome, few or none had ftood againft the Oath) efpecially when as nothing hath bene yet proued by any that haue written of this fubiect, fince the coming of the Breues foure yea fiue yeares agone and more, to be contained in the Oath againft faith?

Sylueft. verb. obedietia.nu. 5.
Syluefter likewife alledging *Panormitane*, agreeable to the former authoritie, faith, that the Pope is not to be obeyed, not onely when his precept is iniuft or fauoureth fin, but alfo when by fuch obedience it may be prefumed, that the ftate of the Church is like to be greatly difturbed, or fome other detriment or fcandall is to enfue, yea although he fhould command vnder paine of excommunication *latæ fententiæ. Nec eft* (faith he) *ei obediendum, fi ex obedientia præfumeretur ftatus Ecclefiæ perturbandus vehementer, vel aliud malum aut fcandalum futurum, etiam fi præciperetur fub pœna ex-*

Panormit. See Felin. in cap. Si quado. nu. 4. & in c. Accepimus.
communicationis latæ fententiæ. Ut notat idem in cap. Si quando, & in cap. Cum à Deo de refcrip. And goeth forward, *Ex quo ipfe in dicto, cap. Si quando infert, Quod fi, &c.* Whereupon he inferreth, that if he (the Pope) command any thing vnder paine of excommunication *ipfo facto*, by execution whereof it is prefumed there will be a fcandall in the citie of foules or bodies, he is not to be obeyed, &c. It followeth: *Imo ex cap. Officij de pœnis & remif. habetur, &c.* Yea it is euident, that the pofitiue law interpreteth, that reftitution, which is *de iure diuino*, fometime is not to be made, by reafon of danger, when it may happen to foules or bodies: then it may be wel inferred, that obedience in like cafe may be petnicious,

Tolet. de 7. pec.mort.cap 15.
and fo ought not to be rendered. The fame writeth Cardinall *Tolet*, citing thefe authors: *Nulli fuperiori præcipienti aliquid, &c.* No fuperiour commanding any thing whereby

fcan-

scandall or any notable detriment of others do follow, is to
be obeyed in such a precept. So say *Panorm.* and *Syluefter*
ver.obed. §.5. where they say, that in this cafe we are not to
obey, although the fuperiour command vnder paine of excommunication : for it bindeth not *quando male imponitur,*
when it is iniuftly impofed. *Emmanuel Sa* likewife : *Obedi-* Aphorif.Sa
endum non eft cum creditur inde malum oriturum : When it is ver.obedien.
thought euill may come by obeying, we are not to obey.
Againe, He is not bound to obey, that thinketh the fuperiour commandeth vpon error (as being mifinformed,) and
that if he knew the truth, he would not command: and alfo,
that fuperiours by their generall edicts intend not to bind
with great detriment. This *Sa.* And had not Catholickes
I pray you, before the Popes fecond Briefe, iuft caufe to be
perfwaded, that the Breues were procured by finifter fuggeftions and wrong informations of fome ouer-haftie and
bufie perfon? and that if his Holineffe had had true and particular notice by fome other true harted fubieĉt, how things
ftand with them here in England, what perturbations they
might breed in the Church, and what loffe and detriment
was vndoubtedly to fall on fuch as fhould obey them, and
thereby refufe the Oath, that he would neuer haue granted
forth the faid Breues in maner and forme as he did ; nor
when he had granted them, intended to bind Catholickes
to obey to their fo great detriment and damage? For that
were *addere afflictionem afflictis;* which kind of crueltie is not
to be thought can proceed from that holy Sea. And this
may fuffife for anfwer to the point, fo much ftood vpon by
many inconfideratly precife, of obeying or difobeying the
Popes Breues prohibiting the iuft Oath of allegiance. Howbeit a word or two more may not be omitted, *vt obftruatur*
os loquentiũ iniqua, to ftop the mouth of flanderous tongues;
and to anfwer a fond, or rather ftrong argument, as fome
thinke and fay, that *in dubys* (as is the Popes power of depofing Princes, in their opinions) we are to haue recourfe
to the Sea of *Peter* for folution, and there to learne what is
truth to be embraced, what is errour to be auoided. Yea,

I 3   what

what is there decided, the Church is bound to beleeue, though it be that vertue is euill, and vice good; as Cardinal *Bellarmine* formerly hath taught (ſtrange doctrine;) but now in his late Recognition retracted, ſaying, that he ſpake of doubtfull acts of vertues or vices. For if in the old law, the deciſion of difficult and doubtfull queſtions and ambiguities *inter ſanguinem & ſanguinem, cauſam & cauſam, lepram & lepram*, were granted to the Prieſts of the Leuiticall ſtocke, and to the Iudge that ſhould be for the time : much more to the Prieſts of the new law, and to Chriſts Vicar, the chiefe Iudge and interpreter in all Eccleſiaſticall controuerſies. Therefore in this caſe of the Oath now controuerted, Catholickes are to require no more but his bare precept; and whoſoeuer diſobeyeth it, taking the oath, ſinneth deadlie. This, ſome wiſe in their owne conceits, and learned in the eſtimation of others, haue ſaid and taught, ʽhowſoeuer otherwiſe verie inconſtant in their opinions & iudgements; but how prudently, charitably, or learnedly, let the diſcreet reader iudge. Theſe haue forgotten who it is that ſaith, *Nolite iudicare, & non iudicabimini: nolite condemnare, & non condemnabimini.* And what *S. Thomas* teacheth: *Eccleſia non debet præſumere de aliquo peccatum, quouſque probetur:* The Church ought not to iudge any of ſin, till it be proued. Indeed if the Popes precept were ſuch as S. *Iohn* Euangeliſt recommended, and often inculcated to his Diſciples at his departure out of this world, which was, as S. *Hierome* writeth: *Filioli diligite alterutrum*, Little children loue ye one another; then (as he ſaid) vpon their tediouſneſſe of hearing it ſo oft repeated, *Præceptũ Domini eſt, & ſi ſolum fiat, ſufficit:* It is our Lords precept, and if it only be done, it ſufficeth; then I ſay, we ſhould not need to diue farther in ſeeking reaſons, but ſimply to obey, *quia præceptum Papæ eſt*, becauſe it is the precept of the Pope : but by reaſon of the infinite difference betweene the commanders and the commandements, we muſt craue pardon if we ſay, *Et ſi ſolum fiat, non ſufficit :* if in this caſe of the Oath, there be but his bare precept, it is not ſufficient.

Marginal notes:
Lib.4.de ſum. Pont.cap.5. §.Vltimo.

Deut.17.

Luc.6.

Supplem q. 47.ar.3.

Hieron.lib.de ſcrip.Eccleſ.

Tou-

Touching the other point, I muſt needes confeſſe that in obſcurities, and doubtfull queſtions, and difficulties in the Law of Chriſt, all Chriſtians are to repaire to him that ſitteth in *Peters* chaire for the light of interpretation and true ſolution thereof: as S. *Hierome* did to Pope *Damaſus*, deſiring, if he had erred in his writings, to be corrected by him. Alſo *Athanaſius* in his diſtreſſes appealed to *Fœlix* and *Iulius* Popes of Rome; S. *Iohn Chryſoſtome* to *Innocentius*, *Calendion* of Antioch to Pope *Fœlix*: and other ancient Fathers in their diſtreſſes and difficult cauſes were wont alway to ſeeke for ſuccour and redreſſe of the Pope of Rome then being : but in caſes perſpicuous, wherin are no ambiguities or doubts to be made, againſt which nothing was euer formally decreed in any generall Coũcell, nor by any ancient Father taught, but is moſt plaine and euident in holy Scriptures, and as cleare as the Sunne in the firmament; that needeth not. And ſuch is the duty of inferiours to ſuperiours, of ſubiects to their lawfull Princes, of children to parents, of rendring to *Cæſar* that is *Cæſars*, and ſo forth : for which there is an expreſſe commandement from the Higheſt, wherein no power created can diſpence or iuſtly command the contrary. Which if any ſhould attempt to do (as his Holineſſe ſeemeth to haue done in prohibiting the Oath of allegiance) it may well be by a Catholik Engliſh ſubiect in all humilitie and reuerence to the Sea Apoſtolicke, yet with Chriſtian courage anſwered: *Non obedio præcepto Regis, ſed præcepto legis.* I obey not the precept of the King (that is, the Pope) but the precept of the law. And, *Obedire oportet Deo magis quàm hominibus.* We muſt obey God rather then men. To conclude, in ſuch a caſe not to do as the Pope commandeth in his Breues, ſo there be no cõtẽpt (as I haue ſaid) of his precept, is no mortall ſinne : *ex fine enim morales actus ſpeciem habent.* For morall acts haue their formality of the end: and ſuch diſobedience being *materialis tantum*, maketh not a deadly ſinne, & cõſequently no ſin at al. And this much as touching obedience to the Popes H. Breues. It followeth now that we treat
briefly

Hieron. ep. ad Damaſum.

Coſte rus in Enchir. de ſum. Pont.

2. Macch. 7.

Act. 5.

See Caiet. 5. Precepti tranſgreſſio. Tho. 2. 2. q. 105. a. 1. ad. 1.

briefly of a fubiects dutie in this point towards his liege
Lord and fecular Prince.

If it muft be granted that Chriftians by the law of
God are ftrictly bound to obey all iuft determinatiue fentences and decrees that proceed from the Sea Apoftolicke,
being the higheft fpirituall tribunall in Gods Church; why
muft it not likewife be granted that fubiects, as wel Clercks
as laicks, are by the fame law no leffe boūd *in foro cōfcientiæ*
to be obedient to the King and his iuft lawes, the chiefeft
tribunall in the common wealth? This (I thinke) no
Chriftian wil deny, as being moft cleare and euident in holy
Scriptures, taught, and practifed by all ancient Fathers and
holy Saints.

Tho.1.2.q.
96.ar.4.

Prou.8

I confeffe (you will fay) that humane iuft lawes haue
their efficacie of binding all fubiects to obey in the Court
of confcience, from the eternall law of God, of which they
are deriued, according to that of *Salomon*: *Per me Reges
regnant* , *& legum conditores iufta decernunt* . By me (faith
God) Kings do reigne, and Law-makers decree iuft things.
But whether this law of the Oath(which you aime at) be
fuch, fome make doūbt; for that Cardinall *Bellarmine*
in *Tortus*, and father *Parfons* in his Catholicke letter
affirme, many things to be contained therein againft the
fpirituall primacie of the chiefe Paftor, and his authoritie
of binding and loofing: and concerning the limitation (to
vfe father *Parfons* owne words) of his Holineffe authoritie,
to wit, what he cannot do towards his Maieftie, or his
fucceffors in anie cafe whatfoeuer. Moreouer, befides promife of ciuill and temporall obedience in the Oath, other
things are interlaced and mixt therewith, which do detract
from the fpirituall authoritie of the higheft Paftor, at leaft
wife indirectly, faith he. Therfore this law is iniuft, as being
preiudiciall to the law of God and holy Church.

Some I know will be carping at me for affirming father
Parfons to be the author of that Catholicke letter; who being afhamed (as may be thought) of the flender and in-
fufficient clearing the important matter of the Oath, by
foure

foure feuerall and diftinct waies according to his promife,
denie that euer he wrote the fame. But will they nill they,
it is fo well knowne to be his, and was to the Inquifition
in Rome (if I haue not bene mifinformed, and by a verie
credible perfon, that heard it from a gentleman, prefent in
the citie in his life time, and at his death) that he could not
denie it; and vpon the acknowledgement thereof (whether with forrow and griefe for fome points vnaduifedlie
or erroneoufly written, and brought in queftion in his old
age; or fomewhat elfe in fome other booke of his againft
Doctor *Morton*, touching the lawfulneffe of the Oath of
Supremacie in fome cafe, I cannot fay) foone after fell ficke,
and died within eight daies. But to returne to our matter.
Then lawes are faid to be iuft, firft when they are made for
the common good: fecondly when they exceede not his
power that maketh them: and thirdly when they haue
their due forme, to wit, when the burdens (or penalties)
are impofed on the fubiects with a certain equalitie of proportion, in order to the common good or vtilitie of the
weale publicke, as S. Thomas noteth.

    Such is this law of the Oath of allegiance, made by full
authoritie in Parliament, for the conferuation of his Maieftie and whole commonwealth in tranquillitie and peace,
which is both priuate and common good. When I fay full
authoritie, I meane, in temporals; for fo the Prince hath,
and onely in temporals in the common wealth: no leffe
the the Pope in fpirituals in the patrimonie of the Church.
Which law was generaly enacted for all Englifh fubiects,
though principally intended as a diftinctiue figne to detect,
not Catholickes from Proteftants, nor fuch as denie the
Kings fpirituall fupremacie in caufes Ecclefiafticall, from
the Popes fpirituall primacy, as Cardinall *Bellarmine* in
Tortus affirmeth; but turbulent fpirited Catholickes (and
thefe to repreffe) from milde and dutifully affected fubiects
of the fame religion: fuch as difliking haply in words that
moft horrible confpiracy of Gunpowder King-flaying,
would in heart haue applauded the euent, from thofe who

K   in

Tho.1.2.q. 96.24.

Tho.22.q.67. 2.4.
Innoc.3.cap.
Per venerabi-
lem: Extra.
Qui filij fint
legitimi.

in affliction for their conscience, with patient perseuerance
to the end, how long soeuer God permit it to continue for
our sinnes, will in word and deede loue their enemies,
beare wrongs without murmuring, and sincerely pray for
the conuersion of their persecutors, if they haue any, following the example and doctrine of our blessed Sauiour
and his holy Apostles.

That our dread Soueraigne in setting forth this Oath by
Act of Parliament, hath not exceeded the limites of his
power, is manifest, in that it was framed onely for this end,
that his Maiesties subiects should thereby make cleare profession of their resolution, (to vse his Maiesties owne
words) faithfully to persist in his Maiesties obediëce according to their naturall allegiance. And so farre was his intent by the same Oath to detract from the Primacy or spirituall authority of the Pope, of binding or loosing by Ecclesiasticall censures or sacraments (as the Cardinall and
father *Parsons* affirme,) that his Maiestie as it were by a
most prudent preuention, to take away all scruples that
might arise in Catholicke subiects consciences, tooke speciall care that that clause inserted by the lower House into
the Oath, which detracted from the Popes spirituall authority of excommunicating his Maiestie, should be forthwith
put out. And withall declared, that the vertue or force of
this Oath was no other, then that the Popes excommunication might not minister a iust and lawfull cause vnto his
subiects to attempt any thing by open or priuie conspiracies against his Maiestie or state. What more I pray you
could he haue done for clearing this controuersie, and sa-
tisfying his subiects?

If then it be so that nothing is contained in this Oath,
but what apperteineth to naturall allegiance, nor more by
his Maiestie required then profession of ciuill and temporall obedience, which nature prescribeth to all borne subiects (as his Maiestie the interpreter of his owne law hath
most sufficiently in his Premonition and Apologie made
knowne to all by his pen) nor that he intended by interla-
cing

(margin) Præfat.monit.
Apolog.Reg

(margin) Præfat.monit.

cing or mingling any thing, to detract from the spirituall authoritie of the Pope, no not indirectly, nor against the law of God, as is likewise manifest, none can iustly say he hath exceeded his limits, or that the law is vniust.

And wheras the Catholick letter hath: That there are some things (but specifying none of those some) concerning the limitation of his Holinesse authoritie (if he meane spirituall, it is vntrue) to wit, what he cannot do towards his Maiestie or his succeffours in any case whatsoeuer. That is a glosse of his owne inuention beside the text, a notorious vntruth; for there are no such words to be found in the Oath, as, *In any case whatsoeuer.* Neither is the Popes spirituall authoritie limited or once touched therein, as by his Maiesties intention sufficiently made knowne vnto vs, doth manifestly appeare. And *Caietan* teacheth that in such like case, if the in- Caietan. ver. præcepti trangreffio. tention of the man that commandeth may be knowne, it is inough; becaufe the force of the precept dependeth of the intention of him that commandeth. Now to end this matter, I wifh you to note the fraude of that Catholicke letter writer: for, to haue set downe in plaine termes, that his Holineffe may depose his Maiestie, dispose his kingdomes to whom he lift, licence subiects to raise tumults, take armes against him, or murther him, and such like, he knew would found to good subiects most odious: therefore he thought it to be a point of policie not to deale plainely, but leaue the Reader perplexed with this obscuritie: What his Holineffe cannot do towards his Maiestie, in any case whatsoeuer. Whose bare affertion without proofe, or truth, can in reason conuince none but such as want their common sense.

Now that it hath bene proued, nothing to be contained in the Oath against the law of God, nor decrees of any generall Councell; and that his Maiestie in making this law, and requiring of his subiects the performance thereof according to his intention (which is but iust and good) hath not gone beyond his bounds: will any yet be so wilfully blind as not to fee, that by the immaculate law of God he is bound in conscience to render to *Cæfar* that is *Cæfars?* to be

obedient

obedient to higher powers , as well the ciuill in temporals,
as the Ecclefiafticall power in fpirituals? Saint *Peter* prince
of the Apoftles taught this doctrine to the Chriftians of the
primitiue Church , that they fhould fubmit themfelues and
be obedient to fecular Princes and Magiftrates,though they
were heathens. *Subiecti igitur eftote omni humanæ creaturæ
propter Deum: fiue Regi quafi præcellenti, fiue Ducibus tamquam
ab eo miffis, &c.* Be fubiect therefore to euery humane creature,for God : whether it be to the King, as excelling, or to
rulers as fent by him to the reuenge of malefactors , but to
the praife of the good : for fo is the will of God, that doing
wel you may make the ignorance of vnwife men to be dum.
And a little after,exhorting the to feare God,his next leffon
is,to honor the King: *Deum timete:Regem honorificate.*How
I pray you is a King honoured,when his iuft precept is neglected or contemned? Some haply without confideration,
both ignorantly & vnwifely wil grant that Catholick kings
are to be honoured and obeyed, but doubt may be made of
fuch as by the Church are reputed , or rather condemned
heretikes, and aduerfaries to the Catholicke faith.

I aske thefe (if there be any fo fimple) whether Emperours, Kings , and Princes , to whom the Apoftles preached
this fubiection and obedience,were not aduerfaries,yea and
perfecutors of the Catholicke faith, and continued fuch the
fpace of more then three hundred yeares? howbeit the
Chriftians of thofe dayes , inftructed both by the doctrine
and example of the Apoftles , in all dutifull humilitie , did
not giue freely,but rendred to *Cæfar* his due , how peruerfe
foeuer their Gouernours were. Which leffon Saint *Peter*
their chiefe Paftor,immediatly after in the fame chapter had
taught them : *Serui fubditi eftote in omni timore dominis , non
tantum bonis & modeftis, fed etiam dyfcolis.*Seruants be fubiect
in all feare to your maifters, not onely to the good and modeft, but alfo to the wayward. This dutifull fubiection likewife teacheth Saint *Paul: Serui obedite Dominis carnalibus
cum timore & tremore, in fimplicitate cordis veftri,ficut Chrifto.*
Seruants,be obedient to yout Lords according to the flefh,

with

1.Pet.2.

Ephef.6.
Colof.3.

with feare and trembling, in the fimplicitie of your heart, as to Chrift, not feruing to the eye, as it were pleafing men, but as the feruants of Chrift, doing the will of God from the heart, with a goodwill feruing as to our Lord, and not to men.

If feruants then commanded by the Apoftle, were bound to ferue and obey their temporall Lords and maifters with fuch care and diligence, were they neuer fo froward and wicked Pagans (for fuch no doubt many Chriftians did ferue) who by their examples, threats, or enticements might hazard to withdraw them from the true worfhip of God: are not fubiects now by the fame law as well bound to be obedient to lawfull Kings and Princes, be they neuer fo wicked in manners, or oppofite to faith and Chriftian religion, as heretikes and apoftates are? Were they not Pagan Princes and Poteftates whom Saint *Paul* willed *Titus* to admonifh Chriftians to obey at a word? *Admone illos* (faith he) *Principibus & Poteftatibus fubditos effe, dicto obedire.* Admonifh them to be fubiect to Princes and Poteftates, to obey at a word. Vpon which place Saint *Ambrofe*: Admonifh; as if he fhould fay, Although thou haft fpirituall gouernment ouer fpirituall matters, yet admonifh them to whom thou preacheft, to be fubiect to Kings and Princes, becaufe Chriftian religion depriueth none of his right. The fame holy Father and alfo Saint *Auguftine* write of the prompt obedience of Chriftians to *Iulian* the Apoftata (which may be a verie good example for Catholickes of thefe latter times to fhew like obedience if they light on like Princes) faying : *Iulianus extitit infidelis Imperator, nonne extitit Apoftata, iniquus, idololatra, &c.* Iulian was an infidell Emperour, was he not an Apoftata, wicked, an idolater? Chriftian fouldiers ferued an infidell Emperour. When they came to the caufe of Chrift, they acknowledged not but him that was in heauen. When he willed them to worfhip Idols, to facrifife; they preferred God before him. But when he faid, Bring foorth your armie, go againft that people, they obeyed incontinently. They diftin-

S. Ambrofe.

Aug. in Pfal. 124. Super illud, Non relinquet Domi nus virgam. Habetur 11. q. 3. c. Iulian

K 3   guifhed

guiſhed the eternall Lord from a temporall Lord : and yet
for the eternall Lord, they were ſubiect alſo to the temporall Lord. Hereby is euident that *Iulian* had right to command Chriſtian ſouldiers in temporals, and they ſhewed
all prompt obedience , knowing that their religion taught
no iniuſtice; that notwithſtanding his Apoſtacie, he being
lawfully called to the Empire, they were not,nor could be
abſolued of their loyaltie and ciuill obedience towards
him.

Was ſo notorious an Apoſtata to be of dutie obeyed,and
not a king, who cannot be iudged an hereticke , becauſe
he doth not *pertinaciter* defend any opinion againſt the
Church of Chriſt , but royally promiſeth to forſake the
religion he profeſſeth, if any point or head thereof belonging to faith can be proued not to be ancient,catholicke,
and Apoſtolicke?

Here Cardinall *Bellarmine* will anſwer , That the Church
in her nouitie or beginning , wanted forces (forſooth
after three, yea foure hundred yeares from her beginning) to depoſe *Iulian* , *Conſtantius*,*Valens*, and other hereticall Princes , and therefore permitted Chriſtians to obey
them in temporals.

Cypr. in De-
metrianum.
Tertul. in
Apologet.
Saint *Cyprian* ſaith, that in his time the number of Chriſtians were verie great. And *Tertullian* writeth thus : Were
we diſpoſed, not to practiſe ſecret reuenge, but to pro-
feſſe open hoſtilitie, ſhould we want number of men , or
force of armes? Are the Moores or the Parthians, or any
one nation whatſoeuer, more in number then we, that are
ſpread ouer all the world? We are not of you, and yet we
haue filled all the places and roomes which you haue. Your
Cities, Ilands, Caſtles,Townes,Aſſemblies,your Tents,
Tribes , and Wards; yea the Imperiall Pallace, Senate,and
Euſeb. l. 3. de
vita Conſtan.
Niceph.l.5.
c.25.
ſeate of iudgement , &c. *Euſebius* likewiſe, and *Nicephorus*
report, That the whole world, as it were, vnder *Conſtantius* was Chriſtian , and the greater part Catholicke.
How then is it true that the Church in her nouitie wanted forces?

                                              And

And therefore fhe permitted Chriftians to obey their
Princes in temporals, faith the Cardinall. Euen fo permitted, as father *Parfons* in his letter to the Catholickes of England againft the Oath of allegiance affirmeth, that Pope
Clement by a Breue had permitted ciuill obedience to our
King, and recommended to all Catholickes foone after his
Highneffe entrance vnto the Crowne. As if ciuill obedience
had not bene otherwife due but by his Holineffe permiffion.
Who would haue thought fuch an imprudent and ftrange
kind of phrafe could haue fo efcaped his pen? But it feemeth he had learned the fame out of Cardinall *Bellarmines*
writings, and fo prefumed it would paffe as current without
controlement. And may not the world maruell (be it fpoken with due reuerence to his great dignitie, which I haue
euer, and in heart ftill do honour) that a man fo excellently
learned will teach, that Chriftian fubiects, vnleffe they be
permitted by the Church, are not bound to render obedience to their lawfull Kings and Princes, if they become heretickes, or aduerfaries to true religion, and perfecutors?
Princes infidels lofe no right, but are the true and fupreme
Princes of their kingdomes, as he himfelfe teacheth: for do- Lib.5.de Ro.
minion is not founded either in grace or in faith; fo as the Pont.c.2.
Pope hath no authoritie to meddle with them. Marry if
thefe become Chriftians, and after fall to herefie, what then?
In that cafe, faith he, *Poteft regna mutare, & vni auferre, &* Cap.6.
alteri conferre: He may change kingdomes, and take from
one, and giue to another, faith he. Then is their condition
worfe as touching temporall poffeffions, then it was when
they were infidels, & worfe then the conditió of the bafeft
of their fubiects. But Chriftian religion depriueth no man
of his right: who had right in infidelitie, cannot lofe the
fame by receiuing the grace and faith of Chrift; which is a-
greeable to the doctrine of the Cardinall, howfoeuer he feemeth fometime to teach contrary to himfelfe. Chrift did not Bellar.lib.5.de
(faith he) nor doth take kingdomes from them to whom Ro.Pont.c.3.
they belong: for Chrift came not to deftroy thofe things
which were well fetled, but to eftablifh them. And therefore
when

when a King becometh a Chriſtian, he doth not loſe his
earthly kingdome which by right he held, but purchaſeth
a new intereſt to an euerlaſting kingdome: otherwiſe the
benefites receiued by Chriſt, ſhould be hurtfull to Kings,
and grace ſhould deſtroy nature. If Chriſtian Kings lawfully attaining to their dominions, by right of nature enioy
the ſame, as cannot be denied, and ſo are to be obeyed;
why not alſo if they happen to fall backe into hereſie or infidelitie, their right not being founded in grace or in faith?
To ſay that ſuch Princes or magiſtrates are not to be obeyed, cometh neare the hereſie charged vpon *Wickliffe*, and
condemned in the Councell of Conſtance, and is repugnant to the doctrine of the holy Ghoſt in ſacred Scriptures,
and practiſe of all bleſſed Saints and Martyrs; who moſt
promptly without any permiſſion of the Pope or Church,
obeyed Pagan Princes, vnder whom they were ſubiect in
all ciuill cauſes; & onely in defence of faith and Gods truth,
made choice rather to ſhed their bloud, then by obeying
Cæſar to diſobey God. And where ſuch a permiſſion was
euer granted (as to obey *Iulian* or other hereticall Emperour) cannot be found in any generall Councell, or ancient
2.2.q.12.a.2. Fathers writings before the dayes of S. *Thomas* of Aquine,
of whom the Cardinall learned his doctrine of *permiſſion*, to
obey till ſuch time as they had forces to depriue them of
their Empire.

Conſider I pray you, that S. *Paul* hauing receiued his doctrine immediatly from heauen, writing to the Chriſtians
in Rome, permitted not for a time, but ſtrictly comman-
Rom. 13. ded them euer to obey higher powers: *Omnis anima poteſta-*
Sap. 6. *tibus ſublimioribus ſubdita ſit*: Let euery ſoule be ſubiect to
higher powers. Was this meant, trow ye, for onely higher
powers Chriſtians, or heathen onely for a time? No; but for
all ſorts of rulers, and as long as there be ſuperiors and inferiors. The holy Apoſtle in this and other his Epiſtles, often inculcateth this neceſſary vertue of obedience, diligently exhorting and commanding as well ſubiects to be obedient to their Princes, as ſeruants to their maſters, and all
infe-

inferiors to their fuperiors. And were not thefe maifters and
higher powers for the moft part Pagans? Were they not e-
nemies to Chriftian religion, whom they were taught to o-
bey? Was any fort of inferiors exempted from obeying?
S. *Iohn Chryfoftome* will put you out of doubt, that fuch fubiection is commanded to all forts, Priefts, Monkes, and fecular men, as the Apoftle himfelfe declareth in the verie beginning : *Omnis anima poteftatibus fublimioribus*
fubdita fit, etiam fi Apoftolus fis, fi Euangelifta, fi Propheta, fiue
quifquis tandem fueris : neque enim pietatem fubuertit ifta fub-
iectio. Let euery foule be fubiect to higher powers, yea if
thou art an Apoftle, if an Euangelift, if a Prophet, or finally
whofoeuer thou art. Marke well. For this fubiection fubuer-
teth not pietie, or religion. And he fpecially noteth, that
S. *Paul* faith not fimply *Obediat,* but *fubdita fit.* And why? becaufe power is of God ; *Non eft enim poteftas nifi à Deo :* For
there is no power but of God. *Quid dicis?* faith this holy Father to S. *Paul: Omnis ergo Princeps à Deo conftitutus eft? Iftud,*
inquit, non dico. *Neque enim de quouis Principum fermo mihi*
nunc eft, fed de ipfa re. What faift thou, O *Paul:* is then euery
Prince conftituted of God? This (faith he) I fay not. For neither of euery Prince do I now fpeake, but of the thing it
felfe: that is, of power. And the Apoftle faith further, *Quæ*
autem funt, à Deo ordinatæ funt: And thofe that are, of God
are ordained. Therefore he that refifteth the power, refifteth
the ordinance of God : adding, contrarie to the loue of
God, in not obeying his commandement: and contrarie to
the loue of his neighbour, withdrawing from his fuperior
obedience due vnto him. And they that do refift, what get
they? They purchafe to themfelues damnation : hauing
committed a deadly finne in refifting. Which kind of purchafe, I wifh many in this our countrey to note diligently,
and in time to take heed of.

But I know fome will inferre that this place of S. *Paul*
may well and ought to be vnderftood of Prelates, and the
chiefe Prelate Chrifts Vicar, who are alfo higher powers:
and therefore toucheth fuch as by obeying the King in the

L   Oath

Marginal notes:

Chryfoft. in
cap. 13. Rom.
hom. 23.
Auguft. in lib.
expofitionis
quorundam
propof. ex e-
pift. ad Rom.

Tho. 1. 2. q.
105. ar. 1.

Oath of allegiance, difobey their fpirituall Paftor the Pope.
Thefe deceiue themfelues, not confidering the drift of the
Apoftle : for if they marke well, they will eafily fee that S.
Paul in this chapter vnderftandeth not the fpirituall dire&-
ly, but the fecular power, as muft needs appeare manifeftly
to him that readeth the text. *Nam Principes* (faith he) *non
funt timori boni operis, fed mali, &c.* For Princes are no feare
to the good worke, but to the euill. But wilt thou not feare
the power? do good, and thou fhalt haue praife of the fame:
for he is Gods minifter vnto thee for good. But if thou do
euill, feare; for he beareth not the fword without caufe: for
he is Gods minifter : a reuenger vnto wrath to him that
doth euill. By whom can all this be meant, but by the fecular power? To whom is tribute due to be rendered, not giuen *gratis*, becaufe it is an act or worke of iuftice, but to the
fecular power? Who carieth fuch a fword to punifh corporally to death, and by the ordinance of God, but Kings and
fecular Princes, who are Gods minifters and vicegerents in
earth for this purpofe ? This fword neuer belonged to *Peter*

D.Kellifon in   nor his fucceffors by Chrifts inftitution, as D.*Kellifon* con-
his Reply to   feffeth againft M.*Sutcliffe*; his words are thefe: If befide this
M.Sutcliffe,   fpirituall power which he hath ouer the whole Church,
cap.1.fo.13.   *Sutcliffe* fuppofe, that either we giue him, or that he challengeth to himfelfe any temporall power ouer Chriftian
Kings and kingdomes, he is foully deceiued ; for we confeffe, and fo doth he, that Chrift gaue him no fuch fword
nor foueraigntie, &c. We acknowledge indeed two fwords
in the Church of Chrift, the one fpirituall, the other temporall, but we giue them not both to the Pope. For the fupreme fpirituall power is the onely fword which he hand-
leth; the fupreme temporall power out of Italie pertaineth
to the Emperour, Kings and Princes.

Idem.fo.14.   For as there are in the Church of God two bodies, the
one politicall and ciuill, the other Ecclefiafticall or myfticall ; the one called the common-wealth, the other the
Church: fo are there two powers to direct and gouerne
thefe bodies, and the one is called ciuill or temporall, the
                                                        other

other Ecclesiasticall : and that ruleth the bodies, this the soules ; that the kingdome , this the Church ; that makes temporall, this spirituall lawes ; that decideth ciuill causes, this determineth and composeth controuersies in religion; that punisheth bodies by the temporall sword, this chastiseth soules with the spirituall glaiues and bonds of excommunication, suspension, interdicts and such like : and the end of that, is temporall peace, the scope and butte of this, eternall felicity; and so that being inferiour, this superiour, that must yeeld to this , when there is any opposition. And so we giue to the Pope one sword onely ouer the Church, and not swords, as *Sutcliffe* saith. They are secular Princes likewise who may exact cust100mes , and to whom tribute ought of dutie to be paied by all subiects, thereby to sustaine and maintaine their dignitie , gouerne their kingdome in peace and iustice , and protect them from all enemies:such excepted as by their priuiledges for the honour of Christ are exempted. *Tributum Cæsaris est, non negetur.* saith S. *Ambrose.* This was neuer due to the Apostles the spirituall Princes of the Church, nor consequently to Bishops now, as they are bishops only:neither did they exercise such a sword, or euer acknowledge to be permitted thē by the institutió of our B. Sauiour, of whó they receiued their cómissió & al power they could practise for gouernmēt of his Church till the worlds end. *Costerus* a reuerend and learned Iesuite *in fidei Demonst.* pag. 95. commendeth *Erasmus* for writing thus : *Nihil vi gerebant (Apostoli scil.) tantùm vtebantur gladio Spiritus , neminem agebant in exilium, nullius inuadebāt facultates, &c. Hæc Erasmus non minus diserte quàm verè.* They (that is the Apostles) did nothing by violence, they vsed only the sword of the Spirit, they droue none into exile, they inuaded no mans possessions, &c. This *Erasmus,* (saith *Costerus*) no lesse wisely then truly. And a litle before in the same booke cap. 12. he teacheth , that the materiall sword belongeth not to any Ecclesiasticall person : *Nulli enim competit Ecclesiastico vel sanguinem fundere , vel capitis quenquam condemnare.* For it appertaineth not to any Ecclesiasticall

Ex. de trad.
Basil.& ep.ad Valentin.

Coste. c.14.

Erasm.ep.ad Vulturium Neocomum.

Cost. propos. 3.cap.12.

clefiafticall perfon either to fhed bloud, or to condemne any man to death. Then not to the Pope as he is an Ecclefiafticall perfon, and fucceffour to *Peter*, doth it belong to vfe fuch a fword. Hereto agreeth Sir *Thomas More* in his

Morus in paf. Dom. pag. 1391.
Bern. de confid. li. 4. c. 3. 4.
See Gratian, 23. q. 8. in princ.

treatife vpon the paffion: *Mitte gladium in locum fuum, &c.* Put vp (faith Chrift to *Peter*) thy fword into his place, as though he would fay: I will not be defended with fword. And fuch a ftate haue I chofen thee vnto, that I will not haue thee fight with this kind of fword, but with the fword of Gods word, Let this materiall fword therefore be put vp into his place, that is to wit, into the hands of temporall Princes, as into his fcabberd againe, to punifh malefactors withall. Adding, that the Apoftles haue to fight with a fword much more terrible then this, that is, the fpirituall fword of excommunication, the vfe whereof pertaineth to Ecclefiafticall perfons alone: as the other to fecular Iuftices. This he, moft learned in his time, and no leffe zelous in Catholicke religion. He goeth on pag. 1393. faying, that

Morus in paffione Domi.

Chrift after this told *Peter*, that he had done very euill, to ftrike with the fword: and that he declared alfo by the example of the ciuill lawes, who faith: *Omnes qui acceperint gladium, gladio peribunt, &c.* For by the ciuill lawes of the Romaines, vnder which the Iewes at the fame time liued, whofoeuer without fufficient authority were fpied fo much as

Matth 26.

to haue a fword about him to murther any mã with, was in a manner in as euill a cafe, as he that had murthered one indeed. If *Peter*, exercifing a materiall fword in defence of Chrift, and at fuch time as the vfe thereof might feeme to him very neceffary, was fharply reprehended, for that he had no lawfull authoritie in fuch wife to fight for him: is it not a fufficient document for his fucceffours not to vfe violence on fecular Princes by exercifing the materiall fword, no not *in ordine ad fpiritualia*, in defence of Chrifts fpoufe the Church, for that fhe hath no warrant fo to do? Our Sauiour a little before his paffion, feeing his Apoftles to contend about fuperiority, teaching them their duties, and in them all their fucceffours, and the different gouernment

ment betweene them and secular Princes said : *Reges gen-* Luc.22.
tium dominātur eorum ; & qui potestatem habent super eos,bene-
fici vocantur,vos autem non sic, &c. The Kings of the Gentiles
ouerrule them : and they that haue power vpon them, are
called beneficials. But you not so: but he that is the greater among you, let him become as the yonger &c.Vpon
which place *Origen, S. Hierome, Chrysostome* and *Basil* with
one assent vnderstand, that secular Princes are not content
onely to haue subiects, but also by ouerruling they vse thē:
but you not so, to wit, you my Apostles and successours after me : for it is your part to serue,to minister, and to feede
by word and example,&c. And in Saint *Matthewes* Gos- Math.20.
pell, our Sauiour said vnto two of his disciples *Iames* and
Iohn: You know that the Princes of the Gentiles ouerrule
them: and they that are the greater, exercise power against
them. It shall not be so among you: but whosoeuer will be
the greater among you, let him be your minister, &c.

Is it not plaine that our Lord Iesus,though he teach not
paritie with Puritans, nor forbiddeth superiority among
Christians neither Ecclesiasticall nor temporall, yet he will
not that his Apostles nor their successors, Bishops and
Priests (being called to the state of a celestiall kingdome,
that differeth from the conditiō of a temporall kingdome)
should rule like vnto Kings and secular Princes, who cary
a materiall sword *ad vindictam malefactorum,* for reuenge of
malefactors? and some now and then imperiously gouerne
their subiects with pride, tyranny, contempt of inferiours,
and for their owne lucre more then the vtility of their subiects. Which kind of gouernement is forbidden both by 1.Pet.5.
the doctrine and example of our Sauiour, and humility Presbyteros
commended to all the Cleargie, yea to *Peter* himselfe; who Compresby-
cōformably to this,likwise instructed such as at any time to ter.so readeth
the worlds end should beare rule in Gods Church (saying; and expoun-
Seniores igitur qui sunt inter vos obsecro,ego consenior. &c. The deth.S.
seniors therefore that are among you, I beseech, my selfe a Hierome ep.
85,So trans-
consenior with them: &c, (or Priests, my selfe a fellow late Erasmus
Priest) feede the flocke of God which is among you, pro- and Beza,
uiding

uiding not by cóstraint, but willingly according to God:
neither for filthy lucre sake, but voluntarily: *neq; vt dominā-*
tes:neither as ouerruling the Clergie, but made examples
of the flocke from the heart. Whereby appeareth that all
violence, coaction, and compulsion by exercising the
temporall sword (which is the sword of Kings) is wholly
forbidden all Ecclesiasticall persons.

To me it seemeth not without a mysterie, that onely
Peter among the rest of the Apostles should not strike any
in all that hellish troupe, coming in fury to lay violent
hands on their Lord, no not the traytor *Iudas* that with a
kisse betraied him, the ringleader of the rest, and so better
deserued to haue had his head cut off: but onely him whose
name is so precisely recorded by the Euāgelist to be *Mal-*
chus : and that he should be checked and reproued by
our Sauiour, of whom haply he expected to be commended for his zeale. But though *Peter* might pretend iust cause
to be moued to strike as he did, yet was his fact reprehen-
sible in two respects. First, for that asking Christ the question whether he and his fellow (for no moe of the eleuen
had swords about them) should strike or no, stroke without his grant, yea against his will. Secondly, because his
fact had rather a shew of reuenge then of defence. For
what might he think to do with 2. swords against so many,
what possibility to preuaile? And as may appeare likwise by
Christs words vnto him: Returne thy sword into his place;
for all that take the sword shall perish with the sword. And
in S. *Iohns* Gospell: Put vp thy sword into the scabbard:
the chalice which my Father hath giuen me, shall not I
drinke it? By all which is cleare that *Peter* was iustly reprehended for striking without commission the high Priests
seruant *Malchus*, which name in Hebrew, or *Malcuth*, signifieth *Rex* or *Regnum*: doubtles in my iudgemēt not without a great mystery, & the admirable prouidence of God,
thereby haply instructing posterity, that no lesse reprehen-
sible is it in *Peters* successours, as they are *Peters* successors,
to dethrone Kings and depriue them of their kingdomes,

(which

Iohan. c. 18.

Math. 26.

Iohan. 18.

(which cannot be done without drawing forth and ſtriking with the materiall ſword) then it was in *Peter* himſelfe for cutting off *Malchus* eare. And that they ought not to vſe ſuch kind of violence on the perſons of Kings, no nor infe-riors to Kings, hauing no commiſſion from Chriſt to puniſh corporally, no more then *Peter* had againſt *Malchus*, but onely ſpiritually.

Now to returne to the authoritie or power meant by S. *Paul* Rom. 13. *Omnis anima.* It is moſt plaine that the Apo-ſtle in that chapter recommended to Chriſtians their dutiful obedience to ſecular Poteſtates: becauſe hauing preached o-bedience to ſpirituall Paſtors, ſome newly conuerted thought themſelues, being Chriſtians, to be freed by Chriſt from al former ſubiection, & now not bound to obey either Emperour, King, or any temporall Lord, for that they were heathens and perſecutors of the Apoſtles and Chriſts reli-gion. For which cauſe, and for that the Apoſtles generally were ſlandered, and ſaid to be ſeditious, and vntruly char-ged of their aduerſaries, that they withdrew men from or-der, and obedience to ciuill lawes and officers: Saint *Paul* here (as S. *Peter* doth in his firſt Epiſtle) to ſtop the mouth of ſuch ſlanderous tongues, cleareth himſelfe, and expreſly chargeth euery man and woman to be ſubiect to their tem-porall Princes and ſuperiors : howbeit in ſuch matters as they may lawfully command, and in things wherein they are ſuperiors.

See S.Chry-ſoſt.in c.13. Ro.ho.23.

Conformable to his doctrine was likewiſe his example, and of the reſt of the Apoſtles, who in all matters not repug-nant to faith and religion, were moſt obedient to their tem-porall Gouernours, though Pagans and cruell perſecutors: yea and their ſucceſſors many hundred yeares after to their lawfull Princes, were they neuer ſo wicked heathens or He-retickes. When Saint *Paul* being accuſed of many crimes by the Iewes, appealed to *Cæſar*, ſaying: *Ad tribunal Cæſaris ſto, ibi me oportet iudicari*: At *Cæſars* iudgement ſeate do I ſtand, there I ought to be iudged: (becauſe this is the place of iudgement, ſaith *Gloſſ. interlin*;) is it to be thought that

Act.25.

he

he would haue said,he ought there to be iudged,if *de iure* he
had not bene subiect to that tribunall ? or that he did it for
feare of death,who was ready before, not only to be bound
and suffer imprisonment, but also to die in Ierusalem for the
name of Iesus?

And who will iudge this holy Apostle to be so readie to
commit such a crime for sauing his life , as by his doctrine
and example to teach and do that which was vnlawfull
to be taught or practised; to subiect against equitie, all
Priesthood to the iurisdiction of a secular Prince? specially
because he was not compelled to go to Ierusalem, to make
a lie so preiudiciall to all the Clergie euer after. But well he
knew that he was then, *de iure*, subiect to *Cæsars* tribunall,
being therein become an imitator of our Sauiour Christ;
who in iudgement submitted himselfe to *Pilate*, *Cæsars*
Lieutenant; and said , that his power to iudge him was not

Ioan.19. onely permitted, but giuen from aboue.And our B.Sauiour
(whose actions are our instructions) in paying tribute for
Math.17. himselfe and *Peter* as due to the Emperour,whose subiect he
acknowledged to be as he was a mortall man, taught vs by
his example that the adopted sonnes of God, (*Peter* not excepted) are not by the diuine law freed from subiection to
secular authoritie in tributes, customes , and such like,
when himselfe the naturall Sonne of his heauenly Father,
King of kings , by yeelding it , shewed it to be *Cæsars* due,
and that it ought to be payed by all that after should beleeue in him: (such excepted as by good Princes grants and
priuiledges should be exempted)howbeit himselfe was not
otherwise bound thereto then for auoyding scandall , for
that he was the naturall Sonne and onely begotten of the
King of heauen(which they knew not who exacted tribute)
and therefore free.

To which purpose Saint *Augustine* writeth thus : *Quod
dixit, Ergo liberi sunt filij, &c.* That he said, Therefore the
children are free, is to be vnderstood, that the children of a
Aug.l.1.qu.
Euan.q.23. kingdóe are in euery kingdome free,that is, are not tributa-
ries.Which S.*Augustine* must needs mean of a kings natural
chil-

children; and not of the sonnes and children of God by a-
doption: for so all vertuous and good Christians should be
freed from paying tribute; which is absurd, and contrarie
to the doctrine of Saint *Paul*, *Omnis anima*, *&c.* euerie soule.
To this agreeth Saint *Thomas*: That such as are made the Tho.2.2 q.
sonnes of God by grace, are free from the spirituall serui- 104.a.6.ad 1.
tude of sinne; but not from corporall seruitude, by which
they remaine bound to their temporal Lords. And such subiection Saint *Gregorie* the Great acknowledged, both by his
example and doctrine, to be due to the Emperour, as to his
superior in temporals; following therein no doubt the steps
of all his predecessors before him. *Ego autem* (saith he in an
Epistle to *Mauritius* and *Augusta*) *indignus pietatis vestræ fa-* Greg.l.2.ep.
mulus: And I an vnworthie seruant of your pietie. And a lit- 61.
tle after: For to this end power was giuen from aboue
to the pietie of my Lords ouer all men. If ouer all men, then
ouer himselfe, though Pope, and the adopted sonne of God
by grace. But some will say, that Saint *Gregorie* submitted
himselfe of humilitie, not of dutie. Which is a great iniury
and derogation to this great Doctor and blessed Saint, who
was *vir simplex, & rectus, ac timens Deum*, Reall and simple Iob. 1.
without any duplicitie, fearing more God then the Emperour, without all fiction or lying; knowing well what a sinne
it would be to him, by such a pernicious fiction to preiudice
greatly all Pontificall dignitie euer after. Old *Eleazarus* in
the Macchabees, he knew, had taught him not so by faining 2.Macch.6.
to leaue an euill example to posteritie, but rather to suffer
martirdome as he did. And Saint *Augustine* saith: That when Aug.ſer.29.
a man maketh a lie for humilitie sake, if he were not a sinner de ver.Apoſt.
before, by lying he is made a sinner. Albeit Saint *Gregorie*
were an Italian and a most noble Romane, yet are we not to
imagine that his Worthinesse would once vse to any, much
lesse to the Emperour, such ceremoniall complements of
courtesie, as many in those parts now adayes do, and not of
the meneſt sort: to wit, *Ton seruitore, anzi sono schiano di vostra*
signoria. I am your seruant, yea, I am a base seruant or slaue
of your Maisterſhip or Worſhip, and other such like; when
　　　　　　　M　　　　　　　they

they meane nothing lesse : or do an vnlawfull act, for feare of the Emperours displeasure. Saint *Gregorie* vndoubtedly *ex animo* obeyed the Emperour commanding him to send a law which he had made, into diuers parts of the world to be promulgated : which he refused not to do, albeit the law in Saint *Gregories* iudgement contained many things against the Ecclesiasticall libertie. *Ego quidem iuſſioni ſubiectus, eandem legem per diuerſas terrarum partes tranſmitti feci,&c.* I being ſubiect to your commandement, haue caused the law to be sent through diuers parts of the world. In the end: *Vtrobique ergo quæ debui exolui, qui & Imperatori obedientiam præbui, & pro Deo, quod ſenſi minime tacui.* On both sides therefore haue I performed my dutie, (or done what I ought, which is to be noted) who haue both obeyed the Emperour, and also for God haue not bene silent what I thought. This obedience Cardinall *Bellarmine* against *Barclai* saith was coacted, and *de facto*, but not *de iure.* By which answer, who seeth not what an imputatió offrailty & weaknesse is laid on him that ought to be and was *murus æneus,* & *petra fortitudinis*, against any power whatsoeuer that commandeth vniustly? A weake defence for so strong a rocke; who both in doctrine and example left a perfect patterne of a most humble Pastor, and glorious Saint burning with the fire of charitie, readie, no doubt, to haue exposed himselfe to martirdome, rather then for sauing his life to consent to a veniall sinne. A mirror may he be to his succeſſours and all Bishops; would God he had many followers in his profound humilitie, which is the vertue that most exaltéth Prelate, Prince, or people to glorie. And this much of ſubiects duties to their Princes in temporals, wherein they ought by the law and ordinance of God to be no leſſe obedient, then to their Pastors and Prelates in ſpirituals.

It followeth now to know what authoritie it is the Pope pretendeth to haue, whether Ecclesiasticall or ciuill, to depose lawfull Kings, and diſpoſe of their temporals, and abſolue ſubiects of their bounden dutie and naturall allegiance. Which queſtion, who ſo deſireth to ſee it more at
large,

In fine epiſt.
61.l.2.

large, he may reade D. *Barclai de poteſtate Papa*, and M. *Widdrington de iure Principum*, where it is moſt ſufficiently and learnedly handled; and before in this my treatiſe pag. 17 I haue briefly touched it, whereto I adde in this place a word or two more for your better ſatisfaction.

Among ſuch Catholickes as refuſe to take the Oath of allegiance, are many who thinke indeed the Pope to haue no power to depoſe Kings or diſpoſe of their kingdoms, howbeit either vpon pretended ſcruple of conſcience, or other humane reſpects, are againſt the taking and takers of the Oath, as if they were little better then Heathens or Publicans. And ſome ſo ſimple and ignorant, as beleeue that no Pope euer challenged or attempted ſuch authoritie on any Kings or Emperors; and that no Ieſuit or other learned man allowed or euer taught ſuch doctrine; ſo odious it ſeemeth vnto them. But the wiſer ſort and more learned know how it hath bene challenged and practiſed by Popes on the perſons of *Henrie, Otho, Fredericke*, Emperours, *Iohn* King of Nauarre, for neither hereſie or apoſtaſie; and ſince on *Henrie* 8. and Queene *Elizabeth*, as by cenſures do appeare. And that it is the moderne doctrine of many both Canoniſts and Diuines in theſe latter ages, which at the firſt teaching thereof (being ſo farre diſſonant from the writings and practiſe of all antiquitie) was generally adiudged to be *noua hæreſis*, as *Sigebert* reporteth. S. *Iohn Chryſoſtome* that great Doctor, vpon that place of S. *Paul*, 2. Cor. 1. *Non dominamur fidei veſtræ*: We ouerrule not your faith; attributeth ſuch power as forcibly reſtraines offenders from their wickedneſſe of life, vnto ſecular Iudges vnder whoſe dominion they are, not vnto the Church: becauſe (ſaith he) neither is ſuch power giuen vnto vs by the lawes, with authoritie to reſtraine men from offences; nor if ſuch power were giuen vs, could we haue wherewith we might exerciſe ſuch power, &c. So in his time, and long after, ſuch power of compelling offenders by temporall puniſhments to conuert to better life; was vnheard of to be in Biſhops of the Church.

Cardinall *Bellarmine* in the catalogue of his ancient writers,

Sigebertus in Chro. ad an. 1088.

Chryſoſt. lib. 2 de dig. ſacerd. c. 3.

ters, which he produceth againſt *Barclai* for the Popes temporall authoritie ouer Princes, beginneth with one who
was iudge in his owne cauſe, *Gregorie* the ſeuenth, that began his reigne in the yeare of our Lord 1073. not able of
like to proue it out of any more ancient Father or generall
Councell. That this Pope was the firſt that challenged or attempted to practiſe ſuch authoritie, witneſſeth *Otho Friſen-*
gen. a moſt learned and holy Biſhop, and highly commended by the Cardinall himſelfe, *lib.4.de Rom.Pont.cap.13.Lego*
(ſaith he) *& relego Romanorum Regum & Imperatorum geſta,*
& nuſquam inuenio quenquam eorum ante hunc à Rom. Pontifice
excommunicatum,vel regno priuatum,&c. I reade and reade
ouer againe the acts of the Kings and Emperors of Rome,
and in no place can I find any of them before this (to wit,
Henrie the fourth) to be excommunicated or depriued of
his kingdome by the Biſhop of Rome; vnleſſe haply any
take this for excommunication, that *Philip* the firſt Chriſtian
Emperor (who ſucceeded *Gordianus*) for a ſhort ſpace, was
by the Biſhop of Rome (or as *Euſebius* reporteth, of the Biſhop of that place where he then reſided) placed among
publicke penitents: and *Theodoſius* ſequeſtred by S. *Ambroſe*
from entrance into the Church, for cruell murther. Whereby we may note, that this learned man could not find no
not one example in all precedent ages of depriuing kings
of their regal ſcepters; though of excommunication he pro-
poſeth onely theſe two, which may haue ſome ſhew of truth
for meere excommunication, howbeit more probable it is
they were not excommunicated at all *maiore excommunica-*
tione. Then this Author in the next chapter following, de-
ſcribeth the inteſtine warres, deſtruction of ſoules and bodies, ſetting vp of Pope againſt Pope, ſchiſmes, and other
manifold lamentable miſeries that enſued vpon that fact of
Pope *Gregory* againſt *Henrie* the 4. who commanded the Biſhops of Ments and Colen to conſtitute *Rodolph* Duke of
Burgundie Emperor, and to put downe *Henrie:* whereupon
followed a moſt grieuous warre, wherein *Rodolphus* was o-
uercome; who dying repentant ſaid: The Apoſtolicall com-
maude-

Otho in chro.
l.6.c.35.

Euſeb.hiſt.
Eccl.l.6.c.25.

Otho ibid.
c.36.

Spec.hiſt l.27.

mandement, and the intreatie of Princes haue made me a trangreffor of my oath; behold therefore my hand, cut off (or wounded) wherewith I fware to my Lord *Henrie*, not trecheroufly to practife any thing againft his life, nor his glorie. Who being ouercome, the Bifhop of Ments by the Popes commandement, and with helpe of Saxons, raifed an other aduerfary againft the Emperor, one *Hermannus Knoflock*: whereupon followed likewife bloudie warres. After this, *Henrie* gathering his armie together, driueth the Pope into France, and fetteth vp the Bifhop of Rauenna againft him, whom he named *Clement*, and fo caufed a fchifme. This *fparfim* out of the hiftory. Such like calamities are more then probable to fall on people and the Church, when Emperors or Kings are fo violently proceeded withall; affured deftruction of many, and no hope of the correction of any by fuch means, is like to enfue. Was fuch power, trow ye, giuen by Chrift to his Apoftles tending to deftruction, not to edification? No, all to edification, according to S. *Paul*, none to deftruction.　2.Cor.10.

Otho Frifengenfis in another place of his workes, writing of the Popes excommunicating the Emperour, fheweth that *Henrie* 4. thought it to be fuch a nouitie, as he had neuer knowne the like fentence to be denounced againft any Romane Emperor before. He liued *an.* 1150.　Li.1. de geftis Frederici, c 1.

And *Sigebert* in *Chronico* 1088. affirmeth the doctrine of Priefts, teaching that no fubiection is to be yeelded to euill Kings, and though they fweare fidelitie, are not bound to performe it, to be *noua hærefis*, a new herefie fprung vp. Howbeit Cardinall *Bellarmine* will tell you, that fuch doctrine and practife began about the yeare of our Lord 700: for before that time there wanted (as he affirmeth) either neceffitie or oportunitie to teach, or vfe fuch power. By reafon, of like, there were no hereticall Princes impugners of the true faith before that time; or that the paucitie of Chriftian Kings to affift the weake forces of the Church againft her perfecutors was fuch, as there could be no hope to preuaile. As if true faith and religion (which is now, befide the　By euill kings he meaneth fuch as are depofed. Cont. Barcl. cap.5.

M 3　Indies

Indies, reftrained into a corner of Europe onely) did not re-
plenifh before that time Europe, Afticke and Afia. No,
there wanted not neceffitie to practife fuch authoritie on
Conftantius, Iulian, Valens, Valentinian, and other like profeffed aduerfaries of Chrift and his Church : nor oportunitie, Chriftians being fo many, fo potent, replete with maruellous zeale and conftant courage in defence of Gods
truth, to the loffe of lands and life, If they had knowne fuch
power of depofing to haue bene in the Church and chiefe
Paftors thereof; and the Paftors knew well what their dutie
was in that behalfe.

But where (I pray you) lay this power hidden for the
fpace of 700 hundred yeares after Chrift by the Cardinals
confeffion (fuppofe I fhould grant fo much vnto him) of
difpofing of temporals *in ordine ad finem fpiritualem,* no Scripture, no tradition, no ancient Father or generall Councell
in all that time teaching it? If he fay, there was; where or how
doth it appeare ? His Grace hath not yet neither in *Tortus,*
nor againft our Kings Apologie, nor in his laft againft *Barclai,* produced any fuch cleare teftimonie as may conuince.
Our Sauiour Chrift himfelfe refufed to intermeddle in deuiding a temporall inheritance betweene two, faying: *Quis
me conftituit iudice aut diuifore fuper vos?* Who hath conftituted me a iudge or a diuider ouer you? difdaining as it were
(as *Ianfenius* noteth) that he fhould be troubled or drawne
fro the celeftiall bufineffe, for which only he was fent by his
Father, to haue care of carnall and bafe things; thereby alfo
to teach fuch as are his, that they ought not to intangle
themfelues in profane bufineffe that gouerne the Apoftolicke office. According to this is that of S. *Paul: Nemo mili-
tans Deo, implicat fe negotijs fecularibus :* No man that is a
fouldier to God, entangleth himfelfe with fecular bufineffe.
What more intangling, what more fecular, then to intermeddle in deuiding and difpofing of temporals ? *Non eft difcipulus fuper magiftrum:* The difciple is not aboue his maifter.
Therefore his Vicar ought not in fuch wife to be iudge ouer
Kings in things terrene, when they are taught by our Sauiours

Luc.12.

Ianfen.conc.

2.Tim.2.

uiours example not to be hindered from celeſtiall affaires, which onely do concerne them:whoſe power is ouer ſinnes of men, not ouer their poſſeſſions, *In criminibus,non in poſ- ſeſſionibus poteſtas veſtra.*

Bern. lib. 1.de conſid.cap. 2.

Againe,S. *Peter* prince of the Apoſtles, hauing receiued of Chriſt all power neceſſary for the gouernement of his Church, which was to be deriued to his ſucceſſors,had not that power which is temporall, but onely ſpirituall; for in the Apoſtles times the Eccleſiaſticall and ciuill were diſtinct and ſeparate, as the Cardinall confeſſeth,*lib. 5.de ſum. Pont.cap. 6.* Which could not be, but were conioyned, if they had any ſuch power, yea indirectly. If then *Peter* had no temporall power directly or indirectly giuen him by Chriſts inſtitution,who doubtleſſe foreſaw that it was neceſſary to be in him and his ſucceſſours for the correction and direction of ſoules to their ſpirituall end; it were abſurd to ſay, that ſucceeding Popes as they are *Peters* ſucceſſors, ſhould haue more ample power then he, or any of the Apoſtles had. And the Cardinals argument which he maketh againſt the Canoniſts,helpeth for confirmation of this matter in hand, to wit: Chriſt (ſaith he) as he was man, while he liued on earth, receiued not, nor would haue any temporall dominion ;but the Pope is Chriſts Vicar, and repreſenteth Chriſt vnto vs, ſuch as he was while he liued here among men; Therefore the Pope as Chriſts Vicar,and ſo as Pope hath not any temporall dominion.

De Ro. Pont. li.5.c 4.

How then cometh it that Popes in theſe latter ages practiſe on exorbitant Princes depoſition,and diſpoſing of temporals,when they ſhall iudge it neceſſarie, or expedient to a ſpirituall end, hauing no commiſſion, no warrant of our Sauiour ſo to do ? Is it by temporall onely,or ſpirituall onely, or by both? By their temporall power, which reacheth no further thē the patrimony of the Church,it is euident they cannot; for ſo they are but equals, not ſuperiours to abſolute Princes : and *Par in parem non habet imperium,* No neither haue they, which is more, being no Monarchs, authority from Chriſt to put any man to death, to baniſh,

or

Coſt.in Oſi-
and propoſ.7. or to depriue any priuate man of his goods, as *Coſterus* a
learned Ieſuite, and other good Authors do hold.

Nemo Pontifex ſanguinis leges tulit, hoc munus Imperatorum eſt, qui varias pœnas de hæreticis ſcripſerunt; quos bonorum ſpoliatione, infamia, exilio, morte, imò igne puniri iuſſerunt, &c.
No Pope hath made lawes of life and death: this is the office of Emperours, who haue written downe diuerſe puniments for heretickes; whom they haue cõmanded to be puniſhed with loſſe of goods, infamie, exile, death, yea with fire, &c. He goeth on, The Pope at Rome putteth no man to death; he hath his ſecular Iudges, who miniſter iuſtice by
Almain.de
dom.nat.&
ciuili.in vlt.
edit,Gerſonis. the lawes of *Cæſar.* To this agreeth *Iacobus Almain: De ratione poteſtatis laicæ eſt pœnã ciuilem poſſe infligere, vt ſunt mors, exilium, bonorum priuatio, &c.* It belongeth to the ſecular power to inflict a ciuill puniſhment, as are death, baniſhment, depriuing of temporall goods. But the Eccleſiaſticall power cannot by the inſtitution of God inflict any ſuch paine: no not impriſon any, as many Doctors hold; but it reacheth onely to ſpirituall puniſhment, that is, to excõmunication: and the other puniſhments which he vſeth, *ex iure purè poſitiuo ſunt*, are onely by a poſitiue law. Who in
Alm.de pot.
Eccleſ.& laic.
c.13.& q.1.
c.9. another place hath thus: *Chriſtus ſecundum humanitatem, &c.* Chriſt according to his humanity had greater power then the Pope hath, as to inſtitute the Euangelicall law: neither had he his power limited to ſacraments, for he could pardõ without application of ſacraments: & his Vicar hath not ſuch, but onely that which is declared in his Vicarſhip; for he gaue him power to remit ſinnes, to preach, to giue indulgences, &c: but it is no where found that he gaue him power to inſtitute and depoſe Kings: therefore by any power giuen him from Chriſt (note well) he hath not foueraigne power of iuriſdiction in temporals. This he. With
Maior in 4.
diſt.24.q.3. theſe may be ranked *Ioannes Maior: Maximus Pontifex non habet dominium temporale ſuper Reges, &c.* The chiefe Biſhop hath not temporall dominion ouer Kings. For the contrary being granted, (ſaith he) it followeth that Kings are his vaſſals, and that he may expell them *de facto* out of their
king-

kingdome, &c. but this is not to be granted. And in the
fame queftion: *Si aliqui Reges*, *&c.* If fome Kings with the
people haue deliuered ouer themfelues to the Popes of
Rome, as it is faid of Englifhmen, it is nothing to vs. Yet
do I not thinke that Englifhmen by any meanes would
permit the Pope to depofe their King, and fet vp another:
for they neuer yet fuffered any of the Bifhops of Rome
to do it.

But left any man here take hold and fay, that King *Iohn*
was brought to yeeld his crowne to the Popes Legate, and
for redeeming it, granted an annuall tribute to the Sea
Apoftolike; let him reade S.*Thomas More* for his better fa- More fupplic.
tiffaction herein, who plainely denieth it thus: If he (the of foules pag.
Author of the Supplication of beggers) fay, as indeed fome 296.
writers fay, (*Platina* and others) that King *Iohn* made Eng-
lad & Ireland tributarie to the Pope & the Sea Apoftolike,
by the grant of a thoufand markes : we dare furely fay a-
gaine, that it is vntrue; and that all Rome neither can fhew
fuch a grant, nor neuer could : and if they could, it were
nothing worth; for neuer could any King of England giue
away to the Pope, or make the land tributarie though he
would.

To conclude this point of depofing Princes, I will note
vnto you onely one place more to this purpofe out of the
Decrees of the Church of France collected by *Bochellus* a Bochel.ex
late writer. *Regnum Franciæ eiufq, pertinentias dare in prædam* Cod.libert.
Papa non poteft, &c. The Pope cannot giue away for a prey Ecclef. Gallic.
the kingdome of France and the appertenances thereof, or li.2.tit.16.c.1.
difpofe therof in any other fort whatfoeuer. And notwithftanding whatfoeuer admonitions, excommunications, or
interdicts, the fubiects are bound to performe due obedience to their King in temporals; neither can they be difpenced or abfolued from the fame by the Pope. The reafon
hereof is, that fuch obedience is due by the law of God and
nature, againft which no man may difpence, according to Tho 2.2.q.88
S.*Thomas*: *In his quæ funt de lege naturæ, &c.* In fuch things ar.10.
as are of the law of nature, and in diuine precepts, no man

N   can

can difp ence. O that French-men (if that their doctrine be
currant in France) would vouchsafe to teach their doctrine
here in great Brittaine. In them it seemeth tollerable, and
would be doubtleffe vnpunishable. But certaine Englifh
priefts, no leffe Catholicke then well affected subiects, for
teaching the like in defence of their King and countrey,
muft be subiect to the loffe of faculties (the onely meanes
that many haue of their reliefe) calumniation & obloquie
of tongues, reputed as fchifmatikes, little better then heretikes; and efteemed of fome vnworthy of foode to maintaine life: diuerfe hauing bene forbidden to vifite fuch in
prifon or relieue them. This is too true: would God it were
not fo. *O tempora, O mores.* Wel may we cry out with S. *Paul,*
1. Cor 15.   *Miferabiliores fumus omnibus hominibus:* we are more misera-
Pfal. 13.   ble then all men. But though the throate of fome be an opē
sepulcher, and with their tongues they deale subtilly, and
the poifon of afpes be vnder their lips: yet we neede not
diftruft the prouidence of almighty God, if we will with
one eye looke to his mercifull and moft wonderfull care of
Daniel, feeding him imprifoned in the middeft of Lions:
and with the other behold his daily relieuing the beafts of
the field, and fowles of the aire, all made for man, as man
for God. Then, *confortamini in Domino, & nolite timere, multis
pafferibus pluris eftis vos.* Comfort your felues in our Lord,
and feare ye not, you are much more worth then many
sparrowes: you I meane that intend not to derogate from
the fpirituall authoritie of Chrifts Vicar, but to render no
leffe vnto him his due, then to *Cæfar* his. But to returne
whence we haue digreffed, if it be true that a Councell may
not iudge, punifh, or depofe the Pope, though he endeuor
Li. 2. de Rom.   to deftroy the Church of God, as Cardinall *Bellarmine* wri-
Pont. c. 29.   teth: which belongeth to none but to a superiour; a Councell not being aboue the Pope, as many hold: why are
Li. 3. c. 19.   we not to beleeue the fame of Kings, though they per-
Tert. ad Sca-   fecute the Church, when as (witneffe the fame Author)
pulam præ-   they acknowledge no superior, no iudge on earth in tem-
fid. Carthag.   porals?

Wel

Well, let such Doctors as teach deposition in schooles, withdraw themselues from speculation to practise, from scholasticall distinctions and disputations to Magistrates examinations, such as haue *potestatem crucifigendi vel dimittendi*; haply they may change their subtile shifts into a simple proposition, that it is small wisedome to band with the supreme Magistrate in a matter so important as is *Cæsars* right, neuer any thing being yet determined by the Church of God to warrant them so to do.

And it may be in my iudgement admired, that catholicke Princes permit such dangerous positions, not onely to be disputed, but also taught for truth within their dominions, and to passe without controlement, knowing that a sparkle of fire lying smothering in combustible matter, if it be neglected and left vnquenched, may cause in short space an vnquenchable flame: so such a speculatiue doctrine litle regarded, is not vnlike in time to breed a wofull practicall ruine of kingdomes and nations. And this of the Popes temporall power.

Is it then by spirituall authoritie alone, or by both, that Princes may be deposed? for it seemeth by later Diuines, that Popes may depose them directly or indirectly. The mirror of this age for diuine literature, Cardinall *Bellarmine*, in his late booke against *Barclai*, cap. 5. and elsewhere, writeth not so plainely as were to be wished, nor so, as he satisfieth his reader, whether it be spirituall onely, or temporall onely, but seemeth to incline more to the spirituall power, yet mixt with temporall. *Iam dixi (inquit) potestatem de* In Barcl.c.5 *qua loquimur, &c.* I haue alreadie said, that the power wherof we speake, is to be found expresly in the Scriptures, but generally, not in particular; to wit, in the 16. of Saint *Matthew: Tibi dabo claues regni cœlorum.* And *Iohn* 21. *Pasce oues meas* : and by these same diuine testimonies may be gathered, that accession and coniunction of power to dispose of temporals, *in ordine ad spiritualia*, as more then once is declared. And may it not I pray you be as well said (with due respect to his dignitie) that by those diuine testimonies

no fuch gloffe of acceffion or coniunction of power may
be gathered : becaufe thofe places were euer vnderftood by
all ancient Fathers of the fole fpiritual authority of the Pope
without acceffion or coniunction of temporall power, yea
in ordine ad fpiritualia?

By the keyes of the kingdome of heauen promifed to
Peter, (yet not for *Peter* alone, but for the * Church) figni-
fying power to be giuen to bind and loofe, to admit the
worthy to the kingdome of heauen, and to exclude the vnworthie; can any other power be vnderftood then meerely
fpirituall? moft certainely there cannot. For aske when this
promife of our Sauiour was performed? No man I thinke
will denie, but then Chrift gaue thefe keyes, when after his
refurrection he vfed this ceremonie of breathing on his eleuen Apoftles, giuing them all like power to forgiue or reteine finnes, by thefe words: *Quorum remiferitis peccata, &c.*
Whofe finnes you fhall forgiue, they are forgiuen them:
and whofe you fhall reteine, they are reteined. By which
words the Fathers often fay, that the keyes were giuen to
all the Apoftles. If any man fo build on that which Chrift
faid to *Peter* : *Quodcunq, ligaueris fuper terram, &c.* Whatfoeuer thou fhalt bind vpon earth, it fhal be bound alfo in the
heauens : and whatfoeuer thou fhalt loofe in earth, it fhall
be loofed alfo in the heauens : that *Peter* and his fucceffors
haue power to fet vp and plucke downe Kings; then muft it
of neceffitie follow, that the reft of the Apoftles had the
fame, becaufe he vfed the like phrafe to them alfo : *Quæcunque alligaueritis, &c.* Whatfoeuer ye fhall bind vpon earth,
fhall be bound in heauen, &c. And fo confequently all Bifhops (who are appointed gouernours likewife of the
Church of God, as Saint *Paul* faith, *Attendite, &c.* Take
heed to your felues, and to the whole flock, wherin the holy
Ghoft hath placed you Bifhops, to rule the Church of God,
which he hath purchafed with his owne blood) may dethrone Kings if they iudge it expedient; which is not to be
granted.

This former interpretatiõ of anciẽt diuines feemes more a-
greeable

* O igen.in
hunc loc. ho. 1
Aug. tract. vlt.
in Ioan. & l. 1.
de doct. Chr.
c. 18.
Cofter. in O-
fiand. c. 4.

Ioan. 20.

Math. 16.

See Ianfeni-
us Concor. c.
72.

Act. 20.

greeable to Chrifts words as *Ianfenius* noteth, to vnderftand bythefe keyes power to bind and loofe (becaufe with thefe two powers as with two keyes, the kingdom of heauē is o-pened to the truly penitēt; & with the other it is fhut againft the vnworthy & impenitēt finner) then is the interpretatió of later Diuines, who fay that Chrift meant of the keyes of knowledge of difcerning *inter leprā & lepram,* who is wor-thy to be abfolued, who vnworthie; and of power to bind & loofe.Howfoeuer they are to be vnderftood, yet therby can-not be gathered power to depofe or difpofe of temporals.

Theophylaɛt vpon this place, hath thus : *(Claues autē intelligas,* | Theoph.in
quæ ligant & foluunt, hoc eft, deliɛlorū vel indulgentias vel pœnas, | 16.Math.
&c; And vnderftand keyes, which bind and loofe, that is, either pardons or punifhments of finnes. For they haue po-wer to remit and to bind, who haue attained to the grace of Epifcopacie as *Peter* hath. Which power he affirmeth was granted to all the Apoftles. *Quamuis autem foli Petro diɛlum fit, Dabo tibi, &c.* And although (faith he) it be fpoken to *Peter* alone, I will giue thee; yet the keyes are granted to all the Apoftles. When? When he faid, Whofe finnes ye remit | Cap.firmiter
they are remitted. For when he faid *dabo,* he fignified a time | defumma
to come, to wit, after his refurreɛlion. So *Theophylaɛt.* If they | Trinit.& fide
were giuen to *Peter,* doth it not follow that the Apoftles | Cath.& c lo-
receiued them of *Peter?* But *Viɛloria* teacheth that they re- | quitur.24.q.1
ceiued them of Chrift, not of *Peter. Rabanus* likewife: Albeit | Viɛt.de claui-
this power of binding and loofing feeme to be giuen onely | bus.nu.4.
to *Peter;* yet it is alfo giuen to the reft of the Apoftles, and is | Rabanus.
now likewife to all the Church in Bifhops and Priefts. But therefore *Peter* fpecially receiued the keyes of the king-dome of heauen, and the principalitie of iudiciarie power, that all beleeuers through the world may vnderftand, that whofoeuer do feparate themfelues in any fort from the vni-tie of his faith and focietie, that fuch can neither be abfolued from the bonds of fins, nor enter into the gate of the king-dome of heauen. This he.

But let it be granted, according to the fentēce of many an-ciēt Fathers, that Chrift fpeaking fpecially to *Peter,* gaue him

more

more ample power then he gaue to the reſt of the Apoſtles, yet all was but ſpirituall, as the words import, and to a ſpirituall end; *in ædificationem, non in deſtructionem,*to edification not to deſtruction: not tending to depoſition or depriuation of the temporall goods of any within his gouernment: but to excommunication, or ſeparation of certaine obſtinate offenders from the common goods of the Church militant, and ſo conſequently from the ioyes of the Church triumphant. And let it be, that *Peter* receiued the keyes of our Sauior when he ſaid vnto him,*Paſce oues meas,*Feed my ſheep; all was but ſpirituall: for the ſame power is required to feed the flocke of Chriſt, that is to open or ſhut the kingdome of heauen. And then was he inſtituted the Vicar of Chriſt on earth: by whoſe inſtitution, and as he is Biſhop or Paſtor of the whole Church, the moſt illuſtrous Card. confeſſeth that he receiued not power to ouerrule (*dominari*) but *paſcere,*to feed. Which kind of ſecular domination was forbidden the Apoſtles, and miniſtration commanded, as Saint *Bernard* ſaith. Who in an other place explicateth what it is, to feed: *Euangelizare, paſcere eſt. Opus fac euangeliſta, & paſtorum opus impleſti.* To euangelize, is to feed. Do the worke of an Euangeliſt, and thou haſt fulfilled the worke of Paſtors. But ſome are forced to ſay, that excommunication of the Pope neceſſarily worketh this temporall effect of depoſition, for that they know not otherwiſe how his Holineſſe can attaine to ſuch power. If this were ſo, then what Biſhop ſoeuer do excommunicate any within his dioceſſe, doth alſo depoſe and depriue them of their temporals : for what the Pope is in the vniuerſall Church, ſuch is a Biſhop in the particular, as Cardinall *Bellarmine* once held, though lately in his Recognitions he retracteth it after this manner: Whereas I ſaid, that a Biſhop was the ſame in a particular Church, as the Pope is in the vniuerſall, it is thus to be taken; that as the Pope is the true Paſtor and Prince of the Church vniuerſall, ſo is a Biſhop a true Paſtor and Prince of a particular Church, not a Vicar or adminiſtrator for a certaine time, &c. Which yet ſerueth well for our purpoſe in hand:

Marginal notes:

Ioan.21.

Vict. de clau. nu.4.

Card. Bellar. de Ro.Pont. l.5.c.10.

Bern. de conſid. l.2.c.5. L.4.c.4. de conſid.

L. 5. de ſum. Pont.c.3.

hand:for if a Bishop a spiritual Prince of a particular church, cannot by vertue of excommunication depose his subiects, neither can the Pope as spirituall Prince ouer all.

And *Victoria* plainly saith thus, That a Bishop *de iure diuino* hath power to excommunicate his subiects *ex officio,* and by ordinary and proper power. And what the Pope can do throughout all the world, a Bishop may also do in his Bishopricke, a few things excepted, as to create a Bishop. Who disagreeth not with the Cardinall in this, that a Bishop is a true Pastor in his particular Church, as the Pope is in the Catholicke and vniuersall: that he may as well excommunicate the subiects committed to his charge, as the Pope may all Princes and people that are sheepe of Christs fold, by the authoritie giuen to *Peter* in those words, *Pasce oues meas.* By which Christ indeed constituted him Pastor ouer his flocke, marry a spirituall Pastor, not a temporall, giuing him all authoritie necessary for that office, which was only spirituall, without coniunction of any other. By vertue then of this spirituall authoritie (the principall part for gouernment in *foro exteriori,* is excommunication, being *grauissima pœnarum,* then which none is more grieuous) no Bishop can depriue any priuate man whatsoeuer within his Diocesse of the least parcell of his lands or goods: (that being the office of the ciuill power) how then can the chiefe Bishop depriue Kings and Princes of their crownes and dignities, the nature of this censure being all one in both?

Excommunication is defined to be *separatio à communione Ecclesiæ, quoad fructum & suffragia generalia, &c.* Excommunication is a separation from the communiō of the Church, as touching the fruite and generall suffrages. The fruite of the Church, cannot be vnderstood of the fruite of temporall goods, because these are not taken away from excommunicate persons. This S. *Thomas:* plainly shewing, that it is beyond the nature of this censure to worke any such effect, as to take away temporall goods. And in the same qu. ar. 3. *Sed quia excommunicatio est grauissima pœnarum, &c.* But because excommunication is the greatest of all punishments,

there-

Victor. de excom. nu. 11.

Tho. in suppl. q. 21. ar. 1. & in 4. dist. 18. q. 2.

therefore excommunication ought not to be inflicted, no
not for a mortall fin, vnleffe the offender be obftinate. *Tunc
enim poftquam monitus fuerit, &c.* For then after he fhall be
admonifhed, if he contemptuoufly difobey, he is reputed
ftubburne, and ought to be excommunicated by the Iudge,
now not hauing any more to do againft him. And the fame
Doctor difputing whether heretickes are to be toilerated,

Tho.2.2.q.11
ar.3.

faith, That after the firft and fecond admonition, if yet he be
found obftinate, the Church not hoping of his conuerfion
(meaning no doubt fuch a one as hauing profeffed the Catholicke faith, hath made fhipwracke thereof, and fallen to
herefie) prouideth for the health of others, feparating him
from the Church by the fentence of excommunication; and
further leaueth him to fecular iudgement to be put to death.
Whereby you fee that in cafe yea of herefie, the Church can

Can. corripi-
antur.24.q.3.

proceed no further then to excommunication after fhe hath
declared and condemned him for his crime.

Mola. de fide
hær. fer.l.2.c.2
& l.3.c 4.

To this agreeth *Molanus*, writing of the condemnation
of *Iohn Huffe* and *Hierome* of Prage by the generall Councel
of Conftance, who (as he faith) hauing excommunicated, a-
nathematized and condemned them for heretickes, and hauing no more to do with them, deliuered them ouer to Imperiall power, by which they were burnt. So that temporall
punifhment of heretickes, whether it be by confifcation of
goods and patrimonie, or death, belongeth and is proper to
the fecular power, as the fpirituall do to Ecclefiafticall perfons. Which we fee manifeft by practife of all Chriftian
countries, yea and our owne, that no man is to be put to
death, nor lofe his goods vpon excommunication, but onely
by execution of the Princes law. And Cardinall *Bellarmine*

Bellarm.in
Barcl.c.23.

himfelfe will confeffe, that *extra cafum hærefis*, out of the cafe
of herefie, by vertue of the fentence of excommunication
there followeth not depriuation of temporall dominion, or
of particular goods, or kingdomes and princedomes: though
(faith he by and by) Kings and Princes may be for iuft caufes depriued by the Pope of their kingdome or princedome.
Varioufly and ambiguoufly infinuating, that there are other
iuft

iuſt cauſes beſides hereſie, but liſteth not, or rather (as may be ſuppoſed) cannot ſet downe what they are: for as yet neuer were any determinately made knowne, more then ſuch as ſhall be deemed worthy of depriuation, *ad arbitrium Pontificis.*

But as farre as I can ſee, his Grace muſt maintaine other cauſes as well as hereſie ; otherwiſe how can the depoſition of *Henrie, Fredericke, Otho,* and other Princes, be defended to haue bene lawfull, who were neuer condemned by the Church for hereſie? And if there be other cauſes current to depriue Princes of temporals then there is for priuate men, ſurely the Chriſtian princely ſtate muſt needs be farre worſe then the plebeian, or then if they were Heathens or Publicans: which were abſurd; when as God the giuer of all power, for correction of men, is not *acceptor perſonarum,* but miniſtreth iuſtice equally or indifferently to all; all, both Princes and people being *populus eius, & oues paſcuæ eius,* his people, and the ſheepe of his paſture. If there be any, as me thinketh I heare one ſay, that he is not yet ſatisfied as touching this point, but deſireth to know the finall cauſe, nature and effects of excommunication; let him note wel what the moſt learned and graue Cardinall *Tolet* of famous memory, and others write thereof.

Eſt autem excommunicatio Eccleſiaſtica cenſura, qua homo Chriſtianus bonis fidelium communibus priuatur. Excommunication is an Eccleſiaſticall cenſure, whereby a Chriſtian man is depriued of the common goods of the faithfull. Which goods, he ſaith are three: 1. externall conuerſation, conſiſting in mutuall talke and ſocietie: 2. participation of ſacraments: 3. prayers and ſuffrages of the Church. And theſe in his opinion, are not ſo much the effects, as the very nature and ſubſtance of excommunication. The end whereof, without controuerſie, is the good and vtility of man, that he may repent, and conuert himſelfe to good, as he ſaith ; when as excommunication is medicinall, not mortall; inſtructing, not plucking vp by the roote. Which agreeth with the Epiſtle of Pope *Vrban,* ſet downe in the Canon law: *Liquido apparet*

Tolet. lib. 1. inſtruc. ſacerd. c. 4. nu. 1.

Lib. 1. c. 11. n. 1
Li. 1. c. 10. n. 14

Cap. Medicinalis de ſent. excom. in 6. Decret. 2. par. 24. q. 3. cap. 36

paret aliud esse excommunicationem,aliud eradicationem,&c. It
euidently appeareth, that excommunication is one thing,
eradication another. For he that is excommunicated (as
the Apostle saith) to this end is excommunicated, that his
spirit may be saued in the day of our Lord. *Disciplina est enim*
excommunicatio,non eradicatio. Now what can here be gathered by the definition, end, effects or substance of this spirituall censure, for deposing Kings, and disposing of temporals? Marry sir, that subiects are bound, obeying the
chiefe Pastors censure, to shun their Prince excommunicated, performing no dutie vnto him, nor in any sort to communicate with him;for an excommunicate person by name,
ought of all to be auoided, to whom *os, orare, vale, commu-*
nio, mensa negatur. And then when all forsake him, is he not
in effect deposed? Yes truly, when all his subiects do forsake him,and he left alone. *Sed quando hæc erunt?* Is a King
more like to be forsaken then a *paterfamilias*, a priuate man?
Almaine saith indeede, that the Pope may forbid the subiects of a Prince,vnder paine of excommunication, to performe any dutie vnto him; whereby in effect he loseth his
kingdome,when no man doth regard him : yet cannot depose him,though he abuse his authoritie to the destruction
of the Christian faith. But if a generall defection of subiects
follow not, if according to their dutie they adhere faithfully vnto him, without regard to his censure, how then?
What his Holinesse may do in this case of excommunication with absolute Princes,being sheepe of Christs fold, to
be directed and corrected with that spirituall rod, when
there is hope of amendment,as well as priuate men, I will
not dispute; but experience of former ages teacheth it is
not expedient, and that such practise breedeth oft schismes,
reuolts, troubles, and tendeth rather to destruction of many, then to edification of any : when as S. *Paul* professeth
power to be giuen to the Church to edifie, not to destroy.
And when this power is exercised in *destructionem*, it is not
that power which cometh from God, but impotencie and
defect.This we may be said to do, that we may lawfully do.
                                                    Which

1.Cor.5.

Alm. de pot.
Eccl.& laica,
q.1.cap.9.

See S.Aug.lib
3.c.2.cont.ep.
Parm.& c.26.

Which power Doctor *Sanders* calleth the sword of the Church, and sheweth how it should be vsed: *Gladius Eccle-* *siæ in ædificationem datus est,&c.* The sword of the Church is giuen to edification, not to destruction;to conferre life,not to inferre death: for defence of the flocke, not for hurt of the sheepe: to driue away the Wolfe, not to deuoure the lambe. This sword being spirituall, and is to worke vpon soules, not bodies or goods of any, may be drawne foorth I must cōfesse by the supreme Pastor against exorbitant Prin- ces(whose superior he ought to be acknowledged but one- ly in spirituals)when there is hope to saue, not to destroy: to do good, no harme: and rather to make a wolfe a lambe, then cause a lambe to become a wolfe ready to deuoure the flocke, as sometimes such censures haue done, which lamē- table experience on the persons of many Princes can testi- fie: whereupon they proceeded further haply in rigor with their subiects then otherwise they would haue done: and not so much for excommunication onely, as for the clauses of depriuation, deposition, and absolution of subiects from their dutifull obedience; which are farre from the nature and substance of a spirituall censure, and exceedeth the li- mites of that power, as very learned Catholike Authors go about to proue. *Excommunicatio (*saith *Ludouicus Richeom)* *non nisi excommunicatum facere potest, eáque fulminatur in Prin-* *cipes , &c.* Excommunication cannot cause one to be but excommunicated, and it is thundred out against Princes, not that they may become tyrants, nor remoued from their possessions, nor to slacken the raines vnto subiects, or that they may be freed from their sworne fidelitie. To this agre- eth *Medina. Excommunicatio non est priuatio alicuius boni pro-* *prij, quod transgressor legis prius possederat : sed est priuatio bono-* *rum communium, &c.*Excommunication is not a taking a- way of any proper good, which the transgressor of the law before had possessed: but it is a depriuing of the common goods which he was to receiue of the Church, as spirituall communion, and receiuing sacraments. By which doctrine is plaine that none, poore or rich, subiect or Prince, may by

Sand de clau. *Dauid,c.9.*

Richeom.in *apolog.*

Medina.in 1. 2.q.96.ar.4. citans Sotum.

vertue of excommunication meerely,be difpoffeffed of any temporall goods whatfoeuer. If they could, then woe to all Chriftians in this refpect, that liue in fuch times as Bifhops and Popes are not faints. Any man excommunicated, vpon repetance may returne to grace, be receiued of the Church, and may recouer thofe fpirituall goods he had loft, as prayers, fuffrages, and facraments of the Church, &c. But if temporals, efpecially kingdomes, be once loft and confifcate; what hope of recouery? Wil it not be too late to cry, *Peccaui?* So then, that punifhment which God hath ordained for the good of foules, would be moft like to turne to the deftruction of bodies, foules, and goods for euer, if excommunication could worke fuch effect, and were not (as it ought to be) *medicinalis*, but *exitialis:* which is not to be granted.

Moreouer if ye looke backe to ancient Canons of generall Councels, yea to the Canons of the Apoftles, you fhall fee for the fame, or like crimes, punifhments to be inflicted on offendors; but depofition inflicted on Clercks, and on Laicks excommunication, or depriuing onely of facraments and communion; making this diftinction, *Si Clericus fit, deponitor; fi Laicus, à communione eijcitor.* Infinuating thereby (as may feeme) that the Church hath fuperioritie directly ouer Clerks to depofition or degradation of perfons, not fo ouer the perfons of Laicks further then to the cenfure of excommunication: and therefore not ouer kingdomes and Kings, who acknowledge no fuperiour on earth in temporals.

But I pray you, if the Popes Holines vpon caufe of herefie do excommunicate a Prince, or priuate man, and all that fhall communicate with him or obey him, is he not then to be auoided and forfaken of his fubiects and inferiours, or others whofoeuer? He that denieth this feemeth to deny the Popes fpirituall authority of binding; & that of S.*Paul: Hareticum hominem poft primam & fecundam correptionem deuita.* A man that is an hereticke after the firft and fecond admonition auoide.

Tit. 3.

What is this to our Oath? Is there any fuch claufe, for herefie,

refie, in it? Are we to adde vnto it by our idle inuentions? or are we vrged to take it otherwise then the words import simply as they lye, framed by act of Parliament? But these and such like fond verball obiections, are the cauilling shifts of such as know not how to giue better answers to the substantiall points of the Oath; and perswade some to the losse of their liues, and others of their lands and goods to their vtter ruine, (if iustice without mercy be executed) that it cannot be taken without deniall of their faith: neuer shewing them any particular point, which it is; for to say truth they cannot. So then their bare word must be beleeued as an oracle; or else in fine with a bat they will beate men downe, The Popes commandement; not hauing ought else to say, which may conuince. It may be admired they make no more conscience in such an important businesse as this is, not hauing the Churches definition, nor ancient Fathers approbations for their assertions. After all, some burst forth in most vncharitable railing & slanderous backbitings against such priests as in conscience haue performed their dutie in taking it, and persist in teaching the lawfulnesse thereof; withdrawing friends, and charitable almes from them, counselling some, and commanding others, not to resort vnto them; as I haue bene credibly told by some that haue themselues bene forbidden, and much more such like dealings which shall not be here rehearsed.

Ignosce illis Deus, quia nesciunt quid faciunt. These ought not to be the proceedings neither of good subiects, nor of discreete guides of mens soules, or true disciples of Christ, who are made knowne to all by a notorious cognisance, commonly called loue or charity, giuen by our Sauiour Christ. *In hoc cognoscent omnes quia discipuli mei estis, si dilecti-* Ioan.13. *one habueritis ad inuicem.* In this all men shal know that you are my disciples, if you haue loue one to another. Which badge were to be wished more visible then it is, in some that pretend to be true followers of Christ.

Now to the authoritie of S. *Paul* may be answered, that an heretick so taken, condemned, and denounced by the

O 3   Church,

Church, is to be auoided in his herefie, to be taken heed of that he be not feduced by him; *hærefis enim ferpit vt cancer*, for herefie creepeth as a canker: and in humane conuerfation alfo, when there is hope to reduce him thereby to a better mind: *Vt fpiritus faluus fit*. But as no Catholike is by the lawes of this realme to be accompted a Recufant till he be conuicted : fo is none by the lawes of the Church to be reputed an hereticke to be auoided, till he be by her admoniíhed, condemned and denounced for fuch ; which is neuer without pertinacie in herefie. And what maketh this for them that fay we denie the Popes authoritie? God forbid that I (by his grace) a Catholicke prieft, íhould euer denie the Popes fpirituall power to excommunicate any, Prince or people, that were once incorporated into the body myfticall of Chrift by Baptifme:but as I haue denied excommunication of her owne nature to extend to depofition and taking away of temporals; fo I may not grant that euery excommunicate perfon is to be abandoned of all, and debarred of all humane fociety and conuerfation. Though humane communication , efteemed one of the common goods, is found alfo among the faithfull, as to eate together, to falute, to talke, negotiate, and fuch like; yet this fort of communication belongeth not to them properly as they are Chriftians and members of the Church, but as they are citizens & parts of the body politick. And as they are fuch, they are bound to adhere vnto the head of this body their Prince, not to forfake, but obey him in all iuft ciuill caufes, notwithftanding any fentence of excommunicatió, as hath bene proued before out of *Syluefter*, *Panormitan* , & others; which is not to deny the Popes power .

No? if you reade *Tortus* and beleeue him, I know you wil change your opinion; for vpon thofe words: That the Pope neither of himfelfe , nor by any authority of the Church or Sea of Rome, hath any power or authority to depofethe king, &c. or to difcharge any of his fubiects of their allegiance and obedience to his Maieftie, &c. He writeth **Tortus par.3.** thus, Here it is manifeftly feene, that this Oath doth not

containe

containe onely ciuill obedience in things meerely temporall,as the Authour of the Apologie(our Soueraigne)so oft
hath repeated; but it containeth also a denyall of the Popes
power,which is not a thing meerely temporall , but a holy
thing and giuen from aboue,which no mortall man can take
away or diminish.

It is strange that his Maiesties oft repetition of a truth,
nothing to be contained in the Oath,or required, but ciuil
obedience,seemeth irkesome to the Cardinal,it being very
necessary whē men will not vnderstand,but his Grace goeth
not about to disproue it. And who I pray you is a better interpreter of a law when doubts or difficulties arise, then he
that made the law?If it containes a deniall of the Popes power, his Grace should haue done well to haue proued it,and
shewed wherein. Though the Cardinall for many respects
ought of me(somtime not vnknown vnto him)highly to be
reuerenced,and his writings credited; yet in this matter to
me most cleare , I must craue pardon if I differ from him in
opinion , and write otherwise : not being able , after study
and diligent search of this matter, to see it so manifest as his
Grace wold make his reader beleeue.It is most manifest the
ancient Fathers neuer taught so, viz. to be in the Popes power to depose Kings,nor discharge subiects of their loyaltie
and dutifull obedience; the Church neuer yet defined it so:
can I then be so credulous to beleeue his bare word without better proofe? His *ipse dixit* in this will not be sufficient.
The other florish to leade away a simple and inconsiderate
reader; forsooth, that the Popes power is spirituall , a holy
thing,from heauen,&c.is somewhat vainely and to no purpose inserted : for no Catholicke denieth it , and we that
haue taken the Oath of allegiance are readie with Gods
grace if need were, to shed our bloud in defence therof and
euerie point of Catholicke faith , albeit we suffer disgraces,
and neuer receiued temporall benefite , nor euer tooke
oath, *vsq, ad effusionem sanguinis inclusiuè*,so to do,as the most
illustrous and most reuerend purple Fathers are accustomed
to take,when in publicke consistory they receiue their hats.

The

The Cardinall in *Tortus* goeth on further, to prooue by subsequent words in the Oath, that the Popes spirituall power is denied; which were enough to terrifie Chriſtian ſubiects, if it were true. The words are theſe: *Alſo I do ſweare from my heart, that notwithſtanding any declaration, or ſentence of excommunication or depriuation made or granted, or to be made or granted by the Pope, or his ſucceſſors, or by any authoritie deriued or pretended to be deriued from him, or his Sea againſt the ſaid King, his heires or ſucceſſours, or any abſolution of the ſaid ſubiects from their obedience; I will beare faith and true allegiance to his Maieſtie, his heires and ſucceſſors.*

Here ſaith the Card. is openly denyed that the Pope hath power to excommunicate Kings, though they be heretikes. Note his proofe. For how (ſaith he) can a Catholicke lawfully and iuſtly ſweare, that he will not obey the Pope excōmunicating an hereticall king, vnleſſe he beleeue that an hereticall king cannot be excōmunicated by the Pope? Nay here in our Oath (with due reſpect to his Grace be it ſaid) is neither openly, no nor couertly denied that the Pope hath power to excōmunicate Kings, though they be heretikes, as the Cardinall beareth his reader in hand: I maruaile he wold in ſuch wiſe adde vnto, & thruſt into the text of the Oath that which no man, no nor himſelfe can find therein. For let it be well viewed and conſidered, it will preſently appeare that there is no mention at al of the Popes excōmunicating Kings, though they be heretiks, or heretical Kings; but onely, if he ſhould excommunicate our King, and abſolue his ſubiects from their obedience, yet I will beare true faith and allegiance to his Maieſtie. What ſincere dealing is this? Such gloſſes or wilfull additions are but manifeſt corruptions of the text, which ought not to be vſed by any that profeſſe ſincerity & truth. So this makes nothing againſt vs, but rather againſt himſelf. Then he cometh with his needles *minor*, which no Catholick denieth: But power to excōmunicate is intrinſecall to the Apoſtolicke primacie, and vnſeparable from it, when as our Lord ſaid to *Peter* as to the firſt ſpirituall Primate; Whatſoeuer thou ſhalt binde vpon earth,

earth, fhall be bound alfo in heauen. What is this to the purpofe? What Catholicke that hath taken the Oath will denie it? It is not vnlike to one that frameth an aduerfarie in the aire to fight withall.

If French Catholickes be demanded, what they will do in this cafe, if the Pope fhould excommunicate their King, and difcharge his fubiects of their obedience? they will forthwith anfwer, that notwithftanding any monitions, ex- comunications, or interdicts, they will not forfake, but obey their King in temporals, from which obedience they can- not be abfolued or difpenced withall by the Pope; as is *in de- cretis Ecclefiæ Gallicana, lib.* 2 *.cap.* 1. Nay they will bring cer- taine priuiledges for them and their King againft the Popes cenfure of excommunication: yet thefe like good Catho- lickes will beleeue that he hath power to excommunicate an hereticall King.

So in our cafe a man of any iudgement may clearely fee, it is neither openly nor couertly, *explicitè* nor *implicitè* denied, but plainely granted of fuch as take the Oath, that the Pope may excommunicate, albeit vpon iuft caufe adhering to his Prince he obey not the fentence. I aske, if his Holineffe in Rome fhould determine to create fome Prieft or Prelate, Cardinall or Bifhop; and he of humilitie or for fome other caufe beft knowne to himfelfe, notwithftanding the Popes determination, refufe to accept of the dignity, (*Quis eft hic, & laudabimus eum?* Who is he, and we will commend him?) doth it follow that therefore he denieth the Pope to haue power to conferre thofe dignities on them? Or if a King be pleafed to extend his mercie toward an offender condem- ned to die, granting him a pardon; can it be faid, though he lift not to accept thereof, notwithftanding the Kings grant, for that he hath a fhrewd wife that maketh him wearie of his life, or for fome other caufe, that he denieth the King to haue power to pardon his offence? It may be admired that one fo excellently learned will argue fo weakely. None would haue thought but the booke bearing the name of *Matthæus Tortus*, had bene in deed his Chaplains, not the

P   Car-

Cardinals, had not his Grace difcouered himfelfe in his anfwer to our Kings Apologie. Whofoeuer faieth or fweareth,
that notwithftanding any fentence of excommunication,
yet he will beare true faith and allegiance to his Prince, no
way denieth it, but fuppofeth fuch a fentence to be, or to
haue bin. When the Pope in his writings putteth this claufe:
Non obftantibus conftitutionibus Apoftolicis contrarijs quibufcun-
que. Notwithftanding any contrary Apoftolicall conftitutions whatfoeuer, &c. as in the Briefe of *Paulus* the fifth to
maifter *George Birket*, dated 1. Febr. 1608. or in others, *Non*
obftantibus priuilegijs quibufcunque, *&c*. Notwithftanding
whatfoeuer priuiledges: Is it not manifeft that fuch priuiledges, or Apoftolicall Conftitutions are fuppofed to be,
or might haue bene before granted? So in our cafe none denieth the Popes excomunication, but chufeth vpo iuft caufe
to adhere to his Prince, notwithftanding the fentence of excommunication againft him, which he prefuppofeth to be,
or elfe may be granted. If any will fay, There can be no iuft
caufe to adhere and obey his Prince if he be excommunicated, it were ridiculous, and falfe, as all writers affirme, fome
cafes being excepted, whether he be excommunicated *à iu-*
*re vel ab homine. Cum omnibus excommunicatis (*faith *Victoria*
among the reft *)quocunque modo fint excommunicati,&c.* With
all excommunicate perfons, in what fort foeuer they are excommunicated, it is lawfull to participate in thefe things
which are contained in this verfe: *Vtile, lex, humile, res ig-*
norata, neceffe. *Nauarre* likewife: *Regulariter participans*,
&c. Ordinarily he that communicateth with one that is excommunicated with the greater excommunication, incur-
reth the leffer: yet it faileth in thefe, *Vtile,lex,&c.* The declaration of which words he that vnderftandeth Latin may
fee in the fame place of *Nauarre*, in *Caietans* Summe, *Ema-*
*nuel Sa,*and other Authors.

	Now who is fo fimple as to thinke that a wife is bound
to abandon her hufband, and not to participate with him;
children to forfake their fathers, feruants their maifters, and
not communicate with them in domefticall affaires, if they
fhould be excommunicated?					If

Vict. de ex-
com. nu. 10.

Tolet. l. 1. inft.
facer. c. 11. n. 7
Nauar. Ench.
c. 27. n. 26.
Tho. 4. dift.
18. ar. 4.

If it be lawfull for fuch,(as it is by *lex* and *humile*)why not alfo for fubiects to communicate in all ciuill caufes with their Prince, there being abfolute neceffitie , befides *vtile* and *humile* to warrant them fo to do , according to the rule as it is in *Nauarre, Quod non eft licitum in lege , neceffitas facit* Nau Ench.c. *licitum?* What is not lawfull in the law , neceffitie maketh 27.nu 35. lawfull.

It is not vnknowne that *Henrie* the fourth,the late French King, obtaining the Crowne of France when he was yet an hereticke, relapfed , and *de facto* excommunicated by the Pope, required an Oath of fealtie of the Clergie of Paris, for the better fecuritie in his dominions, as by their records do appeare: whereupon the chiefe of all the learned Doctors and faculties,both of the fecular and religious Clergie of that citie, willingly without delay performed their dutie, taking a corporall oath of fealtie and true allegiance to his Highneffe notwithftanding the Popes excommunication, with promife to affift him to their power againft all leaguers whatfoeuer (among which his Holineffe at that time was one) that fhould machinate or attempt any thing againft his perfon , hinder his peace and quietneffe, or raife armes to the difturbance of him or his people, &c. This they fo vertuous and learned did with their Prince without refiftance, as knowing it to be their dutie fo to do ; and his cafe to be farre different from that of our Soueraigne (who was neuer excommunicated,nor relapfed, or indeede hereticke, as I haue alreadie faid , and could more largely proue if need were;) yet they did not then, nor euer will denie the Popes fpirituall power to excommunicate. And may not the King of great Brittaine require the like of his fubiects,both Clergie and people, and they performe the fame as well as the French, without preiudicating the Apoftolicall power? When *Monfignore Fontana* Bifhop of Ferrara, knowing well the now Duke of Modina (then vfurping the title and dominion of Ferrara) to be excommunicated by name in moft parts of Italie, did notwithftanding of neceffitie communicate with him, as a fubiect with his Prince, and did refufe to

publifh

publish it in his owne Church without the Dukes consent, notwithstanding the Popes order and commandement vnto him. Will any man say, that this good Bishop denied the Popes spirituall power to excommunicate ? That were ridiculous: or offended in disobedience? No; necessitie (if nought else) excused. So enough of this matter.

There is another knot to be vntied, which seemeth insoluble, to wit, that I do beleeue, that neither the Pope nor any person whatsoeuer, hath power to absolue me of this Oath, or any part thereof, &c. and that I doe renounce all pardons & dispensations to the contrary. Is not this a plaine denying of the Popes spirituall authoritie ? Cardinall *Bellarmine* in *Tortus* plainly teacheth me, that he who a little before by swearing denieth the Popes power to bind, the same doth now denie his power to loose. For of those words of our Lord, *Quodcunque solueris super terram, erit solutum & in cœlis*, all Catholicke men gather, that power belongeth to the chiefe Bishop to absolue, not onely from sins, but also from punishments, censures, lawes, vowes and oathes, when it may be expedient to the glorie of God, and health of soules.

Tortus §.5.

This knot to him that vieweth it well, will not be found to haue more difficultie to vnknit, then the former of binding. For as it is an vndoubted veritie, that no Bishop, no nor the Pope can by vertue of excommunication (lesse by any temporall power out of his owne territories) thrust any priuate Christian man out of his possessions, who before had right thereto, and bereaue him thereof, as hath bene proued: so it is as certaine, that they can no more absolue a subiect of his dutie and naturall allegiance to his Prince, and of his oath of fealtie made vnto him, discharging him of all subiection and obedience, then they can a wife of her dutie to her husband, of childrens honoring their parents, or seruants their maisters, being warranted for the performance thereof by the law of God, *Honour thy father and thy mother, &c.* against which no power in earth can dispence nor absolue them, that is, release them of such dutie.

At

At this word *Abſolue,* ſome ſilly ſoules, yea and others that would be accounted wiſe, are as it were ſcandalized, beleeuing that taking the Oath, they ſhall denie the Popes ſpirituall power of abſoluing a ſinner of his ſinnes in *foro conſcientiæ,* which euery Prieſt hauing iuriſdiction may do: little conſidering that they are not like to confeſſe their ſinnes to him this yeare, or euer in their life; and out of confeſſion, his authoritie ſtretcheth not to remit or abſolue one from deadly ſinne. Theſe in a ſort reſemble ſome good creatures that I haue noted in Italie, when they heare the Preacher in his ſermon vtter this word *Confiteor,* will by and by knocke their breaſts, thinking he is talking of confeſſion; when as the word ſignifieth ſometime to giue thankes. And like people of ſmall vnderſtanding, beleeue, that by renouncing all pardons and diſpenſations to the contrary, they muſt denie the Popes power of granting indulgences or pardons (as the practiſe is) to beades, graines, croſſes, &c. and of diſpenſing in any caſe whatſoeuer, it being ſpirituall, as cannot be denied.

Here I ſtand ambiguous, whether I ſhould follow *Salo-* Prou. 26. *mons* counſell or no, *Reſponde ſtulto iuxta ſtultitiam ſuam, ne ſibi ſapiens eſſe videatur:* Anſwer a foole according to his folly, leſt he thinke himſelfe wiſe. It ſhall not be haply amiſſe for their more ſatisfaction to condeſcend ſomewhat vnto ſuch, letting them to vnderſtand, that to men of any iudgement, it muſt needs be ridiculous, who know it cannot, nor ought ſo to be vnderſtood, but onely of pardoning and diſpencing, or releaſing ſubiects of a lawfull Oath of fealtie and dutifull obedience to their Soueraigne. This is not ſpirituall power which belongeth to the Church; and therefore when ſuch pardons and diſpenſations ſhall be offered by his Holines, (as is neuer like to be) euery good ſubiect is bound to renounce them, as being contrary to the ordinance of almightie God. I aske theſe what they thinke, whether the Pope or any power in earth can command, abſolue in this ſence as we take it, or diſpence againſt the law of God and nature? They muſt needs ſay as truth is, he cannot: and ac-

cording

2.2.q.88.
ar.10.

cording to S. *Thomas* doctrine: *In his quæ funt de lege naturæ,
& in præceptis diuinis, non potest per hominem dispensari.* In such things as are of the law of nature, and in diuine precepts, it cannot be dispensed withall by man. Then I inferre, and it is *Barclaies* argument, not solued by Cardinall *Bellarmine:* But subiection and obedience due to Princes and superiors, is *de iure naturali & diuino*: this cannot be denied, being euident in Scriptures. Therefore neither the Pope, nor any power in earth can command any thing, absolue, or dispense against it; and consequently cannot command subiects not to performe obedience to their Prince or superior, in that wherein he is superior: if he should, it is lawfull for them not to obey him, nor to accept of such a dispensation.

We grant with the Cardinall, that it appertaineth to the Popes spirituall power to absolue from sins, also from paines and censures, lawes, vowes and oathes; *verumtamen non quidquid libet licet*, it is not meant in all lawes, all vowes, nor all oathes. No man I thinke will fay, that he can absolue from the iust ciuill lawes of secular Princes; for that were *in alienam messem falcem mittere*, and to be a monarchicall superior in temporals, which is not to be admitted: but onely in his owne lawes, and the Canons, Decrees, or positiue lawes of the Church. Wherein I confesse he hath *plenitudinem potestatis*: as likewise Princes haue in the commonwealth (and thereby may dispense in their owne lawes) as S. *Thomas* teacheth 2.2.q.6.7.ar.4. *Princeps habet plenariam potestatem in re-*

1.2.q.95.a.5.
ad 3.

publica. Who (according to the same in another place) is said to be freed from the law, as touching the compulsiue force of the law, because no man may giue iudgement of condemnation against him if he do against the law: (if none, then not the people, nobles or commons assembled) where-

Psal.50.

upon on that of the Psalme, *Tibi soli peccaui*, To thee, onely (O God) I haue sinned, the Glosse saith, *Quod Rex non habet hominem, qui sua facta diiudicet*, That a King hath not any man that may determine his facts. But as touching the directiue power of the law, the Prince is subiect to the law by his owne will: as it is said *Extra. de constitut. cap. Cum omnes.*

Quod

Quod quisq, iuris, &c. What law any do decree for another, he ought to vse the same law himselfe. According to that: *Patere legem quam ipse tuleris.* What if a Prince will not do what he ought to do, what then? who may compell him? None but God, to whom onely he is inferiour, as *Tertullian* and other Fathers affirme, who ruleth the hearts of Kings at his pleasure, being his Vicegerents in earth: and other remedy then prayers, teares and patience subiects haue none at all.

I will not deny the Popes Holinesse to haue power to dispence in vowes, yet if I should affirme that in solemne vowes of religion he cannot, I should not disagree from S. *Thomas* and other Diuines. *Papa non potest facere, &c.* The Pope cannot make one that is professed in religion to be no religious man: that is, releafe or free him of the bonds of chastitie, pouertie and obedience vowed. *Abdicatio proprietatis, &c.* The renouncing of proprietie, as also the keeping of chastitie, is so essentially annexed to the monasticall rule (or the state of a Moncke) that against it the Pope himselfe cannot dispence. This is the opinion of S. *Thomas,* as *Caietan* affirmeth, as much as it dependeth of the Decretall, *Extra. de statu Monach. in fine illius cum ad monasterium.* And he concludeth; And therefore in a solemne vow of religion it cannot be dispenced withall by the Church. Who will say that this holy Doctor denieth the Popes spirituall power, though he differ from Cardinall *Bellarmine?* Were he not a great Doctor and blessed Saint that writeth in this wise, I know some of our tender consciences would be much scandalized: for they cannot endure to heare any man talke a word of the limitation of the Popes power, what he cannot do forsooth, as if he were omnipotent. But these are for the most part the ignorant sort, that beleeuing him to be Chrifts Vicar, beleeue also that he is endued with Chrifts power of excellency, and can do all that he could do as man, when he was here on earth. Let these learne that his Holinesse neither challengeth Chrifts power of excellencie, as to institute sacraments, to remit sinnes without

out

out the miniſtery of a ſacrament, to make an article of faith,
and ſuch like; but onely that which it pleaſed our Lord to
communicate vnto him: nor the moſt learned Diuines
yeeld him all authority without limitation. For beſide that

Victoria de ſacram. ord.

which S. *Thomas* writeth of diſpenſation in vowes, *Franciſ-
cus à Victoria*, diſputing whether the Pope may delegate
power vnto a Prieſt who is not a Biſhop, to giue orders?
concludeth that S. *Thomas, Paludanus*, and all ſay, he cannot. And againſt his diſpencing in matrimony before con-

Idem tract. de matrim cland. nu. 282.

ſummatió: *Teneamus cum tota caterua Theologorum, quòd Papa non poteſt diſpenſare in matrimonio rato*. Let vs hold with
the whole troupe of Diuines, that the Pope cannot diſpence in matrimony called *ratum*, that is, before it be con-
ſummate. And Cardinall *Bellarmine* admitteth a limitation;

Bellarm. lib. 5. de Ro. Pont. cap. 4.

Dicimus Papam habere, &c. We ſay that the Pope hath that
office which Chriſt had whē he liued here on earth: but we
cannot giue him thoſe offices which Chriſt had as he was
God, or as a man immortall and glorious, but onely thoſe
which hé had as a mortall man. Whereby you ſee that the
Popes power is not without ſome limitation; howbeit he
exceedeth in yeelding him all that Chriſt had as he was a
mortall man, as is ſaid before. Now remaines to be diſcuſ-
ſed, whether his Holineſſe may abſolue from all oathes, and
ſo from this Oath of allegiance. Which queſtion ſerueth
moſt for our purpoſe in hand.

It is to be noted that euery oath is either aſſertory, that
is, of things preſent or paſt; or elſe promiſſorie, of things to
come: and either of good and lawfull matters, or of euill
and vnlawfull. An vnlawfull thing, and that which cannot
be performed without ſinne, is not matter of an oath, and
therefore requireth no diſpenſation or abſolution from it,
as is manifeſt: for whoſoeuer ſhould ſweare to commit adultery, which is promiſſorie, or neuer to pray, neuer to
faſt, and ſuch like, will any man ſay that he muſt ſeeke to be
abſolued from that oath; and not rather that he is bound *ex*

2, 2. q. 89. ar. 9. ad 3.

natura rei not to performe it, being euill in it ſelfe? S. *Thomas* ſaith: Sometime it happeneth that that which falleth
vnder

vnder a promissorie Oath, is repugnant to iustice; either because it is a sinne, and so is bound not to keepe it; or else
for that it is a hinderer of a greater good (as not to liue a
virgine, not to enter into religion) and such an Oath needeth no dispensation, but is lawfull for him that sweareth to
keepe it, or not to keepe it. And somtime (he saith) somewhat is promised, of which there is doubt whether it be
lawfull or vnlawfull, profitable or hurtfull, absolutely or in
some case: and in this euery Bishop may dispence. But in an
assertorie Oath *Syluester verbo Iuramentum* 5.n.2.S. *Thomas*
in the place aboue said *ad* 1. and all Doctors, hold there can
no dispensation or absolution be granted by any Bishop or
Pope. The reasons such as vnderstand may see in S. *Thomas.*

When in an Oath is any thing sworne or promised to
Prince or priuate man, which is manifestly iust, according
to the law of God, and accompanied with these three asso-
ciates, Veritie, Iudgment and Iustice, that ought duly to
be performed of him that so sweareth: *Reddes Domino iura-* Exod.20.
menta tua; and cannot be dispenced withall, when as the ob- Matth.5.
seruation of an Oath falleth vnder a diuine precept, which
is indispensable, as S. *Thomas* writeth in the place aboue
noted *ad primum.* And in euery such Oath, yea though it be
coacted, riseth an obligation, whereby a man resteth bound
to God, which is not taken away *in foro conscientiæ,* as he affirmeth. To which purpose S. *Bernard* writeth thus: *Illud* Bern. lib. de
quod non ab homine traditum, &c. That which is not deli- præcepto.&
uered vs by man, but is proclaimed from God, admitteth disp.c.5.
no humane dispensation at all, neither is it lawfull for
any man in any sort to absolue from these; that is, diuine Ioan. de Tur-
precepts. recré.in can.
Such I take our Oath of allegiance to be, published and Lector, dist.
proclaimed by God, commanding subiects and all inferiors 34.
to render vnto *Cæsar* and all superiours their due: againft
which no dispensation, no absolution can be of force. And
herein I say not, that his Holinesse cannot dispence or absolue from any Oath, but from this particular Oath, wherein is nothing promised which is not manifestly lawfull, and

Q profitable

profitable and due to him to whom it is made : and in such
an Oath, S. *Thomas* saith, dispensation seemeth to haue no
place; because besides the obligation to Almightie God,
there riseth a new to his Maiestie, which cannot be relea-
sed by Pope, subiects, or any other then by himselfe to
whom it is made. Neither doth the Popes power extend to
the taking away of the right of a third person in matters
which are not Ecclesiasticall, as *Caietan* affirmeth. And
therefore cannot absolue a subiect from an Oath of allegiance to his Prince, for that it would be preiudiciall vnto
him. *Prælatus Ecclesiasticus, etiam Papa, &c.* An Ecclesiasticall Prelate, (saith he)yea the Pope, hath not in such maner power ouer Oathes as ouer vowes. Because it is not in
the Popes power to take away the right of a third man in
matters not Ecclesiasticall, as it is in his power to change (to
wit vowes) into something more acceptable to God; for
that he is Gods Vicar, and is not the Vicar of that man:
neither is he so ouer him as he may depriue him of his
goods at his pleasure. Whereto agreeth Card. *Tolet: Quando iuramentum, &c.* When an Oath is to the vtilitie of some
third person, it cannot be dispenced withall, no not by the
Pope, without the consent of the third person; as also the
Pope cannot take away an other mans goods. Whereto
tendeth our Oath, but to the vtilitie or good of his Maiesty;
and to his great preiudice would it not be, if his subiects
should accept of any absolution from the same ? *Speculator*
likewise denieth that the Pope may absolue any man from
a lawfull Oath, because the bond of keeping an Oath and
performing it to God, is of the law of nature and diuine. By
this appeareth that iust and lawfull Oathes, being such as
may be preiudiciall to a third person, cannot be dispenced
withall.

But the Church vseth to remit an Oath extorted by force
or feare. It may be answered, that if such an Oath extorted
be manifestly vniust, and would be against the law of God
to be taken without force or feare; no violence or feare of
losing goods or life can make it lawfull. Which doctrine is

taught

Sidenotes:

2.2.q.89.ar.9 ad 3.

Caiet. in 2. 2. q.89.ar.9.

Tolet. instr. sacer. li.4. c. 23.nu.3.

Tit.de legato §.nunc osten- dendum,n.24.

taught in the Canon-law, *lib.1.Decretal. de his quæ vi metufue cap.2.in gloffa.*and 15.*c.q.6.*in *gloffa.& Extra.de iureiurando;* that for no feare it is lawfull to incurre a mortall fin. Which C. *fuper eo* in another place is taught alfo of a veniall finne. Therfore an *de vfuris.* Oath extorted of a thing vnlawfull, the Church vfeth not to remit or releafe, when as no man will thinke that vnlawfull Oaths are to be kept, as hath bene faid before. What fay you then to lawfull Oathes, yet compelled by feare of lofing goods, libertie, &c?

If it be iuft and lawfull which thou art required to do, why doeft thou refufe to do it? and why expecteft thou compulfion to make thee to performe that which in dutie thou art bound? I know thou wilt grant that a father may fhake his rod, threaten to correct his child, and beate him, if of ftubburnneffe he will not aske bleffing, or will not do his dutie by obeying him. So may the Magiftrate, who carrieth the fword *ad vindictam malefactorum*, not onely threaten, but really punifh and force thee to performance of that which is lawfull and thou oughteft otherwife to do. And God himfelf the patterne of good gouernment threatneth hell fire, and punifheth feuerely the tranfgreffors of his law with many corporall afflictions, and therby forceth many to obferue and keepe his commandements, which of loue, without any fuch compulfion, they ought in dutie to do. Will any hereof inferre, that the Pope or any power on earth can abfolue thefe from performing their duty to God or man, for that it is extorted by feare? Then I conclude, that lawfull Oathes, fuch as are made by fubiects to Princes of their fidelitie, bind in confcience, although they be forced on them by feare of punifhments, and cannot be difpenced withall. To this purpofe *Caietan* faith; that Oathes of him Caiet. in 2.2 that promifeth, whether they be coacted or voluntarie, *fi habent materiam bonam moraliter*, do binde in the court of confcience.

Whereas fome will fay, that Popes haue practifed this authorie of abfoluing fubiects from lawfull Oaths: it may be anfwered with *Ioan. de Turrecremata*, *Syluefter*, *Soto* and others,

thers, That the facts of Popes make not an article of faith. And it is one thing to do somewhat *de facto*, and another to determine that so it ought to be done *de iure*. *Turrecremata* speaking of vnlawfull dispensations, saith : And if it were so done at any time, by some Pope, either ignorant in diuine learning, or blinded with couetousnesse of mony, which for such exorbitant dispensatiōs is accustomed to be offered, or else to please men: it followeth not that he could do it iustly: (that was, *Clement* 3. dispencing with *Constantia* a professed Nunne, to marrie with *Henrie 6.* Emperor, son to *Fredericke* 2.) The Church is gouerned, or ought to be gouerned, by rights & lawes, not by such facts or examples. Thus you see that it is no denying his Holinesse spirituall power to say, that he cannot dispence in all lawes, all vowes, or all oathes, nor consequently absolue me of this Oath of allegiance.

How I pray you can I sweare truly (as I must if I do well) that which neuer was determined or defined by the Church, but is matter of opiniō, diuersly held of diuers learned men?

Verie well, and without sinne. And you may obserue what is commanded in holy Scripture to such as shall take an Oath; *Iurabis Domino in veritate, in iudicio, & in iustitia.* For then is a man said to sweare truly, that his doctrine of opinion, *v. g.* that the Pope cannot by any authoritie depose Princes, or such a thing is true; not onely when he certainly knoweth it to be so, but also when he is perswaded in his conscience vpon probable reason , and in heart thinketh it to be so as he speaketh. This Cardinall *Tolet* teacheth to be that sufficient truth which is required in euerie Oath. And which is more, both he, *Syluester*, and others hold, that to sweare a thing to be true in his opinion, which indeed is false, is no sinne at all, if he did his best endeuour and vsed due diligence to know the truth. As, if one say as he thinketh, that *Peter* is dead, and should sweare it : he neither speaketh, nor sweareth vntruly, becauſe his words are conformable to his interior mind. Which is sufficient according to Saint *Thomas* also, as *Syluester* noteth, to be accompted truth, the principal point of an oath. The secōd is iudgement.

Ierem. 4.

Tolet. inftru. facer. l. 4. c. 21 nu. 4.
Syl. verb. periurium & 22. q. 2. homines.

Greg. de Val. diſp. 6. q. 7 de iuramento.

ment. For it is required that he who sweareth, sweare not lightly or vainely, but discreetly, vpon consideration of some necessarie or profitable cause. The third is Iustice, to wit, that it be not vniust or vnlawfull which is sworne. Which being so, how can any man be worthily reproued of sinne that taketh the Oath of allegiance, vpon a most necessarie & profitable cause as all know, of remouing therby an imputation of treacherie and treason, and pacifying what in him lieth his Maiesties heauie displeasure, worthily conceiued for the most detestable Gunpowder practise: and further is perswaded, after great diligēce vsed, to be both true, at least in his iudgement, and also verie lawfull, as is a subiects loyaltie to his Prince? Hereupon I see no reason why this Oath may not be taken of all Catholickes without danger of sin, and ought of euery good subiect being required thereto: in the wilfull refusers whereof his Maiestie hath iust cause to suspect a hidden mischiefe to lie, if euer oportunite should serue. By this is cleare, that what a man *ex animo* thinketh to be true, he may truly say, yea and sweare too; it being a most certaine principle, as well in reason as in diuinitie, and noted by father *Parsons* in his Catholicke letter, that what a man may truly say, he may also truly sweare: but he may truly say, that a probable opinion held & maintained by sundry learned men Catholikes, is true, and contradicteth not another probable opinion taught by others as learned and as good. For example, That our blessed Lady the mother of God was free from being conceiued in originall sin: which opiniō was defined in the Councell of Basil Sess. 36. and stifly maintained by the Franscifcan family. The contrary was as earnestly defended by the Dominicans, following the doctrine of Saint *Bernard*, and Saint *Thomas*. This controuersie grew to be so great, that they calumniated each other of mortall sinne, yea of heresie, till such time as *Sixtus* the fourth put them to silence, as appeareth in the Canon law. *Excommunicantur illi qui affirmant, &c.* They are excommunicated that affirme them to sinne deadly, or to be heretikes, who defend the blessed mother of God to be

con-

Extrau. Com.
l.3. de reliq. &
vener. Sanct.
c. 2.

conceiued without originall sin. In like maner they are excommunicated, that affirme them to sin deadly, or to be hereticks, who hold the contrary. The Pope knew (saith *Co-*
sterus) that this question neuer appertained to the doctrine
of faith. And Cardinall *Tolet* writeth thus: Neither part hath
bene defined; *De fide* both may be holden without mortall
sin, although it be much more certaine and truer, that she
was conceiued without any spot, *& ita nos credimus*, and so
we beleeue. Might not (trow ye) each of these without sin
sweare their opinion was true? Yes vndoubtedly.

 The like may be, that the Pope is aboue a generall Councell, as was defined in the Councell of Lateran vnder *Leo*
the tenth, taught and beleeued by the greater part of Diuines at this day. Which definition of the Councell, *Costerus*
maketh doubt, whether it were *de fide*, inclining to the ne-
gatiue part, saying, *Sed an vt negotium fidei, non parum dubi-*
tatur. Yet notwithstanding this definition and opinion of
many learned men besides, such others as beleeue and teach
a generall Councell to be aboue the Pope, are not to be reputed heretickes, nor to sin mortally. For then are the generall Councels of Constance and Basill to be condemned,
who defined it so; wherein were assembled many very learned Bishops and other great Doctors : and likewise the
most learned and renowmed Facultie of Paris, who are euer
ready earnestly to defend it without heresie or sin. *Excusan-*
tur ab hæresi qui aliter sentiunt, vt schola Parisiensis. They are
excused from heresie (saith *Costerus*) that thinke otherwise,
(to wit, then the Councell of Lateran) as the schoole of Paris. And dare not these sweare (trow ye) if need were, their
opinion to be true ? Sir *Thomas More* likewise in his letter
to *Cromwell*, saith: Neuer thought I the Pope aboue the generall Councell. No doubt but this holy and learned man
would haue sworne, if occasion had bene offered, that his o-
pinion was true, because it was such as he thought. So may
any in this our case of the Oath of allegiance, sweare no
lesse truly then they, hauing good Authors, and all antiquitie for their opinion. Many like instances might be here
pro-

Margin notes:

Cost. in Osiād propsoit. 2. pag. 103.
Tolet. instr. sac. l. 3. c. 36. nu. 12. An- suor. 1603.

Cost. in Osiād proposit. 3. pag. 282.

Coster. loco citato.

Tho. More.

produced of the diuerſitie of doctrine betweene S.*Thomas* and *Scotus*, and their ſchollers, who peremptorily will defend their doctrine againſt each others, yet all agreeing *in vnitate fidei*: but theſe ſhall ſuffice.

After all this followeth another point, no leſſe difficult then any of the reſt of the Oath, that is: And I do further ſweare, that I do from my heart abhorre, deteſt and abiure, as impious and hereticall, this damnable doctrine and poſition, that Princes which be excommunicated or depriued by the Pope, may be depoſed or murthered by their ſubiects, or any other whatſoeuer.

Some peraduenture not duly conſidering what they heare or reade concerning this point of the Oath, finding the words (Pope) and (excommunicated,) perſwade themſelues aſſuredly, that to take this clauſe, is abſolutely to renounce the Pope, and denie his power to excommunicate. Others of better vnderſtanding conceiue rightly, that ſuch authoritie is rather preſuppoſed and granted to be in him, then denied: but to abiure (which in this place ſignifieth to denie with an oath) a doctrine as hereticall, that is, to ſweare it is hereſie, which hath not bene determined or defined by the Church, ſeemeth very hard and vnlawfull to be ſworne. For anſwer, you ſhall firſt vnderſtand, that a man may abhorre, or deteſt a doctrine, as he would deteſt yea hereſie it ſelfe, yet not affirme the doctrine which he ſo deteſteth to be hereſie. *V.g.* If any ſhould deteſt the doctrine of S.*Thomas* and of the Dominicans, which deny the conception of our B. Lady to be free from originall ſin; or that of the Sorbons in Paris, holding peremptorily (as I haue ſaid) a Councell to be aboue the Pope; will any man of iudgement ſay, that the poſition is hereſie, and they hereticks? *Coſterus* and other learned men do cleare them from ſuch a note, and they are ſtill ready to defend themſelues againſt any that ſhall accuſe them thereof. Likewiſe if any abhorre drunkenneſſe, detraction, ſowing diſcord betweene brethren and friends, as he abhorreth hereſie; can it be ſaid that drunkenneſſe, detraction, or ſowing diſcord (though they be great

Tho.3.p.q. 27.ar.2.

great fins, and abound in too too many) is herefie? it were
too fond and childifh. This *As*, fignifieth here a fimilitude,
not an equalitie: and all know, that *nullum fimile eft idem;*
which may ferue for one anfwer.

And for a fecond, let it be granted, that fuch as fweare,
thinke it indeed to be heretical doctrine (albeit the Church
hath not defined it fo,) that Princes which be excommunicated or depriued by the Pope, may be depofed or murthered by their fubiects, &c. what abfurditie is like to follow?
I haue already (as I truft) fufficiently proued, that neither
Bifhops nor the Pope, by their fpirituall cenfure, haue authoritie to difpoffeffe any priuate man or Prince, be he neuer fo peruerfe an hereticke, of his lands, goods, or temporall dominions; for that it is againft the effence or nature
of excommunication to worke fuch an effect. It is likewife
proued to be againft the law of God, for children, feruants
and fubiects to difobey their parents, maifters and Princes,
commanding iuftly: notwithftanding any excommunication denounced againft them, which is the Churches period, beyond which fhe may not go; it being onely a depriuing of the common goods of the Church appertaining to
Chriftians. Now what doctrine foeuer is repugnant to
Scripture, euery word thereof being *de fide*, may well be accounted herefie, and as fuch abhorred and abiured: for *hæ-*
Tho.2.2.q.11
ar.2. *refis eft circa ea quæ funt fidei*, herefie is about thofe things
which belong vnto, or are of faith. Such is the dutie of fubiects to their lawfull Prince, and of all inferiors to their fuperiors. Then is it herefie directly to fay, that it is lawfull
for fubiects, or any other whatfoeuer, who is not his Iudge
and fuperior in that kind, to murther him; it being exprefly
againft a diuine precept, *Non occides*, and this faying of our
Matth.26. Sauiour, *Omnes qui acceperint gladium, gladio peribunt*: All
that take the fword, fhall perifh with the fword. By which
Ianfen.in
hunc locum. are vnderftood all fuch, as affume to themfelues authoritie
to vfe the materiall for reuenge, before it be granted them
by the Prince, who onely hath his authoritie by the diuine
ordinance, which ought not to be refifted by fubiects or
others.

others. For, as *Cunerus* writeth : *Nulla pacta vel contractus:* Cun. de offic. No couenants or contracts may preiudicate the diuine or- Princip. l.4. c. dinance, whereby a King hath his power, that the people 12. at any time may take armes againſt their King.

And in my iudgement it may be admired, that any Catholick wil ſtick at this point, here being no mention of the Popes depoſing (that which many ſtand vpon,) but of ſubiects, or any other whatſoeuer; vnleſſe they will ranke him among theſe, *whatſoeuer*, which ought not ſo to be vnderſtood. But if they will vnder this generall word vnderſtand alſo the Pope, yet may it be ſaid, it is hereſie, to wit, *May be murthered;* which cannot be vnderſtood but of killing vniuſtly, and without authoritie. If you ſay, that the other part, *May be depoſed*, was neuer declared, nor adiudged hereſie, and therefore the Oath cannot be taken, becauſe *bonum* is *ex integra cauſa*, and *malum ex ſingulis defectibus* : then one part not being hereticall, how can this clauſe be lawfully ſworne, *that Princes which be excommunicated, may be depoſed*, to be damnable and hereticall doctrine?

This indeed is ſuch an obiection, as in the iudgement of diuers cannot be anſwered, and whereupon many pretend to haue great reaſon to ſtand : but let all paſſion be layd aſide, lending me an indifferent eare, & with Gods aſſiſtance ſuch a ſolution may be framed, as ſhall ſatisfie I truſt and ſolue the difficultie.

In our Oath, no man ſweareth, nor is vrged to ſweare, nor by the law ought to ſweare further then the expreſſe words of the Oath, which are after this ſort; as is alſo noted before, pag. 119.

And I do further ſweare, that I do from my heart abhorre, deteſt and abiure as impious and hereticall, What? Note wel, *this damnable doctrine and poſition,* What poſition? Forſooth, *that Princes which be excommunicated or depriued by the Pope, may be depoſed or murthered by their ſubiects, &c.* This poſition is ſworne, not *per partes*, by peecemeale, but coniunctiuely and wholly as it lieth : and ſo, it cannot be denied but it is impious and hereticall doctrine; hereſie here being affirmed,

R med,

med, not on the parts of the position separated, but on the whole together.

For in a sentence affirmatiue, disiunctiue proposition, or booke, if any part be defectuous, false, or hereticall, albeit some part thereof be true, and found doctrine; it may wel be said, that the whole sentence, proposition or booke is defe-
Gretf.l.1.con- sider. pag. 47. ctuous, false, or hereticall, as *Gretserus* writeth. Then that, *May be deposed,* closed in one proposition with the other part, *or murthered,* which is hereticall; the whole position as it lieth must needes be said, and may be sworne to be hereticall. For example, The Inquisition vseth to condemne as a scandalous or hereticall booke, if there be but one onely Chapter or sentence of scandalous or hereticall doctrine contained therein, though all the rest be found and Catholicke. And may not any man lawfully sweare, that booke so condemned, to be scandalous or hereticall, albeit all the whole is not such? or that man to be an hereticke, which erreth against one onely article of the Catholicke faith?

But if the two parts of the proposition you thinke are sworne *diuisim* and by parts, not *coniunctim* or totally together; then let *impious* go with the first part *may be deposed,* and *hereticall* with the latter *or murthered;* and I cannot see how you can deny, but so it may be sworne.

If any will yet stand vpon the word *abiure,* as I heare many do, saying, It signifieth not onely simply to deny a thing with an oath, as al Dictionaries vnderstand the word, but by oath to deny that which once he held before: then, he that neuer held the doctrine and position aboue named, cannot take this Oath, because he may not abiure that opinion which he neuer held.

But this will manifestly appeare, to him that hath any experience in the practise of the Church, to be false. For, let any be conuented into the Inquisition for any one heresie whatsoeuer, as Anabaptisme, Brownisme, &c, if afterwards he repent and conuert to the Catholicke faith, he shall be required, and must of necessitie abiure, not onely that impious opinio or heresie of Anabaptisme or Brownisme, which

he

he held before, but alſo all other hereſies, as Pelagianiſme, Arianiſme, Neſtorianiſme, &c. which haply he had alwayes before deteſted. This therefore is but a vaine verball ſhift of ſome who not knowing what to ſay againſt the maine points of the Oath, are driuen out of the profundity of their wits to ſeeke a knot in a ruſh, to inuent a difficultie where none is, therby to intrap the ſoules of ſcrupulous conſciences, and deterre them from performing their dutie to their Prince, making no conſcience to ouerthrow them alſo in their temporals.

If any inſiſt ſaying, that they thinke indeed the doctrine, which teacheth it to be no ſin to depoſe or murther a good and lawfull King, ſuch a one as gouerneth for the good of the common-wealth, to be hereticall : but if he become a tyrant, ſuch a one as hath more care of his owne vtilitie then of the weale publicke, and ſeeketh to ſubuert the State, perſecuteth the profeſſours of the true religion, and ſets vp idolatrie in ſteed of Chriſtian faith in the iudgement of the people; it is not hereſie to teach, that he may be depoſed by the State aſſembled, or lawfully murthered by any man whatſoeuer.

And is not this pernicious doctrine of many ſectaries of this age hereſie? It being directly repugnant to the doctrine and example of our Sauiour Chriſt and his Apoſtles, againſt the law giuen to *Moſes, Thou ſhalt not kill;* as alſo againſt that ſaying of our Lord, *Qui acceperit gladium, gladio peribit:* Whoſoeuer ſhall take the ſword (to ſtrike withall without authority) ſhal periſh with the ſword. This was that dangerous poſitiō worthily condēned as heretical in the Councel of Conſtance: *Quilibet tyrannus poteſt, & debet licitè & meritoriè occidi, &c.* Euery tyrant may, and ought lawfully and meritoriouſly to be murthered, by any his vaſſall or ſubiect whatſoeuer, either by cloſe trechery, or by ſmooth practiſes and inſinuations, notwithſtanding any Oath taken or promiſe of allegiance made vnto him; nay not ſo much as expecting the ſentence or warrant of any Iudge whatſoeuer.

Againſt which error this holy Synode endeuoring to a-

Conc. Conſtant. ſeſſ. 15. an. 1415.

riſe

rife,and vtterly to extinguifh the fame , after mature deliberation doth declare , and define , that this doctrine is erroneous in faith and manners, and doth reiect and condemne
it,as hereticall and fcandalous,opening a gap to fraude, de-
ceipt,diffimulation, treafon and periury. It doth moreouer
declare,and define,that they who fhall obftinatly maintaine
this pernicious doctrine,are heretikes,and as fuch to be punifhed,according to the canonicall decrees.And that this is

*Molanus de
fide hæret.
fer.lib.5.c.6.*

the intent and purpofe of the Synode, *Molanus* fheweth
thus: *Patres indiftincte de quolibet tyranno loquuntur : & doctri-
na illa de vtriufque generis tyranno, eft in fide & moribus erronea.*
The Fathers fpeake indiftinctly of euery fort of tyrant : and
that doctrine of (killing) a tyrant of either fort,is in faith &
manners erroneous, and it giueth way to fraudes,deceipts,
lyings,treafons, periuries;for thofe things which concerne
the commonwealth are not to be handled or accomplifhed
of priuate perfons : among which is the occifion of an in-
uader.Thus farre he.This doctrine or pofition was alfo long
fince,two yeares before the Councell, condemned as impious,hereticall and damnable by 141. Diuines of the Faculty
or fchoole of Paris,anno 1413.December 13.and now lately againe by the fame facultie,anno 1610. fince the bloudie
parricide of the French king Henry the fourth. The decree

*The decree
of the Do-
ctors of Sorb.*

is this,as it is fet downe in *Antimariana: Cenfet feditiofum,im-
pium & hæreticum effe.*The facred Facultie iudgeth or decreeth, that it is feditious, impious, and hereticall for any fubiect,vaffall or ftranger,vpon what occafion,pretence,or di-
uifed colour foeuer,*facris Regum perfonis vim inferre* , to do
any violence(note wel)againft the facred perfons of Kings.
Whereunto accordeth S. *Thomas*, that yea a tyrant may
not be flain by his fubiects, otherwife he fhould be contra-

*Tho.de re-
gim.prin.lib.
1.c.6.*

ry to himfelfe, for thus he writeth. *Effet multitudini periculo-
fum & eius rectoribus.* It were dangerous to the people and
their gouernhours,that any fhould attempt to take away the
life of Princes, though they were tyrants : for commonly
not the well difpofed, but the ill affected men do thruft
themfelues into that danger.And the gouernement of good
Kings

Kings is as odious to bad men, as the rule of tyrants to good people. Wherefore the kingdome by this presumption would be rather in danger to forgo a good Prince, then a wicked tyrant. So S. *Thomas*. By this Catholicke censure of that famous Vniuersitie, and by the definitiue sentence of the generall Councell, and the doctrine of S. *Thomas*, you see it to be condemned as hereticall and damnable doctrine, that Princes (as in our Oath) which be excommunicated, (or tyrants by the Councell) may be deposed (which cannot be effected without violence to their persons, and slaughter of many men) by their subiects (Nobles or commons) or any other whatsoeuer. Whereby you may secure your conscience, this part of the Oath to be lawfull, and may be taken without feare or preiudicating the Popes spirituall authoritie.

Sir, what say you then to the Friars killing his liege Lord Henrie the third of France, the most Christian King, supposed to be a tyrant in gouernement, and a fauourer of heretikes; applauded or allowed of (as seemeth to some) by Pope *Sixtus* 5. in his oration made in a secret Consistorie before the Cardinals, anone after the certaine newes of the act, and the Kings death?

My opinion is, that as the doctrine teaching to be no sinne to kill a tyrant, is worthily condemned as impious and hereticall: (which you haue heard sufficiently proued in the precedent pages,) so such a fact, of such a one, in such sort, must needs be most impious and damnable: yea supposing we should grant, that King to haue bene such a one as is aboue said; albeit the French know right well he was their true and rightful King, and besides liued and died a member of the Catholicke Romane Church. And whosoeuer will go about to excuse this inexcusable fact, and to say, that he did it, either out of a great zeale to deliuer the commonwealth from such a supposed wicked and tyrannicall King: or else that he did it by diuine inspiratió, being ordained and appointed by God so to do; Saint *Paul* teacheth otherwise, to wit, *Non faciamus mala, vt veniant bona.* Let vs Rom. 3.

not

not do euill, that there may come good. And *Dauid*, a man acc•rding to Gods owne heart, elected to be King of the Iewes, both by his example proceeded, and in his doctrine taught otherwife.For when *Dauid*, perfecuted by *Saul*,yea who at that time fought his life, came euen to *Sauls* Tent whileft he was fleeping, and was counfelled by his Chiefe-taine *Abifai* to kill him:faying, *Conclufit Deus inimicum tuum hodie in manus tuas : nunc ergo perfodiam eum lancea in terra,fe-mel , & fecundò opus non erit.* God hath this day deliuered thine enemie into thine hands ; I will now therefore pierce him with a lance in the earth, once, and the fecond time it fhall not need.*Dauid* made him anfwer in this fort,charging him not to lay hands on the King to hurt him: *Ne interficias eum : quis enim extendet manum fuam in chriftum Domini , & innocens erit?*Kill him not : for who , or what is he that fhall reach out his hand againft the annointed of our Lord , and fhall be innocent? It followeth a little after : Our Lord be mercifull vnto me (faith *Dauid*) that I may not ftretch out my hand againft the annointed of our Lord.In faying,who, or what is he; and teaching that himfelfe, who beft might, could not without offence lay violent hands on King *Saul*, gaue vs inftruction that it could not be lawfull for Friar *Clement* to extend his bloudie hands as he did , againft his true and lawfull Prince the annointed of our Lord : and Chrift himfelfe after commanding,not to touch his annoin-ted. Such kind then of furious zeale of taking the fword, is to be detefted in any , and to be repreffed with great fe-ueritie ; left way be giuen to euill difpofed perfons to per-turbe, yea ruine whole kingdomes and commonwealthes, whileft vnder a prepofterous zeale they embolden them-felues to perpetrate any villany.

And no leffe dangerous & impious it is to fay,that he did that horrible murther by diuine infpiration;for then fhould be iuftified a moft wicked Parricide , and likewife a gap o-pened to all mifcreants to commit any outragious crueltie, againft any fuperiour , Prince or King whatfoeuer. And fo whileft they machinate their mifchiefe , if this be granted,

they

Reg.26.1.

Nolite tan-gere chriftos meos.

they may cloake it with the mantle of diuine infpiration, thinking thereby to paffe blamelelfe before God and men. But who can enter into the fecret iudgements of almightie God to know this? according to the holy Scripture , *Quis cognouit fenfum Domini , aut quis confiliarius eius fuit?* Who hath knowne the iudgement of our Lord, or who hath bene his counfellor? This affertion of this truly ignominious and wretched Friars being infpired from God to do fo finful, and execrable an outrage, is no leffe to be reiected then the former. For the righteous God of heauen, neither appointed, nor excited, but onely permitted him to put in practife his diuellifh inward fuggeftions, againft the facred perfon of his dread Soueraigne, for caufes to man vnknowne , as he permitted *Adam* to fall, *Iudas* to betray his Lord and maifter.

Now touching the Popes oration, fome make a doubt whether euer any fuch, fpecially of approuing the Friars act, were pronounced by his Holines, & in Confiftorie, as hath bene reported, and is extant in *Anti-Sixtus*, or no: and the rather for that Cardinall *Bellarmine* in his anfwer to our clement and moft gracious Kings learned Apology writeth, that no fuch oration is extant but only among the enemies of the Church, who fet forth *Anti-Sixtus*, and therefore is of no credit. Neither (faith he) did any take this oration made in priuate Confiftory; nor was publifhed by the Pope himfelfe, or by his order and appointment, by any other.

Tortus. p. 54. edit. Colon.

Whether the enemies of the Church haue fet forth the oration made by Pope *Sixtus* in the Confiftorie I know not; but this I know, that I haue lately feene fuch a one both in Latin and in French , printed according to a copie fet forth at Paris 1589. the yeare of the Kings death , by *Nicholas Niuelle*, and *Rollin Tierry*; *Sur la Copie imprimée à Paris chez Nicholas Niuelle & Rollin Tierry foy difans Imprimeur & Libraire de la fainte Union, auec Priuilege de la dite Union & approbation de la faculté de Theologie de Paris.* And fet forth with approbation of three Doctors of the facultie of Paris, as followeth.

Nous foubfignez Docteurs en Theologie de la faculté de Paris,
certifions

certifions auoir conferé ceste Harangue prononcée par sa sainĉteté auec l'exemplaire Latin enuoyé de Rome, & auoir trouué conforme l'vn à l'autre.

BOVCHER. DECREIL. ANCELIN.

Which oration who so is desirous to see, may here reade it according to the Latine copie printed as aboue: it followeth thus:

Sixti Quinti Pont. Max. de Henrici
Tertij Morte, Sermo.

Romæ in Consistorio Patrum habitus, 11. Septembris, 1589.

Abac.1.

*A*Nimo meo sæpe, ac serió reuoluens, mentisque aciem intendens in ea, quæ nuper Dei voluntate acciderunt, videor mihi verè posse illud Prophetæ Abacuch* vsurpare: Quia opus faĉtum est in diebus vestris, quod nemo credet, cum narrabitur. *Mortuus est Rex Francorum per manus Monachi. Nam ad istud potest reĉtè applicari: licet de alia re, nempe de incarnatione Domini, quæ omnia mira, ac mirabilia superat; Propheta propriè locutus sit; sicut & Apostolus Paulus eadem verba Aĉtorum 13. ad Christi resurreĉtionem verisimè refert. Quando Propheta nominat opus, non vult innuere aliquid vulgare, vel ordinarium, sed rarum, insigne, ac memorabile facinus; quomodo de creatione mundi,* Opera manuum tuarum sunt cœli. *Item,* Requieuit die septimo ab omni opere quod patrarat. *Cum verò faĉtum ait, eo verbo tale aliquid in Scripturis exprimi, quod non temerè, casu, fortuna aut per accidens euenire dicitur; sed quod expressa Dei voluntate, prouidentia, dispositione, ac ordinatione obuenit. Vt cum dicit Saluator,* Opera quæ ego facio,

vos

vos facietis, & maiora horum facietis : *& similia in
sacris litteris plurima. Quod autem loquatur in præterito
factum esse, id more aliorum Prophetarum facit, qui propter certitudinem euentus solent sæpe de futuris, ac si iam
facta essent, prædicere. Dicunt enim Philosophi, res præte-
ritas esse de necessitate, præsentes de inesse, futuras de pos-
sibili tantùm : ita illi loquuntur. Propter quam certitudinem Isaias Propheta longè antè vaticinatus de morte
Christi, sic dixit, sicut in Act. Apostolorum cap. 8. etiam
recitatur,* Tanquam ouis ad occisionem ductus est,
& sicut agnus coram tondente se non aperuit os suum
*&c. Atque hoc, de quo nunc verba facimus, & quod his
diebus nostris euenit, verè insigne, memorabile, & penè
incredibile opus est, nec sine Dei opt. Max. particulari prouidentia, & dispositione perpetratum. Occidit Monachus
Regem, non pictum aut fictum in charta, aut pariete; sed
Regem Francorum in medio exercitus sui, milite & custo-
dia vndique septum, quod re vera tale est, & eo modo effectum, vt nemo nunc credat, eum narrabitur, &
fortasse apud posteritatem pro fabula reputabitur.
Quod Rex sit mortuus, vel etiam peremptus, facilè
creditur, sed eum sic sublatum, vix est credibile : sicut
Christum natum ex fœmina statim assentimur : sed si ad-
das porro ex fœmina Virgine ortum esse, tunc secundum
hominem non assentior: ita etiã quod mortuus sit Christus
facilè credimus, sed quod mortuus iam resurrexerit ad
vitam, quia ex priuatione ad habitum non sit regressio,
redditur secundum intellectum humanum impossibile, &
propterea incredibile : quod homo ex somno, ex morbo,
etiam ex syncope, vel extasi resuscitatur, quia id sæpe secundum naturam sit, humanitus credimus; sed resurrexisse
à mortuis, ita secundum carnem videbatur incredibile.Vt*

S   *Paulo*

Paulo apud Philosophos Athenienses de hac resurrectione differenti, improperarent, quòd esset nouorum dæmoniorum annunciator : & alij, sicut D. Lucas narrat, irridebant, alij dicebant, Audiemus te de hoc iterum. *De talibus igitur, quæ secundum naturæ leges, & ordinarium cursum fieri non solent, dicit Propheta : quòd nemo credet, cum narrabitur; sed huiusmodi tantùm fidem adhibemus ex consideratione omnipotentiæ diuinæ, & per subiectionem intellectus nostri in obedientiam fidei, & obsequium Christi. Nam hoc modo quod erat incredibile naturaliter, fit credibile. Igitur qui secundum hominem non credo Christum de virgine natum, tamen quando additur hoc factum esse supra naturæ terminos per operationem Spiritus sancti, tunc verè assentior, & credo. Ita quando dicitur Christum ex mortuis resurrexisse, humanitus non credo; sed cum id factum esse per diuinam (quæ in ipso erat) naturam affirmatur, tunc omnino credo. Eodem modo licet tantum Regem in medio exercitus, tot stipatum militibus, ab vno simplici, & imbelli Religioso occisum esse, secundum prudentiam carnis, & intellectum humanum sit incredibile, vel omnino improbabile ; tamen considerando ex altera parte grauissima Regis peccata, & specialem Dei omnipotentis in hac re prouidentiam, & quàm inusitato, & mirabili modo iustissimam voluntatem suam erga ipsum impleuerit, omnino, & firmiter credo. Rem etenim istam tam grandem, & inusitatam aliò referre, quàm ad particularem Dei prouidentiam (sicut quosdam ad alias caussas ordinarias, vel etiam ad fortunam, & casum, aut similes accidentarios euentus perperam referre intelligimus) prorsus non licet; sicut ij, qui totius facti seriem pressiùs obseruant, facilè videre possunt, vbi plurima interuenerunt, quæ ab homine, nisi Dei speciali concurrente auxilio, expediri non*

quiue-

quiuerant. Et fanè Regum,ac Regnorum rationes,cæterá-
que tam rara, tantíque momenti negotia à Deo temerè ad-
ministrari non eft existimandum. Sunt in sacra historia
nonnulla huius generis, nec eorum quidquam poteft aliè,
quàm ad Deum authorem referri: tamen nihil eft, vbi
magis claret superna operatio, quàm in ifto, de quo nunc
agimus. Lib. Maccha. 1.cap. 6. legimus, Eleazarum, vt
Regem populi Dei perfecutorem, ac hoftem tolleret, feipfum
certæ morti obtuliffe. Nam in conflictu confpiciens Ele-
phantem cæteris eminentiorem, in quo videbatur Rex
effe, concito curfu in mediã hoftium turmam fe coniÿciens,
hinc inde viam vi fternens, ad belluam venit, atque fub
eam intrauit, fubiectóque gladio peremit, quæ cadens op-
prefsit Eleazarum & extinxit. Hic quoad zelum, & a-
nimi robur, reíque tentatæ exitum, aliquid huius noftri fi-
mile cernimus, tamen in reliquis nihil eft comparabile. Ele-
azarus erat miles, armis & pugna exercitatus, in ipfo præ-
lio conftitutus, ardóréque animi, & furore (vt fit) accen-
fus : ifte Monachus prælÿs ac pugnis non erat affuefactus,
& à fanguine, vitæ fuæ inftituto ita abhorrens, vt nec ex
venæ incifione fufum cruorem forfan ferre potuerit. Ille
nouerat genus mortis, fimúlque locum fepulturæ fuæ, nempe
quòd ruina belluæ inclufus magis, quàm oppreffus, fuo fepe-
liretur triumpho : ifte mortem, ac tormenta crudeliora,
& incognita expectabat, fepulchróque fe cariturum non du-
bitabat. Sed & alia multa difsimilia funt. Nota quoque
eft infignis illa hiftoria fanctæ mulieris Iudith, quæ & ipfa,
vt obfeffam ciuitatem fuam, ac populum Dei liberaret, ce-
pit confilium, Deo fine controuerfia fuggeftore, de interi-
mendo Holopherne hoftilis exercitus principe; quod & per-
fecit. In quo opere licet plurima, & apertifsima fupernæ
directionis indicia appareant, tamen longè maiora diuinæ

S 2 *proui-*

prouidentiæ argumenta, in istius Regis occisione, ac ciuita-
tis Parisiensis liberatione conspicere licebit, sicut certe quo-
ad hominem, hoc fuit illo magis difficile, vel impossibile.
Nam illa sancta fœmina intentionem suam aliquibus vrbis
presbyteris aperuit, portámque ciuitatis, & cuſtodiam per-
tranſiit illis præſentibus, ac approbantibus, vt proinde ſcru-
tationi, vel explorationi, quæ obſidionis tempore ſolet eſſe
tam exacta, vt ne muſca fere ſine examine egredi queat,
non potuerit eſſe ſubiecta. Apud hoſtes vero, per quorum
caſtra, & varias excubias tranſeundum erat, ſæpius ex-
plorata, & examinata cum fœmina eſſet, nec quidquam
haberet vel litterarum, vel armorum, vnde ſuſpicio oriri
potuit, déque aduentu in caſtra, & à ſuis, fugæ probabiles
reddens rationes, facile dimittebatur. Sicut tam propter
eaſdem cauſſas, quàm propter ſexum, & formæ excellenti-
am ad Principem impudicum introduci, & in temulen-
tum, facile, quod deſignauit, perficere valuit. Ita illa.
Hic vero Religioſus aggreſſus eſt, & cõfecit rem longè ma-
iorem, pluribúſque impedimentis, ac tantis difficultatibus,
periculíſque obſitam, vt nulla prudentia, aut aſtutia hu-
mana, nec alio modo, niſi aperta Dei ordinatione, ac ſuc-
curſu confici potuerit. Debebant obtineri litteræ commen-
datitiæ ab ijs, qui erant contrariæ factionis, tranſeundum
erat per eam vrbis portam qua itur ad caſtra hoſtium, quæ
ita ſine dubio in illis obſidionis anguſtiis cuſtodiebatur, vt
cuncta haberentur ſuſpecta, nec cuiquam ſine curioſiſſima
exploratione de litteris, nunciis, negotiis, armis pateret exi-
tus. Sed iſte (res mira) vigiles pertranſiit ſine examine
etiam cum litteris credentiæ ad hoſtē, quæ ſi fuiſſent inter-
ceptæ à ciuibus, ſine mora, ac ſine vlteriori iudicio de vita
fuiſſet actum. atque apertum hoc diuinæ prouidentiæ argu-
mentum : ſed maius miraculum eſt illud, quod idem mox

ſine

fine omni exploratione tranfierit quoque caftra hoftium,
varias militum excubias, ipfamque corporis Regis cuftodi-
am, ac totum denique exercitum, qui ferè erat conflatus ex
hareticis, ipfe Religiofus exiftens, & in habitu Ordinis fui,
qui ita erat exofus talibus hominibus, vt in illis locis, quæ
paulo ante prope Parifios vi ceperant, ⲥMonachos quofque
vel occiderint, vel pefsimè tractauerint. Iudith erat fœmi-
na, minimèque odiofa; tamen examinata fæpe, illa nihil fe-
cum tulit, vnde fibi oriretur periculum: ifte ⲥMonachus,
& propterea odiofus, ac fufpectifsimus, etiam cum cultello
ad hoc propofitum præparato, non in vagina condito (vnde
poterat effe probabilis excufatio) fed nudo, ac in manica
abfcondito, quem fi inueniffent, mox fuiffet in crucem
actus. Ifta omnia clariora funt particularis prouidentiæ di-
uinæ argumenta, quàm vt negari queat: nec aliter fieri
potuit, quàm vt à Deo occæcarentur oculi inimicorum ne
agnofcerent illum. Nam, vt antea diximus, licet quidam
ifta abfurdè tribuant fortunæ, aut cafui, tamen nos hoc
totum non aliò referendum cenfemus, quàm in diuinam
voluntatem. Nec profectò aliter factum crederem, nifi cap-
tiuarem intellectum in obfequium Chrifti, qui hoc modo
admirabili, & liberare ciuitatem Parifienfem (quam vari-
is viis intelleximus fuiffe in fummo difcrimine, maximif-
que anguftiis conftitutam) & iftius Regis grauifsima pec-
cata punire, eumq; tam infaufta, & infami morte è medio
tollere ftatuit. ⲥAtque nos, dolentes fanè, aliquoties præ-
diximus fore, vt quemadmodum erat familiæ fuæ vltimus,
ita aliquem infuetum, & dedecorofum vitæ exitum effet
habiturus. Quod me dixiffe non folum Cardinales Ioiofa,
Lenocortius, & Parifienfis, fed etiam, qui tunc apud nos
refidebat Orator, teftes effe poffunt. Neque enim hic mor-
tuos, fed viuentes in teftimonium huiufmodi verborum no-

ftrorum

ſtrorum adhibemus, quorum iſti omnes probè meminiſſe
poſſunt. Quidquid tamen in hunc infœlicem Regem hoc
tempore dicere cogimur, nullo modo volumus,vt pertineat
ad nobiliſsimum illud Galliæ Regnum, quod nos impoſterũ,
ſicut hactenus , ſemper omni paterno amore,ac honore pro-
ſequemur. De perſona ergo Regis tantùm iſta cum dolore
diximus, cuius infauſtus finis eximit quoque ipſum ab ijs
officijs, quæ ſolet hæc ſancta ſedes (quæ eſt pia Mater om-
nium fidelium,& maximè Chriſtianorum principum)Im-
peratoribus & Regibus poſt mortem exhibere: quæ pro iſto
libenter quoque feciſſemus , niſi id fieri in hoc caſu ſacræ
Scripturæ vetarent. Eſt, *inquit S. Ioannes,* peccatum ad
mortem, non pro illo dico vt roget quis: *quod vel intel-*
ligi poteſt de peccato ipſo, ac ſi diceret, pro illo peccato,vel
pro remiſsione illius peccati nolo vt quiſquam roget, quo-
niam non eſt remiſsibile: vel, quod in eundem ſenſum re-
dit , pro illo homine, qui peccat peccatum ad mortem,
non dico vt roget quis. De quo genere etiam Saluator a-
pud Matth. quòd illi,qui peccat in Spiritum ſanctum,non
remittetur, neque in hoc ſæculo,neque in futuro. Vbi facit
tria genera peccatorum,nimirum in Patrem,in Filium,&
in Spiritum ſanctũ,atque priora duo eſſe minus grauia,&
remiſsibilia,tertium verò irremiſsibile.quæ tota differen-
tia, ſicut ex ſcripturis ſcholæ tradunt,oritur ex diſtinctio-
ne attributorum,quæ ſingula ſingulis Perſonis ſanctiſsimæ
Trinitatis appropriantur. Licet enim, ſicut eadem eſt eſ-
ſentia,ſic eadem quoque eſt potentia,ſapientia, & bonitas
omniũ perſonarum(ſicut ex Symbolo S .Athanaſii didici-
mus,cum ait,Omnipotens Pater, omnipotens Filius,omni-
potens Spiritus ſanctus,) tamen per attributionem, Patri
applicatur Potentia,Filio Sapientia,Spiritui ſancto Amor.
quorum ſingula eo modo,quo attributa dicuntur , ita ſunt
                                   pro-

propria cuiufque perfonæ, vt in aliam referri non queant.
Ex quorum attributorum contrariis, & distinctionem, &
grauitatem peccatorum dignofcimus. Contrarium Poten-
tiæ, quæ attribuitur Patri, est infirmitas, vt proinde id
quod ex infirmitate, feu naturæ nostræ imbecillitate com-
mittimus,dicatur committi in Patrem.Oppofitum Sapien-
tiæ est ignorantia, ex qua cum quis peccat, dicitur peccare
in Filium, ita vt ea, quæ vel ex humana infirmitate, vel
ignoratione peccamus , faciliùs nobis condonari foleant.
Tertium autem attributũ quod est Spiritus fanctus,nem-
pe Amor,habet pro contrario ingratitudinem , vitium
maximè odibile.Vnde venit, vt homo non agnofcat Dei
erga ipfum dilectionem,aut beneficia,fed obliuifcatur,con-
temnat, ac odio etiam habeat. Ex quo tandem fit, vt obsti-
natus reddatur,atque impœnitens.Atque his modis multo
grauius & periculofius peccatur in Deũ,quàm ex ignoran-
tia,aut imbecillitate, proinde huiufmodi vocantur peccata
in Spiritum fanctum:& quia rarius,ac difficilius, & non
nifi abundantiori gratia condonantur , dicuntur irremif-
fibilia quodammodo, cum tamen fola impœnitentia fit om-
nino, & fimplicititer irremifsibilis. Quidquid enim in
vita committitur, licet contra Spiritũ fanctum,potest per
pœnitentiam deleri ante mortem:fed qui perfeuerat vfque
ad mortẽ, nullum locum relinquit gratiæ ac mifericordiæ.
Atque pro tali peccato,feu pro homine fic peccante,noluit
Apostolus vt post mortem oraremus.Iam ergo quia magno
nostro dolore intelligimus , prædictum Regem ex hac vita
fine pœnitentia,feu impœnitentem exceffiffe, nimirum in
confortio hæreticorum;ex talibus enim hominibus confece-
rat exercitum fuum : & quòd cõmendauerat moriens reg-
num in fuccefsione Nauarræ declarato hæretico,& excom-
municato;necnon in extremis,ac in vltimo ferè vitæ fpiri-

*tu ab eodem,& similibus circumstantibus petierit,vt vin-
dictam sumerent de ijs, quos ipse iudicabat fuisse caussas
mortis suæ. Propter hæc, & similia manifesta impœniten-
tiæ indicia, decreuimus pro ipso non esse celebrandas exe-
quias.non quod præsumamus quidquam ex hoc de occultis
erga ipsum Dei iudiciis, aut misericordijs, qui poterat secundum beneplacitum suum in ipso exitu animæ suæ con-
uertere cor eius, & misericorditer cum illo agere; sed ista
locuti sumus secundum ea,quæ nobis exterius patent.Faxit
benignissimus Saluator noster,vt reliqui hoc horrendo iu-
stitiæ supernæ exemplo admoniti,in viam salutis redeant,
& quod misericorditer hoc modo cœpit, benignè prosequa-
tur,ac perficiat,sicut eum facturum speramus:vt de erepta
Ecclesia de tantis malis, & periculis ,perennes illi gratias
agamus.*

In quam sententiam cum dixisset Pontifex, dimisit
Consistorium cum benedictione.

L A V S D E O.

An Oration of Pope Sixtus the fift
vpon the death of King Henry the third,
in Rome,in the full assemblie of the Cardinals.

COnsidering oftentimes with my selfe, and applying my whole vnderstanding vnto these
things , which now of late by a iust iudgement
of God, are come to passe : I thinke I may with right
vse the words of the Prophet Abacuck, saying: *I haue
wrought a worke in your daies, which no man will beleeue
when it shall be told him.* The French King is slaine by
the

the hands of a Friar, for vnto this it may fitly be compared, although the Prophet fpake of another thing, namely of the incarnation of our Lord, which exceedeth and furmounteth all other wonders and miracles whatfoeuer: as alfo the Apoftle S. Paul referreth the fame words vnto the refurrection of Chrift. When the Prophet fayd *a worke*, his mind was not to fignifie by it fome common or ordinarie thing, but a rare & notable matter, and a deede worthy to be remembred, as that of the creation of the world, The heauens are the works of thine hands: And againe, He refted the feauenth day, of all the works which he had made. When he faith, *I haue wrought*, with thefe wordes the holy Scripture is wont to expreffe things not come to paffe by cafualtie, fortune, or accident, but things befallen by the determined prouidence, will, and ordinance of God, as our Sauiour fayd: The works which I do, ye fhall do alfo, and yet greater; and many more fuch like wherewith the holy Scriptures are replenifhed. And that he faith that it is done in times paft, herein he followeth the vfe and order of the other Prophets, who for the certainty of the euent are wont to prophefie of things to come as if they were paft alreadie. For the Philofophers fay, that things paft are of neceffitie; things prefent, of being: and things to come onely of poffibilitie. For which certaintie the Prophet Ifay long before prophefying of the death of Chrift, hath thus fpoken: He was led as a fheepe to the flaughter, and like a dumbe lambe before his fhearer, fo opened he not his mouth, &c. And this whereof we fpeake at this prefent, and which is come to paffe in thefe our dayes, is a famous, notable, and an vncre-

T   dible

dible thing, not done or atchieued without the particular prouidence and diſpoſition of the Almightie. A
Friar hath kild a King, not a painted one, or drawne
vpon a peece of paper, or pictured vpon a wall, but the
King of France, in the midſt of his armie, compaſſed
and enuironed round about with his Guard and Souldiers : which truely is ſuch an act, and done in ſuch
a manner, that none will beleeue it, when it ſhall be
told them, and perhaps our poſterity and the age to
come will account and eſteeme it but a fable.

That the king is dead or elſe ſlaine, it is eaſily to be
beleeued; but that he is kild and taken away in this ſort,
is hardly to be credited: euen as we preſently agree vnto this, that Chriſt is borne of a woman; but if we adde
vnto it of a woman virgin, then following naturall reaſon we can no in wiſe aſſent vnto it. Euen ſo we lightly
beleeue that Chriſt died; but that he is riſen vp againe
from death to life, it falleth hard vnto mans vnderſtanding, and therefore not lightly digeſted. That one is
wakened againe out of a ſleepe, extaſie, or a ſound, becauſe it is not againſt nature, we naturally beleeue it;
but to be riſen againe from death, it ſeemeth ſo vncredible vnto the fleſh, that S. Paule diſputing in Athens
of this point, was miſliked greatly, and accuſed to be
a ſetter forth of new Gods, ſo that many (as S. Luke
witneſſeth) did mock him, and many for the ſtrange-
neſſe of the doctrine ſayd, We will heare thee a-
gaine of this thing. Of ſuch things therefore which befall not according to the lawes of nature, and the ordinarie courſe thereof, ſpeaketh the Prophet, That none
ſhall beleeue it when it ſhall be told them. But we giue
credit vnto it by conſideration of the omnipotencie of
                                                    God,

God, and by fubmiffion of our vnderftanding vnder
the obedience of faith, and feruice which we owe vnto
our Sauiour Chrift. And by thefe meanes this that
was incredible by nature, becometh credible by faith:
therfore we that beleeue not after the flefh that Chrift
is borne of a virgine, yet when there is added vnto it,
that this was done fupernaturally by operation of the
holy Ghoft; then truly we agree vnto it, and faithfully
beleeueit. So likewife when it is faid that Chrift is rifé
againe from the dead, as we are flefh onely we beleeue
it not; but when it is affirmed that this was done by the
power of the diuine nature which in him was, then
without any doubting we beleeue it. In the fame maner whé it fhal be told vs, that fuch a mighty King was
kild by a poore, fimple, and a weake Friar, euen in the
midft of his armie, and enuironed with his Guard and
Souldiers; to our naturall reafon and flefhly capacitie it
will feeme vncredible; yet cófidering on the other fide
the great & grieuous finnes of this King, and the fpeciall prouidence of the Almightie herein, and by what
accuftomed & wonderfull meanes he hath accomplifhed his moft iuft will and iudgment againft him, then
moft firmely we will beleeue it. Therfore this great &
miraculous worke I may but onely afcribe it vnto the
particular prouidence of God, not as thofe that referre
all things amiffe vnto fome ordinarie caufcs, or vnto
fortune, or fuch like accidentarie euents : but as thofe
who (more neere obferuing and looking in the courfe
of the whole matter) eafily-fee that here in this befell
many things, which could in no wife haue bene
brought to paffe and difpatched without the fpeciall
helpe of God. And truely the ftate of Kings and king-

domes

domes, and all other fuch rare and weightie affaires
fhould not be thought to be gouerned of God rafhly
and vnaduifedly. In the holy Scripture fome are of this
kind, and none of them can be referred vnto any other
thing, but vnto God the only author thereof: yet there
are none wherein the celeftiall operation more appeareth then in this whereof we fpeake at this prefent. We
reade in the firft booke of the Macchab. chap. 6. how
Eleazar offered himfelfe vnto a certaine death, to kill
the king that was an enemie and perfecutor of the people and children of God. For in the battell efpying an
Elephant more excellent then any of the other beafts,
whereupon it was like that the king was, with a fwift
courfe cafting himfelf in the midft of the troups of his
enemies, here and there making a way perforce, came
to the beaft at laft, and went vnder her, and thruft his
fword in her belly and flue her, who falling, with the
great weight of her body preft him to death, and kild
him out of hand. Here in this we fee fome things not
vnlike vnto ours, as much as toucheth the zeale, vali-
antneffe of mind, and the iffue of the enterprife, yet in
the reft there is no comparifon to be made. Eleazarus
was a Souldier, exercifed in weapons, and trained vp in
warres, fet in battell, emboldened with courage, and
inflamed with rage and anger: this a Friar not inured
to the fight, and fo abhorring of bloud by the order of
his profeffion, that perhaps he could not abide the cutting of a veine. He knew the kind of his death, as alfo
the place of his buriall, namely that he fhould be in-
tombed vnder the fall of the beaft, and fo buried in the
middeft of his triumph and victorie. This man did
looke for death onely, and expected nothing but vn-
                                                    knowne

knowne and moft cruell torments, and did not doubt before, but that he fhould lacke a graue to reft within. But in this are yet many other things that can fuffer no comparifon. The famous hiftorie of the holy woman Iudith is fufficiently knowne, who tooke counfell with her felfe, that fhe might deliuer her Citie and the people of God (no doubt by the infpiration of the holy Ghoft) to murther Holophernes chiefe Captaine and Prince of the enemies forces, which fhe alfo moft valiantly accomplifhed. Wherein although appeare many and moft manifeft tokens of heauenly direction, yet farre greater arguments of Gods prouidence, are to be feene in the killing of this King, and the deliuering of the citie of Paris, farre more difficult and harder to be brought to paffe, then was the enterprife of Iudith. For this holy woman difclofed part of her intention before vnto the Gouernors of the Citie, and went not without great commendation of young and old, through the gates of Bethulia, & by the watch, in fight and prefence of the Elders and Princes of that place: and by that meanes was not fubiect vnto their examination and fearching, which is alwayes vfed fo ftrictly in time of fiege and warre, that a flie can hardly without examining get by. She being come to the enemy, through whofe campe and watches fhe was to go, and now oftentimes examined and fearched, being a woman, carrying no letters nor weapons about her, from whence any fufpition might grow, and yeelding probable reafons of her coming there, and abandoning of her countrey, was eafily difcharged. As alfo for the fame caufes, and for her fexe and exquifite beautie being brought before this lewd Prince, whom luft, wine,

and

and good cheare had rockt afleepe, might lightly performe that which fhe had determined before. But this
religious man had vndertaken a matter of greater
weight, and alfo performed it, which was compaffed
with fo many impediments, difficulties, and dangers,
that it by no earthly meanes could haue bene brought
to paffe without the manifeft ordinance, and fpeciall
aid of the Almightie. Firft letters of commendation
were to be procured from the enemie; then was he
conftrained to go through that gate of the city, which
directly went to the enemies campe, the which without doubt was fo narrowly kept & watched in the extremitie of that fiege, that euerie trifle bred fufpition,
and none were fuffered to go foorth without curious
fearching before, touching their letters, bufineffe, and
affaires they had. But he (a wonderfull thing) went by
the watch vnexamined, yea with letters of commen-
datiõ vnto the enemie, which if they had bin intercep-
ted by the citizens, without delay and further fentence
he fhould haue bene executed prefently; and therefore
this is a manifeft argument of Gods prouidence. But
this is a farre greater miracle, that he without fearching
went alfo through the enemies campe, by diuerfe watches and fentinels, and, which more is, through the
Guard of the Kings body, and finally, through the
whole armie, which was compacted almoft of none
but Hugonots and Heretickes, he being a religious
man, and apparelled afrer the order of his profeffion,
which was fo odious vnto them, that they killed, or at
leaft greatly mifufed all thofe Friars, whom they found
in thofe places, which not long before they had taken
perforce about Paris. Iudith was a woman, & nothing
                                                    odious

odious, yet examined oftentimes, she carried nothing
about her that might haue turned to her danger & destruction. This man, a Friar, & therfore hated, and most
suspected, hauing also a knife prepared for that purpose,
not put vp in a sheath, (which might haue made his
excusation probable) but bare & hidden in his sleeue,
which if it had bene found about him, presently without any further iudgment he should haue bin hanged.
All these are such cleare arguments of the particular
prouidence of God, that they cannot be denied or dif-
prooued: and it could not be otherwise, but that God
blinded the eies of the enemies, so that they could not
see nor know him. For as we haue said before, although
some absurdly ascribe this vnto fortune, or vnto some
other such like accident, yet we thinke good to referre
all this to none else, but vnto the holy will and ordinance of God. And truly I could not beleeue this to
haue bene done otherwise, vnlesse I should captiue &
submit my vnderstanding vnder the obedience of
Christ his doctrine, who had determined by these miraculous meanes to vnset and deliuer the citie of Paris,
(which as we haue heard hath bene in great danger &
extremitie) and iustly punish the hainous and notorious sinnes of that King, and take him away out of this
world by such an vnhappie and infamous death. And
we truly (not without great inward griefe) haue oftentimes foretold, that as he was the last of his name and
familie, so was he like to haue, and make some strange
and shamefull end of his life. Which, that I haue oftentimes said it, not onely the Cardinals *Ioiofa*, *Lenocar-*
tius, and he of Paris, but also the Oratour at that time
here resident, can sufficiently witnesse and testifie. We
will

will not feeme to call here to affirme our wordes, for thofe that are already deceaffed,but the liuing,& fome of them at this time prefent do yet well remember the: yet notwithftanding we will not vnrip all that we are able and forced to fpeak againft this vnfortunate king, for the moft noble realme of France it fake, which we fhall profecute and fofter hereafter,as we haue done alwaies before with al fatherly loue,honor and affection. This therefore which we with griefe haue fpoken, toucheth onely the kings perfon, whofe vnhappie and vnluckie end depriueth and exempteth him alfo of thofe duties and honors,which this holy fea(the tender and gentle mother of all faithfull,but chiefly of chriftian Princes) is wont to offer vnto all Kings and Emperours, which we moft willingly would likewife haue beftowed vpon him, if the holy Scriptures in this cafe had not altogether forbidden it.There is,faith S.Iohn, a fin vnto death; I fay not that any fhould pray for it: which may be vnderftood, both of the fin it felfe, as if he fhould fay, for that fin,or for the remiffion or forgiueneffe thereof,I will that none fhould pray,becaufe it is not pardonable. Or elfe in the fame fence,for that man who committeth fuch a fin vnto death, I fay not that any fhould pray for.Whereof our Sauiour himfelf hath fpoken in S. Matthew,faying,that he that finneth againft the holy Ghoft,fhal not be pardoned,neither in this world nor in the world to come. Where he fetteth down three forts or kinds of fin, to wit, againft the Father,the Sonne,and the holy Ghoft; and that the two firft are leffe hainous,and pardonable,but that the third is altogether vnpardonable,and not to be remitted.All which difference proceedeth from the diftinction of

the

the attributes, as the Diuines teach vs, which feuerally are appropriated vnto euery feuerall perfon of the holy Trinitie. And although as the eſſence of all the three perfons is but one, ſo alſo is their power, wiſedome, and goodneſſe, as we haue learned in the ſymbole of Athanaſius, where he ſaith, almightie is the Father, almighty is the Sonne, and almighty is the holy Ghoſt: yet by attribution, power is aſcribed vnto the Father, wiſdome vnto the Sonne, and loue vnto the holy Ghoſt; whereof euery feuerall as they are tearmed attributes, ſo are they ſo proper vnto euery feuerall perfon, that they can not be attributed and referred vnto any other. By the contraries of which attributes, we come to diſcerne the diſtinction and greatneſſe of ſinne. The contrary to power, which is onely attributed vnto the Father, is weakeneſſe, and therefore that which we do amiſſe through infirmity of nature, is ſaid to be committed againſt the Father. The oppoſite vnto wiſdome, is ignorance and blindnes, through which when any man ſinneth, he is ſaid to ſinne againſt the Sonne: therefore that which we commit through naturall infirmity, and ignorance, is more eaſier forgiuen vs. The third attribute, which is the holy Ghoſtes, is loue, and hath for his contrary ingratitude and vnthankfulneſſe, a vice moſt deteſtable and odious, which cauſeth men not to acknowledge the loue of God, & his benefites beſtowed vpon them, but to forget, deſpiſe, yea and to hate them. Whereout briefly, and finally proceedeth, that they become altogether obſtinate and impenitent. And this way ſinne is committed againſt God with greater danger and perill, then if it were done through ignorance and weakeneſſe of the fleſh, and therefore it is tearmed a ſinne against

V

gainſt the holy Ghoſt. And becauſe ſuch ſinnes are
ſeldome and difficultly pardoned, and not without
great abundance of grace, in ſome ſort they are ſaid to
be vnpardonable: whereas altogether through vnrepentance onely, they become ſimply vnpardonable.
For whatſoeuer is done amiſſe in this life: although it
be againſt the holy Ghoſt, by repẽtance it may be wipt
out and defaced before death; but they that perſeuere
therein till death, are excluded from all grace and
mercy hereafter. And therefore for ſuch ſinners and
ſins the Apoſtle hath forbidden to pray after their de-
ceaſſe. Now therfore becauſe we vnderſtand, not without our great griefe, that the ſaid king is departed out
of this world, without repentance and impenitent, in
the companie, to wit, of heretickes, (for all his armie
was made almoſt of none other but of ſuch men) and
that by his laſt will he hath commended and committed his crowne and kingdome to the ſucceſſion of Nauarre, long ſince declared an hereticke, and excommunicated; as alſo in his extremitie, and now readie to
yeeld vp his ghoſt, deſired of him, and ſuch like as he
was there ſtanding by, that they would reuenge his
death vpon thoſe whom he iudged to be the cauſe
thereof. For theſe and ſuch like moſt manifeſt tokens of
vnrepentance, we haue decreed not to ſolemnize his
death with funerals: not that we would ſeeme to con-
iecture by theſe any thing concerning the ſecret iudgements of God againſt him, or his mercies, who could
according vnto his good pleaſure in the departing of
his ſoule from the body conuert and turne his heart,
and deale with him mercifully: but this we haue ſpoken, being thereunto moued by theſe externall ſignes
and

and tokens. God grant therefore that all, being admoniſhed and warned by this feareful example of heauenly iuſtice, may repent and amend, and that it may further pleaſe him to continue and accompliſh that which he hath mercifully begun in vs , as we do put our truſt in him, to the end we may giue euerlaſting thankes to him, to haue deliuered his Church from ſuch great and imminent dangers.

Whereof when his Holineſſe had ſpoken, he brake vp the Conſiſtorie, & hauing giuen his bleſsing, let them al depart.

Whether that the Pope in this his Oratió applauded or approued the Friars murthering his Prince, I would rather the learned reader ſhould be iudge thereof then my ſelfe : his wiſdome doubtleſſe was too great to approue by any cleare and direct ſentence, ſo vile and deteſtable a fact. Howbeit this I can witneſſe, that it was commonly ſpoken by many in Rome, that had the Friar bene a Franciſcan, as he was a Dominican, he might haply haue bene then declared a Saint. And this is moſt certaine, which my ſelfe liuing in the court of Rome ſaw, that as it were to retaine a pious memory of ſuch a deed, the Friars picture was drawne on paper together with the Kings, in one ſquare or *quadro* in Italian, and publikely ſold without controlement (to my knowledge,) which many admired to ſee.

Beſides, this likewiſe is true, that M. *William Reynolds* then being in the Low countries (to whó as to my ſpeciall friend I ſent a copie of the Oration) eſteemed it (ſo did many others) as an approuing of the Friars act . For, returning me an anſwer to my letter, he gaue me heartie thankes for it, ſaying, that I could not haue gratified him with any thing more , then by ſending him the approbation of the Sea Apoſtolicke, which came in very good ſeaſon, he being at that time writing his *Roſſæus Peregrinus,* a booke of ſuch a like ſubiect.

If any deſire to know how I ſhould light on a copie thereof,

of, when as it is moſt true,that neither the Cardinall,whoſe
office it was to haue noted the Popes oration, was not prouided of paper nor iṅke, as he ſhould haue bene, had any
ſuch occaſion of vſing it bene thought of before; and therefore was not taken by any,as Cardinall *Bellarmine* ſaith well:
let him vnderſtand, that the Oration and Conſiſtory being
ended, and the Pope departed toward his chamber,certaine
Cardinals,among which (if my memory faile me not) were
Cardinall *Gallo* , and my moſt honorable patron Cardinall
Borromeo Archbiſhop of Millan,who are yet liuing , with a
greedie deſire flocked about Cardinall *Alan* there in the
chamber,intreating him that he would cal to remembrance,
and write what they had heard there ſpoken,to the end they
might after at more leiſure reade and conſider it better,and
that ſo worthy a ſpeech of his Holineſſe might not periſh.
Cardinall *Alan* crauing pardon, beſought them not to impoſe on him a matter of ſuch difficultie,for that he acknowledged himſelfe vnable to effect it;yet at laſt wonne by their
importunitie (they being his friends) promiſed to do the
beſt he could, hoping they would when they ſaw it, with
their memories helpe to ſupply his defects. The ſame after-
noone he began to ſet downe in writing the Popes ſpeech
in his owne phraſe and ſtile,as neare as he could remember:
and when he had done, he commanded me, being one of
his Chaplains,and two other of his gentlemen,to write out
copies thereof; which he after preſented to the Cardinals
his friends,who had importuned him to that labour. Afterwards they gaue him thankes,ſaying,that it was the very O-
ration which *Sixtus* had vttered in Conſiſtory : and as I was
enformed, the Pope himſelfe liking his doing therein,ſaid,
it was his ſpeech indeed.

　　By this meanes the Oration was ſet forth, and publiſhed
among diuers particular friends, and ſo I reſerued to my ſelf
a copie,which I ſent(as I haue ſaid)ſoon after to my beloued
friend M.*William Reynolds.*And as far as my memory ſerueth
me, this here printed according to the Pariſian copie, doth
well agree with the originals firſt written in Rome : for I do
　　　　　　　　　　　　　　　　　　　　　　　　　　yet

yet perfectly remember the beginning out of *Abacucke* to be the fame, likewife the facts of *Eleazar* and of *Iudith*, with the circumftances to haue bene in that Oration; as alfo the citcumftances of the Friars going to certaine aduerfa- Brifac then ries of the league for letters of credence to the King, his go- prifoner in ing forth of the gate fo dangeroufly, and his paffage through the Baftile. the heretickes campe to his Maieftie, with other like circumftances there fpecified. But whether the Pope in this his Oration approueth or alloweth of the Friars fact killing his King, for that he had caufed the Cardinall of Guife Archbifhop of Rhemes to be put to death, & was efteemed of fome a tyrant, and fauourer of heretickes; or onely admired the prouidence of almightie God, as Cardinall *Bellarmine* in *Tortus* affirmeth, I do not prefume to define, but leaue it to the confideration of each prudent reader.

What if the Pope vpon wrongs done to himfelfe, as a temporall Prince in Italy, fhould authorize fome of his vaffals or feudatary Princes to wage warre againft our King, and inuade his dominions, is not this lawfull for him by the law of nations? How then doth the Oath fay, *that the Pope neither of himfelfe, nor by any authoritie of the Church or fea of Rome, or by any other meanes with any other, hath any power or authoritie to depofe the King, or to difpofe any of his Maiefties kingdomes or dominions, or to authorize any forrein Prince to inuade or annoy him or his countries?* That his Holineffe as he is a temporall Prince in Italy, may vpon iuft caufe reuenge iniuries offered, by attempting the various euents of warre, and thereby feeke to annoy his Maieftie or his countries, no man I thinke will doubt: but can any man hereby inferre, that fo doing he hath more authoritie to depofe our King, or difpofe any of his Maiefties kingdomes, or inuade his dominions, then hath the Emperour, French King, King of Spaine, or any other fecular Prince? And in cafe he fhould attempt in hoftile manner (not as he is a fpirituall Paftor, but a fecular Prince) by himfelfe, or by the helpe of any forreine Prince, to inuade or annoy his Maieftie or his countries; euery good fubiect may lawfully, and in dutie is bound

V 3 to

to take armes in defence of his King and countrey against him, no lesse then he ought to do against any other secular Potentate whatsoeuer. But our Oath speaketh not of the secular power of the Bishop of Rome, which he hath onely by the bountie and liberalitie of temporall Princes, or by prescription in the temporall dominions he possesseth: but of any authoritie whatsoeuer receiued from Christ or his Apostles, as he is Christs Vicar, and *Peters* successor; as the words of the Oath seeme to import, viz. *That the Pope, neither of himselfe,* that is, as he is Pope, *nor by any authoritie of the Church or sea of Rome.* For thus his authoritie is onely and meerly spirituall, which was neuer ordained by God to produce such effects, as waging of warre, inuasion of kingdomes, deposing and dethroning of Princes, as hath bene said before; but onely to practise spirituall censures, to wit, excommunication, suspension, interdiction, and such like, which maketh nothing for such as refuse the taking of the Oath.

Another obiection some vse to make for their iustification against the Oath, viz: That he who sweareth, must do his best endeuour to disclose and make knowne vnto his Maiestie, his heires and successours, all treasons and traiterous conspiracies, which he shall know or heare of to be against him, or any of them. But to be a Priest, to reconcile, or to be reconciled to the Church of Rome, is treason by the statutes of this kingdome. Therefore he is bound by this Oath to reueale Priests, and all reconciled persons; which no man can do without committing a most grieuous and hainous crime.

Anno 23, 27.
Elizab.

Are not these men narrowly driue to their shifts trow ye, when after labouring their wits to defend their refusall of the Oath, they can find no better arguments? The words of the Oath import, that such as take it must make knowne all treasons, and traiterous conspiracies, which he shall know to be against him. How I pray you can this be vnderstood of any who is not disposed to cauill, to be meant of Priesthood, and confession of sins, or reconcilement to

the

the fauour of God, or vnitie of his Church; and not rather of such like treasons and traiterous conspiracies as were inuented, and should haue bene practised by those late wicked sulphurean traitors? These indeed, and others of like nature and qualitie are directly against his Maiestie, his h:eres and successours; & for repressing and detecting such, this Oath was inuented, and the Act framed; not for disclosing Priests or reconciled persons, who according to the intentio of the Act, are no such traitors, as long as they enter not into any treasonable practise against his Maiestie and the State: whereof God forbid all Priests should be guiltie.

And I trust, both his Maiestie most learned and wise, together with his graue and prudent Councell, in their wisedomes know, that besides some few, who haue already giuen good proofe of their loialtie and dutifull affection (though to their great temporall detriment for the same) there are many moe, who beare likewise a true English heart to their King and countrey, and would be ready to make also proofe thereof if occasion were offered.

Wherefore supposing it were true, that by the letter of the law, all Priests, Iesuites, &c. mentioned in the statute, are to be reputed traitors, and all reconciling treason; yet I dare auouch it was neuer his Maiesties, nor the lawmakers intent, to bind any called to the Oath to reueale such kind of traitours or treasons: which is made further manifest, for that no Magistrate ministring the Oath doth euer interprete the law in that sence, or giue charge to any for detecting such. So that these are but ridiculous, and the cauelling shifts, of some, to withdraw men from performing their dutie to his Maiestie: whereby they cause a confusion and perturbation in the whole realme, bring many families to ruine, hinder the conuersion of many soules, and minister iust occasion vnto the State to suspect little fidelitie in their hearts, what faire shew soeuer they make in words.

Here, by reason of such an interpretation made of reuealing and detecting Priests and reconciled persons, it shall not

not be amiffe to know how an Oath is to be interpreted:
and in what fort euery one is to fweare that taketh an oath
before a Magiftrate. *Molanus* writeth, that an oath ftret-
cheth not to things vnlawfull:*Omne iuramentum iuris inter-*
*pretatione ad licita tantum,non vero ad mala fe extendit.*Euery
oath by the interpretation of the law extendeth to lawfull
things onely, and not to fuch as are euill. The cafe is moft
perfpicuous and plaine, that in the Oath of allegiance it
cãnot be drawn to be meant of reuealing Priefts as Priefts,
not otherwife traitours; becaufe it fhould be extended to
that which is to be reputed euill according to the knowne
Catholicke Romaine faith, which his Maieftie in his
learned Apologie profeffeth no way to preiudice by taking
this Oath. When *Herod Tetrarch* of Galilee fware to giue
Herodias daughter what fhe would aske, though halfe his
kingdome: who will fay that it extended to the cutting off
S. *Iohn* Baptifts head, it being manifeftly euill in it felf? Yea,
but in this matter of our Oath, what if the cafe be doubtfull? *Emanuel Sa* a Iefuite teacheth you, that *in pœnis*, in punifhments a milde interpretation is to be made, and being
doubtfull, it is to be interpreted to the better part, and more
benigne, and more probable. Then what reafon haue thefe
that wil make the cafe doubtfull, to interprete this claufe of
the Oath not to the better, but to the worfe, and more
improbable? Now a word or two how an oath is to to be
taken before a lawfull magiftrate.

Whofoeuer fweareth to an officer being required, ei-
there fweareth guilefully, or without guile, which is not to
be denied: Then, faith S. *Thomas*, He who fweareth fincerely without guile, is bound according to the intention
of him that fweareth: he that fweareth with guile, ought to
fweare according to the found vnderftanding of him to
whom the oath is made. And to this purpofe faith *Innocen-*
tius in Cap.*Veniens de iureiurando*,That an oath giuen generally of performing obedience to commandements, is fo interpreted as it may not be extended but to thefe things
which were thought of, or indeed ought to be thought of.
                                                                              Which

Marginal notes:
Mola. de fide
hær.fer. lib.2.
c.7.

Marc. 6.

Sa. Apho. verb
Interpretatio.

Tho. 2.2. q.
89. ar. 7. ad 4.
Sylueft. verb
Iuramentũ 3.

Innocentius.

Which is to be meant of things lawfull. Then it followeth a little after: And if he that requireth (the oath) be a Iudge *in bona fide*, requiring it in a lawful cafe, according to the order of law; then that taketh place 22.q.5. to wit, *Quacun-* Ifido.li. 2. de *que arte verborum quis iuret, Deus tamen qui confcientiæ teftis* fum.bo.c. 31. *eft, ita hoc accipit, ficut ille cui iuratur intelligit.* With what cunning fort of words foeuer any fweare, yet God who is witneffe of the confcience, fo accepteth it, as he before whom the oath is made vnderftandeth: and he that wittingly fweareth not according to the intention of him that requireth it, finneth deadly, and is periured : and is bound to performe it as he vnderftood it. This is meant, as S. *Thomas* faith, of a guilefull oath ; and fuch a one is made guiltie in two forts, for that firft he taketh the name of God in vaine, and with fubtiltie deceiueth his neighbour. Hereupon I inferre, that to fweare to reueale all treafons and traiterous confpiracies, cannot be extended to be meant of Priefts, Priefthood, or reconciling, becaufe it was neuer thought of, nor ought to be thought of in the Oath . Neither is it his Maiefties or his officers intent, as I affure my felfe, to draw any thereby further, then to make profeffion of their allegiance; and not to entangle any mans confcience in matters of faith and religion : which is fufficient for iuftification of his Maieftie in requiring it, and for fatiffaction of Catholickes lawfully to take it.

After all this that hath bene faid , there remaineth yet one ftumbling ftone more to be remoued, and fo I will end, which is commonly called Scandall. For that fome there be that vfe to fay, being preffed with ftronger argumēts then they can well anfwere, they could be content to take the Oath, (as either holding it lawfull, or elfe not able by any important reafons to difproue it, vnleffe they borrow fome one, or all foure of the Catholicke letter deemed to be father *Parfons*, to little purpofe) were it nor for offending many Chatholicks, who are much fcandalized at the taking and takers thereof.

And is it not ftrange for Chriftian men profeffing charitie,

X

tie, to take ſcandall where none is giuen? Are not alſo many other Catholikes no leſſe, but rather more iuſtly ſcandaliʒed at ſuch as refuſe it? yea and the whole ſtate beſide, both Nobles and commons together with his Maieſtie, cannot but reſt much ſcandalized, not onely at ſuch perſons, but alſo at their religion for their ſakes.

If they will ſay vnto ſuch as take the Oath, as *Achab* King of Samaria ſaid vnto *Elias* the Prophet: *Tunè es ille, qui conturbas Iſraël*: Art not thou he that troubleſt Iſraël? For ſo ſome, *Quorum os maledictione & amaritudine plenum eſt*: whoſe mouth is full of malediction and bitterneſſe haue ſaid in effect, That ſuch Prieſts as haue performed their dutie in taking the Oath of allegiance, and ſought thereby to pacifie the Kings wrath worthily conceiued againſt Catholickes for the demerite of a few, haue cauſed a trouble and great perturbation in the Church; which vndoubtedly would neuer haue bene (ſay they) had all Catholickes and Prieſts ſtood conſtantly againſt the Oath. But ſuch loyall ſubiects, Prieſts or Laickes, may well retort vpon them, as *Elias* did vpon King *Achab*: *Non ego turbaui Iſraël ſed tu, & domus patris tui*. It is not I that haue troubled Iſraël, but thou and the houſe of thy father, who haue forſaken the commandements of our Lord. It is not ſuch as haue taken the Oath, that cauſe trouble in the Church, nor forſake the commandements of our Lord; but ſuch Prieſts and people as wilfully refuſe it, and perſwade others againſt it, to the hazard yea loſſe of ſome of their liues, and of the lands and goods of others: and alſo of the ſoules of ſuch as louing more the glorie of men then the glorie of God, obſtinately refuſe to performe their dutie in obeying that precept of our Sauiour: *Render vnto Cæſar that which is Cæſars*: and that of S. *Peter, Regem honorificate*: and alſo the commandement giuen to *Moyſes: Honour thy father and thy mother*. Theſe, aſſure you, are they who giue cauſe of ſcandal indeed, wherby their perſecution (if ſo they pleaſe to cal it) is continued, the Church perturbed, Catholicke religion little regarded, and many a ſoule loſt. But *Væ illi, per quem ſcandalum venit*.

Woe

3.Reg. 18.
Pſal. 13.

Woe to him, by whom scandall cometh. Time will make triall who it is, whether they or we.

In the meane while we say, that the proper and true definition of scandall, as it is defined by S. *Thomas* and others, most aptly agreeth with the doctrine and example, or words and deedes, of such English subiects as withdraw men from performing their dutie to their dread Soueraigne: not on such as perswade it, and yet remaine no lesse Catholicke, then they do pretend in euery point of faith. Scandall is a word or deed not right, giuing occasion of ruine; that is, of spirituall ruine or sinne. Now what euill or shew of euill or sin is there in those, who by their deedes and words, example and doctrine, teach and labour to induce all to do that which is right and due by the law of God? What scandall or offence, or occasion of sinne do they giue, who perswade nothing against any one article or point of faith, but meere allegiance to their Prince? Doth this offend or scandalize any ? If they will be scandalized for well doing , and take offence where none is giuen, do they not shew how imperfect they are in the loue of God? *Pax multa diligentibus legem tuam; & non est illis scandalum.* To such as loue thy law (ô God) there is great peace : and to them there is no scandall. May not these be well likened to the Pharisies, that of enuie and malice were offended or scandalized at the sayings and doings of our Blessed Sauiour? who, being told by his disciples of their scandall taken, answered : *Omnis plantatio quam non plantauit Pater meus coelestis, eradicabitur.* All planting which my heauenly Father hath not planted, shall be rooted vp. Let them alone; blind they are , guides of the blind. And if the blind be guide to the blind, both fall into the ditch. Such are to be pitied and praied for, not enuied; whom we may answer in the same sort, and with *Haimo : Si pro veritate scandalum oriatur, magis veritas eligenda est, quàm scandalum vitandum.* If for truth scandall do arise (as it doth in this our case) rather truth is to be chosen , then scandall sought to be auoided. The same affirmeth S. *Gregorie* the Great, as before,

Definition of scandall.
Tho. 2. 2. q. 43. ar. 1. & Ieron. in comment. su- per Math. c. 15.

Psal. 118.

Math. 15.

Haimo in Math. c. 18. Greg. ho. 7. in

Ezech. pag. 2.

pag.

Tho.1.2.q.
43.ar.7.

pag.45. And S.*Thomas* difputing whether fpirituall goods are to be pretermitted for paffiue fcandall,faith: That fuch goods as are *de neceſſitate ſalutis*, ought not to be omitted for auoiding fcandall: becaufe they cannot be pretermitted without mortall finne : (as in our iudgements we take allegiance in the Oath to be;) but it is manifeft (faith he) that none ought to finne mortally, to faue an other from finne: becaufe according to the order of charitie, a man ought to loue more his owne fpirituall health then another mans.

Pupil.oculi.

The fame likewife hath *Ioannes de Burgo*: *Opera neceſſaria ad ſalutem non ſunt omittenda ad vitandum ſcandalum proximi, ex quacunque radice procedat.* Workes neceſſarie to faluation are not to be omitted for auoiding the fcandall of our neighbour, out of whatfoeuer roote it proceedeth. Herby, deare brethren in our Lord Iefus, I truft you reft fatisfied, that fuch as haue taken the Oath of allegiance, wherein nothing hath bene hitherto proued by any learned man to be contained againft any one point of faith, haue not giuen caufe of fcandall (as they haue bin flandered to haue done) but by that their fact, performing their bounden dutie to their dread Soueraigne according to the law of God, haue fought to take away that horrible fcandall giuen indeed, by a few vngracious Catholikes in the gunpowder treafon; and which others daily giue to his Maieftie and the State in refifting the law made vpon fo great reafon, and for the commō good of the realme. Befides, I truft your wifdomes will confider, that to take the Oath being *bonum ſpirituale*, wherein no euill thing againft religion is contained, they are not to pretermit it for the imperfections of fome, who are readie to fuffer or take fcandall where none is giuen.

Wherefore I exhort you all moft dearely beloued Catholikes in the bowels of our Sauiour Iefus Chrift., (as the very Reuerend and learned maifter *George Blackwell* fometime our Archprieft, did in his letter to his Affiftants, and you all both Clergie and Laitie) for abolifhing and ending this controuerfie which hath fcandalized the whole State, you wold defift to impugne fupreme authoritie in this cafe

of

of the Oath moſt lawfull and iuſt, as hath bene proued:and ceaſſe any longer to prouoke to wrath his Maieſty our moſt clement Prince:clement I ſay,for I dare boldly auouch,that neither the Pope,nor any King or Prince in Chriſtendome, had he had the like cauſe offered by any his ſubieĉts, eſpecially of a contrarie religion, and finding others of the ſame religion to refuſe to make profeſſion of their loyalty by an Oath required at their hands,would ſhew ſuch mercy and clemencie as his Maieſtie hath done, and doth. Conferre the faĉt or enterpriſe of the Moores in Spaine now two years agone, who wēt about(as report goeth)treacherouſly to bring in Turkes and forreiners to inuade the countrey, with this *Cateſbeyan* and *Percian* moſt barbarous treaſon: and I doubt not but you will iudge them both worthy condigne puniſhment. Compare againe the two Princes, who by Gods ordinance carie the ſword *ad vindiĉtam malefaĉtorum*, to take reuenge on malefaĉtours;you ſhall find them both iuſtly prouoked to indignation againſt the delinquents : yet the one, viz. King *Philip*, with great ſeueritie chaſtiſeth the innocent with the nocent , old & yong, men, women and children,expelling all alike out of his dominiós,to the number of nine hundred thouſand, as appeareth by his ediĉt, within the ſpace of xxx. dayes,to the loſſe of all their immoueables . Whereas the other, our dread Soueraigne, of his pitifull inclination,did not puniſh in ſuch ſort the guiltles, nor all the offendours according to their deſerts,but repreſſed by his ediĉt the furie of his people, readie to haue taken reuenge yea on many innocent perſons, for their ſakes that had offended.Embrace then, deare brethren,the mercie and long ſufferance of this our milde and clement Prince whileſt time is granted you , leſt through your default it be turned into furie ; for oft times *patientia læſa*, ſpecially of a King, *vertitur in furorē*.And reſiſt no longer,but cóforme your ſelues to his Maieſties iuſt demand in this caſe of the Oath, that wherein they (that is) ſuch as are of a different religion,miſreport of you as of malefaĉtours, by the good workes conſidering you,they may

1.Pet,ai

X 3   glorifie

glorifie God in the day of vifitation. Alfo with this bleffed Apoftle S. *Peter* I wifh you to be fubiect to euery humane creature of God, whether it be to the King, as excelling: or to rulers as fent by him to the reuenge of malefactours, but to the praife of the good : for fo (note well) is the will of God, that doing well you may make the ignorace of vnwife men dumbe. I defire likewife with S. *Paul*, that obfecrations, prayers, poftulations ;thankefgiuing be made for all men; for Kings, & all that are in preeminence: that we may leade a quiet and peaceable life in all pietie and chaftitie. If *Tertullian* were liuing and thofe ancient Fathers of the primitiue Church, they would queftionleffe, following the doctrine and example of the Apoftles, exhort you likewife to pray for the long life of our Soueraigne, no leffe then they did the Chriftians of thofe dayes for their Emperours or Kings, howfoeuer they differed in religion.

.1 Tim. 2.

Tertul. Apologet. c. 50.
See mafter Blackwels letter.

Finally as *Baruch* the Prophet wifhed fuch Iewes as were left in Ierufalem after the captiuitie, to pray for the life of *Nabuchodonozor* King of Babylon, and for the life of *Balthafar* his fonne, that their dayes might be as the dayes of heauen vpon the earth: fo do I defire all Catholickes profeffing with me the Romane faith, heartily to pray for the long life and profperous reigne of King *Iames* of great Brittaine, together with his deare Spoufe our moft gracious Queene *Anne*, and the hopefull yong Prince *Henrie* his fonne, with the reft of his moft roiall iffue, that in this world they may long continue to the glorie of the eternall God; and afer this mortality euer to enioy that felicitie which neuer fhall haue end.

Baruch. 1.

Vni Trinoque Deo omnis honor & gloria.

STRANGE

STRANGE REPORTS
OR NEWES FROM ROME.

His my diſcourſe of the Oath of Allegiance being fully complete & ended, written ſpe-cially for ſatisfying and perſwading ſuch Catholickes of our countrey as thinke it not lawfull to be taken, at leaſt by reaſon of the Popes Breues prohibiting the ſame; be-hold, certaine ſtrange newes diuerſly ſpread aboade, from diuers parts and perſons, haue miniſtred me occaſion to continue on my labour by adding this briefe Treatiſe fol-lowing, for and in defence of my ſelfe and ſome others my brethren Prieſts, who for no crime committed in our iudge-ments, but onely for performing our duties to God and man, haue bene and are calumniated to be depriued of all faculties granted by any authoritie from the Sea of Rome; whereby we are vtterly diſabled to liue, for not being any longer regarded; but forſaken and in affection abandoned by ſuch as formerly vſed of charitie to releeue vs.

Audite ergo cœli quæ loquor : audiat terra verba oris mei. Heare therefore ô ye heauens what I ſpeake : let the earth hearken to the words of my mouth. For I am to vtter that which to Saint *Peter* and Saint *Paul*, and to the bleſſed A-poſtles, and to all glorious Saints, will ſeeme ſtrange and wondrous tidings, and whereat all good Chriſtians on earth that ſhall enter into conſideration of the caſe, may ſtand a-mazed, and poſteritie will ſcarce beleeue when it ſhall be told them.

Talking not long ſince with a friend that came newly from beyond the ſeas, I asked him what newes in thoſe parts, and what was ſaid of vs that had taken the Oath of al-legiance:

legiance: he told me, the report was there, that we had loſt
our faculties, but could not tell by what meanes or by whō.
And here at home in our country the ſame is bruted abrode
by many, and in many places, but in ſundrie manner, the re-
porters diſagreeing ſo much in their tales, as no certaine
truth can be gathered by thē. For ſome ſay, that fiue Prieſts
onely of the Clinke were by name depriued of their faculties, (one of which is lately deceaſſed) and maiſter *Blacke-
well* was not mentioned, becauſe he was thought to be dead.

Others haue reported that he alone was named, but all o-
ther Prieſts likewiſe had loſt them that did concurre with
him.

Others againe, that ſuch were depriued of their faculties
(that is, vnabled to exerciſe certaine priuiledges granted
Prieſts at their miſſion into England) as hauing taken the
Oath, do conſtantly perſiſt or perſeuere in teaching or al-
lowing the lawfulneſſe thereof. Now which of theſe reports ſo much differing, is true (for all cannot be true) I
greatly deſire to know, but cannot learne any certaintie.

Then as touching the manner, how, and by what meanes
they be taken away, little agreement do I find, but ſuch varietie in relation thereof, as wiſe men may well admire to ſee
ſuch proceedings in a matter ſo important as this is: and, that
ſome of our owne profeſſion and religion, ſhould receiue ſatisfaction and contentment in beholding our miſeries, by
being in ſuch wiſe puniſhed; who haue (as it may ſeeme)
long expected, and *Tantalus* like hungred and thirſted after
the ſame.

Firſt, ſome ſay that we haue loſt them, and had long ſince
by vertue of the Archprieſts *Admonition* directed, To all the
ſecular Prieſts of England; which anon ſhall be ſet downe
verbatim, that all diſcreete perſons may iudge thereof.

Another report is, that the Cardinals of the Inquiſition
haue giuen their iudgement, and cenſured our faculties to
haue bene loſt by the Archprieſts *Admonition* at the firſt.

A third report is, that the Cardinals of that congregation
haue themſelues taken them from all ſuch Prieſts as either
haue

haue taken,or ſhall hereafter take our Oath of allegiance.

From theſe, the fourth ſort diſagree, ſaying, That the Viceprotector of his owne authoritie that he hath ouer our nation, in his priuate letters writing to the Archprieſt, ſignified his depriuing ſuch of their priuiledges, as had taken the ſaid Oath,and do perſiſt in defending it.

Fifthly,that indeed he did it,but by order from the Popes Holineſſe.

And laſtly, that the Pope himſelfe hath ſent to the Archprieſt a Breue,wherein he commandeth him *in virtute obedientiæ*, to depriue all thoſe Prieſts of their faculties which do concurre with maiſter *Blackwell*, or elſe haue taken, or ſhall teach it lawfull to take the Oath of allegiance. Yea and in ſuch ſeuere ſort,as the like was neuer ſeen *ab initio naſcentis Eccleſiæ*; viz. *Omni excuſatione poſthabita : etiam ipſis delinquentibus non admonitis : & nullo iuris ordine ſeruato.* That is, all excuſe ſet aſide: yea the delinquents not admoniſhed; and no order of law obſerued in proceeding with vs. That this is true, by mine owne knowledge I can teſtifie, and proue ifneed were.

Which of all theſe reports deſerue moſt credite and is trueſt, were greatly wiſhed might be made knowne to the parties whom it concerneth; otherwiſe how can they tell what to do in this important buſineſſe,and what is required at their hands, to retaine ſtill, or recouer their faculties being once loſt? How ſhall they obey, if they know not what is commanded them? *Etenim ſi incertam vocem det tuba,* (ſaith Saint *Paul*) *quis parabit ſe ad bellum?* For if the trumpet giue an vncertaine voice, who ſhall prepare himſelfe to battell? 1.Cor.14.

Therfore it is moſt requiſite,that ſuch as haue bin in poſſeſſion of their faculties,granted thē by authority of the Sea of Rome,ſome 20.ſome 30.yeares agone, and ſome more, ſhould know how,and by whom they are taken from them, and for what cauſe; which ought to be for ſome great fault, becauſe the paine is moſt grieuous : & ſhould ſee moreouer not onely an authenticall copie of the originall letters, but also

alfo the originals themfelues , if the Churches orderly proceedings be obferued ; otherwife all may be thought idle
reports not to be beleeued. For Saint *Thomas* faith , That
when the Church depriueth heretickes and fchifmatickes,
and other fuch like, withdrawing fubiects from them, either
fimpliciter , or *quantum ad aliquid*, fimply, or touching fome
particular thing; they cannot put in practife or haue vfe of
the keyes, touching that which they are depriued of. Then
I fay, it is verie neceffarie that Priefts , not heretickes, nor
fchifmatickes, or fuch like, but moft conftant in euerie leaft
article of the Romane faith , fhould know whether they be
forbidden fimply all , or elfe but fome particular faculties
receiued at their miffion: whereby they may in all humilitie
fhew themfelues obedient to his Holineffe , in furceafing
from exercifing what they fhall perceiue to be by him forbidden them.

Now whereas the firft report of the manner of taking a-
way faculties, is , That Priefts conftantly perfifting in teaching the lawfulneffe of the Oath , had loft their faculties &
were difabled to abfolue their penitents from deadly fin, by
vertue of the Archpriefts admonitió:I wifh the difcreet reader not to giue credite thereto , becaufe doubt may well be
made thereof, feeing diuerfe learned Priefts, yea fuch as
haue not taken the Oath,haue iudged otherwife, viz : That
they were not loft;and amongft the reft, an Affiftant efteemed of many to be one of the graueft and beft iudgement
in fuch cafes. Which will alfo moft perfpicuoufly appeare to
him, that fhall with iudgement reade the Admonition , and
duly confider the Archpriefts act and proceeding therein,
whether it be (as it ought to be)in euery refpect conformable to that of the Popes Breues authorifing him, which was
as followeth : *Tibíque iniungimus & mandamus , ac fpecialem*
facultatem ad hoc tribuimus , vt authoritate noftra omnes & fin-
gulos Sacerdotes Anglos ,qui quoddam iuramentum (in quo multa
continentur quæ fidei atque faluti animarum aperte aduerfantur)
præftiterunt: vel ad loca ad quæ hæretici ad eorum fuperftitiofa mi-
nifteria peragenda conuenire folent; confultò accefferunt , aut qui
talia

Tho.3.p.q.
19.ar.6.

Ex Breui fum
Pont.

talia licitè fieri posse docuerunt, & docent, admonere cures,vt ab
huiusmodi erroribus resipiscant & abstineant : quod si intra tem-
pus (extraiudicialiter tamen) arbitrio tuo illis præfigendum hoc
facere distulerint, seu aliquis illorum distulerit, illos seu illum fa-
cultatibus & priuilegijs omnibus ab Apostolica sede, seu illius au-
thoritate à quocunque alio illis vel cuiuis illorum concessis, eadem
authoritate priues,ac priuatos esse declares,&c.Datum Romæ a-
pud S.Petrum sub annulo piscatoris die 1.Februarij, 1608.Ponti-
ficatus nostri anno 3. And we enioyne and command you, and
for this we giue you speciall facultie, that by our authoritie
you take care to admonish all and singular English Priests,
who haue taken a certaine Oath (wherein many things are
contained which are manifestly against faith and the health
of soules, &c.) or haue taught, and do teach such things may
lawfully be done, that they may repent and abstaine from
such errors: and if within the time(*extraiudicialiter* notwithstanding) by you to be prefixed vnto them, they shal deferre
to do this, or any one shall deferre, that you by the same authoritie depriue, and declare them or him to be depriued of
all faculties and priuiledges granted them, or any of them,
from the Sea Apostolicke , or by her authority from any o-
ther whatsoeuer. Dated at Rome the first of Frebruary,
1608.

This much out of the Popes Breue to the reuerend Archpriest M. *Birket*, touching his facultie or commission giuen
him, first to admonish, then after the time prefixed was expired, no satisfaction being giuen of repenting or abstai-
ning, to depriue such, and declare them depriued of their
faculties. Whereupon the Archpriest indeed sent a letter of
admonition to the Priests then of and in the Clinke, endor-
ced, To all the reuerend Secular Priests of England. Which
was as followeth : *Most dearely beloued brethren, whereas I* The Arch-
haue alwayes desired to liue without molesting or offending others, priests letter
it cannot be but a wonderfull corsiue, sorrow and griefe vnto me, of the Clinke.
that against mine owne inclination I am forced (as you haue seene
by the Breue it selfe) to prescribe a certaine time for such as do
find themselues to haue bene contrarie to the points which are tou-

ehed

ched in the said *Breue*, concerning the *Oath* and going to *Church*;
that they may thereby returne and conforme themselues to the doctrine declared by his *Holinesse*; both in this and the other former
Breues. And therefore now by this present do giue notice vnto you
all, that the time which I prefixe and prescribe for that purpose, is
the space of two moneths next ensuing after the knowledge of this
my admonition. Within which time, such as shall forbeare to take,
or allow any more the *Oath*, or going to *Church*, I shall most
willingly accept their doing therein; yet signifying vnto you withall, that such as do not within this time prescribed giue this satisfaction, I must (though much against my will for fulfilling his *Holinesse* commandement) depriue them, and denounce them to be depriued of all their faculties and priuiledges granted by the Sea *A-
postolicke*, or by any other, by authoritie thereof vnto them, or to
any of them, and so by this present do denounce; hoping that there
is no man will be so wilfull or disobedient to his *Holinesse* order, but
will conforme himselfe as becometh an obedient child of the *Catholicke Church*. And so most heartily wishing this conformitie in
vs all, and that we may liue and labour together vnanimes in do-
mo Domini, I pray God giue vs the grace to effect that in our a-
ctions, whereunto we are by our order and profession obliged. This
2. of *May*, 1608.

> Your seruant in Christ
> *George Birket Archpriest of England*,
> and *Protonotarie Apostolicall*.

After which admonition, the Archpriest proceeded no
further, nor euer afterwards did depriue, nor declare any
one to be depriued of his faculties, as he should haue done
strictly, according to the order and commission granted
him by his Holinesse that now is *Paulus* 5: and not to denounce them lost during the time of the admonition, exceeding his bounds, as he did, saying, *And by this present do
denounce*. Therefore most certaine it is, that the Priests to
whom knowledge of the admonition came, did not then
lose their faculties by vertue thereof. Neither is it to be credited, that the Cardinals of the Inquisition, who are both
wise and learned, can iudge them lost by that act, as the second

cond report affirmeth, if they were truly informed, and as
well experienced in the cafe, as fome here, their inferiors in
euery refpeƈt are. If they haue bene of that opinion, and iudged fo, yet is the contrary opinion of other learned men
rather to be beleeued and followed, being much more prō-
bable then theirs. But fuppofe we fhould grant, which is
not to be granted, that thofe Priefts who receiued and tooke
notice of the admonition, were iuftly depriued, and had loft
their faculties; at leaft fome others who haue taken the Oath
fince that generall letter, being neuer admonifhed, nor euer
feeing that, or any other letter from the Archprieft to any
fuch end, are free and haue not loft them: the Archprieft being bound by his faculty *admonere fingulos*, to admonifh each
one in particular, at leaft to giue him knowledge thereof,
that fhall take the Oath, or teach it lawfull; or to go to the
Proteftants Churches to their Seruice. Befides, why I pray
you, fhould not that Prieft be exempted from lofing his faculties, albeit he faw and read the admonition, who wrote,
and endeuoured what he could poffibly to fend to the Archprieft (as in his letter he required) to giue him fuch fatisfa-
ƈtion, as might haue caufed his Reuerence to ftay from cen-
furing him when the time prefixed fhould haue bene expired, but could not find any meanes to conuey letters vnto
him, which fome (if need were) can teftifie? This all know,
quod ad impoffibile nemo tenetur, that none is bound to a thing
impoffible to be effeƈted. So then confequently, neither did
that Prieft lofe his facultiesby the admonition. Howbeit all
without exception, and without any excufe (for no excufe
muft be admitted) are depriued, all abandoned of Catholickes, and as if they were the greateft offenders that euer
were in Gods Church, adiudged vnworthy of the charitable
almes and poore meanes which they had to fuftaine their
painfull and tedious life.

And if the moft illuftrious and moft reuerend Cardinals
of the congregation of the holy Office, haue taken them a-
way, (as it is in the third report) then is it requifite that the
Priefts whom this matter toucheth, fhould fee and know

with

with what authoritie they do it, whether by facultie from his Holineſſe, or of themſelues by their owne power; and alſo, the forme of their ſentence: all which lieth hidden in the clouds, and cannot be ſeene.

Whereas the fourth report hath, that the Viceprotector of his owne authoritie by his letters written to the Arch-prieſt, depriued ſuch Prieſts as are aboue mentioned, of their faculties, is moſt vaine, and worthy to be exploded as a for-ged fable. For it is not to be credited, that a ſage Prince and pillar of the Church wil euer attempt to do that which is not in his power, vnleſſe it be giuen by him whom we acknow-ledge to haue *plenitudinem poteſtatis in ſpiritualibus*, ſpecially in ſuch a caſe as ours is.

What if his Grace hath done it by order from his Holi-nes, as the fift report ſaith, is not his ſentence then to be ac-cepted and obeyed? Yes, I acknowledge as a child of the Church ought, that a ſentence or cenſure proceeding medi-ate or immediatly from the chiefe Paſtor, is to be reſpected and feared, as S. *Gregorie* teacheth me. Yet I thinke none wil denie but it ought orderly to be made knowne to the par-ties whom it concerneth; and that vntill it come by orderly meanes to their knowledge, it bindeth not: nor then nei-ther, if the cenſure be manifeſtly vniuſt, as procured by ob-reption, falſe information, or any ſiniſter meanes which may vitiate the proceſſe. Whereto agreeth *Petrus Gregorius* in his

Pet.Greg.de
repub.l.26.c.5
bookes *de Repub.* ſaying, *Sed neque reſcripta omnia, aut impe-trata, ſeu extorta à ſummo Pontifice per ſuggeſtionem falſam, vel obreptionem, aut in præiudicium alterius, debent effectum vel con-ſequentiam habere, quia hæc Sedem Romanam (quæ inſtitiæ cul-trix eſt) redderent ignominioſam, ſæpe præter intentionem Ponti-ficum; quorum reſcriptis perpetuò duæ clauſulæ adijciuntur, vel*

L.1.§.Si quid
à principe ne-
quid in loco
publico p.
omiſſæ adiecta cenſentur: Si preces veritate nitantur, & ſine præ-iudicio tertij inauditi. But neither all reſcripts, or matters ob-tained, or rather wreſted from the Pope by falſe ſuggeſtion or obreption, or to the preiudice of another, ought to haue any conſequence or take effect, becauſe ſuch like procee-dings would make the Sea of Rome (which is a louer of iu-ſtice)

ftice) ignominious,oftentimes befide the intentió of Popes,
to whofe writings alwaies two claufes are added , or being
omitted, are adiudged to be added,(to wit) *If the petitions
are grounded on truth , and without preiudice of a third perſon
that is vnheard.*

Now that this cenſure of fuſpenſion from faculties (if
there be any ſuch extant) hath bene obtained , or wre-
fted out by ſome finifter meanes, to wit, by falſe ſuggeftion
or wrong information of one or other ouerhaftie ſolicitor,
that is greedie to ſee what will be the euent and finall iſſue
of this our controuerſie, is very probable . The cauſe that
maketh me ſuſpeꞔt falſe information in this our caſe,is,that
to my knowledge a certaine prime Prieſt in a letter to his
friend affirmed,he had ſent information to Rome of as much
as any of vs that haue taken the Oath , can ſay in defence
thereof,yea and more.Which doubtleſſe is a moft falſe ſuggeſtion,if he hath ſo informed , and farre beyond his talent
to performe.What elſe (I pray you)is this,but by obreption
to procure or extort that from either the Cardinall Vice-
proteꞔtor,or from the Pope, which would neuer haue bene
granted (as may be preſumed) againſt reuerend Prieſts,ne-
neuer heard what they can ſay for themſelues , and to their
great preiudice?Therefore if the ſoliciter and informer haue
ſo egregiouſly erred in deceiuing his Holineſſe, the cenſure
or ſentence ſo procured is of no validitie at all.

The ſixt and laſt report is,that the Pope in a Breue to the
Archprieſt commanded him to depriue all thoſe Prieſts of
their faculties , which do or ſhall concurre with maifter
Blackwell, without giuing any admonition , admitting any
excuſe,or obſeruing any order of law.So that the Archprieſt
may ſit quietly in his chamber , and but ſay the word , that
the Prieſts of the Clinke or elſe where , that ſhall concurre
with maifter *Blackwell* (they know not wherein)are depriued of their faculties,and ſo forthwith they are, and muft be
depriued.This report ſeemeth to me more improbable then
any of the reft; becauſe it raifeth an imputation and ſlander
againſt the chiefe Paſtor of the Sea of Rome, to wit, that he

fhould giue eare onely to one aduerfe part, and not be content to lend alfo another eare, to heare what the other part
accufed can fay in defence of their actions : to condemne
them before they come to their anfwer, and before any
crime to their knowledge be proued againft them, which
would be an act of iniuftice, and contrarie to the laudable
cuftome of the ancient Romanes, yea heathens, as is in the
Actes of the Apoftles: *Non eft Romanis confuetudo damnare a-*

Act.25.

liquem hominem, priùs quàm is, qui accufatur, præfentes habeat
accufatores, locumq̃ defendendi accipiat ad abluenda crimina. It
is not the Romane cuftome (faid *Feftus* Prefident of Iurie,
to king *Agrippa*) to yeeld vp (or condemne) any man, before that he which is accufed haue his accufers prefent, and
take place to make his anfwer for to cleare himfelfe of the
crimes. Is it not ftrange that any fhould be fo prefumptu-
oufly bold, as to impute vnto his Holineffe, that he, who
fhould be a louer of iuftice, and louing father of all his children, fhould inflict fo grieuous a punifhment on Priefts, as
to bereaue them of their life? their life I fay, for that to take
faculties from them, is to take all reliefe from fome of them,
and to take reliefe, is to driue them into extreme miferie,
fickeneffe, famine, and death: yea and fuch Priefts who for
no hope of temporall emoluments, or fpirituall benefices,
but only, as we are perfwaded, for gaining foules vnto Chrift
their Redeemer; and after haue laboured fome 20. fome 25.
fome 30. yea and more yeares to that end; during which
time, without expectation of preferment in this world, they
haue fuffered many fharpe fhowers of tribulation, fome by
imprifonment, in fundry prifons many yeares, and fome
many yeares banifhment from their parents and friends and
and natiue countrey too. That thefe fhould be thus cenfured
and depriued by the common Father and chiefe Paftor of
the Church, as if they had committed a crime fo hainous &
fo notorious, in taking the Oath, as needed no admonition,
might admit no excufe, nor deferued any orderly proceeding in law, I cannot be perfwaded, nor will beleeue it is fo,
till I fee more euident fignes thereof then hitherto I haue
feene.

                                                        The

The materiall caufe of fufpenfion (faith Cardinall *Tolet*) is finne, for which it is inflicted: for none may be fufpended without finne. His words are: *Non enim abfq, peccato quis fufpendi poteft. Cap. Satis peruerfum. d. 56.* And this fin (faith he) moft commonly is mortall. *Poteft autem pro veniali aliqua fufpenfio imponi, vt dicit Caietanus. Dummodo tamen fit lenis fufpenfio, ficut & culpa.* Yet for a veniall finne fome fufpenfion may be impofed, fo for all that the fufpenfion be light, as the fault is light. *Argum. text in l. refpiciendum. in prim. ff. de pœn.*

If none ought to be fufpended grieuoufly but for fome grieuous finne, then I truft it is vntruly giuen forth, that his Holineffe hath inflicted fo feuere a punifhment on fuch Priefts as haue taken the Oath, becaufe it hath not yet bene proued by any to haue bene a deadly, yea or veniall finne in them. And then *Ecclefia non debet prefumere de aliquo peccatum donec probetur:* as Saint *Thomas* faith. Neither can they after due fearch and examination of their owne confciences, accufe themfelues to haue committed any finne at all in fo doing, but rather difcharged their duties, as good fubiects & good Catholickes ought: and haue not denyed by taking it any one point or *Iota* of faith at all: nor difobeyed his Holineffe Breues of contempt, which maketh a finne; but vpon well grounded reafons, and authorities of good writers, haue refufed (as lawfully they might) to obey them.

Befides, when as the end for which the pain of fufpenfion or loffe of faculties is inflicted, is the vtilitie of foules, as Cardinall *Tolet* affirmeth: *Finis fufpenfionis eft idem, qui & excommunicationis; Ecclefia enim animarum vtilitatem intendit, quando corrigit & caftigat.* The end of fufpenfion (faith he) is the fame as is of excommunication; for the Church intendeth the vtilitie of foules, when fhe correcteth and chaftifeth: I cannot be induced to beleeue that his Sanctitie, (who in all weightie affaires, as this is, vfeth the affent of his Senate of Cardinals) will fo rigoroufly proceed with Priefts, that haue alwayes liued, and do defire nothing more in this world, then to continue and end their dayes in that faith they haue hitherto profeffed, and in the feare of God. Who

Z knoweth

Materialis caufa proxima.
Tolet. inftr. facerd. l.1.c.44
Caietan. verb. fufpenfio.
Nauar. in fum. c 27. nu. 159.

Tolet. inftr. fac l.1.c.44. in fine.

knoweth not that oft times neceſſitie driueth men to do that which they neuer thought? *Durum telum neceſſitas.* And now lately ſome Prieſts, vpon theſe reports giuen foorth of hauing no faculties, haue in ſuch ſort felt the alienation of Catholickes, and the withdrawing their charitie from them, (for on the eight of this moneth, for an addition to our affli-ctions, it was written vnto vs by him that hath had the di-ſtribution of the common almes many yeares, that from hencefoorth you may ſeeke to be relieued elſewhere, for, for my part I finde I ſhall not be able to helpe you any more hereafter;) as if neceſſitie could haue ſhaken them, they might haue, not onely ſaid with *Dauid*, *Penè moti ſunt pedes mei,* My feete were almoſt moued, but had bene moued indeed.

Pſa.71.

Great reaſon we might thinke there was for vs to expect that his Holineſſe would, conſidering this pouertie of Ca-tholickes of England to relieue, and the multitude of priſo-ners to be relieued, knowing we are ſuch Prieſts as were made *ex indulto Apoſtolico,* without title of benefice, or patri-mony, rather haue taken ſome order according to the Coun-cell of Trent, to haue bene ſuccoured and relieued in pri-ſons, then to expoſe ſuch to famine, by taking from the the only meanes ſome of them had to vphold & maintain their vnpleaſant life. Yet if it be true that is reported, and that it is the Popes pleaſure we muſt ſuffer more, & ſharper ſhowers of calamities, and that orderly courſes are not in this our caſe to be kept with vs, let vs with patience comfort our ſelues in our Lord, and ſay with Saint *Paul: Benedictus Deus & Pater Domini noſtri Ieſu Chriſti, Deus totius côſolationis, qui conſolatur nos in omni tribulatione noſtra.* God be bleſſed and the Father of our Lord Ieſus Chriſt; who comforteth vs in all our tribulation. And do wiſh that theſe our afflictions may be cautions to all our countrimen to conſider well the ſequele of things and times, before they make them-ſelues Prieſts beyond the ſeas, leſt the like fall to them as to vs.

FINIS.

Faultes escaped.

Preface A 2.line 8.reade ouermuch.page 24.line 4.reade,Emanuel.p.30.
l.12.reade pa.24. Pa.34.l.5. pro defenfione.Ibidem l.15.occupandam.p.
42.l.26.poffunt.p.56.l.11.reade can not get it.p.70.l.10.wanteth in the mar-
gent. Præfat. mon.Regis feren.p.62.Lat. p.71.l.27. faith he, is fuperfluous.
p.73.l.26. adding, reade, doing.p.81.l.35.fon feruitore.ibid,fchiauo.p.86.
l.13. hundred, is fuperfluous.p.65.l.26. put out, only in temporals. Ibidem.
l.27. reade, in fpirituals in the Church, and in the patrimony of the Church
onely in temporals. p. 116.l.22. of, reade or opinion.p.125.l.14. or, reade
of preiudicating.p.126.l.25.and Chrift himfelfe,reade, and the fame Prophet
prefiguring Chrift himfelf,after commanded.p.136.l.27.reade,a worke hath
bene wrought.p.137.l.12.of,reade from all.Ibid.hath bene wrought.Ibid.l.
17.reade, as when our. p.138.l.31.fhall,reade,will.p.168.l.11.Roman,reade,
Romans.

ST. JEROME
Certaine Selected Epistles
1630

CERTAINE
SELECTED EPISTLES
OF
S. HIEROME
AS ALSO
THE LIVES OF
SAINT PAVL
THE FIRST HERMITE,

Of Saint H I L A R I O N the firſt Monke of Syria, and of S. M A L C H V S :

VVritten by the ſame Saint .

Tranſlated into Engliſh .

Permiſſu Superiorum , M . DC . XXX .

THE
PREFACE
TO THE READER.

 Haue beene requeſted by a Friend, whome I know not how either to deny, or delay; that I would tranſlate ſome choyce Epiſtles, and the three liues of S. Paul the Hermite, S. Hilarion the Monke, and S. Malchus, who was alſo a moſt holy man. They were written by that great famous Doctour S. Hierome, and now here you haue them in our English tongue. I thinke I need not ſay (for they who will haue the wit to vnderſtand me, do already know) that if it were not for the ſeruice of God, and for that duty which a man owes his friends, he would take no great pleaſure in tranſlating the workes of ſuch perſons, as are extraordinary and eminent, both in knowledge, and in the expreſsion thereof. For when the conceptions are choice, & the power of ſpeech is great in any authour,

his

The preface to the Reader.

his tranflatour is likely enough to find his hands full of worke . S . Hierome is fo well knowne, and fo generally acknowledged, to haue beene rare in both thefe kindes whereof I fpake, that I make account my pardon of courfe is already vnder Seale, though I may haue robbed the Saint of life in many of his paffages ; for I haue done it againft my will, and (as we vfe to fay) but in myne owne defence. As for any aduife which you may expect, you fhall haue but this from me If when you read thefe Epiftles and Liues, you obferue any particulars which may eyther be beyond your beliefe in regard of the miracls which are recounted, or elfe befids your beliefe in refpect that you haue been taught fome doctrines otherwife ; do but caft your mind vpon confidering, that it is no leffe then S. Hierome who is fpeaking to you. Who liuing in the Primitiue Church, within foure hundred years after Chrift our Lord, and hauing flourished with vncontrolled fame throughout the whole world, for incomparable fanctity and wifedome, and for learning alfo in all fciences, as well diuine, as humane ; it is fit that you fhould deferre much to him, both in the beliefe of thefe miraculous thinges, and in the admittace alfo of thefe doctrins, which are fo expreffly infinuated by him to haue beene practifed by the Catholicke Church of his tyme. I hope you will thinke fo too : & in this hope I leaue you.

THE

THE EPISTLE

OF

S. HIEROME

TO RVFFINVS.

T HOVGH I knew before by the teſtimony of holy Writ, that God beſtowes
more then is deſired at his handes, yea &
that he graunts ſuch thinges, *as neyther the
eye hath ſeene, nor the eare hath heard, nor
haue aſcended into the hart of Man:* yet now,
moſt deare *Ruſſinus,* I haue found by experience in myne owne perſon, that this is
true. For I, who thought that my greateſt ambition was ſufficiently to be ſatisfyed, if we might counterfeit a kind of preſence to one an other, by meanes of letters; do now vnderſtād
that you are entring deep into the moſt ſecret parts of Egypt,
and that you are viſiting the Quires of Monkes and making a
kind of progreſſe, to ſee that heauenly family which liues on
earth. O that our Lord Ieſus, would now ſuddenly grant me
ſuch a kind of tranſport of my ſelfe, as *Philippe* made to the Eunuch, or of *Abacuke* to *Daniel!* How would I euen claſp in
your necke with ſtraight imbracements! How would I euen
print a kiſſe vpon that mouth of yours, which either erred or
was in the right, togeather with me: But becauſe I leſſe deſerue to go ſo to you, then you do to come to me, and that this
poore body of myne (which when it was at the beſt, is but
weake) hath beene lately euen broken in pieces with conti-

A 3

nuall

nuall ficknefse.; I haue fent this meffenger of my mind to meet
you, which tying you vp faft in a knot of loue, may bring you
hither to my felfe. The felicity of this vnexpected ioy, was
brought me firft by our brother *Heliodorus* . I belieued not that
to be certaine, which I defired it might be fo; both becaufe he
had it but by the relation of another, and efpecially becaufe
the ftrangenes of the thing depriued me of power to giue it
credit . But then (whileft my mind was in fufpence through
the vncertainty whether I fhould haue my wifh or no) a certaine Monke of *Alexandria*, who had beene fent long before,
through the pious deuotion of that people, to thofe Confef-
fours of *Egypt*, who already in their defire were Martyrs, inclined me greatly to belieue it . Yet I confeffe I was ftill in a
kind of wauering: though he being ignorant both of your coūtry and of your name, did euen thereby make the matter more
probable; for that in other circumftances he affirmed the felfe
fame thinges, which already had beene fayd by another . At
length the truth broke out with a downe waight . For the frequent multitude of trauailers related to vs, both that *Ruffinus*
had been at *Nitria*, and was paffed on to the Bleffed *Macharius:*
and then I gaue full way to my beliefe, and then indeed I har-
tily grieued to fee my felfe a ficke man . And vnles my weaknes had beene fuch, that after a fort it tyed me vp in chaines;
neither had the heat of the hoteft part of Summer, nor the Sea
which is neuer certaine to fuch as faile, beene able to hinder
me from going towards you, with a holy kind of haft . Belieue
me Brother, that the Sea-faring man, who is toffed with tempeft, doth not fo earneftly looke towardes his Port; nor do the
thirfty fieldes fo defire fhowers of rayne; nor doth the paffionate Mother fitting on the fhoare, fo expect the arriuall of her
fonne, as I doe to imbrace you . When that fudden tempeft
fnatched me away from your fide; when that wicked feparation diftracted me, who was cleauing to you with the faft
knot of Charity; then did the gloomy ftorme hang ouer me;
then did the sky and fea rage bitterly..

At length whileft I was wandring in that vncertaine pe-
regrination, when *Tracia*, *Pontus*, and *Bithynia*, and the whole
Iourney ouer *Galatia*, and *Cappadocia*, and that Country of the
Cælicians

Galicians had euen confumed me with that fcorching heat; the
land of *Syria* occured to me, as a moſt fafe and faythfull hauen
after ſhipwrack. Where yet (hauing felt as many difeafes in my
perfon as can be conceiued) of my two eyes I loſt one. For the
fudden fury of a burning feauer fnatched away *Innocentius* ,
whom I accounted a part of my very hart . And now I only
enioy *Euagrius,* who is the one and only eye which I haue left;
to whofe labours otherwife , my continuall infirmity may be
accounted to ad a new heap of care. There was alfo with vs
Hylas the ferúant of holy *Melanius* , who by the purity of his
conuerfation , hath waſhed away the ſpot of ſlauery to which
he had been fubiect; and his death did agayne open the wound
which fcarce was skined before. But becaufe we are forbidden
by the Apoftles commandement to be afflicted for fuch as are
departed; and to the end that the exceffiue force of forrow
may be tempered by the arriuall of a ioyfull newes , I alfo declare it to you , to the end that , if you know it not, you may
know it , and that if you know it already, we may reioyce together at it .

　Your *Bonofus* , or rather myne , or (that I may fay more
truly) *Bonofus* who belongs to vs both , is now climing vp that
ladder , which *Iacob* faw in his fleepe. He carryes his Croffe ,
and neither is troubled with that which may fucced, nor with
that which is paft. He fowes in teares, that he may reape in ioy;
and accord ng to the miftery of *Moyfes* , *He hangs vp the ferpent in
the Defert.* Let all thofe falfe *Miracles,* which are founded in lyes,
whether they be written either in the Greek or Latin tongue,
giue place to this truth. For behould this young man, who was
brought vp with me in the liberall arts of this world , who had
plenty of eftat & honour, amongſt the men of his owne iácke;
hauing contemned the delight and comfort of his mother, his
fifters, and his brother, who was moſt dear to him, doth now
inhabit a certaine Iland which is haúted by nothing but ſhip-
wracks, and a fea roareing loud about it; (where the craggy
rockes , and bare ſtones , and euen filence it felfe giues terrour)
as if he were fome new kind of Inhabitant of Paradice. There
is no hufband man to be found, no Moncke , no nor yet doth
that little *Onefimus* (in whome you know he delighted dearely

as

as in a brother) affoard him any society in this fo vaſt ſolitudè
of his. There doth he all alone, (or rather not alone, but now
accompanyed with Chriſt) behould the glory of God, which,
euen the Apoſtls could not ſeę, but in the Deſert. He lookes not
indeed, vpon the towring Cittyes of this world; but he hath
giuen vp his name in the numbring of the new Citty : his body
is growne horrid with deformed ſackcloath ; but he will ſo, be
the better able to meet Chriſt our Lord in the cloudes . It is
true that he enioyes no delitious gardens there ; but yet he
drinkes of the very water of life, from the ſide of our Lord .
Place him before your eyes, moſt dear friend , and let your
whole mind , and cogitation, procure to make him preſent to
you . Then may you celebrat his victory, when you haue coir-
ſidered the labour of his combat .

The mad Sea is roaring round about the whole Iland,
and doth euen rebel againe , in regard it is broken backe , by
thoſe mountaines of wreathed rockes. The ground is not there
adorned with graſſe ; and there are no freſh fields ouerſhadow-
ed with delightfull groaues . Theſe abrupt rude hills contriue the place into a kind of hideous priſon ; where he, all ſe-
cûre (as being without any feare , and armed by the Apoſtle
from head to foot) is now hearkening to God, when he reades
ſpirituall things, and then ſpeaking to God when he is praying
to him ; and perhaps alſo he hath ſome viſion after the example
of *Iohn*, whileſt he is dwelling in the Iland . What plots can
you thinke the Diuell to be deuiſing now ? What ſnares can
you conceaue that he will be laying ? Will he perhaps (being
mindfull of his ancient fraude) giue him a temptation by hunger ? But already he hath his anſwere, *Man liues not by bread a-*
lone . Will he perhaps offer wealth or gloiy ? But then he ſhall
be tould, *That ſuch as deſire to be rich , fall into temptations and traps.*
And ; *All my glory is in Chriſt* . Will he take aduantage of his body , which is weakned by faſting, and which may be aſſalted
by ſome diſeaſe ; but he ſhall be beaten backe by this ſaying of
the Apoſtle : *When I am weake , then am I ſtrong* ; and *ſtrength is*
perfected in weaknes . Will he threaten death ? but he ſhall heare
Bonoſus ſay : *I deſire to be diſolued and to be with Chriſt*. Will he caſt
fyery , darts at him ? *Bonoſus* will receiue them vpon the *target of*
                                                                 fayth .

fayth. And that I may proceed no further, Satan will impugne him ; but Chriſt will defend him.

Thankes be to the, O Lord *Ieſus*, that I haue one in thy preſence, who may pray to the for me . Thou knoweſt (for to the all our thoughtes are knowne, who ſearcheſt the ſecret of our harts, and who ſaweſt thy Prophet ſhut vp in the ſea, euen in the belly of that huge beaſt) how *Bonoſus* and I, grew vp together from our tender infancy, till we were in the ffouriſhing prime of youth ; and how the ſame boſome of our nurſes, & the ſame imbracements of our foſter-fathers did carry vs vp and downe the houſe . And how, after we had ſtudyed, neer to thoſe half barbarours bankes of the Rhine, we liued vpon the ſame food, and paſſed our time in the ſame houſe ; and how I was the firſt of the two, who had a good deſire to ſerue thee . Remember I beſeech thee, how this great warryer of thyne, was once but a green ſouldier in my company . I haue the promiſe of thy Maieſty, *He who ſhall teach others, and not do thereafter, ſh all be accounted the leaſt in the kingdome of heauen ; but he who ſhall both teach, and do, ſhall be called the greateſt in the kiugdome of heauen* . Let him enioy the crowne of his vertue, and let him follow the lambe in his long whit robe, for the daily martyrdome which he vndergoes. *There are many manſions in the Fathers houſe; and one ſtarre differs in clarity from another* . Impart thou to me , that I may lift vp my head amongſt the feet of thy Saints ; that when I may haue had a good deſire, and he may haue performed the good worke, thou mayeſt pardon me becauſe I was not able to fulfill it, and thou mayeſt giue the reward to him , which he deſerues. Perhaps I haue produced my ſpeech into a greater length, then the breuity of an Epiſtle would permit ; and this is euer wont to happen, when I am to ſay any thing in praiſe of our *Bonoſus* . But (to the end I may returne to that, from which I had digreſſed) I beſeech you, that together with your ſight, your mind may not conſent to looſe a friend; who is long ſought, rarely found, & hardly kept . Let any man ſhine neuer ſo brightly in gold, and let his glittering plate be muſtered out in as great pompe as pleaſeth him; charity cannot be bought, nor can there be any price ſet vpon loue. That friedſhip which can euer fayle, was neuer true . Farewell in Chriſt

Saint

Saint Hierome to Asella.

IF I would imagine my selfe able to giue you such thankes as
you deserue, I should be deceiued. God is able to repay that
to your holy soule, which you haue merited at my hands; but
I, vnworthy man could neuer conceiue, or euen desire that
you should impart so great affectiō to me in Christ. And though
some hold me to be wicked, and euen ouerwhelmed with
crimes (and considering my sinnes towards God, euen these
crosses are too light;) yet you do wel, in that, measuring others
by you selfe, you esteem euen such to be good, as indeed are
wicked. For a dangerous thing it is, to pronounce iudgment
vpon the seruant of another: and it is not easily pardoned, if a
man speake ill of good men. The day will come, when together with my selfe, you will lament to see, that so many are
tormented in fire. I must be a slaunderous person, I false and
lasciuious, I a lyer, and a deceiuer by diabolicall art. But whether is it safer to haue deuised such things as these of innocent
persons, or not so much as to haue belieued them, of such as are
guilty? They were dayly kissing my hands; & yet, with teeth
of vipers, were detracting from me: with their tongues they
wery sory; but in their harts they reioyced. Our Lord saw it
and scorned them for it, and reserued mee his poore miserable
seruant, to be hereafter iudged together with them. One man
calumniated my gat and laughter; another detracted from me
by occasion of my countenance; another suspected some what
by my playnenes. I remayned with them vpon the point of
three years; I was often euen enuironed by a whole troupe of
virgins; I expounded holy Scriptures to many, the best I
could. This exercise bred frequence of conuersation, conuersation familiarity, and familiarity confidence. But yet, let thē
say what other thing they euer found in me, then might become a Christian? did I euer take any of their moneyes? did I
not despise al Presents, whether they were great, or smal? Was
any of their mettall euer found to gingle in my hand? Was my
speech indirect, or myne eye wanton? No other thing is obiected

iected to me but my Sexe, & euen not fo much as this was e-
uer obiected , but onely when *Paula* and *Melania* tooke their
Iourney to *Ierufalem* .

These men belieue the flaunderer, when he tels the lye;
but why do they not belieue him, when he denyes it? He is the
felfe fame man , he was . He now auowes me to be innocent,
whom formerly he made guilty ;and furely torments do rather
exact the confelfion of a truth , then good fellowfhip, & fport ;
fauing that men vfe more eafily to belieue that, which being
fayned , is gladly heard, or rather which is procured to be fayned . Before I was acquainted with the houfe of holy *Paula*, the
affections of the whole Citty fell vpon me , and I was almoft
generally efteemed worthy of the higheft place of Priefthood.
Damafus of Bleffed memory fpake of no body but me. I was fayd
to be holy, I was fayd to be humble, and eloquent . Did I enter into the houfe of any one who was counted immodeft? Did
gay cloathes, or bright gemmes , or paynted faces, or the ambi-
tious defire of gold , carry me away ? Was there no other Ma-
tron in all *Rome*, who could tame this vnruly mind of myne, but
one who was all lamenting, and fafting , and neglecting her
felfe euen to extremity, and who was almoft blind with teares,
and who imploring the mercy of God all night long, was often
taken in the manner by the next dayes funne ? Whofe fonges
were the pfalmes , whofe difcourfe was of the Ghofpel, whofe
delights were Chaftity , and whofe life was a continuall Faft?
Could no other creature pleafe me , but fhe whom I did neuer
fo much as fee at meat . But as foon as I began to efteem, to honour, and to reuerence her , for the merit of her chaftity, I was
inftantly depriued of all vertue. O enuy which firft doeft euer
feed vpon thy felfe! O craft of Satan, which euer is perfecuting
holy things! There were no other which made talke to the
whole Citty of *Rome*, but *Paula*, and *Melania* ; who contemning their fortunes, and forfaking all that which might challenge loue at their hands, did exalt the Croffe of our Lord, as
the enfigne of piety,

If they had frequented the Bathes , if they had made vfe of
oyntments, if they had wedded riches and widowhood together, as the matter both of lafciuioufnes & liberty, they might

B 2 ftill

ſtill haue bene called great Ladies,and Saints; but now , they being in ſackloath and aſhes, will needs haue the reputation of beauty , and deſcend into hel fyer , with faſting and vtter ne-glect of themſelues;belike, becauſe it was not lawfull for them to periſh in company , with applauſe of the people .

If they were Pagans who carped at this kind of life , or yet if they were Iewes , we ſhould haue ſome comfort in not pleaſing them, who are diſpleaſed with *Chriſt*. But now (O infamous crime!)ſome who carry the name of Chriſtiãs, laying aſide all care of their owne houſes , and neglecting the beame in their owne eyes , looke for motes in the eyes of others. With their teeth they teare the holy vowe of chaſtity ; and eſteeme it to be a remedy for their owne fault, if there be not a Saint in the world, if all men be ſubiect to their detraction, if there be a multitude of ſuch as ſinne , and a troupe of ſuch as periſh .

Thou takeſt pleaſure to bathe daily; another houlds ſuch kind of cleanlines to be meer filth. Thou feedeſt vpõ pheaſants, till thou doeſt euen regorge againe, & thinkeſt thy ſelfe a great man , when thou haſt eaten vp ſome dainty foule ; but I ſtuffe my body with beanes . Thou art delighted in great companies of people , who laugh loud ; and I take guſt in *Paula*, and *Me-lania* mourning. Thou coueteſt the goods of others;theſe con-temne their owne . Thou art pleaſed with drinking wine dreſ-ſed with honey; & they find more ſauour in cold water. Thou accounteſt thy ſelfe to looſe whatſoeuer thou poſſeſſeſt not, thou eateſt not, thou deuoureſt not, for the preſent; but they deſire future things, and belieue that to be true which is writ-ten. Say they do it fooliſhly & idly,as belieuing the reſurrectiõ of bodies; what haſt thou to do with that ? for to vs, on the other ſide is thy life diſpleaſant . Much good may it do thee with thy fatnes; but I had rather be leane and pale . Thou hol-deſt ſuch people to be miſerable; and we eſteem thee to be ſo much more . We are euen with one another, and either of vs thinkes his fellow mad .

Theſe words my Lady *Aſella*, did I write to you in great haſt , both with greif & teares, euen when I was taking ſhip; and I giue thankes to my God, for being thought worthy by him , that the world ſhould hate me . But do you pray, that I

may

may retorne to *Ierusalem* out of *Babylon*, that *Nabuchodonozor* may not gouerne me, but *Iesus* the some of *Iosedech*. Let *Esdras* come, and carry me back into my country. Foole that I was, who would needs be singing the cáticle of our Lord, in a ſtrág land; and forſaking Mount *Sina*, would needs craue ſuccour of *Ægypt*. But I remembred not the Ghoſpell : becauſe he who went out of *Ierufalem*, fell inſtantly into the hand of theeues, and was ſtripped and wounded, and almoſt ſlayne. But though the Prieſt, and Leuite deſpiſed him ; yet that Samaritan is mercifull. To-whom when it was ſayd, *That he was a Samaritan, and that he had a deuill*, he denyed not himſelfe to be a Samaritan : becauſe looke what a Guardian or keeper is with vs, that is a *Samaritan* in the Hebrew tongue. Some there are who baſely giue me out to be a Witch. I who am no better them a ſeruant, am content to weare this badge of my fayth ; for the Iewes cald my Lord, Magitian. The Apoſtle was alſo ſayd to be a ſeducer. Let no temptation light on me other then humane How ſmall a part of aſliction haue I endured, who yet ſerue vnder the enſigne of the Croſſe ? They haue layd the infamy of falſe crimes vpon me ; but I know that a man may get to heauen, both with a good name and a bad. Salut *Paula* and *Euſtochium*, who are myne in *Chriſt*, whether the world will or no. Salut our mother *Albina*, and our ſiſter *Marcella*, as alſo *Marcellina*, and holy *Felicitas*. And tell them, that one day we all ſhall ſtand before the Tribunall of *Chriſt*, and there will it appeare what our intentions haue been here. Remember me, O you excellent patterne of chaſtity, and modeſty, and appeaſe the Sea waues, by you prayers.

To Marcella in praiſe of Aſella.

LET no man reprehend me, in that I either praiſe or reproue ſome in my Epiſtles: ſince by reprouing ſome wicked men, others of the ſame kind are taxed thereby ; and by celebrating the praiſes of the beſt, the affections of ſuch as be good, are ſtirred vp to vertue. Some three dayes ſince, I ſaid ſomewhat of *Lea* of bleſſed memory, and ſtraight I found my ſelfe

moued ; and my mind gaue me , that I was not to be silent, of a
Virgin ; since I had spoken of one, who was but in the second
degree of chastity. I will therefore briefly declare the life of
Asella, to whom yet I will pray you not to reade this Epistle ;
for she is troubled with hearing her owne praises ; but rather
vouchsafe to reade it to some others of the younger sort, that so
addressing theselues according to her exaple, they may know
they haue a conuersation to imitat, which carryes in it the very
rule of a perfect life. I omit to say, that before she was borne,
she had a blessing in her mothers wombe; and that the virgin
was shewed to her father, as he was taking his rest, in a violl of
criftall, and more pure then any looking glasse : That being ,
yet, as it were in the cradle of her infancy, and scarce exceeding the tenth yeare of her age, she was consecrated to the honour of her future happines. But let all this be ascribed to grace,
which did preced any labour of hers: though God, who fore-
knowes future things, did both sanctify *Ieremy* in the womb ,
and made *Iohn* exult in his mothers bowels, and seperated *Paul*
for the Ghospell of his sonne, before the creation of the world.
But I come to those things, which after the twelfth year of her
age she chose, she apprehended, she held fast, she begane, & she
perfected by her owne great labour.

Being shut vp within the straightes of one little Cell, she
enioyed the large liberty of a paradice. The same spot of groud
was the place both of her prayer, and of her sleepe. Fasting was
but a sport with her, and hunger was her food. And when not
the desire of feeding, but the necessity of nature would draw
her to eat, she would, by the taking of bread and salt and cold
water, rather stirre vp hunger, then take it downe . And I
had almost forgotten that which I should haue said before; whē
she first resolued to enter vpon this kind of life, she tooke that
ornament of gold which is vsually called a lampry (becaufe
the mettal being wrought into certaine wyers a chaine is made
in such a wreathing forme) and sould it, without the knowledge of her parents . And hauing so procured and bought a
courser coat, then she was able to obtayne of her mother, she
did suddenly, by that pious and fortunate begining of her spirituall negotiation , consecrat her selfe to our Lord, in such sort,
that

that al her kinred might quickly know, that no change of mind could be exorted from her, who by her cloathes had already renounced the world. But as I was begining to fay, she euer carryed her selfe with such referuation, and fo contained she her selfe within the priuate limits of her owne lodging, as that she would neuer put her selfe in publicke, nor know what belonged to the conuerfation of any man. And, which yet is more to be admired, she did more willingly loue then fee euen her owne fifter, though she were alfo a virgin. Somewhat she would worke with her owne handes, as knowing that it is written ; *They who will not labour, let them not eat.* She would euer be fpeaking to her *Spoufe*, either in the way of praying, or finging. To the *Shrines of Martyrs*, she would make fuch haft, that she would fcarce be feen. And as she would be euer glad, for that she had vndertaken this courfe of life, fo would she more vehemently exult in that she was vnknowne to all the world. Throughout the whole yeare, she would be fed with a continuall kind of faft, eating nothing till after two or three dayes. But then in Lent, she would hoife vp the fayles of her ship, and with a cheerfull countenaunce, would knit one weeke to another, by one onely meale. And (which perhaps will feeme impoffible to be belieued, though by the fauour of God it be poffible) she is now arriued in fuch fort to the fiftieth yeare of her age, as that she hath no payne in her ftomacke, & no torment in her bowels. Her lying vpon the ground, hath not wafted any of her limmes; her skinne growne rugged with her fackcloath, hath contracted no ill condition, or offenfiue fmell; but being healthfull in body, and yet more healthfull in mind, she holdes her retirednes to be delicioufnes, and in a fwelling and tempeftuous towne, she finds a wildernes of Moncks. But thefe things you know better then I, from whom I haue learned fome particulars, & whofe eyes, haue feen, that the knees of her holy body haue the hardnes of a camels skinne, through her frequent vfe of prayer. As for me, I declare that which I haue bene able to know. There is nothing more pleafing then her feuerity; nothing more fad then her fweetnes; nor more fweet, then her fadnes. So is palenes in her face, as that it difcouers her abftinence, but yet yeeldes no ayre of oftenta-
tion

tion. Her speech is silent , and her silence full of speech . Her
pace is nether suift , nor slow. He countenance is still the same.
A careles cleanlynes , and an incurious cloathing; and her dressing is, to be without being dressed . And by the onely temper
of her life , she hath deserued , that in a Citty full of pompe , of
lasciuiousnes , and of delicacy , wherein humility is a misery ,
both they who are good proclaime her , and the wicked dare
not detract from her . Let widowes and virgins imitate her, let
marryed woemē reuerence her, let such as are faulty feare her,
and let Priests looke with much respect vpon her .

Saint Hierome to Marcella, by occasion of the sicknes and true conuersion of Blesilla .

ABRAHAM was tempted concerning his sonne, and was
found so much the more faithfull : *Ioseph* was sould into
Ægypt, that he might feed his Father and his brethren : *Ezechias*
was frighted by the sight of death at hand, that so pouring himselfe forth in teares, his life might be prolonged for fifteen years:
The Apostle *Peter* was shaken in the Passion of our Lord , that
weeping bitterly he might heare those wordes , *Feed my sheepe*:
Paul , that rauening wolfe , and who withall grew to be a second *Beniamin* , was blinded in an extasis , that so he might so
afterwards; & being compassed in by a sudden horrour of darkenes, he called vpon God, whom he had persecuted long as
man . And so now, O *Marcella*, we haue seem our *Blesilla* boyle
vp for the space of almost thirty dayes in a burning feauer , to
the end that she might know , that the *Regalo* of that body, was
to be reiected, which soon after was to be fed vpon by worms ,
Our Lord *Iesus* came also to her , and touched her hand, and
behould she rises vp, and doth him seruice. She had some little
tincture of negligence, & being tyed vp in the swathing bads
of riches , she lay dead in the sepulchre of this world. But *Iesus*
groaned deepely , and cryed out in spirit saying, *Come forth Blesilla* . As soon as she was called she rose , and being come forth ,
she eates with our Lord . Let the Iewes threaten and swel, let
them seeke to kill her , who is raised vp to life , and let the A-
                                                                    postle

poftles onely reioyce at it. She knowes that fhe owes him her
life, who reftored it to her. She knowes that fhe now imbra-
ces his feet, of whofe iudgment fhe formerly was affrayd. Her
body lay euen almoft without life, and approaching death did
euen shake her panting limmes. Where were then the fuccours
of her friends? Where were thofe words which vfe to be more
vayne, then any fmoke? She ows nothing to thee, O vngratefull kinred of flefh and blood ; fhe who is dead to the world,
& who is reuiued to Chrift. Let him who is a Chriftia reioyce,
and he who is offended at this, declares himfelfe not to be a
Chriftian. The widow, who is free from the tye of marriage,
hath no more to do, but to perfeuer. But you will fay, that
fome will be fcandalized at her browne coat. Let them he fca-
dalized alfo at *Iohn*, the whome there was none greater amogft
the fonnes of men, who being called an Angel, baptized our
Lord himfelfe, and was clad with a camels skinne, and was
girt in, by a girdle of haire. If meane fare difpleafe them, there
is nothing meaner then locufts. Nay let Chriftian eyes be fca-
dalized rather at thefe woemen, who paint themfelues with
red, and whofe plaftered faces being deformed euen with extreme whitenes, make them like Idolls: from whome it before they be aware, any drop of teares breake out, it makes a
furrow in their cheeks: whome euen the number of their years
cannot teach them how old they are; for they ftrew their
crowne with ftrange haire, and they dreffe vp their paft youth
in wrinckles of their prefent age; and in fine, though they treble with being fo old, yet in prefence of whole troupes of their
grand-children, they will ftill be tricked vp, like delicate and
tender maides. Let a Chriftian woman be afhamed, if fhe
would compell Nature to make her handfome, *if fhe fullfill the*
care of her flesh towardes concupifcence : for they who reft in that, can-
not pleafe Chrift, as the Apoftle fayth. Our widow formerly
would be dreffing her felfe with a ftiffe kind of care, & would
be inqniring all day long of the glaffe, what it might be that
fhe wanted. And now fhe confidently fayth : *But all we, contem-*
plating the glory of our Lord with a cleare face, are transformed into the
fame image, from glory to glory, as by the fpirit of our Lord. Then did
her maides marfhall her haire in order, and the crowne of her

C   head

head, which had made no fault, was imprifoned by certaine Coronets, crifped with irons. But now her head is fo much neglected, as to know that it carryes inough, if it be but vay-led. In thofe dayes, the very foftnes of downe would feeme hard, and fhe would fcarce be content to ly in beds when they were euen built vp to giue her eafe; but now fh: ryfes vp full of haft to pray, and with her fhrill voice fnatching the *Allelluia* out of the others mouthes, her felfe is the firft to prayfe her Lord. Her knees are bent vpon the bare ground, and that face which formerly had beene defiled and daub'd with painting, is now often wafhed with teares. After prayers they rattle out the Pfalmes, and her very necke, her weake hammes, and her eyes pointing towardes fleep, can hardly yet (through the ex-ceffiue ardour of her mind) obtaine leaue that they may take reft. Her browne coat is leaft fowled, when fhe lyes vpon the ground. She is poorely fhod, and the price of her former guil-ded fhooes, is now beftowed vpon the poore. Her girdle is not now diftinguifhed by ftuddes of gold and precious ftone; but it is of woll, & as fimple & poore as can be made, & fuch as indeed may rather tye in her cloathes, then gird her body. If the ferpent enuy this purpofe of hers, and with faire fpeech perfwade her to eat againe of the forbidden Tree; let him be ftricken with an *Anathema* ; & let it be fayd to him, as he is dy-ing in his owne duft : *Goe backe Sathan,* which by interpretati-on is *aduerfary.* For an *aduerfary* he is of Chrift, and he is an Antichrift, who is difpleafed with the Precepts of Chrift. Tell me, I pray you, what fuch thing euer did we, as the Apoftles did ; vnder the colour whereof men fhould be fcandalized at vs? They forfooke an old Father, *and their nets and ships.* The Publican ryfes from the cuftome-houfe, and followes our Sa-uiour ; & one of the Difciples being defirous to returne home, and declare his purpofe to his friends, is forbidden by the com-mandment of his Mafter. Euen buriall not giuen to one by his Father; and it is a kind of piety to want fuch piety, for the loue of our Lord. Becaufe we weare no filke, we are efteemed to be Monkes; becaufe we will not be drunke, nor diffolue our fel-ues in loud laughter, we are called feuer and fad people. If our coat be not faire and white, we are prefently encountred

with

with the by-word of being *Impaſtours* and *Greekes*: Let them ſlander vs with more ſly cunning if they will, and carry vp & downe their fat-backes with their full panches . Our *Bleſilla* ſhall laugh at them, nor will ſhe be ſory to heare the reproaches of theſe croaking frogs, when her Lord himſelfe was called *Belzebub* .

Saint Hierome to Pope Damaſus

BECAVSE the Eaſtern part of the world being battered by the auncient fury of that people, doth teare euen into fitars the ſeameles coat of our Lord , which is wouen from the top to the bottome : and ſince the foxes do root vp the vine of Chriſt; ſo that in the mideſt of thoſe leaking lakes , which hold no water, it is hard to find where that ſealed fountaine, & that ſhut garden is ; therefore haue I thought fit to conſult with the chayre of *Peter*, and that ſayth which was prayſed by the Apoſtles mouth, demãding food from thence for my ſoule, where formerly I had taken the baptiſmal habit of Chriſt. For neither could the vaſtity of that watry element , nor the interpoſition of thoſe long tracts of earth, prohibit me frõ inquiring after that precious pearle, *Whereſoeuer the body is , thither will the Eagles reſort*. The patrimony hauing beene waſted by the prodigal ſon, the inheritance of the Father is only preſerued incorrupt by you . There doth the earth which is a fruitfull ſoyle, returne our Lords ſeed with purity, & that a hundred ſould ; but here the corne being ouerwrought by the furrow, degenerates into cockle and wild oates . Now doth the Sunne of iuſtice ryſe vp in the Weſt , and that *Lucifer* who is fallen , doth place his throne aboue the ſtarres in the Eaſt: *You are the light of the world* ; *you, the ſalt of the earth* ; *you , the golden and ſiluer veſſels* , and here the veſſels are of earth, or wood, which do but expect the iron rod, and eternall fire . Therefore though your greatnes fright me, yet doth your humanity inuit me . I deſire a ſacrifice of ſaluation from the Prieſt, and the ſuccour which belongs to a ſheep from his paſtour . Let Enuy auoyd, let the Ambition of that high Roman ſeat recede, I am ſpeaking with the ſucceſſor of a Fiſherman, and a diſciple of the Croſſe . I, who in the firſt

C 2   place

place follow none but Christ, am ioyned by communion to your *Beatitude*, that is, to the chayre of *Peter*. *Vpon that rocke doe I know that the* Church *is built*. Whosoeuer *eateth the Lambe out of this house, is a profane person*. Whosoeuer *is not in the* Arke *of* Noe, *shall perish, when the flood growes to be in height*. And becaule, for my grieuous finnes, I haue betaken my selfe to that desert, which deuides *Syria* from the barbarous confines on the other side, nor can I alwayes be crauing the *Holy of our Lord* from your Sanctity, being so hugely distant from you in place: therfore here do I follow the Confessours of *Egypt* your colleagues and like some poore barke, I lye vnder the lee of those great shippes. I know not *Vitalis*, I reiect *Meletius*, I haue nothing to do with *Paulnus*: VVhosoeuer *doth not gather with you, scatters, that is to say, he who is not of* Christ, *is of Antichrist*. But now (O excessiue cause of griefe!) after the *Nicen fayth*, after the decree of *Alexandria* against three *Hypostasies*, wherein the Westerne Church did also ioyne, there is a new name exacted of me, being a man of *Rome*, by the Prelate of the *Arians*, and the *Campensians*. What Apostles I pray you were they, who declared this? What new Maister of the *Gentiles*, which was *Paul*, taught this? Let vs enquire what they may be thought to vnderstad, by three *Hypostasies* They say, they do but meane *three subsisting persons*. We answere that we also belieue iust so. The sense will not serue their turne, but they must haue the very name, because I know not what poison lyeth hid in the sillables of those wordes. And we cry out, that if any man will not confesse *three Hypostasies*, or *Enypostata*, that is, *three subsisting persons*, let him be accursed. And becaule we do not learne words, we are iudged to be Heretikes. But if any man vnderstanding *Hypostasis* to be *Vsia* or *Substance*, shall say that there is any more then one *Hypostasis* in three persons, he is an aliene from Christ; and vnder this confession we are marked togeather with you, by the burning iron of the same cōmuniō. Determine therfore, if it please you; I will not feare to say there are three *Hypostasis* if you bid me. But yet if you bid me, then let a new fayth be found out, different from that of *Nice*, and let vs, who are Orthodoxall, confesse our Fayth in such wordes, as the *Arians* vse. All the schooles of learning know no other signification

of

of *Hypostasis*, but *Substance*. And now who is he, who with a sacrilegious mouth, will speake of three *Substances in God*? The nature of God is *one*, and only *one*, and it is most truly fo ; for that which subfifts of it felfe, hath not his being from any other, but it is his owne. Other thinges which are created though they may feeme to be, yet indeed they are not; for fometymes they were not, and that may againe not be, which once was not: God only who is eternall, that is, who hath no beginning, doth properly enioy the name of *Effence*. And therfore he fayd thus out of the bush to *Moyfes*: *I am he that I am*. And againe: *He that is fent me*. It is true that then, there were Angels, Heauen, Earth, and Sea: and how then can God challenge the name of *Effence* as proper to himfelfe, which is common to others? But becaufe that only Nature is perfect, & one Deity doth fubfift in three perfons, which truly is, and is *one Nature*; whofoeuer he be, that will fay they are three, namely three *Hypoftafies*, that is, three *Subftances*, doth endeauour vnder a colour of piety, to affirme that God hath three *Natures*. And if that be fo, why are we feparated by Church-walls frō *Arius*, who are vnited to him in falfe beliefe? let then *Vrficinus* be ioyned to your Holynes, and let *Auxentius* keep fociety with *Ambrofe*. Let this be farre from the *Roman fayth*, let not the harts of Religious people fucke in fo great a facriledge as this. Let it fuffice for vs to affirme *one fubftance*, and *three fubfisting perfons*, perfect, equall, aud coeternall. Let there be, if it pleafe you, no more talke of three *Hypoftafies*, but let vs fticke to one : It is fufpitious when words are differing, the fenfe being the fame. Let the aforefayd beliefe fuffice for vs ; or if you thinke it fit, that we fpeake of three *Hypoftafies* with their interpretations, we will not refufe to do it. But belieue me, there lyes poyfon vnder the hony, and Sathan hath transfigured himfelfe into an Angell of light. They interpret the word *Hypoftafis* well, and yet when I profeffe my felfe to belieue it as they expound it, I am held an Heretike for my labour. But why do they hold faft that one word with fuch anxiety? Why ly they hid vnder that ambiguous manner of fpeech? If they belieue it as they expound it, I do not condemne that which they imbrace. If I belieue fo as they pretend themfelues to hold, let them giue me

leaue

leaue to expreſſe myne owne ſenſe, in myne owne wordes.
And therefore I beſeech your Holyneſſe by Chriſt crucifyed,
by the ſaluation of the world, by the ſelfe-ſubſtantiall Trinity,
that by your letters you will giue me authority, either to reiect
or to vſe the name of ſeuerall *Hypoſtaſies*. And leaſt the retyred-
nes of this place where I liue, ſhould diſappoint you, voutch-
ſafe to ſend to me by the letter-carryers, & direct yours for me
to *Euagrius* the Prieſt, whome you know well; and ſignify to
me withall, with whome you would haue me keep communion at *Antioche*. For the *Campenſians* being coupled with the
Heretikes of *Tharſis*, affect nothing els, but that being vpheld
by the authority of communicating with you, they may pu-
bliſh three *Hypoſtaſies*, in the auncient ſenſe.

Saint Hierome to Pope Damaſus.

THE importunate woman in the Ghoſpell, deſerued to
be heard at laſt. And one friend obtained bread of another, though himſelfe and his ſeruants had ſhut vp their doores,
and though it were midnight. God himſelfe whome no power
can ouercome, was conquered by the prayers of a Publican.
The citty of *Niniue* which was to periſh by ſinne, ſtood on foot
by tears. But why do I fetch the matter vp ſo high? To the end
that you being great, may looke on me who am little; that you
being a rich ſhepheard, may not contemne me, who am a ſicke
weake ſheep. Chriſt conducted the murdering Theef from the
croſſe into Paradiſe: and leaſt any man ſhould thinke that this
conuerſion was too late, he made that puniſhment of his mur-
der, to be a Martyrdome to him. Chriſt, I ſay, doth ioyfully
imbrace the prodigall Sonne, when he returnes; and leauing
ninety nine ſheep, that ſingle poore one which remayned, is
brought home vpō the ſhoulder of the good ſhepheard. *Paul* of a
perſecuter is made a preacher; his carnall eyes are blinded, that
he may ſee the better with his mind; & he who carryed the ſeruants of *Chriſt* bound before the Counſell of the Iews, did glory afterward, to ſee himſelfe in bonds for *Chriſt*. I therfore, who
as I wrote before, receiued the garment of *Chriſt* in the Citty o

Rome , do now remayne in the barbarous confines of _Syria_. And leaſt you ſhould thinke, that I do it in obedience to the ſentēce of ſome other , my ſelfe was obliged by my ſelfe , to vnderge this taske, which I had deſerued. But as the heathen Poets ſay, _he changes the Clyme not his mind_ , _who paſſes ouer the Seas_ . So hath my inceſſant enemy followed me , as that now I endure greater aſſalts in the wildernes . For here , the rage of the _Arians_ being vpheld by the pillars of the world, doth rage. Here, doth the Church , deuided into three parts , vſe al diligence to draw me to it; the auncient authority of the troupes of Monkes which are round about me , riſes vp againſt me . But I , in the meane time cry out, that if any man be in coniunction with the chaire of _Peter_ , that man is myne. _Meletius_, _Vitalis_, and _Paulinus_ ſay that they adhere to you. I might belieue it, if onely any one of them did affirme it; but now , either all of them lye, or two at leaſt . Therefore I beſeech your _Holynes_ , by the Croſſe our Lord, by the glory of the world which was crucified , & by the Paſſion of Chriſt, that as you follow the Apoſtls in honour, ſo yow wil follow them alſo in merit . So may you ſit in that Throne , to iudge with thoſe twelue ; ſo may there be another , who may gird you, like _Peter_, when you are old ; ſo may you become a Citizen of heauen with _Paul_; as you ſhal ſignify to me by your letters, with whome I ought to communicate in _Syria_. Do not deſpiſe that ſoule, for which _Chriſt_ dyed .

_S_ aint _Hierome_ to a Mother and a daughter, by way of caution againſt keeping ill company .

ACertaine Brother coming out of Fráce relates to me, that he hath a Siſter , who is a virgin , and a Mother who is a widow, and that they liue in ſeuerall habitations , and yet in the ſame Citty ; & that, either becauſe their dwellings are ſolitary, or els for the conſeruing of their little meanes , they had ſeuerally taken certaine Prieſts , to gouerne them ; ſo that they were ioyned to others, with leſſe reputation, thē they had bene ſeperated between themſelues. And (when I had ſighed deeply, and ſignifyed much more by ſilence, then I could haue

done

done by fpeech,) I befeech you faith he, reproue them by your letters, and draw them backe to good agreement, that the mother may acknowledge the daughter, & the daughter the mother. I afwered him thus; you put me indeed to a faire taske; that I being a ftranger fhould reconcile them, when a fonne and a brother could not do it . As if I fat in fome Epifcopall chaire, and were not fhut vp in a little Cell; and being farre remote from troups of men, do not either lament my fins paft, or procure to auoid fuch as are at hand : befides the ill fauourednes of it for a man to he hid in body, and to wander ouer the whole world, with his tongue. Then fayd he, you are to fearfull. And where is now that courage, wherewith you haue fo wittily touched the whole world, for you haue bene a kind of *Lucilius*. This, faid I, is that which puts me of, and fuffers me not fo much as to opē my mouth. For fince by reprouing the faults of others, my felfe am growne faulty, and according to the vulgar faying, *VVhen euery man doth fo wrangle, and contradict me, me thinkes I do neither heare nor touch,* and euen the very wals beat reproaches backe vpon me, & drinkers of wine make fonges of me, I being conftrayned by fad experience, haue learned to hold my peace, efteeming it better *to place a guard before my mouth, & a ftrong doore before my lippes, then that my hart fhould decline towards the wordes of malice* for feare leaft whileft I taxe vice in others my felfe fhould fall into the vice of detraction. When I had faid thus much, he anfwered me after this manner . To fay truth, is not to detract; nor doth a priuate reprehenfion amount to make a generall doctrine; fince they are few, or none who fal within the compaffe of that fault. I befech you therefore not to permit me to be come in vayne, who haue bene vexed by fo long a iourney . For our Lord knowes, that next after my vifiting thefe holy places, my chief occafion was, that by meanes of your letters, I might cure both my Sifter and my mother . Well then faid I, I am content to do as you bid me; for both my letters ferue for the other fide of the Sea, & that fpeech which is dictated vpon fo particular an occafion as this, will hardly find any other whom it may offend . But as for you, I befeech you that the matter may be carryed with great fecret, that when you fhall haue taken it with you by way of proui-

fion

fion, if my aduice be harkened to, we may reioyce together ;
but if it be contemned (which I rather feare) yet I may haue
loft but my words, and you the labour of a long Iourney .

Firſt O you mother and daughter, I deſire you may know ,
that I write not therfore to you, as ſuſpecting any thing ill of
you; but I deſire your agreement, leaſt others ſhould grow
to haue ſuſpition. For otherwiſe, if I thought you had bene
ioyned together by any tye of ſinne ;(which God forbid,) I
ſhould neuer haue written, as knowing that I were talking to
deafe perſons. In the ſecond place, I would deſire, that if I ſhal
write any thing which may be of the ſharper ſort, you will not
thinke it to ſauour ſo much of my auſtere condition, as of the diſeaſe in hand. Rotten fleſh muſt be cured with a burning iron ,
and the poyſon of ſerpents, driuen away with an Antidot. And
that which giueth much payne, muſt be expelled by a greater .
In the laſt place this I ſay, that although the conſcience may
haue no wound in it of any crime, yet fame ſuffers ignominy
thereby. Mother and daughter are names of a Religious kind of
tendernes, they are wordes of obſeruance, they are bondes of
nature, and they are of the higheſt leagues vnder God. It deſerues no prayſe if you loue; but it is extreme wickednes, if you
hate one another. Our Lord *Ieſus Chriſt* was ſubiect to his parents, he carryed veneration to his Mother, whoſe very Father
he was. He was obſeruant of his foſter-father, whom yet himſelfe had nouriſhed; and he remembred that he had beene carryed in the wombe of the one, and in the armes of the other.
Whereupon, when he was hanging on the Croſſe, he commē-
ded his Mother to his Diſciple, and he neuer forſooke that mother till his death.

But you O daughter (for now I forbeare to ſpeake to the
mother, whome perhaps either age, or weaknes, or deſire of
ſolitude may make excuſable) you, I ſay, O Daughter, can
you hold her houſe too ſtraight. You liued ten monethes ſhut
vp in her wombe, & can you not endure to liue one day with
her in one chamber? Are you not able to like, that ſhe ſhould
haue an eye vpon you? and doe you fly from ſuch a domeſticall
witneſſe as ſhe is, who knowes euery motion of your hart; as
ſhe who bare you, who brought you vp, and lead you on to be

of

of this age. If you be a Virgin, why mislike you to be diligently kept? If you be defiled, why doe you not marry in the sight
of the world? This is the second planche, or table, after ship-
wracke; let that which you haue ill begun, at least be tempered by this remedy. But yet neither do I say thus much, to the
end that after sinne I may take away the vse of Pennance, or
that she who hath begun ill, may perseuer to do ill; but becaufe
I despaire of any separation, after such coniunction. For o-
therwise, if you go to your mother, after you shall haue beene
subiect to that ruine, you may in her presence, more easily lament your selfe for that which you lost by being absent from
her. If yet you be entire, and haue not lost it, take care to keep
it. To what purpose are you now in that house, where it will
be neceffary for you, either to perish, or to fight continually,
that you may ouercome? What creature did euer sleep securely
neere a Viper, who though she do not bite, yet she will keep
him awake? It is a point of more safety not to be in danger of
perishing, then being in danger not to perish. In the one there
is tranquility, in the other there must be labour and skill : in
the former we ioy ; and in the later we do but escape. But perhaps you will answere: *My mother is of a harsh condition, she desirs*
worldly thinges, she loues riches, she knowes not what belonges to fa-
sting, she paintes her eyebrowes blacke, she takes care to be curiously dref-
sed, and hinders my purpose of chastity, and I cannot liue with such an
one. But first, if she were such as you pretend, you should haue
the greater merit, if you forsook not such an one as she. She
carryed you long in her wombe, she nursed you long, & with
a tender kind of sweetnes did endure the vntowardnes of your
infancy. She washed your fowle cloutes, and was often defiled with your filth. She sate by you when your were sicke ;
and did not only endure her owne incommodities, but yours
also. She brought you to this age, and she taught you how to
loue Christ our Lord. Let not her conuersation displeafe you,
who first did confecrate you, as a Virgin, to your spoufe.

But yet, if you cannot endure her, but will needs fly away
from her delicacies, and if (as we vse to fay) she be a kind of fecular mother; in that cafe you may haue other Virgins, you
will not want some holy quier, where chastity is kept. Why,
forfa-

forfaking your Mother, haue you taken a liking to one, who perhaps hath alfo forfaken his Mother, and his Sifter? She is of a hard condition : but this man forfooth, is fweet & kind. She is a chider, but he is therefore eafily appeafed. I aske whether you followed this man at the firft; or whether you found him afterward? For if you followed him at the firft; the reafon is plaine, why you forfooke your mother. If you found him afterward; you fhew plainly what it was, which you could not find in your Mothers houfe.

This is a sharp kind of griefe for me, which woundes me with myne owne fword. He who walkes fimply or plainly, walkes bouldly. I would faine hold my peace, if myne owne confcience did not giue remorce; and if now I did not reprehend myne owne fault, in the perfon of another, and if by the beame of myne owne eye, I faw not the mote which is in an others. Bu now, fince I am farre off among my brethren, and whileft, éioying their fociety, I live honeftly vnder witneffes of my conuerfation, and I fee, and am feene very feldome, it is a moft impudent thing, if you will not follow his modefty, whofe example you haue followed otherwife. Now if you fay: *Myne owne confcience is fufficient for me, I haue God for my iudge, who is the witneffe of my life; I care not for the talke of men.* Heare what the Apoftle writes : *Prouiding to do good thinges, not only before God, but alfo before all men.* If any man will detract from you, in regard that you are a Chriftian, or that you are a Virgin, let it not trouble you, though you haue forfaken your Mother, to the end that you may liue in fome Monaftery with Virgins. Such detraction will be a praife to you, as when feuerenes, and not too much loofenes is reproued in the Virgin of God. Such kind of cruelty is piety : for you preferre him before your Mother, whome you are commanded to preferre before your life it felf; and whome if she will alfo preferre, fhe wil acknowledge you both to be her daughter, and her fifter.

But what, is it fuch a crime to liue in fociety with a Holy man? You make a wry necke, and now you draw me into a kind of quarell : and fo, as that either I muft allow the thing which I like not; or vndergo the enuy of many. A holy man doth neuer feuer the daughter from the Mother; he refpects

them

them both, he carryes veneration to them both. Though the daughter be holy; yet if the Mother be a widow, she giues a good teftimony of chaftity. If that man of whome you know, be of equall age to your felfe, let him honour your Mother as his owne. If he be elder then you, let him loue you as his daughter, and make you fubiect to the difcipline o a Father. It becomes not the fame of either of you, that he fhould loue you better then your mother; leaft it may feem, that he choofes not fo much to loue you for other refpects, as becaufe you are younge. And all this I would fay, if you had not a brother of your owne, who is a Monke, or if you wanted other domefticall helpes. But now (O exceffiue caufe of griefe!) betweene a Mother, and a brother, a mother who is a widow, and a brother who is a Monke, how comes it to paffe, that a ftranger interpofes himfelfe? It were good for you, that you knew your felfe both to be a daughter, and a fifter : but if you cannot do both, at leaft let your brother pleafe you ; and if your brother be ill conditioned, she will be gentler, who bare you. Why do you waxe pale? Why are you fo much troubled? Why do you now grow to blufh ; and by your trembling lippes, declare the impatience of your hart? There is no loue, but only that of a wife, which outftrips the loue of a mother, and of a brother. I heare befides that you are walking vp and downe by houfes in the country, & fuch other places of delight, with your Allies and kindred, and fuch kind of people as that ; nor do I doubt, but that it is fome Cofen or Sifter, for whofe folace you are lead about like a Page after this new cut. For God forbid, that I should fufpect you to affect the conuerfation of men, howfoeuer they may be neer you, either in Neighbourhood, or blood.

I befeech you therefore, O Virgin, to anfwere me. Do you walke in this company of your friendes, either with your louer or without him? Without faile, how impudent foeuer you may be, you dare not produce him, before the eyes of fecular perfons. For if you should doe thus, all the neighbours would make fonges both of him, & you ; nay the world would point at you both, by fignes. Yea that very Sifter, or Ally, or kinfwoman, who to flatter you will often mention him in your

prefence,

preſence, as if they held him for a ſaint; when they ſhall find
themſelues out of your ſight, will ſcoffe at ſuch a prodigious
kind of husband. But now if you go alone (which I rather
thinke) amongſt that younger ſort of ſeruants, among woemen
who either are marryed, or to be marryed, among thoſe wanton maides, and thoſe ſpruſe and well apparelled young men;
if I ſay, you goe like a maid in meane apparell, euery young
beardles fellow, will be reaching forth his hand towards you,
and will be ſupporting you when you are weary, & then ſtrai-
ning his fingers, he will either tempt you, or be tempted by
you. You ſhall be at ſome banquet among men, and matrons;
you ſhall ſee them kiſſe, and taſt their meat, to one another; &
not without danger to your ſelfe, you ſhall admire the ſilke, &
cloath of gold which others were. In the banquet, you ſhall
alſo be compelled as it were, againſt your will, to eat fleſh. To
the end that you may be drawne to drinke wine, they will be
prayſing it, as a creature of God. That you may be induced to
frequent bathes, they wil ſpeake againſt being vncleanly. And
whenſoeuer you ſhall do any of thoſe things, which they perſwade you to, with any kind of vnwillingnes, they will pu-
bliſh you with a full mouth to be pure, and ſimple, a great Lady, and an ingenuous creature. The while, ſome man ſhalbe
ſinging to you, when you are at table, and whileſt he is running ouer his ditty with ſweet diuiſion, he wil be often caſting
an eye towards you who haue no guardian, not daring to look
vpon mens wiues. He will ſpeake to you by geſture, and that
which he dares not expreſſe by wordes, he will by ſignes. A-
mong ſo many ſhrewd incitements to pleaſure, euen mindes as
hard as iron are made ſoft towards luſt; which moues with
greater appetite in Virgins, who thinke that to be ſweeteſt,
which they know not. The fables of Heathen Poets relate,
that Mariners are driuen headlong vpon rockes by the ſinging
of *Syrens*; and that trees and beaſts were inchanted, and euen
hard flintes made to yeeld, vpon the hearing of *Orpheus* harpe.
Virginity is hardly kept, at feaſting tables. A ſmooth ſkinne,
ſhewes a ſordid mind. We haue read whileſt we were boyes
at Schoole, & we haue ſeene the ſtory grauen in braſſe, ſo wel
that it ſeemed euen to breath with life, of one who had no-

thing.

thing vpon him but skine and bone, and yet being fired with
vnlawfull loue, that plague did no sooner leaue him, then his
life. And what then will become of you, O mayd, who are
healthfull, delicate, fat, high complexioned, boyling vp in
meate, in wine, in bathes, amongst marryed woemen, and
young men? who though you should not doe that which will
be desired of you, may yet hold it to be an vgly kind of eui-
dence against your selfe, euen that you are desired. A lustfull
mind doth very eagerly hunt after dishonest thinges, and for
the very reason of being vnlawfull, it is suspected to be the
more delightfull. Euen a poore and blacke vest, if it be drawne
close, and haue no wrinkles in it, is an argument of a consen-
ting will; and if it be worne so long, as to be drawne after vp
on the ground, that she may seeme the taller; and if the coat
be left vnstitched of purpose, that somewhat may appeare, and
if any thing which is ill fauoured must be concealed, and that
which is handsome be disclosed. The buskin also of her that
walkes, if it be daintily shining and blacke, serues for a call
to young men, by the noise thereof. The little brests are pressed with strippes, and the wast is straitned with a wretched
girdle. The haire of the head fals downe either vpon the forehead, or about the eares. The little cloake fals off sometymes,
that she may shew her naked shoulders, and instantly she maks
hast to hid them, as if she would not haue that seene, which yet
she willingly discouered. And when going in publick, she hids
her very face with a pretence of modesty, she only shewes that
after the manner of the Stewes, which being shewed may delight the more.

But you will answere me thus, and say: How come you
to know me so well? And how, being seated so farre of, doe
you come to cast your eyes on me? The teares of your Brother,
& those intolerable deep sighes, which euery minute he was
sending forth, haue declared thus much. And I wish he had
rather fayned it, & had spoken more out of feare, then knowledge. But belieue me, a man lyes not, when he weepes. He
grieues that a yong man is preferred by you before himselfe,
yea and he, no delicate creature, nor one who treates himselfe
neatly; but a brawny fellow, who is but a slouen with all his
                                                    delicacy,

delicacy, and who ſhuts the purſe, and holdes the worke with his owne handes, and diſtributs the taskes, and gouernes the family, & buyes all thinges neceſſary in the market. He is the ſteward, and the Lord; and yet he preuents the inferiour ſeruants in their Offices: at whome the whole houſe rayles exclaming againſt him as detayning all that, which the Lady doth not allow & giue. Theſe ſeruants are a complaining kind of people, and how much ſoeuer you affoard, it is ſtill too little with them. For they conſider not out of what meanes, but how much is giuen them, and they comfort themſelues the beſt they they can, in all their griefe, by deeraction only. One cals him a Paraſite, another an Impoſtour, a third an Vnderminer of the eſtate, and a fourth will find ſome new name for him. They ſay he ſits at her beds ſide, that he fetches midwiues, when ſhe is ſicke, that he reaches her the baſon, warmes her cloathes, and foulds her ſwathing bandes. Men are apt to belieue the worſt, and whatſoeuer is deuiſed at home, turnes a broad into common fame. Nor muſt you wonder, if your maids and men giue out theſe thinges of you; when euen your mother and your Brother make the ſame complaint. Do therefore this, which I aduiſe and euen begge of you: be firſt reconciled to your Mother; and if that be not poſſible, to your Brother at leaſt; or if yet you will needes implacably deteſt theſe names of ſo great dearnes, at leaſt deuide your ſelfe from him, whome you are ſayd to haue preferred before them. If you cannot doe euen thus much, yet reſpect the honour of your friends, and if you cannot forſake your companion, yet make more honeſt vſe of him. Keep ſeuerall houſes, and doe not eat at the ſame table, leaſt men of ill tongues prooue to ſlaunder you with ſaying, that you lye both in one bed, when they ſee that you liue both in a houſe. You may, for your neceſſary occaſions, take what kind of ſolace you will, and yet want ſome part of this publicke infamy. Though yet you had need take heed, of that other ſpot, which according to the Prophet *Ieremy,* is not to be remoued by any *Niter,* nor by any *Diers* herbe.

When you haue a mind, that he ſhould ſee and viſit you, let it be in the preſence of witneſſes, friends, free ſeruantes, ſlaues. A good conſcience feares the eyes of none. Be without
feare

feare when he comes in, and fecure when he goes out . Eueri
ftill eyes, filent fpeech, and the habit of the whole body, doth
fometymes difcouer, either fecurity or feare . I befeech you o-
pen your eares, & hearken to the clamour of the whole Citty .

You haue loft your owne names , and now you are called
by the names of one another; for you are faid to be his, and he
yours . Thefe thinges do your Mother and your B rother heare
of you; and they are ready to receaue you, and befeech you to
deuid your felues betweene them two, that fo this particular
infamy of your coniunction, may redound to the prayfe of all .
Be you with your Mother , and let him be with your Brother.
More fafely may you loue the companion of your Brother , &
more honeftly may your Mother loue the friend of her fonne
then of her daughter ?

But if you will come to no reafon , if you will needes
contemne my counfell with a frowning brow , this letter fhal
proclaime thefe thinges to you with a loud voice . Why doe
you thus befiege the feruantes of another ? Why make you
him, who is the feruant of Chrift, to be a houfhould-feruant of
yours ? Looke vpon the people , and behould the faces of
euery one . He reads in the Church, and all men caft their eyes
on you ; fauing that you do euen glory in your infamy, as if
you had the priuiledge of marryed people . Nor are you any
longer now content with fecret infamy . You call faucy bouldnes by the name of liberty ; you are growne to haue the face of
an Harlot , and you know not how to blufh . Againe you will
be calling me maligne, againe fufpitious, and a liftner and pu-
blifher of tales . Am I fufpitious? am I malitioufly difpofed ?
who as I tould you in the beginning of this Epiftle, did therefore write, becaufe I did not fufpect. But it is you who are negligent , diffolute, and who defpife counfelle, and who being
fiue and twenty yeares ould, haue taken a young fellow with
little haire vpon his face ; and you haue wrapt him vp in your
armes, as if it were in netts . A rare inftructer indeed, who may
admonifh and fright you, euen with the feuerity of his countenance . And though in no age one be fafe from luft , yet when
the head is gray, a body is defended from publicke infamy .
The day will come, it will come (for tyme flides away whileft
you

you thinke not of it)when this dapper deare man of yours (becaufe woemen grow quickly old, and efpecially fuch as liue
in company with men) will find either a richer, or a younger
then you . Then will you repent your felfe of this courfe, and
you will be weary of your obftinacy; when you fhall haue loft
both your goods, and fame; and when that which was ill ioyned, fhall be well deuided. Vnles perhaps you be fecure, that
your loue getting the growth of fo long tyme, you fhall need
to feare no feparation .

And you alfo, O Mother, who by reafon of your age wil
be afrayd of no malediction, yet be not you fo bould as to fin.
Let your daughter rather be feparated from you, then you be
feuered from her. You haue a fonne, and a daughter, and a
fonne in law, yea and alfo a companion in houfe for your
daughter. Why do you go in queft after forraine comforts, and
ftirre vp that fire which now lyes vnder afhes? At leaft it is
more handfome for you to beare with the fault of your daughter,then to feeke any occafion through committing faults your
felfe. Let your fonne, who is a Monke be with you, as the ftay
of your widowhood, and the entertainement of your tender
loue. Why doe you feeke out a ftranger, efpecially to be in that
houfe, which is not able to hold your fonne, and daughter in
it? You are now of fuch age, as that you may haue grand-children by your daughter . Inuite them both to you, and let her
returne to you in company of her man, who went out alone.I
fayd her man, not her husband. Let no man flaunder me, I
meant but to expreffe the fexe; not the ftate of mariage . Or if
fhe blufh, and fhrinke, and conceaue that the houfe wherein
fhe was borne, is growne too little for her houfe; go you to her
houfe, though it be ftrait, it will more eafily be able to receaue
a Mother and a Brother, then a ftranger, whith whome fhe
cannot certainly remaine chaft in one houfe, vnleffe fhe haue
another chamber . Let there be in one habitation, two woemen & two men. But if that third party, that dry nurfe of your
old age, will not be gone, but will needs make a ftirre and dif-
quiet the houfe, let the Cart be drawne by two, or els let it be
drawne by three, your brother, and your fonne, and at leaft
you fhall thus allow your fonne both a fifter and a Mother . O-

E   there

thers will call thefe new commers, a fonne in law & a Father in law; but your fonne may call them a fofter-father & a Brother .

I haue dictated this with fpeed, at a fhort fitting vp, being defirous to fatisfy the entreaty of him who fought it, & by way of exercifing my felfe, after a fcholaftical maner . For he knocked at my doore the fame day in the morning, when he was to take his iourney : and I did it alfo to let my detracters fee, that I alfo can vtter whatfoeuer comes into my mouth . For which reafou I haue taken little out of Scripture , nor haue I wouen my difcourfe with the flowers thereof, as I vfe to do in my other workes . I dictated it *ex tempore*, & it flowed from me by the light of my little lampe, with fo great facility, that my tongue outftript the hand of the writers, and fo as that the volubility of my fpeech, did euen ouerwhelme the letters which ftole the words out of my mouth. This I haue fayd, to the end that he, who will not pardon my little wit, may excufe me in refpect of my little tyme .

Saint Hierome to Rufticus the Monke, to whome he prefcribes a forme of liuing.

NOTHING is more happy then a Chriftian, to whom the kingdome of heauen is promifed . Nothing is more laborious, then he who is daily in hazard of his life . Nothing is more ftrong, then he who ouercomes the diuell ; & nothing is more weake, then he who is ouercome by the flefh. We haue very many examples, on both fides . The theefe belieues vpon the Croffe, and inftantly deferues to heare ; *Verely I fay to thee, this day thou shalt be with me in Paradife*, Iudas, from the high dignity of *Apoftolate*, flips downe into the deep darke pit of deftruction ; and could not be drawen backe from betraying him, as a man, whom he knew to be the fonne of God, either by the familiarity of eating at the fame table, or by the dipping of that morfell of bread, or by the dearnes of the kiffe, which was giuen him . What is meaner, then that *Samaritan* woman , and yet not onely did the belieue, and after the hauing fix husbands found

found one Lord , and knew that Messias at the fountayne;whō
the people of the Iewes knew not, in the Temple ; but did also
become the authour of saluatiō to many;& whilst the Apostles
were buying meat , did refresh him who was hungry and sus-
tayne him who was weary . Who was wiser then *Saloman* , &
yet he was besotted by the loue of woemen ? Salt is good , and
no Sacrifice is receiued without the aspersion thereof . Where-
upō the Apostle prescribes thus . Let your speech be euer seasoned in grace , with salt . If that be infatuated , it is cast forth, &
so farre doth it loose the dignity of the name it had , that it is
not of any vse , so much as to a dunghill ; whereby yet when it
is good , the feildes of belieuers are seasoned , and the barren
soile of soules is made fruitfull .

These thinges I say , O my sonne *Rusticus,* to the end that
at the first entrance , I may teach you , that you haue begun to
do great things, & that your endeauours are high,and now that
you haue troden vpon the *incentiues* , or temptations , of the
sprouting and budding of youth , you must clyme vp to the
steps of perfect age. But the way whereby you go is slippery,&
you will not reape so much glory, by obtayning a victory , as
ignominy , if you be ouercome . My busines must not be now
to deriue the streame of my discourse, through the fieldes of the
vertues ; nor must I labour to shew you the beauty of seuerall
flowers , and what purity the Lillyes haue , what a bashfullnes
the Rose possesses, what the purple of Violets doth promise ,
in that kingdome ; and what we may expect from the repre-
sentation of those glittering gemmes . For already , by the fauour of God, you are holding the plough ; Already you haue
mounted vp the house with the Apostle *Peter,* who thirsting
after the Iewes,was satisfyed by the fayth of *Cornelius,* & killed
the hunger which was bred in him through their incredulity,
by the conuersion of the Gentils ; and by that foure cornered
vessell of the Ghospels which came downe from heauen to
earth, he was taught , and he learned that all kindes of men
might be saued. And againe that , which he saw in the forme
of a most pure white sheet , is carryed vp on high, and carryes
vp also with it the troupe of belieuers from earth to heauen ,
that the promise of our Lord may be fullfilled. *Blessed are the*

pure

pure of hart , for they shall ʃee God .

All the matter which I deʃire to inʃinuate to you is , that I
like an old ʃea man , being taught by hauing ʃuffered many
ʃhipwrackes , taking you now by the hand, may guide you ,
who are but a new paʃʃenger . That is to ʃay, that you may
know, vpon what ʃhoare the Pirate 'of chaʃtity lyes ; where
the *Charybdis* of auarice is,that root of al euill; where thoʃe barking Dogs of *Scylla* are ; wherof the Apoʃtle ʃpeakes thus : *Leaʃt
biting one another, you be conʃumed by one another* ; and how , when
we thinke our ʃelues ʃafe in the mideʃt of a calme, we are ʃom-
tymes ouerwhelmed by the vnʃtable quickeʃandes of vice ; &
finally that I may declare to you , what venemous beaʃts are
nouriʃhed in the deʃert of this world . They who ʃaile in the
red Sea (wherein it is to be wiʃhed by vs , that the true *Pharao*
with his army may be drowned) muʃt arriue through many
difficulties , and dangers , at the great Citty . Both ʃides of the
ʃhoare are inhabited by wild, yea and they moʃt cruell beaʃtes .
Men are there euer full of care , and being well armed, do alʃo
carry the prouiʃion with them of a whole yeare . All places are
full of hidden Rockes, and hard ʃhallowes, in ʃuch ʃort that the
skillfull Maʃter muʃt keep himʃelfe ʃtill vpon the top of the
Maʃt, and from thence conuey his directions,how the ʃhip is to
be conducted , and ʃteered . And it is a proʃperous voyage , if
after the labour of ʃix moneths , they come to the port of that
Citty, for the place where the Ocean begins to open it ʃelfe, &
and whereby a man doth 'ʃcarce arriue at the *Indies* in a whole
yeare, & to the riuer *Ganges*, which the Holy Ghoʃt doth mé-
tion by the name of *Phiʃon*, and which enuirons by the name of
Euelath, and is ʃayd to produce many kindes of odoriferous ʃpi-
ces out of that fountaine of Paradiʃe , where the Carbuncle &
the Emerand is gotten , and thoʃe other shining Gemmes , and
thoʃe Orient pearles, towardes which the ambition of great
Ladyes doth ʃo much aʃpire , and thoʃe mountaines of gold ,
which it is impoʃʃible for men to approach, by reaʃon of thoʃe
Dragons, and other furious Beaʃts of monʃtrous bignes , that in
fine we may ʃee, what kind of guard , couetouʃnes hath gotten
for it ʃelfe .

Butte what purpoʃe doe I ʃay all this ? It is cleare, that if
men

men, who negotiat the businesses of this world, do vndergo ſo
great labour, that they may obtayne riches, which both are not
certaine to be gotten, and are certaine either to leaue vs, or to
be loſt, and they are kept with hazard to the ſoule, and they are
alſo ſought through many dangers; what is that man to doe,
who negotiates the affaires of Chriſt, & who ſelling al things,
goes in purchaſe of that moſt pretious pearle ; and who, with
the ſubſtance of his whole eſtate buyes a field, wherein he may
find that treaſure, which neither the picklocke can fingar, nor
the violent theef carry away? I know I ſhall offend many, who
will interprete my generall diſcourſe againſt vice, to be a per-
ſonall reproach to themſelues. But in being angry with me,
they declare what kind of conſcience they haue, and they paſſe
therby a worſe iudgment vpon themſelues, then vpon me. For
I will name no man, nor (by that liberty which the ancient
Comedians were wont to take) will I ſet forth, and ſting any
indiuiduall perſon. It is the part of prudent men and woemen,
to hide their diſguſt, or rather to amend that which they find
to be amiſſe in themſelues ; and indeed rather to be offended
with themſelues, then me ; and not to caſt reproach vpon him,
who giues them good counſelle: who although he were ſubieƈt to the ſame crimes which poſſeſſe them, yet certenly he is
the better, in that he is not pleaſed with vice.

I heare you haue a deuout woman to your Mother, a widow of great age, who kept and brought you vp from infancy,
and that after you had paſſed your ſtudies in *France* (which
flouriſh greatly there) ſhe ſent you to *Rome*, not ſparing to ſpéd;
and enduring the abſence of her ſonne, through the hope of future good, that ſo you might ſeaſon the plenty, and elegancy
of ſpeech, which is gotten in *France*, by giuing it the graue maner of *Rome* ; and how ſhe did not vſe the ſpurre towardes you,
but the bridle ; which we haue alſo read of the moſt eloquent
men of *Greece*, who dryed vp that ſwelling *Aſyatike* humour
of ſpeech, with the ſalt of *Athens*, & did cut off with the hooke
thoſe luxuriant tops of the vines, that ſo the preſſes of eloquéce
might not be ſtuffed vp with the rancke leaues of wordes, but
with ſolid matter and ſenſe, as it were with the expreſſion of
the iuyce of the grape. See you reuerence her as your Mother;

loue

loue her as your nurfe, and exhibite veneration to her , as to a
Saint . And do not imitate the example of others, who forfake
their owne mothers,and defire to be with the mothers of other
folkes, whofe shame is publicke; fince they feeke fufpected co-
uerfations, when they haue cloaked them vnder the names
of fo pious affection . I know certaine woemen who are now
of yeares ripe inough , who take pleafure in young men, who
were bond-flaues freed , and who feeke fpirituall children, &
then fhortly after (all modefty being deftroyed in them) thofe
fayned names of Sonne and Mother, haue broken out into the
liberties of man and wife . Some others forfake their fifters
when they are virgins,and adhere to widowes who are ftrangers . There are fome who do euen hate their friends in blood,
and are not taken by any naturall affection , whofe impatience
difcouers of what mind they are ; and fo they are capable of no
excufe , and they breake through all inclofures of modefty, as
if they were but cobwebs . You fhall fee fome man well girt ,
in a courfe ruffet coate , and with a long beard , and yet can
neuer get himfelfe out of the company of woemen , but he
dwells with them in the fame houfe, and eates at the fame table, and is ferued by young maides, and enioyes all that which
belonges to mariage, fauing the only name . But it is not the
fault of Chriftian profeffion, if an Hypocrite be to blame , but
rather it is a confufion to the Gentils , when they fee, that
Chriftians are difpleafed with thofe thinges, which are vnplea-
fing to all good men .

But you, if you meane , not only to feeme to be a Monke,
haue care, I fay, not of your temporall eftate (by the renunci-
ation whereof you haue begun to be what now you are) but
of your foule . Let your meane cloathes, be the *index* of a fayre
mind in you . Let your courfe coate fhew your contempt of the
world ; but fo, as that your mind do not fwell , and that your
habite and your fpeech differ not from one an other . Let not
him feeke the *regalo* of Bathes, who defires to quench the heat
of flefh and blood, by the coolenes of fafting . Which fafts muft
be alfo moderate , leaft being exceffiue, they grow to weaken
the ftomacke; and fo requiring a more liberall refection , they
breake out into crudities, which are the breeders of luft. A
fparing,

sparing, and temperate dyet is profitable both to body & foule. Looke so vpon your Mother, as that by occasion thereof, you grow not to behould other woemen, whose countenance may sticke close to your hart; & so it may receaue an inward woud. Make account that the maides who serue her, are so many snares which are layd for you, becaufe how much more their condition is meane, so much more easy is the mischiefe. And *Iohn* the *Baptist* had a holy Mother, & he was the sonne of a Bishop, yet would he not be wonne, either by the loue of that Mother, or by the wealth of his Father, to liue in their house, to the danger of his Chastity. In the desert he liued, & hauing eyes which desired to behould Christ, he vouchsafed not to looke vpon any thing els. His garment was courfe, his girdle made of haire, his food locusts and wild hony; all which did carry proportion to vertue and chastity. The sonnes of the Prophets (whome we find in the old Testament to haue beene Monkes) did build themselues little houses neere the waters of *Iordan*, and forsaking the crowdes of Cittyes, did liue vpon meale, and wild herbes. As long as you are in your owne coutry, haue you a cell which may be a paradise to you. Gather sundry fruites of scripture, let those be your delights, and let them enioy your imbracements. If your eye, your foot, or your hand endanger you, throw it away. Spare none, that you may be good to your owne soule: *He* (sayth our Lord) *who lookes vpon a woman in the way of concupifcence, hath already beene vncleane with her in his hart*. Who will vasit himselfe to haue a chast hart? The starres are not cleane in the fight of our Lord, and how much lesse are men cleane, whose very life is a temptation? Woe be to vs, who as often as we haue impure desires, so often do we commit fornication. *My sword* (sayth he) *is inebriated in heauen;* and much more on earth, which breedes thornes, and brambles. That *Vessell of election*, whose mouth did found forth Christ, *doth macerate his body, and makes it subiect to seruitude,* and yet he findes, that the naturall heat of his flesh, doth so resist his mind, that he was forced to that, to which he had no mind; & to cry out, as suffering violence, and to say: *Miserable man that I am, who shall deliuer me from the body of this death?* And doe you thinke that you can passe through, without any fall, or woud,

                                                            vnles

vnles you keep your hart with a most straight custody, and vnlesse you say with our Sauiour: *My mother and my brethren, are they who do the will of my Father*. Such cruelty is piety. Or rather what c..n fauour of more piety, then that a holy Mother should keep her sonne holy? She also desires, that you may liue, and that she may not see you for a tyme, to the end that she may euer see you with Christ. *Anna* brought forth *Samuell*, not for her selfe, but for the Tabernacle. The sonnes of *Ionadab*, who drunke neither wine, nor any other thing which could inebriate, who dwelt in Tents, and had no other places to rest in, then where the night layd hold vpon them, are sayd in the Psalme to haue beene the first, who sustayned captiuity and were constrayned to enter into Citties by the Army of *Caldeans*, which ouerran *Iudea*. Let others consider what they will resolue, for euery man abounds in his owne sense. To me a towne is a prison, and a solitude is a Paradise. Why should we desire the frequent concourse of men in townes, who are already sayd to be single? *Moyses*, that he might gouerne the people of the Iewes, was instructed forty yeares in the Wildernes: from being a pastour of sheep, he grew to be a pastour of men. The Apostles from fishing the lake of *Geneseretb*, passed on to fish for men. Hauing then their Father, their net, and their ship, they followed our Lord; they left all thinges outright, they daily carryed their crosse, without so much as a sticke in their handes. This I haue sayd, that if you be tickled with desire of being ordained Priest, you first may learne what you are to teach, and may offer a reasonable sacrifice to Christ, that you esteeme not your selfe to be an old souldier, before you haue first carryed armes, and that you be not sooner a Master, then a scholler.

It belonges not to my poorenes, and small capacity to iudge of Priests, or to speake any thing of ill odour, concerning such as minister to the Churches. Let them hold their degree and ranke, to which you also arriue; that booke which I wrot to *Nepotianus*, will be able to teach you how you are to liue therein. We do now but consider as it were the cradle and coditions of that Monke, who being instructed from his youth in liberal sciences, hath layd the yoke of Christ vpon his neck.
And

And first it is to be considered, whether you were best liue in the Monastery alone, or in the company of others. For my part, I shall like well that you haue the society of holy men; that you do not teach your selfe, nor euer vpon that way without a guide, which you neuer knew; for so you may decline either to one hand or other, and be subiect to errour: and that you may not walke either faster, or slower, then is fit; least either running, you be weary, or loytering you be sleepy. In solitude pride creeps on apace; and if a man grow to fast a little, and then see none but himselfe, he will thinke he is some body; and forgetting both whence, and to what end he came, his hart wanders within, and his tongue without: *He iudges the seruant of an other*, against the Apostles mind; he reaches forth his hand as farre as gluttony bids him; he sleepes as much as he will; he feares no man; he doth what he lists; he thinkes al men to be his inferiours; and is oftener in Citties, then in his Cell. And yet when he finds himself among others of his owne profession, he takes vpon him to be so maydenly, as if the crowd of the streetes pressed him to death. But what? Do we reprehend a solitary life? No, for we haue often praysed it. But we desire that such men may go out from the discipline of Monasteries, as the hard lessons of the wildernes may not fright, they who haue giuen a long allowable testimony of their conuersation, who made themselues the lowest and least of all, and so grew to be the greatest; who haue not beene vanquished eyther by eating, or abstayning; who reioyce in pouerty; whose habite, speech, countenance, gate, is the very doctrine of piety; who know not how, after the custome of some fond people, to deuise certaine phantasticall battailes of Diuells, as if they were fighting against them; that so they may grow to be woundred at, by the ignorant vulgar, and make some commodity thereby. We saw lately, and we lamented, that the goods of *Crasus* were found vpon the death of a certen man, & that the almes of the Citty, which had beene gathered to the vse of the poore, was left by him to his posterity, and stocke. Then did the iron, which had lyen hide in the bottome, swimme vpon the top of the water; & the bitternes of Myrh was seene to be among the palmes. Nor is this strange: for he had such a companion,

F   panion,

companion , and such a Master, as made his riches grow out of
the hungar of poore men ; and the almes which had beene left
to miserable persons , he reserued for his owne misery . For at
last , their cry reached to heauen, and did so ouercome the most
patient eares of God, that an Angell *Nabal Carmelo* was sent ,
who sayd : *Thou foole this night shall they take thy soule from thee , &*
the goodes which thou hast prouided , whose shall they be? I would not
therefore, vpon the reasons which I haue declared already, that
you should dwell with your Mother ; & especially, least whe
she offers you delicate fare, you should either make her sad by
refusing it, or adde oyle to your owne fire, if you accept it. And
least also, among those many woemen, you should see somewhat by day, which you might thinke vpon by night . Let
your booke be neuer layd out of your handes, and from vnder
your eyes . Learne the Psalter, word for word . Pray without
intermission ; haue a watchfull mind , and such a one as may
not lye open to vaine thoughts . Let both your body and soule
striue towardes our Lord . Ouercome anger with patience ;
loue the knowledge of Scripture , and you will not loue the
vices of the flesh . Let not your mind attend to the variety of
perturbations, which, if they find a resting place in your hart ,
will grow to exercise dominion ouer you, and bring you at
last, to any grieuous sinne . Be still doing somewhat , that the
Diuell may euer find you imployed . If the Apostles , who
might haue liued vpon the Ghospell , laboured with their hads
least they should ouercharge others , and gaue almes to them,
from whome they might haue *reaped carnall thinges for their spi-*
rituall , why should not you prouid those thinges, which are fit
for your owne vse ? Either make some baskets of reedes , or els
of small wicker ; let the ground be raked , and the garden beds
diuided by some straight line ; into which as soone as you haue
cast the seed of Kitchin herbes, and other plants be set in order,
the springing waters may be brought, and you may sit by , as
if you did euen see the contents of those most excellent verses ,

The water on the brow of that steep passage playes .
VVhich falling on the pibles, a soft noyse doth rayse ,
And by those liuely springes, the Sunne-burnt fieldes allayes .
Let your vnfruitfull tree either be inoculated or ingraffed ,
that

thas fo in a fmall tyme, you may eat the fauoury fruit. of your
labours. Take order to make Bee-hiues, to which the Pro-
uerbes of *Salomon* fend you; and learne in thofe little bodies,
the order both of Monafticall, and Monarchicall difcipline.
Knit nets for taking of fifh, and write alfo fomewhat,that both
your body may get food, and your mind may be filled with
reading. The lafy perfon contents himfelfe with bare defires.
The Monafteries of *Egypt* haue this cuftome, that they admit
of no man, who will not vfe corporall labour; and that, not fo
much for the neceffity of corporall food, as for the good of the
foule. Let not your mind wander vp and downe in pernitious
cogitations, nor be like to fornicating *Hierufalem*, which partes
her feet to all corners. When I was a young man, and when
the deferts of folitude compaffed me in, I was not able to endure the *incentiues* of vice, and the ardour of my nature,which
though I tamed with often fafting, yet my mind would be
boyling vp in other thoughts. For the fubduing whereof I
committed my felfe to one, who of a Iew was become a Chriftian; and I made my felfe fubiect to his difcipline, to the end,
that after I had paffed by the fharpnes of *Quintilian*, the eafy
flowing of *Cicero*, the graue ftile of *Fronto*, and the fmoothnes
of *Pliny*, I might begin to ftudy the Alphabet, and meditate vp
on thefe hiffing, and broken-winded wordes. What labour it
coft me, what difficulty I endured, how often I defpaired,
how often I ceafed, and how I began againe with a defire and
ftrife to learne, both my confcience, who felt it, is the witnes,
and fo is theirs alfo, who liued with me. And I thanke our
Lord, that now I gather fweet fruit frō the bitter feed of thofe
ftudies.

I will tell you alfo of another thing,which I faw in *Egypt*
There was a young man,a *Grecian*, in the Monaftery,who neither by abftinence of diet, nor by any aboundance of the pains
he tooke, was able to extinguifh the flame of flefh and blood.
This man being thus in danger, the Father of the Monaftery
did preferue by this deuife. He commanded a certaine graue
perfon of the company, that he fhould haunt the other, with
brables and reproaches, in fuch fort,that after the iniury was
offered, that other might be the firft, who alfo made cōplaint.

The witnesses being called, did testify in his behalfe, who had done the wrong. The other would weep against that lye, but no man was found who would belieue the truth; only the Father would subtilly come in to his defence, that so the brother might not be swallowed vp by too excessiue griefe. What shal I say more? There passed a yeare after this manner. Vpon the ending whereof, the young man being interrogated about his former thoughts, whether yet they ̓gaue him any trouble? *Father*, sayth he, *I haue much adoe to liue, and should I haue a mind to fornication*? If this man had beene alone, by what meanes would he haue beene able to ouercome. The Philosophers of this world are wont to driue away an old loue, with a new, like one naile with another : which the seauen Persian Princes did to King *Assuerus*, that the concupiscence which he had towards Queen *Vasthi*, might be moderated by the loue of other Virgins. They cure one vice and sinne by another; but we conquer vice by the loue of vertue : *Decline* , sayth he, *from euill, & do good*; *Seeke peace and pursue it* . Vnles we hate euill, we cannot loue that which is good : or rather we must do good, that we may decline from euill; we must seeke peace, that we may fly from warre. Nor doth it suffice vs to seeke it, vnles we follow it with all endeauour, when it is found; for it is still flying from vs; but being obtayned, it exceeds all imagination, and God holdes his habitation therein according to that of the Prophet, *And his place is in peace* . And it is elegantly sayd, that *Peace is persecuted*, according to that of the Apostle, *Persecuting hospitality* . For we must not inuite men with a sleight and complementall kind of speech, and (as I may say) from the teeth outward, but we must hold them fast, with the whole affection of our mind, as persons who after a compendious manner come to make vs rich.

No art is learnt without a Master. Euen dumbe creatures, and the heardes of wild beasts, follow their leaders. The Bees haue their Princes: Cranes follow one of the flocke after a kind of learned manner. There is but one Emperour, and one supreme Iudge of a Prouince. *Rome* as soone as it was built, could not endure two brothers togeather, for Kinges; and so it was consecrated in paricide. *Esau* and *Iacob*, fought battailes

in

in the wombe of *Rebecca*. Euery Church hath one Biſhop, one Arch-Prieſt, and euery Eccleſiaſticall order relyes vpon his owne gouernours . In a Ship, there is one man who ſteeres; in a houſe, one Lord; and the VVord comes but from one perſon, how great ſoeuer the Army be .

And that I may not make my Reader weary by repetiti- ons, my whole ſpeech tends but to this, that I may teach you , that you are not to be committed to the gouernement of your owne wil! ; but that you muſt liue in the Monaſtery, vnder the diſcipline of one Father; and in the conuerſation of many, that you may learne humility of one, & patience of another : one man may teach you ſilence , another meeknes. Do not that which you deſire; eat that which you are bidden ; cloath your ſelfe with that which they offer; performe the taske, which is impoſed; be ſubiect to him, to whome you deſire not to be ſub- iect; come weary to your bed, ſo that you may ſleep euen as you go ; and as ſoone as you are ſleeping ſoundly, be compel- led to riſe. Recite the Pſalmes in your turne; wherein, not the ſweetnes of your voice, but the pious affection of your mind is ſought by the Apoſtle, ſaying : *I will ſing with the ſpirit ; and I will alſo ſing with the mind*, and, *ſinging to our Lord in your hartes* ; for he had heard that it was thus commanded, *ſing wiſely* . Serue your brethren ; waſh the feet of ſtrangers ; be ſilent when you ſuffer wrong; feare the chiefe Father of the Monaſtery, as you would do your Lord, and loue him as your Father. Belieue that whatſoeuer he commandes is good for you, and iudge not the direction of your Superiours ; you, whoſe office it is to o- bey, and to execute the orders which are giuen, according to *Moyſes: Hearken Iſrael, and hould thy peace* Hauing ſo great things to thinke of, you will not be at leaſure for idle thoughtes ; and when you paſſe from one thing to another, and when the later action followes the former , your mind will be imployed vpon that alone, which you are bound to do . I haue knowne ſome, who after they renounced the world, not in their deedes', but in their cloathes, and wordes, made yet no change in their cō- uerſation . Their eſtate or fortune was rather augmented, then diminiſhed . They vſed the miniſtery of the ſame ſeruantes, & kept the ſame ſtate at their table ; in a plate of glaſſe, or earth

　　　　they

they eat gold; & being hemmed in with swarmes of seruants,
they yet will needes take the name of being solitary vpon the.
They who are of the poorer sort, and of weake fortune, and
seeme to themselues to be shrewd Schollers, walke forth in publicke, like as many Pageants, that they may exercise their
snarling kind of eloquence. Others shrugging vp their shoulders, and chattering I know not what, within themselues, &
fixing their eyes firmely vpon the ground, meditate deeply
vpon certaine swelling words; and if they had but a cryer, you
would sweare the *Prefect* were passing by. There are some, who
by a certaine humour, to which they take, & by the immoderate fastes, which they vse, and by the wearynes of solitude, &
much reading (whilest day and night they make a noyse in
their owne eares) grow into such a kind of melancholy, that
they haue more need of *Hypocrates* his medecines, then my admonition. Many cannot forbeare their auncient artes, and ne-
gotiations; and changing the names of their broker, they still
exercise the same trafficke; not seeking food, and cloathing, according to the Apostles, but aspiring to improue their states,
more then worldly men. Heretofore this rage of sellers was
repressed by those *Ædiles*, whome the *Grecians* call ἀγορανόμυς,
nor was sinne so vnpunished then, as now it is. For now, vnder the title of Religion, vniust hudling gaynes are exercised,
and the honour of the name of Christian, is rather deceiuing,
then deceiued. And (which is a shame to be sayd; but there is
no remedy, that so at last we may blush at our owne shame)
when we stretch our handes forth publikly, we hide the gold
within our cloaths, and against the opinion of all men, we dye
rich with full bags, who liued in the estimatiō of being poore.

Neither must you be lead away, by the multitude of sin-
ners, or be sollicited by the troupe of such as are in the way to
perdition, nor thinke thus within your selfe. *VVhat ? Shall
therefore all they be damned, who dwell in Cittyes?* Behould, they
enioy their fortunes, they serue in Churches, they frequent the
Bathes, they refuse not odoriferous oyntments, and yet they
are celebrated in the mouthes of all men. To this I answered
before, and now I answere briefly againe, that in this present
worke, I speake not of Priests, but I instruct a Monke. Priests

are

are holy, and euery profeſſion is laudable. Doe you therefore ſo proceed, and liue in the Monaſtery, that you may deſerue to be a Prieſt, that you may not defile your youth with the leaſt ſpot; that you may paſſe on to the Altar of Chriſt, as a virgin would do from her bed, chamber; that you haue a good repucutation from abroad, and that woemen may know you by name, but not know you by ſight. When you come to a perfect mans eſtate, if your life be anſwearable, and either the people, or the Biſhop of the Citty make choice of you, into the clergy, doe you thoſe thinges, which belong to a Prieſt, and let the beſt Prieſts be your patterne. For in all conditions and eſtates, the worſt are mingled with the beſt. Do not ſtart forth to write ſuddenly, and be not carryed away with light madnes. Be long in learning that, which you may teach. Do not belieue them who prayſe you, or rather do not lend your eare to them who ſcoffe at you. For when they ſhall haue ſtroked you with flattery, and put you after a ſort out of your wits; if you looke ſuddenly backe ouer the ſhoulder, you ſhall ſee them either ſtretch out their neckes at you, like ſo many ſtorkes, or moue the eares of an Aſſe, which they haue framed with their fingers, or thruſt out their tongues at you, as if it were at ſome panting Dog.

Detract from no man, nor conceaue your ſelfe to be therefore a Saint, for tearing other men in pieces. We accuſe others oftentymes for that which we alſo do, and we inueigh againſt thoſe vices; they who are dumbe, giuing ſentence againſt vs who are eloquent. *Grunnius* ſtauked on toward his ſpeech, with the pace of a *Tortois*, and by certaine pauſes would be hardly able to ſpeake a few wordes, ſo that you would rather thinke he ſwallowed, then ſpoke; and yet when he had layd a heap of his bookes abroad vpon the table, and had compoſed his face to ſeuerity, and had contracted his noſe, and caſt his forehead into a frowne, he would ſnap with two of his fingers beſpeaking the attention of his Auditours by that ſigne, & then would he powre out meere toyes by heapes, and declayme againſt all the world; and you would ſay he were *Longinus* of *Creete*, and the *Cenſor* of the roman eloquence; he would taxe whome he liſted, & expell them from the Senate of Doctours.

But

But this man being wel moneyed, gaue men more contentmēt
at the dinners he made. Nor was it any marueile, that he who
was wont to inueigle many, would proceed in publicke with
a crowd of clamorous parasites round about him; and indeed
he was a *Nero* in substance, and yet a *Plato* in shew. He was all
ambiguous, as being framed of seuerall yea and euen contrary natures. You would say that he were some monster, or new
beast, deuised according to that of the Poet. The first part hath
of the Lyon, the last of the Dragon, and the middle part is a
very *Chymera*. Neuer visit you any such men as these, nor apply your selfe to them, *Nor let your hart decline to the wordes of
malice*, nor doe you heare these wordes : *Sitting downe thou
spakest against thy brother, and thou laydst a scandall before the sonnes
of thy Mother*. And againe. *Sonnes of men, theyr teeth are weapons,
and arrowes*. And elsewhere: *Their speech is more supple then oyle,
and yet they are dartes withall*. And more clearely in Ecclesiastes:
*As the serpent bites secretly; so doth he, who detracts priuatly from his
brother*.

But you will say, I detract not : but if others doe, how
can I help it ? We pretend these thinges, for the excuse of our
sinnes. Christ is not to be ouerreached by trickes. It is no sentence of myne, but of the Apostles : *Be not deceaued, God is not
mocked*. He lookes into the hart; we looke but vpon the face.
Salomon sayth in the Prouerbs: *A Northern wind scatters the clouds,
and so doth a sadd countenance, detracting tongues*. For as an Arrow,
if it be shot against a hard obiect, doth oftentymes returne vp
on him, who sent it forth, and woundes him that wounded it;
and that is then fullfilled; *They are made as a crooked Bow to me*.
And elsewhere; *He who throwes a stone vp on high, it shall returne
vpon his owne head*: So the detracter, when he sees that the face
of his hearer is sad (or rather of him who should not be his hearer, but the stopper of his eares, least he chance to heare the
iudgment of blood) is presently put to silence, his countenance
growes pale, his lips will not part, his mouth is dryed. Whereupon the same Wise man sayth : *Doe not mingle thy selfe with detracters, for suddenly their perdition will arriue*, and who knowes
the ruine of them both. That is it to say, both of the speaker,
and of the hearer. Truth seekes no corners, nor doth it desire
any

any whifperers . It is fayd to *Timothy* : *Be not eafy in receauing an accufation againft a Prieft*. But if indeed he finne, reproue him publikely, that others alfo may be affrayd. You muft not be light in belieuing any thing of a man in yeares, who is alfo defended by the fame of his former life, and who receaues the honour of any eminent title. But becaufe we are men, and fometymes we difhonour our mature yeares by falling into the errours of children : therefore if thou wilt correct me, when I offend, reproue me publickly, and only do not bite me behind my backe. *The iuft man will correct, and reproue me in mercy, but let not the oyle of the finner bedaube my head*, And our Lord cryes out by *Ifaias* : *O my people, they who fay you are happy, feduce you, and fupplant your fteppes*. For what doth it profit me, that thou relate my faults to others, if whileft I know nothing of the matter, thou woundeft another with my fin, or rather with thyne owne detractions, and when thou makeft hafte to recount it to all the world, thou fpeakeft it fo to euery one, as if thou hadft not fayd it to any other. This is not to reforme me, but to humour thy felfe in thyne owne finne. Our Lord commandes that finners fhould be fecretly admonifhed face to face, or els before witneffe; & if they refufe to obey, that account fhould then be giuen of it, to the Church; and that if they would be obftinate in doing ill, they fhould be held for Publicanes, and Pagans.

I haue beene the more expreffe in this, to the end I may free my young man from the itch both of eares, and tongue, and that fo being regenerate in Chrift, *I may exhibite him without wrinkle or fpot*, like a modeft virgin who is chaft, both in body and mind. Leaft els, he fhould glory in the only name he beares, and then his lampe being extinguifhed, for lacke of the oyle of good workes, he fhould be excluded by the fpoufe. You haue there, the moft holy and learned Bifhop *Proculus*, who will excell thefe letters of ours, with his admonitions, by word of mouth; and will direct your courfe, by his daily directions; and not fuffer you, by declyning on either hand, to forfake the Kinges high way. Ifrael haftening to the land of repromifion, affures him that he will go. And I pray God, that voice of the Church may be heard, *O Lord graunt vs peace, for*

them

thou hast giuen vs all thinges. God graunt that our renouncing the world, be an act of our will, and not of necessity ; and that our pouerty being desired by vs, may haue glory ; and not that being imposed, it may giue torment. But after the rate of the miseries of these tymes, and the swords which are euery where vnsheathed, he is rich inough, who hath bread to eat; he is but too powerfull, who is not constrained to be a slaue. Holy *Exuperius* the Bishop of *Tolosa,* the imitatour of that widow of *Sarep'a,* feeds others, though himselfe be hungry; and hauing his face pale with fasting, he is tormented with the hunger of others ; & hath bestowed his whole substance vpon the bowells of Christ. There is nothing richer then this man, who carryes the body of our Lord, in a basket made of little twigs; & his blood in a glasse ; who hath cast auarice out of the Temple; & without any whip or reproofe, hath ouerthrowne the chaires of them , that sould doues (that is to say , the gifts of the holy Ghost) and the tables of riches ; and hath dispersed the money of the changers, *That the house of God may be called the house of prayer, and not a denne of Theeues .* Follow the steps of this man close at hand , and of the rest who are in vertue like him, whome Priesthood makes humbler, and poorer, then he was before. If you desire to be perfect , go with *Abraham* out of your owne conntrey, and from your kindred, and go forward, without so much as knowing whither. If you haue an estate sell it , and giue it to the poore ; if you haue none, you are already rid of a great deale of trouble. Be naked in following Christ, who is nacked. It is heauy, it is high, it is hard, but the rewardes are great.

S . Hierome against Vigilantius the Heretike .

THERE are many Monsters brought forth in the world. *Centaures* and *Syrens, Harpyies,* and other prodigious birds are mentioned in *Esay . Leuiathan* and *Behemoth* are described by *Iob,* in a mysticall kind of language. The Poets in their fables speake of *Cerberus,* and the *Stymphalides,* the *Boare of Erymanthus, the Nemean Lion ,* the *Chimara ,* and the *Hydra* of many heades :
Virgil

Virgil defcribes *Cacus*; and the countryes of *Spaine*, haue ſhewed
vs, that three formed *Geryon* . *France* alone hath brought no
Monſters, but hath euer abounded with moſt valiant, and moſt
eloquent men . Only *Vigilantius* is ſuddenly ſtart vp, who more
truly may be called *Dormitantius*, ſince he fights with his impur
ſpirit, againſt the ſpirit of Chriſt; and, *Denyes that veneration is to
be exhibited to the tombes of Martyrs* . He ſayth alſo ; *That Vigills are
to be condemned; that Allelluia is neuer to be ſung but at Eaſter ; That
Continency is herefy; and chaſtity but a ſeminary of luſt* . And as *Eu-
phorbus* is ſayd to haue beene reuiued in *Pythagoras*; ſo is the wicked mind of *Iouinian* riſen vp againe in this man : ſo that we
are conſtrayned to anſwere to the ſleights and ſubtilties of the
Diuell, in the perſon both of that man, and this, to whome it
may be iuſtly ſayd, O thou wicked ſeed prepare thy children
to be ſlaine, by the ſinnes of thy Father . The former man being condemned by the authority of the Church of Rome, is not
ſo properly to be ſayd to haue giuen vp his Ghoſt, as to haue
caſt it out in the middeſt Pheaſants, & Swines fleſh; but this
Tauerne-keeper of *Callagura*, who by nickename, in reſpect of
the towne where he was borne, was called the dumbe *Quintilian* , ſophiſticates his wine with water; and out of the ſtocke of
that ancient fraud, he ſtriues to mingle the poyſon of his perfidious doctrine with the Catholike fayth, to impugne virginity,
to hate chaſtity ; and at the full table of ſecular perſons, to de-
claime againſt the faſting of Saints, whileſt himſelfe is playing
the Philoſopher, among his cuppes; and feeding licoriſhly vpon fine cakes, he will needes be ſtroked with the ſweet ſinging
of Pſalmes . In ſuch ſort as that, in the middeſt of his bankets,
he voutchſafes not to heare any other ſonges then of *Dauid, I-
dithus, Aſaph,* and the ſonne of *Chorah* . Theſe thinges do I vtter
with a ſad and grieued mind, not being able to containe my
ſelfe, nor to paſſe by the iniuries, which are done to the Apoſtles and Martyrs, with a deafe eare . O vnſpeakable abuſe! he
is ſayd to haue found Biſhops, who are partakers with him of
his crime ; if they may be called Biſhops, who ordaine no Dea-
cons, but ſuch as firſt haue marryed wiues ; not belieuing that
any vnmarryed man can be chaſt; and ſhewing thereby how
holily themſelues liue, who ſuſpect all men of ill; and vnles

they

they fee that Prieſts haue wiues with great bellyes, and that their children be crying in their Mothers armes, they giue the not the facraments of Chriſt.

But what ſhall then become of the Orientall Churches? What of the Churches of *Egypt*, & of the Sea Apoſtolike? which receiue men to Prieſthood, either before they are marryed, or when then are widowes; or if ſtill they haue wiues, yet they leaue to do the part of husbandes. But this hath *Dormitantius* taught, releaſing the raynes to luſt, and doubling by his exhortations, that ardour of fleſh and blood, which vfually boyles vp in youth, or rather quenching it, by the the carnall knowledg of woemen. That fo now, there may be nothing, wherein we differ from horfes, and ſwine, and fuch brute beaſts, of whom it is written, *They runne towardes woemen as horſes, which are mad with luſt do to their kind ; and euery man goeth euen neying after his neighbours wife*. This is that which the Holy Ghoſt fayth by *Dauid*, *Do not grow like the horfe and mule, in whome there is no vnderſtanding*. And againe he fayth of *Dormitantius*, and his companions, *Keep in, with the bridle and bit, the iawes of them who draw not neere to thee*. But now it is tyme, that ſetting downe his owne words, we procure to make them a particular anſwere. For it is poſſible, otherwiſe, that fome maligne interpreter, or other, will againe alleadge, that my felfe haue deuifed matter to which I may anſweare with a Rhetoricall kind of declamation, like that which I wrote into *France* to the Mother and Daughter, who were in diſcord. The holy Prieſtes *Riparius*, and *Defiderius* are the occaſions of this Epiſtle, for they write that their Pariſhes were infected by the neighbourhood of this man; and by our brother *Sefinnius*, they haue fent vs thofe bookes, which fnorting vpon a furfet, he hath vomited out. And thefe men affirme, that many are found, who fauouring the vices of his life, are content to heare the blafphemies of his doctrine. The man is ignorant both in knowledge and wordes, he is of vngratefull fpeech, and who cannot fo much as defend a truth: but yet in regard of worldly men, and poore woemen who go loaden with their finnes, and who *are euer learning, and neuer arriue to the knowledge of the truth*, I wil make anſweare to his traſh, in this one ſingle fitting vp at night,

leaſt

leaſt otherwiſe I might ſeeme to deſpiſe the letters of thoſe holy men, who haue entreated me to do thus much .

But this man followes the kind of which he comes, as
being deſcended from murdering theeues, and from a people
made vp of many natiōs ; Whome *Cnæus Pompeius* (hauing conquered *Spayne*, and haſtening to celebrate his triumph) thruſt
downe from the top of the *Pyrenean* hills, and gathered them
together into one towne, whereupon the Citty was called
by no other name, but of *Conuena* , that is to ſay of *People gathe-*
red together . Thus farre doth he reach now, in exerciſing murdering thefts vpon the Church of God, and deſcending from
the *Vectonians,* the *Arabatians,* and *Celtiberians* he ouerrunnes the
Churches of *France* ; not carrying in his hand the enſigne of
Chriſt, but the ſtandard of the Diuell. *Pompey* did the ſame in
the Eaſterne parts alſo . And the *Cilician,* and *Iſaurian* Pirates, &
murdering theeues, being ouercome, he built a Citty for them
betweene *Cilicia* , and *Iſauria*, bearing his owne name . But
that Citty doth ſtill liue vnder the lawes of their forefathers,
and no *Dormitantius* is ſprung vp there . The Countreyes of
Fraunce haue a domeſticall enemy, and now they ſee a man of a
troubled brayne, and fit to be bound vp, as *Hipocrates* directed
that mad men ſhould be, hauing a ſeat in the Church, and a-
mong other wordes of blaſphemy deliuering alſo theſe ; *To*
what purpoſe is it for thee , with ſo great reſpect, not only to honour, but
to adore alſo , that (I know not what I ſhould call it) which thou wor-
ſhippeſt in that little portable violl . And againe in the ſame booke;
VVhy doeſt thou adoringly kiſſe that duſt, wrapped vp in a little cloath .
And afterward ; *VVe ſee that almoſt after the manner of the Gentils ,*
it is introduced into our Churches, vnder the pretence of Religion , to
light huge heapes of waxen tapers ; and euery where they kiſſe , and a-
dore I know not what little duſt in a little violl, wrapped about in ſome
pretious linnen cloath. Such men as theſe do doubtles impart great honour
to the moſt bleſſed Martyrs in thinking that they may be illuſtrated by
thoſe moſt baſe waxe lights, whome the Lambe , who is in the middeſt
of the Throne doth illuminate, with the whole brightnes of his Maieſty .

But who, O you mad headed man. Did euer adore the
Martyrs ? Who thought that a man was God ? Did not *Paul* and
Barnabas , when they were thought by the *Lycaonians* to be Iu-

piter ,

piter, and *Mercury,* and had a mind to offer them ſacrifice, teare their garments, and declare that they were but men? Not but that they were better then *Iupiter* or *Mercury,* who were dead long before; but becauſe, vnder the errour of Paganiſme, the honour which was due to God, was deferred to them. This we alſo read of *Peter,* who when *Cornelius* deſired to adore him, rayſed him vp by the hand, & ſayd; *Riſe vp, for I am alſo a man.* And dare you ſay, *That ſame, I know not what, which you worſhip iǹ that little violl to be carryed vp and downe?* What is that thing which you call by the name of *I know not what?* I would faine vnderſtand what you meane by it. Speake plainely that you may with perfect liberty blaſpheme, *That ſame I know not what kind of little duſt, in that little violl, wrapt about with a precious linnen cloath.*

He is grieued that the Relikes of Martyrs are precouſly couered, and wrapped vp, and that they are not foulded in cloutes, or courſe haire clouths, or caſt in fine into ſome dunghill, that ſo *Vigilantius* alone, being drunke aſleep, might be adored. So that belike we commit ſacriledge when we go into the temple of the Apoſtles. *Conſtantine* the Emperour was alſo ſacrilegious, who transferred the holy Relikes of *Andrew, Luke* and *Timothy* to *Conſtantinople*; at the preſence of which Relikes, the Diuels roare, and the Inhabiters of *Vigilantius* confeſſe, that they feele the preſence thereof. Yea and *Auguſtus Arcadius,* is not only to be accounted ſacrilegious, but *a ſot alſo,* who hath carryed *a thing moſt baſe, and euen looſe aſhes in ſilke, and in a caſe of gold.* The people of all Churches muſt be alſo fooles, who went to meet thoſe holy Relickes, and entertayned them with ſo much ioy, as if they had beheld the Prophet preſent, & liuing with them, in ſuch ſort, as that the ſwarmes of people, did euen reach from *Paleſtine* to *Chalcedon,* and did ſound forth the praiſe of Chriſt with one voice. Belike they adored *Samuel,* & not Chriſt whoſe, Prieſt & Prophet *Samuel* was. You think he is dead, and therefore you blaſpheme. But read the Ghoſpel. *The God of Abraham, the God of Iſaac, the God of Iacob, is not the God of the dead but of the liuing.* If therefore they be aliue, they are ſhut vp, belike according to your opinion, in ſome honeſt priſon. For you ſay, *that the ſoules of the Apoſtles, and Martyrs, are iǹ*

the

the boſome of Abraham, or in a place of repoſe, and eaſe, or vnder the Al-
tar of God, and that they cannot be preſent at their tombes, and where
els they will. So that belike they are endewed with the dignity
of Senatours, who are not condemned to be kept in ſome ab-
hominable priſon; but ſhut vp in ſome honeſt and free cuſto-
dy, in the fortunate *Ilands*, and *Eliſian fields*.

But will you preſcribe a law for God? Will you tye vp the
Apoſtles in chaines, in ſuch ſorte as that they ſhall be kept in
priſon, till the day of iudgment, and not be with their Lord;
they of whome it is written, *They follow the Lambe whereſoeuer*
he goes? If therefore the Lambe be euery where, they alſo who
are with the Lambe, are to be belieued to be euery where.
And if *Lucifer*, & the reſt of the Diuells wäder ouer the whole
world, and by their too exceſſiue ſwiftnes, be euery where at
hand, ſhall Martyrs after the effuſion of their blood, be ſhut vp
in a cheſt, and not be able to go forth?

You ſay further in your booke, *that whileſt we liue, we may*
pray mutually for one anhoter; but after we ſhall be dead the prayer of
noe one is to be heard for another, eſpecially *ſince Martyrs, deſiring the*
reuenge of theyr blood were not able to obtayne it.

But if the Apoſtles and Martyrs, being yet liuing in theſe
mortal bodies, might pray for others, when ſtill they ought to
be ſolicitous for themſelues; how much more can they do it
after they haue obtayned their crownes, their victories, & tri-
umphes? That one man *Moyſes*, obtayned pardon of God for
ſix hundred thouſand armed men: and *Steuen* the imitatour of
our Lord, and the firſt Martyr of Chriſt, begges fauour for his
perſecuters; and ſhall they be of leſſe power when they haue
begun to be with Chriſt? *Paul* the Apoſtle affirmes, that two
hundred ſeuenty ſix mens liues were ſaued in the ſhip at his
ſuit, and when *being diſſolued, he ſhall be with Chriſt,* ſhall his
mouth be ſtopped, and ſhall he not dare to ſpeake a word for
them, who throught the whole world did belieue, vpon his
preaching the Ghoſpell? And ſhall *Vigilantius* this liuing dog,
be better then that dead Lyon? I might rightly alleadge this
out of *Eccleſiaſtes*, if I ſhould confeſſe that *Paul* were dead in
ſpirit, but Saints in fine *are not ſayd to be dead, but to be ſleeping.*
Whereupon *Lazarus,* who was to riſe againe, was ſayd to ſleep,
and

and the Apoſtle forbiddes the *Theſſalonians to be afflicted for ſuch as ſleep.* But you ſleep euen when you wake, and you write whē you ſleep; & you propound to me an *Apocriphall* booke, which is read by you, and ſuch as you are, vnder the name of *Eſdras,* where it is writtē that after death, no one muſt dare to pray for any other, which booke I neuer read. For to what purpoſe ſhould I take that booke in hand, which the Church doth not receaue? Vnleſe perhaps you will produce *Balſamus* to me, and *Barbelus,* and the treaſure of *Manichæus,* and the ridiculous name of *Leuſibora* ; and becauſe you dwell at the foot of the *Pirenean* mountaines, and are a neighbour to *Spayne,* you aduance thoſe incredible monſters of opiniō which were vented by *Baſilides,* that moſt auncient, but ignorant, vnskillfull Heretike; & you propound, that which was condemned, by the authority of the whole world. For in your little Commentary, you take a teſtimony out of *Salomon,* as if it made for you; which, *Salomon* indeed neuer wrote: to the end that, as you had then another *Eſdras,* ſo now you may haue another *Salomon.* And if you will, go read thoſe fayned Reuelations of all the Patriarches and Prophets; and when you ſhall haue learnt them, you may ſing them in the weauing houſes of woemen; or rather propound them to be read in your tauernes: that ſo by meanes of theſe bables, you may the more eaſily prouoke the vnlearned vulgar to drinke hard.

But as for tapers of waxe, we light them not in cleere day, as you idly ſlaunder vs; but to the end, that by this comfort, we may temper the darknes of the night, and that we may watch by light, leaſt otherwiſe being blind, we ſhould ſleep in darknes like you. And if any either through the vnskillfullnes, or ſimplicity of ſecular men, or yet of deuout woemen (of whome we may truely ſay, *I confeſſe they haue the zeale of God, but not according to knowledge*) do this for the honour of Martyrs, what are you the worſe for that? The Apoſtles did alſo, long a go, complaine that a pretious oyntment was caſt away, but they were reproued by the voice of our Lord. For neither did Chriſt need that oyntment, nor the Martyrs *this light of tapers;* and yet that woman did that in honour of Chriſt, and the deuotion of her mind was accepted. And whoſoeuer light ta-

pers,

pers, *haue their reward according to their fayth,* as the Apostle sayth
Euery one aboundes in his owne sense. But do you call such persons
as these, Idolaters? I deny not, but that all we, who belieue
in Christ, came from the errour of Idolatry : for we are not
Christians by generation, but by regeneration. And belike,
because we once worshipped Idols, we should not now worship God, least we may seeme to exhibit the same honour to
him : which formerly we exhibited to Idols. That was done to
Idols and therefore it was to be detested ; but this is done to
Martyrs, and therefore it is to be receaued. But abstracting frō
Martyrs Relickes, there are tapers lighted, through all the
Churches of the East, when the Ghospell is to be read ; how
brightly soeuer the Sunne then shine. Not forsooth to driue a-
way darkenes, but to declare our ioy by that testimony. Wherupon those Euangelicall Virgins *haue their lampes euer lighted.*
And it is sayd to the Apostles : *Let your loynes be girt, & your lam-*
pes burning in your handes. And of *Iohn Baptist* it was sayd; that *Ho*
was a lampe which did both burne and shine, that vnder the tipe of
visible light, the other light might be shewed, wherof we read
in the Psalme. *Thy word, O Lord, is a lanterne to my feet, and a light*
to my steps.

So that the Bishop of Rome doth ill, who ouer the bones
of the dead men, *Peter* and *Paul* (which according to our beliefe
are venerable, and according to you are *vile poore dust*) doth offer sacrifices to our Lord, and holdes their tombes to be the Altars of Christ. And not only he of one Citty, but the Bishops of
the whole world erre, who contemning this Tauerne-keeper
Vigilantius, enter into the Churches of these dead men, wherein
this *most base dust, and I know not what kinde of ashes, lyes wrapped*
vp in linnen, that it selfe being defiled, may defile all thinges els;
and which are like those Pharisaicall sepulchres, exteriourly
adorned, when within, the ashes being impure according to
you, all other thinges may be also vnsauoury and impure. And
then casting vp that base vncleanes out of the profound hell of
your stomach, you dare say thus, *Therfore belike the soules of Mar-*
tyrs loue theyr ashes, and houer about them, and are euer present
with them ; least perhaps if some petitioner might come thither, they
should not be able to heare them, if themselues were absent.

H O

O prodigious Monſter, fit to be poſted away into the furdeſt foot of the whole earth ! you ſcoffe at the Relickes of Martyrs, & together with *Eunomius* the authour of this hereſy, you procure to caſt a ſcandall vpon the Churches of *Chriſt.* Nor are you frighted by finding your ſelfe in ſuch company as that; & you ſpeake thoſe very things againſt vs, which he ſpake againſt the Church. For none of his followers will go the Churches of the Apoſtles, and Martyrs; that forſooth they may adore the dead *Eunomius,* whoſe bookes they eſteeme to be of more authority then the Ghoſpells ; and in him they hold the light of truth to be; as other hereſies affirmed, that the holy Ghoſt came into *Montanus,* yea and they ſay, that *Manichæus* is that very holy Ghoſt. That moſt learned man *Tertullian* (that you may not vaunt your ſelfe to be the firſt finder out of this wickednes) writes againſt this hereſy of yours, which broke out long ago againſt the Church, an excellent booke, which he termed *Scorpiacum,* vpon a moſt iuſt reaſon ; becauſe by a circling kind of wound, that Heretike ſpread his poiſon vpon the body of the Church, by that hereſy, which anciently was called of *Cain,* and which ſleeping, or rather lying buryed a long tyme, is now by *Dormitantius* raiſed to life. It is a marueile, you ſay not, that Martyrdomes are not to be endured, becauſe God doth not ſeeke the blood of ſo much as goates, or bulles, and much leſſe will he require that of men. Which when you ſhall haue ſayd, yea although you ſhall not ſay it, you ſhall be ſo accounted of, as if you ſayd it. For he who affirmes, that the Relicks of Martyrs are to be troden on ; forbids that blood to be ſhed, which is vnworthy of any honour.

Concerning *Vigils,* and ſitting vp at night, which are often to be celebrated in Martyrs Churches, I haue giuen a briefe anſwere in another Epiſtle, which I wrote almoſt two yeares ſince, to *Riparius* the holy Prieſt If therefore you thinke that they are to be reiected, leaſt otherwiſe we may ſeem to celebrate many ſeuerall Eaſters; and that we keep not ſolemne *Vigils* at the end of euery yeare : by the ſame reaſon no ſacrifices ſhould be offered to Chriſt vpon the Sundaies, leaſt we ſhould ſeeme to celebrate the Eaſter of the Reſurrection of our Lord often ; & ſo we ſhould not haue one Eaſter, but many. Now that abuſe ufe and fault, which is many tymes committed in the night, betweene young men, and the bafeſt forte of woemen, is not to be imputed to deuout perſons; becauſe ſome ſuch thing is many tymes found to be committed, euen in the *Vigil* the Eaſter; but now the fault of few, muſt not preiudice this Act of Religion; For euen without *Vigils*, men may commit that ſinne, either in their owne or others houſes. The treaſon of *Iudas*, deſtroyed not the fayth of the Apoſtles, and ſo the ill *Vigills* of others, muſt not deſtroy our *Vigils*; but rather let them be conſtrained to watch to chaſtity, who ſleep to luſt. For that which was good being done once, cannot be euill, if it be done often. And if it be culpable through any fault, it is not culpable becauſe it was done often, but becauſe it was done at all. Let vs not therfore, belike, watch at Eaſter, leaſt the long entertained deſire of ſome adulterer, may chaunce to be fullfilled then, leaſt the wife find occaſion of committing ſinne; leaſt ſhe exempt her ſelfe, from being ſhut vp by her husbandes keys. Whatſoeuer is rare, is ſo much the more ardently deſired.

I cannot runne ouer all thoſe particulers, which are mentioned in the letters of thoſe holy Prieſts; but ſome I will produce out of his owne bookes. He frames arguments againſt thoſe wonders, and miracles, which are wrought in *Martyrs Churches*, and he ſayth, *they are good for vnbelieuers, but not for belieuers*. As if now the queſtion were, for whoſe ſake, and not by what power they are wrought. But well, let *Miracles* be wrought for Infidells, who becauſe they would not belieue ſpeech, and doctrine may be brought by *Miracles* to the fayth. Our Lord wrought *Miracles* for ſuch as were yet incredulous; and yet the *Miracles* of our Lord are not be taxed, becauſe they were for Infidels, but they were to be admired ſo much the more, becauſe they were of ſo great power, as to tame euen the ſtifeſt mindes, and oblige them to imbrace the fayth. Therfore I will not haue you tell me, *that miracles are for Infidels*: but anſwere me how there comes to be ſo great a preſence of wöders and miracles, *in moſt baſe duſt, and I know not what kind of aſhes?* I find, I find, O you the moſt vnhappy of all mortall men, what grieues you, and what frights you? The impure ſpirit which compels you to write thoſe thinges, is often tormented with

thu

this most base dust, yea and is tormented this very day ; and he, who diffembles the wounds, which he giues to you, confeffes thofe which he giues to others . Vnles perhaps, after the manner of *Gentiles* , and prophane perfons (fuch as *Porphyrius* and *Euuomius* were) you will pretend that thefe are but trickes of the Diuells ; and that indeed the Diuells cry not out, but only that they fayne themfelues to be in torment . Take my counfaile , goe to the Martyrs Churches, and you fhall be one day difpoffeft . There fhall you find many of your fellowes, and you fhall be burnt , not *by the tapers of Martyrs* , which difpleafe you , but by inuifible flames : and then you will confeffe what you now deny ; & you wil freely publifh your owne name, though now you fpeake in the name of *Vigilantius* ; and fay, that either you are *Mercury*, for your defire of money, or *Nocturnus* according to the *Amphitryo* of *Plautus*, who fleeping in adultery with *Alcmena, Iupiter* made two nights of one, that *Hercules* might be borne full of ftrength . Or els that you are *Father Bacchus* for your drunken head, and you tankard hanging at your backe , and your face euer red , your lips foming, and your vnbridled tongue rayling . Whereupon there being a fudden earth-quake in this Prouince, which rayfed all men from their fleep, you being the moft difcreet, & wife of mortall men, were praying naked, and reprefented to vs an *Adam* and an *Eue*, as they were in Paradife . Sauing that they hauing their eyes open, and feeing themfelues naked, did blufh and couer their fecret partes with leaues of trees, but you being as naked of cloathes as voyd of vertue, and frighted with a fudden feare, hauing fomewhat in you of the furfet of the former night , did expofe the obfcene parts of your body , to the eyes of the Saints, that you might fhew how difcreet a man you were .

Such enemyes as thefe hath the Church. Thefe are the Captaines who fight againft the blood of Martyrs; fuch Oratours as thefe, thunder out againft the Apoftles, or rather fuch madd Dogs as thefe barke againft the difciples of Chrift . I confeffe my feare, leaft perhaps in your opinion it might feem, to grow from fuperftition When I haue bene angry, when I haue had any ill thought in my mind, and haue beene deluded by any imagination in the night, I dare not goe into the Martyrs Churches ;

ches; I doe all fo tremble both in body aud minde. Perhaps
you will fcoffe at me for this, as if it were the dotage of fome
old woman. But I blush not to hold faſt the fayth of thofe
woemen, who were the firſt in feeing our Lord after his refurrection, who were fent to his Apoſtles, and who in the perfon
of the Mother of our Lord & fauiour, were recomended to the
fame holy Apoſtles . Go you belching on, with the men who
lead a worldy life. I will faſt with thofe woemen, yea and alfo with thofe Religious men, who carry chaſtity euen in their
countenance; and hauing their faces pale, through continuall
abſtinence, declare the modeſty of Chriſt.

Me thinkes you alfo feem to be troubled at another thing
and that is ; leaſt if chaſtity, fobriety, and faſting should continue to take deep footing in *France*, your Tauernes would
make little gayne; and fo you should not be able to continue
thofe *Vigills* of the Diuel, & thofe drunken feaſts, all night lóg.

It is related to me befides, in the fame letters, that you
forbid men to be at any charge, for the vfe and comfort of
thofe holy men, who liue at *Ierufalem*, againſt the authority of
the Apoſtle *Paul*, yea and of *Peter* alfo, and of *Iames* and *Iohn*,
who gaue handes to *Paul* and *Barnabas*, in *teſtimony of their confent with them, and required them to be mindefull of the poore*. But
now if I should anfwere thefe thinges, you would prefently
barke out and fay, that I am pleading myne owne caufe; you
who haue been fo liberall to all the world, as that if you had
not come to *Iefuralem*, & had not powred forth your own money, or that of your Patrons, we should all forfooth haue bene
in danger to ſtarue. For my part, I will but fay that which
the bleſſed Apoſtle *Paul* deliuers almoſt in all his Epiſtles, and
enioyneth the Churches, which had bene conuerted among
the Gentiles, namely that vpon the firſt day after the Sabboth,
(that is to fay, vpon the Sunday) men were all to conferre a-
bout that alms, which should be fent to *Hierufalé* either by their
difciples, or by others, whome they should appoint ; and that
if it proued to be of moment, himfelf might either carry or fend
it. In the Acts of the Apoſtles, fpeaking to *Fœlix* the Gouernour, he fayth thus ; *After many yeares, being to giue much almes to
the men of my nation, and to make oblations and vowes, I came to Ie-*

rufalem

rusalem, where they found me purifyed in the Temple. But had he
not also power, to dispose of some part of that, which he had
receaued of others, vpon the Churches in other parts of the
world, which growing to be Chriftian, he had inftructed by
his preaching? But yet he defired to impart the almes to the
poore of thofe holy places, who leauing their fortunes for
Chrift, had deuoted themfelues wholly to the feruice of our
Lord. It were a long bufineffe, if I would reflect vpon all the
teftimonies which might be brought out of euery one of thofe
Epiftles, wherein the Apoftle endeauours, and with his whole
affection makes haft to ordaine, that money fhould be addreffed
to the faythfull at *Hierufalem*, and to the holy places; not to fatisfy couetoufnes, but for their neceffary comfort; not for the
gathering together of riches, but for the vphoulding of their
weake bodies, and for the auoyding of hunger and cold; this
cuftome continuing in Iury euen to this day, not only among
vs Chriftians, but among the Iewes alfo, that they who meditate vpon the lawes of our Lords day and night, and who haue
no Father vpon earth, but only God, fhould be cherifhed by the
charities of the Synagogues of the whole world, with a fit e-
quality; not that fome fhould be at eafe, and fome in mifery,
but that the aboundance of fome might ferue to fupply the wat
of others. But you will anfwere, that euery man may do this
in his owne country, and that poore people will not be wanting to be mainteyned vpon the charity of the Church.
And fo alfo neither doe we deny, but that almes is to be giuen
to all kind of poore people, yea though they be euen Samari-
tans, and Iewes, if there be enough for all. But the Apoftle
directeth indeed, *that we should giue almes to all, but especially to
them of the houshold of fayth, in respect of whome our Lord fayd in the
Ghospell: Make your selues friendes by the Mammon of iniquity, who
may receaue you in the eternall Tabernacles.* Now I pray you, can
thofe poore people, who among their rags and corporall
miferies haue burning luft ruling ouer them, can they, I fay,
haue any eternall Tabernacles, who poffeffe neither prefent, nor
future thinges? For not abfolutly fuch as are poore, but fuch as
are poore in fpirit, are called happy; of whome it is written:
Bleffed is the man, who vnderftandingly confiders the poore and needy,
   our

our Lord will deliuer him in the euill day . Now for the reliefe of the generality of poore people, there is no ſuch need of *Vnderſtan-ding* , but of the almes it ſelfe. In the caſe of ſuch poore as are holy, there is a kind of beatitude of *Intelligence*, that a man may giue to him , who will bluſh to receaue, and euen be ſory when he is on the taking hand, *reaping carnall thinges, and ſowing ſuch as are ſpirituall* .

But in that you affirme them to do better who ſtill make vſe of theyr owne goodes & diſtribute the reuenues of their eſtates by little & little, then they who by ſelling their landes, giue all at once, no anſwere ſhall be giuen you to this by me, but thus by our Lord, *If thou wilt be perfect, go and ſell all that thou haſt & giue it to the poore , and come thou and follow me* . He ſpeakes to him who will be perfect, and who in company of the Apo-ſtles will diſmiſſe himſelfe of his father, of his ſhip, and of his net. This other man whome you comend, is of the ſecond and third ranke, whereof we alſo allow ; ſo as yet we may know withall, that the firſt is to be preferred before the ſecond and the third .

Nor are Monkes to be frighted from their courſe by your viperous and moſt cruell biting tongue, againſt whome you argue thus, and ſay, *If all men ſhould ſhut themſelues vp, and be-take themſelues to the deſert , who ſhall dōe Offices in Churches, who ſhall gaine ſecular men to God, who ſhall exhort ſinners to a courſe of ver tue* ? And ſo alſo if euery body ſhould be a ſot with you, what wiſe man would there be in the world? And by this reaſon al-ſo virginity muſt not be approued . For if euery body ſhall be chaſt, there will then be no mariages, and then mankind will periſh ; noe infants will be crying in their cradles, Midwiues muſt goe begg without meanes to liue ; and *Dormitantius* muſt ly awake in his bed in the coldeſt wether which can come, al alone, and ſhrunke vp together.

But vertue is a rare thing, and not ſought by mauy. And I would to God all men were that, which few are ; of whome it is ſayd, *Many are called but few are choſen.* The priſons then would be empty. But as for the Monke it is not his Office to teach, but to lament and bewayle, either himſelf , or the world, and to expect the comming of our Lord with profound feare : who

knowing

knowing his owne weakenes, and how brickle the pott is which he beares about him , is affrayd to offend , leaft firlt he ftumble, aud then fall, and fo it be broken . And for this reafon, he declines the fight of woemen, and efpecially of the younger forte; and is fo farre a chaftifer of himfelfe, that he shrinkes euen at thofe thinges, wherein there is no danger .

But you aske me, why I go to the *Defert*? Euen to the'end that I may neither heare, nor fee you; that I may not be offended by your madnes, nor endure the troubles which you put me to ; that the harlots eye may not take hold of me , nor that great beauty of hers bring me to vnlawful embracements . But you will fay ; This is not to fight, but to fly . Stand faft in the battaile, be in armour, and refift your ennemy, to the end that you be crowned when you haue conquered . I confeffe my weaknes, I will not fight through a hope of victory, leaft at fome tyme or other , I may chaunce to loofe it. If I fly, I auoyd the fword ; if I ftay, I muft either conquer, or be killed . But what need haue I to let goe that which is certaine, and to feek after that which is vncertaine ? Death muft be auoided, either by the targuet , or by flight . You who fight, may both ouercome, and be ouercome . I , when I fly away, fhall euen therfore not be ouercome . There is no fafety in fleeping neere a ferpent . It may be, he will not bite; but fo perhaps, there may be a tyme, when he will . We call them our Mothers, our Sifters, and our Daughters, & we are not afhamed to cloake our vices by fuch names of piety as thofe . But what doth the Monke in woemens chambers ? What meane thefe fingle and priuate conferences, and thefe countenances which are afraid of witneffes ? A holy loue, is not fubiect to impatience; & that which we haue fayd of luft, may be applyed to couetoufnes, or any other vice which is auoided in the defert . And therefore do not we decline the frequent refort of Citties, leaft we fhould be obliged to do thofe thinges , to which nature doth not compell vs fo much as our owne will .

Thefe wordes (as I was faying) I haue dictated in the fitting vp of one night, at the requeft of thofe holy Prieftes ; our brother *Sifinus* making much haft , and going towardes *Egypt* with all fpeed, to carry almes to the Saints there . For otherwife,

wiſe, the matter it ſelfe is full of expreſſe blaſphemy , which
rather would require indignation, in the writer, then any mu-
ſtering vp of proofs againſt him . But if *Dormitantius* keep himſelfe awake to rayle at me , and with the ſame blaſphemous
mouth , wherewith he teares the Apoſtles and Martyrs, ſhall
thinke alſo fit to detract from me ; I will not keep my ſelfe wa-
king in ſome ſhort ſitting vp , but all night long , both for him
and his companions ; or rather for his , either diſciples, or Maſters ; who vnles they may ſee the woemen with great bellies,
thinke their husbands to be vnworthy of the Miniſtry of Chriſt

The Epitaphe of S . Paula the Mother , directed to Euſtochium by S . Hierome .

I F all the parts of my body were conuerted into tongues, &
all my limmes were able to expreſſe theſelues by the voice
of man, I ſhould not yet be able to ſay any thing, which might
be worthy of the vertues of the venerable and holy *Paula* . She
was noble by extraction, and much more noble by her ſanctity ; powerfull ſhe had once beene in riches, but now more il-
luſtrious by the pouerty of Chriſt . She who was of the ſtocke
of the *Gracchi* , of the race of *Scipio's,* the heire of *Paulus* (whoſe
name ſhe bore,)the true vndoubted progeny of *Martia, Papyria,*
and the mother of *Africanus*, preferred *Bethleem* before *Rome*, &
made an exchãge of her houſes brightly bunrniſhed with gold,
for the baſenes of ill fauoured durt . We grieue not for hauing
loſt ſuch a one ; but we giue God thankes, in that we had her ,
or rather in that we haue her ſtill . For all thinges liue to God ,
and whatſoeuer returnes to our Lord , is ſtill reputed as a part
of his Family . For our loſſe of her , is the peopling of that celeſtiall houſe ; of her I ſay, who when ſhe was in her body, *was
in pilgrimage from our Lord* ; and would ſtill be ſaying with a lamenting voice ; *VVo be to me becauſe my Pilgrimage is prolonged , I
haue dwelt with the Inhabitants of Cedar, my ſoule hath beene farre off
in pilgrimage.* Nor is it marueile if ſhe bewayled her ſelfe, as being in darkenes (for ſo is the word *Cedar* interpreted) ſince the
world is placed in malignity , and the very light of it is like darke-

nes ; but true light *shines in that darkenes, and darkenes comprehendt
it not .* Whereupon she would very often inferre these wordes ;
A stranger I am, and a pilgrime as all my Fathers were . And againe ;
I desire to be dissolued and to be with Christ . But then, as often as she
was vexed by any infirmity of her body , which she brought
downe by incredible abstinence & doubled fasting, she would
take this saying into her mouth ; *I subiect my body , and I bring it
into seruitude, least whilest I preach to others, my selfe may become a
reprobate .* And ; *It is good not to drinke wine, nor to eat flesh ; and I
haue humbled my soule in fasting .* And ; *Thou hast made my whole bed
in my sicknes ; and I haue beene conuerted in my misery, whilest the
thorne stucke in my sides .* And in the middest of those sharp pangs
of payne , which she endured with admirable patience, she
would be saying, as if she had seene heauen open , *VVho
will giue me the winges as of a Doue , that I might fly vp , and rest ?* I
take Iesus and his Saints so witnes ; and that particular Angell
who was the keeper, and companion of this admirable woma,
that I will say nothing of her for fauour, nothing after the custome of flatterers ; but whatsoeuer I am to say, shall be as if it
were vpon myne oath ; and yet still it will fall short of her merits, whome the whole world celebrates, whome Priests admire, whome the quiers of Virgins want, and the troupes of
Monkes, and poore people, lament .

Do you , O Reader , desire to know her vertues in few
wordes ? She left all her friendes poore, her selfe being more
poore, then any of them all . Neither will it be strange , that
we should say thus much of them, who were next her , as namely her family (the slaues and hand-maydes whereof, in both
sexes, she had exchanged into the name of brothers and sisters)
since she left the virgin *Eustochium* , her daughter deuoted to
Christ (for whose comfort this booke is made) farre off from her
illustrious friendes, and only rich in fayth and grace . But let
vs speake of thinges in order . Let others fetch them higher ; &
from her cradle, & euen in her swadling cloutes (as I may say)
produce her mother *Blesilla* , and *Rogatus* her father , wherof the
Mother was the ofspring of the *Scipio's* , and the *Gracchi* ; & the
Father is sayd to haue drawne downe his blood , through the
best nobility of all *Greece* , by descending from the stemme of
that

that *Agamemnon*, who deſtroyed the Citty of *Troy*, in that ten yeares ſiege . As for vs we will prayſe nothing in her, which was not her owne, and which is not to be deriued out of that pureſt fountaine of her holy mind.

Although our Lord and Sauiour taught his Apoſtles in the Ghoſpel, when they askehim, *what he would reſtore to them who should part with their fortunes for his ſake, in this world they should receaue a hundred fold , & eternall life in the next* : wherby we come to vnderſtand, that it is no prayſe to poſſeſſe riches, but to contene them for Chriſt; not to ſwell vp with honour, but for the fayth of God to deſpiſe it. What our Sauiour promiſed to his ſeruāts, he hath truly performed in the preſent caſe. For ſhe, who contemned the glory of one Citty, is celebrated by the fame of the whole world; ſhe whom as long as she dwelt in *Rome*, none knew but they who were at *Rome*, lying now hid in *Bethleem,* both the *Barbariā* & the *Romā* world hath admired. For of what nation are there any men, who come not to viſit the holy places ? And who findes any thing in theſe holy places, which he may admire more then *Paula* ? For as the moſt pretious Gemme doth outſhine other little gemmes, and as the Sunne beames do ouerwhelme and obſcure the brightnes of the little ſtarres , ſo doth ſhe with her humility, ouercome the excellencies and vertues of all the reſt, and she is growne the greateſt, becauſe ſhe would needs be the leaſt of them all, and ſo much more as she deiected her ſelfe, ſo much more was she eleuated by Chriſt our Lord. She lay hid , and she lay not hid . By flying from glory she deſerued glory, which follows vertue like a shadow; and forſaking ſuch as honoured her , she ſought after ſuch as might contemne her . But what am I doing, now that I omit to ſpeake of things in order; for whileſt I take hould of ſo maany particulers, I obſerue not the rules of good diſcourſe .

Paula being thus deſcended, was marryed to *Toxotius* her husband, who was extracted from that high blood of *Æneas* & the *Iulio's*; whereupon alſo her daughter, the virgin of Chriſt, *Euſtochium*, is called *Iulia*; and that *Iulius* had his name deriued from the great *Iulus* . Now we ſpeake of theſe thinges , not becauſe they are great in them who haue them ; but becauſe they may be wondred at, in ſuch as deſpiſe them. The men of

this

this world admire such persons, as are adorned with these priuiledges; but we praise such others as contemne them, for the loue of our Sauiour; but we who esteeme little of those who haue them, do after a strang fashiō proclaime those others, who cōtemne, & care not for them. She being borne, I say, of those parents, was approued both in fecundity, & modesty, first by her husband, then by her friendes, and by the testimony of the whole Citty; and when she had brought forth fiue children, *Blesilla* (vpon whose death I comforted her at *Rome*,) *Paulina* (who left behind her that holy and admirable man *Pammachius*, the heire both of her holy purpose and her estate, to whome we addressed a little booke vpon the occasion of her death,) *Eustochium* (who is now in the holy places, euen the very pretious Iewell of virginity, and of the Church,) *Ruffina* (who by her vntimely death did euen astonish the tēder hart of the mother,) & *Toxotius*, after whome she had no more children, that we might know she had no mind to attend to the office of a wife for any long time; but only to bring children; till the husbandes longing were satisfyed, in his desire of a sonne. When her husband dyed, she bewayled him so as that it had almost cost her her life; and yet withall shee did so giue her selfe away to the seruice of our Lord, that she might seem to haue desired her husbandes death.

What shall I stand to tell of her ample & noble house, which formerly was most abundantly rich, & whereof now all the wealth was spent vpon the poore? What, of her mind, which was so mercifully enclined to all? and of her goodnes which would be wandring, euen to the help of them, whome she had neuer seene? What poore man dying, was not shrowded in cloathes of her giuing? What cripples were not maintayned by her purse? whome causing to be sought for with extreme curiosity, ouer the whole citty she would hold it to be her owne losse in particular, if any weake or hungry person were sustayned by any food, but hers. She euen stript her owne children; & to her friends, who would be chiding her for this excesse; she would say, she meant to leaue them a greater inheritance, then she found, namely the mercy of Christ. Nor could she long endure the visits, and courting which was due to her most noble house,

house, and to that high stock of hers, according to the account of the wold. She grieued at the honour which was done her, and made hast to decline, and fly from the face of such as gaue her prayse. And when the Imperiall letters had brought the Bishops both of the East, and West to *Rome* for composing the dissentions of some Churches, she saw those admirable men, and Bishops of Christ, *Paulinus*, the Bishop of the Citty of *Antioch*, & *Epiphanius* of *Salamina* in *Cyprus*, of whome she had *Epiphanius* for her owne guest, and *Paulinus* though lodging in an other house she possessed as her owne, by the care she had of him.

Being inflamed by the vertues of these men, she deuised, from one minute to another, how to forsake her country. And not being mindfull of her house, not of her children, not of her family, not of her estate, not of any thing which belonges to this world, she had an earnest desire to be going on, euen a-lone, and vnaccompanyed (as a man may say) to the desert of those *Anthonies* and *Pauls*. At length the winter being spent, and the sea being open; the Bishops returning to their Churches, she also, in her desire, and with the vowes of her hart, went sayling with them. Why shall I deferre it longer? She went downe to the Sea port, her brother, her kinred, her allyes & (which is more then this) her children following her, & striuing with their earnest suits, to ouercome that most tender mother.

The sailes were by that time spread, and by stretching of the Oares, the ship was drawne into the deepe. Little *Toxotius* cast forth his begging hands, vpon the shoare. *Ruffina*, who then was marriageable, did in silence craue with teares, that she would expect to see her bestowed. But *Paula* the while, cast vp her dry eyes towards heaue, surmounting her dear affectiō towards her children, by her deuotion towards God. She knew not her selfe to be a mother, that she might approue her selfe, for a hand-mayd of Christ. Her very bowels were racked within her, and as if she had bene torne from the very parts of her owne body, so did she fight with grief, in this so much the more admirable to all, as she carryed a great loue to them which was to be conquered. When people are in the hands of enemyes, & in the sad condition of captiuity, there is no one thing more

cruell,

cruell,then for parents to be separated from their children. And
yet euen this, did her full faith endure, against the rights of
nature; nay her ioyfull hart did desire it, and contemning the
loue of her children through her superiour loue towards God,
she contented her selfe with onely *Eustochium*, who was the có-
panion, both in her holy purpose, & nauigation . In the meane
time the shippe plowed vp the Seas, & all the passingers who
were embarked with her, looking backe vpon the shoare, she
only turned her eyes from thence; that so she might not see the,
whom she could not behould without torment . I confesse that
no woman could more loue her children, to whom, before she
went, she gaue away whatsoeuer she had best .

Being arriued at the Iland of *Pontia* which auciently had
bene ennobled by the banishment of that most excellét of woemen *Flauia Domitilla*, vnder the Emperour *Domitian*, for confessió
of the name of Christ, & beholding those Coles wherin she had
suffred a long martyrdome she then tooke vp the wings of faith
and desired to visit *Ierusalem* and the holy places . The windes
were thought sluggish, and all speed was slowe . Committing
her selfe to the Adriaticke Sea, between *Scylla* and *Carybbis*, she
came, as by a lake, to *Methona* ; and there refreshing her selfe a
little, & laying her seasicke limmes vpon the shoare, by *Malea*,
& *Cythera*, and the *Cyclads* (which are sprinkled ouer that Sea)
and those waues being the more furious by the often indenting
of the land and hauing also passed by *Rhodes*, and *Lycia*, at
length she came to *Cyprus*, Where casting her selfe at the feet of
the holy and venerable *Epiphanius*, she was deteyned by him
ten dayes, not for her regalo as he meant it, but for the worke
of God, as indeed it proued . For vewing all the Monasteries
of that quarter, she left to the vttermost of her power, certeyne
almes to beare the charge of those brothers, whom the loue of
that holy man had drawen thither from the seuerall parts of
the whole world From thence she made a short cut ouer to *Se-
leucia*, & then going vp to *Antioche*, & being deteyned a while
by the charity of the holy Confessour *Paulinus*, in the hart of
winter, (her owne hart being most hot with a liuely faith) the
noble creature who auntiently vsed to be carryed by *Eunuches*
hands, did put her selfe now to trauaile, vpon an asse. I omit to
speake

fpeake of *Cales*, the way to *Syria* and *Phenices* (for I meane not
to writ her Iournall) but will only name thofe places, wherof mention is made in holy Scripture . And leauing *Berytus*,
the *Colony* of *Rome*,as alfo the auntient Citty of *Sidon*, fhe went
into the little tower of *Elias* vpon the fhoare of *Sarepta*; Wherin
hauing adored our Lord our Sauiour, fhe came to *Coph*, which
now is called *Ptolemais*, by thofe fandes of *Tyrus*, where *Paul*
prayed vpon his knees . And pafling by the fields of *Mageddo*,
which were priuy to the death of *Iofias*, fhe entred into the land
of *Philiftim*, & wondred at the ruines of *Doe*, which was once
a moft powerfull Citty, and on the contrary fide fhe faw the tower of *Strato*, which was called *Cefarea* by *Herod*, King of Iury,
in honour of *Auguftus Cefar*, wherein fhe beheld the houfes of
Cornelius, which grew to be a Church of Chrift; and the little
houfes of *Phillip*, and foure chambers of the prophetifing virgins; and then *Antipatris*, a towne halfe ouerthrouen, which
Herod had called by the name of his father, and *Lidda*, changed
into *Diofpolis*, made famous by the refurrection of *Dorcas* to life,
& of *Æneas* to health . Not farre from thence was *Arimathea* the
little towne of *Iofeph*, who buryed our Lord, and *Nobe* which
autiently was the Citty of Priefts, now a fepulture of the dead,
and *Ioppe* alfo the hauen of *Ionas*, when he fled, and (to the
end that I may giue fome little touch of the inuention of Poets)
which was the fpectatrix of *Andromade* when fhe was tyed to
the rocke. And then renewing her Iourney, fhe went on to *Ni-
copolis*, which formerly had bene called *Emaus*, where our Lord
being knowen in the breaking of bread, did confecrat the houfe
of *Cleophas* a Church.

Departing from thence, fhe afcended both into the vper
and lower *Bethoron*, which were Citties built by *Salomon*; but
were afterward deftroyed, through the tempeft which was
drawen vpon them, by feuerall warres; beholding vpon her
right hand, both *Haialon*, and *Gabaon* where *Iefus* the fonne
of *Naue*, fighting againft fiue Kinges, commanded both the
funne and moone; and condemned the *Gabaonites* to be water
carryers, and wood-cutters, for their trechery, and falfhood
in breaking the league, which themfelues had obtayned . In
Gabaon (which had bene a Citty, but was then deftroyed eue

to the very ground) she paufed a while; remembring the finne it committed , and the concubine cut in peices, and the three hundred men of the tribe of *Beniamin*, who were referued for *Paul* the Apoftles fake .

Why make I any longer ftay? Hauing left the tombe of *Helena*, on the left hand (who being the Queen of the *Adeabenians*, had relieued the people with corne in a time of famine , she entred into *Hierufalem* that citty of a treble name ; *Iebus, Salem*, and *Hierufalem*, which afterward out of the ruines, and a-shes of the Citty, was raifed by *Helius Adrianus*, and called *Helia*. And when the *Proconful* of *Paleftine* (who excellétly well knew her Family) had fent her Officers before, and comman-ded the Pallace to be prepared , she rather chofe an humble Cell; and went round about to all thofe places with fo great ardour, and affection of mind , that vnles she had haftened to haue feene the reft , she would neuer haue beene drawne from the former . And lying proftrate before the Croffe, she adored our Lord , as if she had feene him hanging on it . Being entred into the Sepulcher, she kiffed the ftone of the Refurrection , which the Angell had remoued from the doore thereof. And that very place, where our Lord had lyen , shee licked with a faythfull mouth, as any thirfty creature would do , the moft defired waters . What teares , what groanes , what griefe she there powred forth, all *Hierufalem* is a witnes ; and indeed our Lord himfelfe is the beft witnes, to whome she prayed. Going out from thence, she went vp to *Syon*, which now is turned into a watch-tower, or lanterne. This Citty, *Dauid* did anci-ently, both deftroy, and build againe . Of this , when it was deftroyed, it is written thus ; *VVoe be to thee, O Citty Ariel that is, thou Lyon of God, and once of excefsiue ftrength, which Dauid tooke .* And of that Citty being reedifyed, it is fayd; *Her foundations are in the holy hills, our Lord loueth the gates of Sion, aboue all the Tabernacles of Iacob :* not thofe gates which now we fee diffolued in-to duft, and ashes ; *but the gates, againft which hell cannot preuaile ,* and by which the multitude of belieuers go into Chrift. There was shewed to her, a pillar of the Church houlding vp the porch, which was fpotted by the blood of our Lord, to which he was fayd to haue beene bound , and whipt, and that place

also

alſo shewed where the holy Ghoſt *deſcended vpon the ſoules of more then a hundred and twenty belieuers,* that the prophecy of *Ioel* might be fullfilled .

After this hauing diſpoſed of her little meanes to the poore who by that tyme were growne to be her feilow-ſeruants, ſhe went on towards *Bethlem,* & ſtayed on the right hand of her way, at the ſepulcher of *Rachel,* wherin the mother of *Beniamin* brought him forth, not *Benoni* as ſhe called him when ſhe was dying, that is, *the Sonne of my griefe,* but as the Father prophecyed of him in ſpirit, which is, *the ſonne of my right hand .* And from thence going to *Bethleem ,* and entring into that hollow place of our Sauiour, as ſoone as ſhe ſaw the ſacred lodging of the Bleſſed Virgin, & that ſtable *wherin the Oxe knew his owner, and the Aſſe the manger of his Lord* (that it might be fulfilled which was written by the ſame Prophet; *Bleſſed is he who ſoweth vpon the water, where the Oxe and Aſſe do tread.*) She ſwore in my hearing, that ſhe ſaw with the eyes of Fayth, the child wrapped in his cloutes, and our Lord crying in the manger , the *Magi* adoring, the Starre shining from aboue, the Virgin Mother , the diligent Foſter-father, the Paſtours comming by night; *that they might ſee the VVord which was made* (and ſo dedicated euen then , the beginning of *Iohn* the *Euangeliſt; In the beginning was the word, and the word was made fleſh ,) Herod* raging , the young Infants ſlaine , *Ioſeph* & *Mary* flying into *Egypt.* And then with teares mixed with ioy ſhe ſayd; *All haile , O Bethleem, the houſe of bread, wherein that bread was borne , which deſcended from heauen; All haile , O Ephrata , thou.moſt abundant, & fruitfull Region, whoſe fertility, God is . Of thee* Micheas *prophecyed of old . And thou Bethlem the houſe of Ephrata, art not the leaſt among ſt thoſe thouſand of Iuda; out of thee ſhall he come forth to me, who is the Prince in Iſraell ; & his going forth is from the beginning , from the dayes of eternity . Therefore ſhalt thou giue them, till the tyme of bringing them forth arriue . She ſhall bring them forth , and the relikes of her brethren , ſhall be conuerted to the ſonnes of Iſrael . For of thee is borne a Prince, who was begotten before* Lucifer, *and whoſe birth on the Fathers ſide, doth exceed all ages . And ſo long did the beginning of* Dauids *ſtocke remaine in thee, till a Virgin did bring forth, and till the relickes of the people belieuing in Chriſt , were conuerted to the ſonnes of Iſraell , and did freely preach in*

K   *this*

this manner. To you first it was fit to preach the word of God, but be-
cause you haue reiected it, and iudged your selues vnworthy of eternall
life, behold we are conuerted to the Gentils. For God had sayd, I came not
but to the lost sheep of the house of Israell. And at that tyme, the words
of Iacob *were fulfilled: A pr nce shall not be wanting out of the house*
of Iuda, *nor a Captaine out of his loynes, till he come, for whome it is*
layd vp ; and he shall be the expectation of the Gentiles. Dauid *swore*
truly, and made his vowes well, saying: If I enter into the tabernacle
of my house, if I ascend into the bed of my couch if I graunt sleep to
myne eyes, and slumbring to myne eye-lids, till I find a place for our
Lord, *and a tabernacle for the God of* Iacob. *And instantly he decla-*
red what he desired, and with his propheticall eyes discerned that he was
to come, whome now we see to be come already : Behold we haue heard
him in Ephrata, *we found him in the fieldes of the wood. For* Vau *the*
Hebrew word (as I haue learned by your teaching) doth not
signify Mary the mother of our Lord, that is ‹αυλον›, but him,
that is ‹αυτον›. Whereupon she confidently sayd ; *VVe will go into*
his Tabernacles ; we will adore in the place where his feet haue stood.
And, I miserable and sinnefull creature, am I held worthy to kisse the
manger wherein my Lord *being an infant cryed ; to pray in that stable,*
where the Virgin Mother *was deliuered of our* Lord, *being made a child?*
This is my rest because it is in the country of my Lord ; here will I dwell
because my Sauiour *made choice thereof. I haue prepared a lampe for*
my Christ, *my soule shall liue to him, and my seed shall serue him .•*

Not farre from thence, she went to the tower *Ader,* that is
to say, *Of the flocke,* neere which *Iacob* fed his flockes, and the
shepheardes, who watched by night, deserued to heare; *Glory*
be to God on high, and peace on earth, to men of a good will. And whilest they kept their sheep, they found the Lambe of God, with
that cleane & most pure fleece, which when the whole earth
was dry, was filled with celestiall dew, and whose blood
tooke away the sinnes of the world, and droue away that exte-
minatour of *Egypt,* being sprinkled vpon the posts of the house.
And then presently with a swift pace she began to go forward,
by that old way which leades to *Gaza,* to the power of the riches of God ; and silently to reuolue within her selfe, how the
Ethiopian Eunuch (prefiguring the Gentiles) did change his
skinne, and whilest he was reflecting vpon his old way found
the

the fountaine of the Ghoſpel . From thence ſhe paſſed towards the right hãd . From *Bethſur* ſhe came to *Eſcoll,* which ſignifyes a Bunch of grapes, and from whence (in teſtimony of the extreme fertility of that ſoile, & as a type of him who ſayd: *I haue trod the wine preſſe alone, & not one of the Gentils was with me*) thoſe diſcouerers , or ſpyes carryed home a bunch of Grapes of a wõderfull bignes . Not farre from thence , ſhe entered into the little houſes of *Sarah,* and viewed the antiquities of the infancy of *Iſaac,* and the relikes of *Abrahams Oake,* vnder which *he ſaw the day of Chriſt, and reioyced* . Riſing vp from thence, ſhe aſcended vp to *Chebron,* which is *Cariath Arbe* , that is to ſay , the towne of the foure men, *Abraham, Iſaac, Iacob,* and the great *Adam,* whome according to the booke of *Ieſus Naue* , the Iewes conceiue to be buryed there, although many thinke that the fourth man was *Caleb,* whoſe memory they continue by ſhewing there a part of his ſide. Hauing viewed theſe places, ſhe would not proceed to *Chariath Cephor,* that is to ſay, *the little towne of letters,* becauſe contemning the killing letter, ſhe had found the quickning ſpirit . And ſhe wondered more at thoſe ſuperiour and inferiour waters, which *Othoniel* the ſonne of *Iephone Kenaz* , had gotten , inſteed of that Southerne Land, & dry poſſeſſion ; and by Aquiducts had moiſtened thoſe fieldes of the old teſtament, that he might find the redemption of old ſinnes, in the *water of Baptiſme* . The next day, the Sunne being riſen, ſhe ſtood vpon the brow of *Chaphar Barucha* , that is, *the Towne of benediction* , to which place *Abraham* followed our Lord, looking downe from thence vpon a large deſert, & that Land, which of old was belonging to *Sodomah,* and *Gomorrah* , *Adamah,* and *Seboim.* She then contemplated thoſe Vines of *Balſamum in engaddi,* and the Calfe of *Segor* ; and *Zoara* , which in the *Syrian* language ſignifyes, *Tle little one.* She remembred the little hollow caue of *Lot* ; and being all bathed in tears, ſhe admoniſhed the Virgins who accompanyed her, to take heed of Wine, *wherein Luxury is* : and whoſe fruites are the *Moabites,* & *Ammonites* .

I make too long ſtay in the South, where the ſpouſe found out her fellow ſpouſe, as he was layd ; and where *Ioſeph* was inebriated with his brethren . But I will now returne to *Hie-*

ruſalem; and betweene *Thecua* and *Amos*, I will behold the bightly shining light of Mount *Oliuet*, from whence our Sauiour aſcended vp to his Father; and vpon which mountaine, a red Cow was yearely burnt by way of Holocauſt to our Lord; the aſhes whereof did expiat the people of *Iſrael* : wherupon alſo the *Cherubin* paſſing away from the Temple; according to *Ezechiel*, there was founded a Church to our Lord. After this , going into the Sepulcher of *Lazarus*, ſhe ſaw the houſe of *Mary*, and Martha; and *Bethphage* , the towne of *ſacerdotall iawes*; and that place, where the wanton aſſes coult of the *Gentiles* accepted the bridle of God ; and being ouerſpred with the Apoſtles garments , gaue an eaſy ſeat to the rider. Then did ſhe deſcend by a ſtraight way towards *Iericho* reuoluing in her mind, that wounded man of the Ghoſpell; and withall, the clemency of the *Samaritan*, which ſignifyes a *Guardian*, who layd the man being halfe dead , vpon his beaſt, and brought him to the ſtable of the Church, whileſt the Prieſts and Leuites, with vnmercifull harts paſſed by . She alſo ſaw the place called *Adonim* , which is by interpretation , *of blood*; becauſe much blood was wont to be ſhed there , by the frequent incurſion of murdeing theeues. She ſaw the *Sicomore tree* of *Zacheus*; that is to ſay the good workes of penance, whereby he trod vnder foot his former ſinnes, which were full of extortion and cruelty;& beheld that high Lord of ours, from the height of vertue . And neer that way , ſhe ſaw thoſe places of the blind men , where receiuing their ſight, they prefigured the myſteries of both thoſe people , which were to beliue in our Lord.

Being entred into *Iericho*, ſhe ſaw that Citty, which *Hazell* founded in *Abyram* , for his eldeſt ſonne ; and whoſe gates were placed in *Segub*, for his youngeſt. She beheld the tents of *Galgala*, and the whole heape of foreskinnes and the myſtery of the Circumciſion, and the twelue ſtones which being transferred thither out of the bottome or bed of *Iordan*, did ſtrengthen the twelue fomdations of the Apoſtles; and that fountayne of the lawe, which auntiently was moſt bitter and barren of waters, but now the true *Elizeus* had ſeaſoned it with his wiſedome, and indued it both with ſuauity, and plenty . The night was ſcarce paſſed when ſhe came with extreme feruour of deuotion

to

to *Iordan*. She ſtood vpon the bancke of the riuer ; and as ſoon as the Sunne was vp, ſhe remembred the Sunne of *Iuſtice*; and how the Prieſts had formerly ſet their dry feet in the middeſt of the riuer, when the ſtreame made a fayre way, by the ſtaying of the water halſe or the one ſide, and halſe on the other, vpon the commandement of *Elias* and *Elizeus* ; and how our Lord, by his baptiſme clenſed thoſe waters, which had bene inteſted in the tyme of the flood, by the death of all mankind. It will be a long buſineſſe, if I ſhall take vpon me to ſpeake of the valley of *Achor*, that is to ſay, *Of troubles* and *tumults*, wherin couetouſnes and theft were condemned; and of *Bethel*, the houſe of God, wherin the poore & naked *Iacob* ſlept vpon the bare ground, and (laying that ſtone vnder his head, which in *Zachary* is deſcribed to *haue ſeuen eyes*, and in *Eſay* is called *the corner ſtone*) ſaw a ladder reaching vp to heauen, toward which our Lord inclined from aboue, reaching forth his hand to ſuch as were labouring to get vp; and precipitating from on high, ſuch as were negligent. She alſo exhibited veneration, to the Sepulchres of *Ieſu* the ſonne of *Naue* vpon mount *Ephraim*, and of *Eleazarus* the ſonne of *Aaron*, which was there hard by, whereof the one was built by *Tannath*..... on the northſide of the Mount *Goas*, the other in *Gabaah* belonging to *Phinees* his ſonne: ſhe much wondered, that he who had the diſtribution of thoſe poſſeſſions in his hands, had choſen the mountaynous & barreyne parts for himſelf. What ſhall I ſay of ... whereof the altar was pulled downe, and is ſhewed to this day, where the tribe of *Beniamin* did forerunne the rapt of the Sabines, which was made by *Romulus* She paſſed by *Sichem* which now is called *Neapolis* (for it is not *Sichar*, as ſome erroneouſly affirme) and ſhe entred into that Church, which is built neer the well of *Iacob*, vpon the ſide of the mountaine of *Garizim*, & vpon which well, our Lord ſitting downe, and being hungry, and thirſty, was ſatisfyed with the faith of the *Samaritan* woman ; who leauing both her fiue husbands vnder the law of *Moyſes*, and the ſixt whome then ſhe auowed her ſelfe to haue, & giuing ouer that errour, to which *Doſitheus* was ſubiect, found the true *Meſſias*, and the true Sauiour. And turning aſide from thence, ſhe ſawe the tombes of the twelue Patriarchs, and *Sebaſtes* that is

Samaria

Sameria, which in honour of *Auguſtus* was called *Auguſta* in the *Grœcian* language. There are the Prophets *Helizeus*, and *Abdias*, *Iohn* the *Baptiſt*, then *whom there was none greater among the ſonnes of men*. There did ſhe euen tremble, and was aſtoniſhed with many wōderful things. For ſhe found the diuels roare through ſeuerall torments; and that, before the Sepulchres of the Saints, men howled after the manner of wolues, and barked like dogs, and foamed like Lyons, hiſſed like ſerpents, and roared like Buls: Others did ſhake, and wheeled their heades about, & bent their crownes behind their backes to the ground; and woemen would be hanging vp by their feet, with their cloathes flying downe about their faces. She had pitty on them, and powred forth her teares, ſhe begged mercy at the hands of Chriſt, for them all.

Now though ſhe were but weake, yet ſhe went vp the hill on foot; in two concauities whereof, *Abdias* the Prophet fed a hundred Prophets, with bread and water, in a time of famine and perſecution. From thence, ſhe went with a ſpeedy pace to *Nazareth*, that nurſery of our Lord, and to *Canaan* & *Caphernaum*, where his Miracles were ſo familiarly wrought. And ſhe ſaw the lake of *Tyberiadis*, which was ſanctifyed by our Lordr ſayling on it, & the wildernes wherein many thouſands of people were ſatiſſyed with bread; & where the twelue baskets of the twelue tribes of *Iſraell* were filled with the reliques of them who were fed. She climed vp to *Mount Thabor* wherein our Lord was tranſfigured. She ſaw a farre off, the hils of *Hermon* and *Hermonym*, and thoſe large wild fields of *Galilee*; wherein *Siſara* and all his Army, was ouercome vnder the conduct of *Barach*; the torret of *Ciſon* which deuided that plaine by the middle; and the towne neer *Naim*, where the widowes ſonne reuiued, was ſhewed to her.

The day wil ſooner faile me then difcourſe, if I ſhal ſpeake of all thoſe places, which the venerable *Paula* viſited with an incredible faith. I will paſſe on to *Egypt*, & I will ſtay a while in *Socoth*, and at the fountayne of *Sampſon*, which he produced out of a great iaw tooth; and I will waſh my dry mouth, and being ſo refreſhed, will looke vpon *Moraſtis*, which auciently was the Sepulchre of the Prophet *Micheas*, & is uow a Church.

                                                                        And

And I will leaue, on the one ſide, the Chorreans, the Geiheans, Mareſa, Idumea, and Lachis; and by thoſe deepe ſands which euen draw the feet of trauailers from vnder them, and by that huge vaſtity of the deſert, I wil come to Sior that riuer of Egypt which by interpretation is, Troubled; and I will paſſe by the fiue Citties of Egypt, which ſpeake the Cananean tongue, and the land of Geſſe, & the fieldes of Tanaiſ, wherin God wrought wonderfull things; and the Citty of No, with grew afterward to be Alexandria; and Nitria, that towne of our Lord, where the filthines of many is daily waſhed away with the moſt pure Niter of vertue. Which when ſhe ſaw, the holy and venerable Biſhop and Conteſſour Iſidorus coming to meet her, together with innumerable troupes of Monckes (amongſt whome there were many, who were ſublimed ſo farre, as to be Leuites and Prieſts) ſhe reioyced indeed at the glory of our Lord, but confeſſed her ſelfe to be vnworthy of ſo great honour. How ſhall I be able to relate, of thoſe Machario's, Arſenio's, Serapions, and the reſt of the names of thoſe pillars of Chriſt. Into whoſe cell did ſhe not eter? Before whoſe feet did ſhe not fal? In euery one of the Saints ſhe côceiued her ſelfe to ſee Chriſt our Lord: & whatſoeuer ſhe gaue thê, ſhe reioyced in that ſhe gaue it to our Lord. She expreſſed a ſtrange ardour of minde, & a courage which was ſcarce credible to be in a womâ. Being forgetfull of her ſex, and of her corporall indiſpoſitions, ſhe wiſhed that ſhe might dwell with her virgins, among ſo many thouſands of Monckes. And perhaps ſhe had obtayned it, through the great reſpects which they carryed to her, vnleſſe a more earneſt deſire to reuiew the holy places had drawen her backe And by reaſon of thoſe moſt exceſſiue heats ſhe put her ſelfe to Sea, from Pelluſium, to Maioma; and retourned with ſo great ſpeed, that ſhe might be thought to fly Soon after reſoluing to remayne for euer in the holy Bethlem, ſhe entertayned herſelfe for three yeares in that ſtraight lodging, till ſhe had built Cels, and Monaſteries, and diuers habitations for pilgrimes, neer that way, where Mary and Ioſeph could find no place of entertainment. And this ſhall ſuffice for the deſcription of her Iourney, which ſhe performed with many virgins one of the being her daughter.

But

But now let her vertue, which is properly her owne, be deſcribed more at large : in the declararation whereof, I pro-feſſe before God , who is both my witnes , and my iudge, that I will adde nothing to the truth ; nor amplify , after the man-ner of men who praiſe others;but rather ſay leſſe,then I might, leaſt els I may ſeem to ſpeake incredible things; and be concei-ued to deliuer vntruthes , and to adorne *Eſopes* crow with co-lours belonging to other birds , in the conceit of my detracters, who are euer gnawing vpon me with a ſharp tooth.She aba-ſed her ſelfe with ſo great humility (which is the chief vertue of Chriſtians)that whoſoeuer had not ſeen her before,and had deſired to ſee her then , for the fame of her perſon, would ne-uer haue belieued that ſhe was her ſelfe , but the very pooreſt of her maydes . And when ſhe was hemmed in with quiers of virgins, ſhe would be the meaneſt of them all , both in cloa-thing, and ſpeech, and behauiour , & rancke . From the death of her husband to the time of her owne death , ſhe did neuer eat with any man, how holy ſoeuer he were; no not although he were placed in Epiſcopall dignity . She went not to any bathes, in but caſes of danger of her life. Euen when ſhe was oppreſt with the moſtſharp feauers ſhe lay vpō no ſoft beds;but ſhe reſted vpon the hard ground being only ouerſpred with certeyn little poore cloathes of haire , if that indeed may be ac-counted reſt , which coupled the dayes and nights,with almoſt continuall praiers , fulfilling that of the Pſalme ; *I will wash my bed euery night , and I will water my couch with teares* . And euen in that time of reſt , you would take her eyes to be as ſome ſluces of water ; and ſo would ſhe lament her leaſt ſinnes , as that you would eſteeme her thereby to be guilty of moſt grieuous cri-mes . And when we would be often warning her , that ſhe ſhould take care of her eyes , and preſerue them for the reading of holy ſcripture ; ſhe would vſe to ſay, *That face is to be made vgly , which againſt the precept of God I haue ſo often daubed ; That body is to be afflicted , which hath been treated with ſo much delicacy . A long laughter is to be recompenced with a conſtant lamentation . Soft li-men , and pretious ſtuffes of ſilke muſt be changed into ragged haire cloathes : I who haue pleaſed a husband and a world,deſire now to pleaſe Chriſt* .

I

If, in the company of her ſo many and ſo great vertues I ſhall praiſe chaſtity in her, I may well ſeem ſuperfluous. For in this vertue, euen when ſhe was a ſecular womā, ſhe was the example of al the Matrons in *Rome.* Where ſhe behaued her ſelſe ſo , as that the report euen of wicked tongues , did neuer preſume to deuiſe any thing againſt her . There was nothing more pittifull then her minde , nothing more benigne towardes meane people . She courted not ſuch as were mighty , neither yet did ſhe faſtidiouſly deſpiſe ſuch as were proud , & affected the vanity of glory . If ſhe ſaw a poore body, ſhe reliued him; if a rich man , ſhe exhorted him to vſe charity . Only in liberality , ſhe exceeded meaſure ; and whileſt ſhe was paying intereſt , ſhe would often borrow of one to diſcharge another, that ſo ſhe might ſtill haue ſome meanes , not to deny an almes to him who asked it . I confeſſe my errour : When I found her too open handed , I reprehended her with that ſaying of the Apoſtle , *Let not others be ſo comforted , as that your ſelues be aff cted thereby ; but doe it with diſcretion and weighing of circnmſtances ; that your abundance may be the relief of others wantes & their abundāce of yours.* And that of our Sauiour in the Ghoſpell , *Let him who hath two coates , giue one to him who hath none*; and I would tell her that we muſt procure, not to do that willingly, which we may not alwayes do ; and many thinges of this kind . Which ſhe with an admirable modeſty , and moſt ſparing ſpeech , would yet diſcharge , calling God to witneſſe , that ſhe did all things for his ſake , and that ſhe had this earneſt deſire , that ſhe might dye begging ; and that ſhe might not haue one penny to leaue her daughter ; and that at her death , ſhe might be ſhrowded in the ſheet of anothers gift . For concluſion , ſhe ſaid , If I ſhal aske almes , I may find many who will giue it me, but if this begger haue not that of me, which I may affoard him, euen out of anothers ſtore, and ſo ſhall chance to dy for want thereof, at whoſe hands ſhall his life be required ? For my part I deſired her to be more cautious in the diſtribution of her temporall eſtat; but ſhe being more ardent in her faith, flew cloſe to her Sauiour, with her whole hart , & being poore in ſpirit, did follow her poore Lord ; repaying him what ſhe had receiued, ſince he had bene made poore for her . In fine , ſhe obtayned what ſhe deſired,

L

and

& left her daughter in great debt, which hitherto she is owing; and confides not in her owne strength , but in the mercy of Christ , that she shall be able to pay it .

It is vsuall with many of our Matrons , to bestow their gifts at the sound of the trumpet , and carrying a profuse hand towardes some few , to withdraw their bounty from the rest; from which vice she was wholy free . For so did she deuid her Charity among them all, as was necessary for euery one , not towardes excesse , but for necessity . No poore man could goe empty from her , which yet she was not able to compasse by the greatnes of her estate, but by her prudence in dispensing; and this she would euer be repeating, *Blessed be the mercifull; for they shall obtaine mercy*. And; *As water quenches fire , so doth almes extinguish sinne* . And againe ; *Make your selues friendes of the vniust Mammon, that they may receaue you into eternall Tabernacles* . And : *Giue almes , and behold all thinges are cleane to you* . And the wordes of *Daniel* admonishing *Nabuchodonezor* the King , *that he was to redeeme his sinnes with almes* . She would not cast away her money vpon these stones , which are to passe away with this world , but vpon those liuing stones which rowle vp & down the earth ; and wherof , in the *Apocalips* of *Iohn,* the Citty of the great King is built ; and which, as the Scripture sayth , must be conuerted into *Saphires* and *Emmerolds,* and *Iaspers,* and other gemmes.

But these thinges may be common to many : and the Diuell knowes, that the top of vertue is not placed in this Whereupon he sayd to our Lord (after *Iob* had lost his substance, after his house was ouerthrowne , after his children were slaine .) *A man would giue a skin for a shinne ; and whatsoeuer he hath , for the sauing of his life ; but stretch forth thy hand , and touch his flesh and bones, and see if he will not curse thee to thy face* . We know that very many haue giuen almes, who gaue nothing of their owne body ; who haue stretched forth their handes to the poore, but yet haue beene ouercome by the pleasures of the flesh ; to haue painted the outside, whilest that within hath beene all full of dead bones. But *Paula,* was no such person but was of so great abstinence, that almost she exceeded measure , and contracted weakenes of body , by excessiue fasting & labour. For except

cept vpon holy dayes, she did ſcarce vſe oyle in her meat; that
by this one inſtance, it may be knowne what iudgment she
made of wine, of ſewet, or larde, and fish, & hony, and egges,
and other things which are delightfull to the taſte. For the very eating whereof, ſome take themſelues to be extremely abſtinent; and if they ſtuffe their belly with theſe thinges, they
thinke their honeſty is in ſafety.

But enuy euer followes vertue; and lightning ſtrikes the
higheſt hils . Neither is it any wonder, if I ſay this of men, ſince
euē our Lord was crucified, through the zeale of the *Phariſees;*
and ſince all Saints haue had Emulators, and ſince there was a
ſerpent euen in Paradice, by whoſe enuy, *death entred into the
world.* Our Lord had raiſed vp *Adad* the *Idumean*, who might
giue her now and then a knocke, leaſt she should extoll her
ſelfe; and he admonished her often, and as it were with a kind
of goad of the flesh, leaſt the greatnes of her vertue might
ſnatch her vp too high, and conſidering the vices of other woemen, she might thinke her ſelfe to be placed out of all reach .
I would be ſaying to her, that she muſt yeild to that bitter enuy
and giue place to madnes, which *Iacob* had done in the caſe of
his brother *Eſaw;* and *Dauid*, in that of *Saull* who was the moſt
implacable of all enemyes; whereof the one flede into *Meſopo-
tamia,* the other deliuered himſelfe vp to ſtrange people; choo-
ſing rather to be ſubiect to enemyes, then to enuyous perſons.
But she would be anſwering me thus . You might iuſtly ſay
theſe thinges, if the diuell fought not euery where againſt the
ſeruants and handmayds of God; & if he got not the ſtart of
them, in being the firſt at all thoſe places whitherſoeuer Chriſtians went to fly. Though I were not deteyned here, by the
loue of theſe holy places, and if I were able to find my *Bethlē*
in any other part of the world but this, yet whh should not I
ouercome the bitternes of enuy with patience ? Why should I
not breake the necke of pride by humility ? and to him who
ſtrikes one of my cheekes, offer him the other? *Paul* the Apoſtle,
ſaying; *Ouercome you euill with good.* Did not the Apoſtles glory,
when they *ſuffered contumely for our Lord* ? Did not our Sauiour
humble himſelfe, taking the forme of a ſeruant & being made
obedient to his father, euen to the death, and that the death of

the

the croſſe, that he might ſaue vs by his *Paſſion*? If *Iob* had not fought and ouercome in the battell, he had not receiued the crowne of iuſtice, nor heard this word of our Lord, *Doeſt thou thinke I had any other mind in prouing thee, then that thou mighteſt appeare iuſt*? They are ſaid to be bleſſed in the Ghoſpell, who ſuffer perſecution for iuſtice. Let our conſcience be ſecure, that we ſuffer not for our ſinnes; & then our afliction in t his worl doth but ſerue vs for matter of reward.

If at any time any enemy of hers had bene malepert, and had proceeded ſo farre, as to offer her any iniury of words, ſhe would reſort to that of the Pſalme, *VVhen the ſinner ſet himſelfe before me, I held my peace, and was ſilent euen from good thinges.* And againe; *I was like to a deafe perſon who heard not; and like one who being dumbe did not open his mouth; and I became as a man, who doth not heare, and hath not in his mouth, any word of reproofe.*

In temptations ſhe would frequent thoſe wordes of Deutronomy, *Your Lord God tempteth you, that he may know whether you loue the Lord your God with your whole hart, & with your whole ſoule.* In aflictions and troubles ſhe would repeat the words of *Eſay. You who are weaned from milke; and taken from the tet, muſt expect tribulation vpon tribulation, and hope vpon hope. Yet expect a little, for the malice of lips, and for the wicked tongue.* And ſhe would bring this teſtimony of ſcripture for her comfort, becauſe it belongs to ſuch as are weaned, and come to an eſtat of ſtrength, to endure tribulation vpon tribulation, that they may deſerue to haue *hope* vpon *hope. As knowing that tribulation works patience, patience probation, probation hope, and hope makes not aſhamed; and that if the outward man grow into decay yet the inward man may be renewed. And that this light and momentary tribulation of yours at the preſent, may worke an eternall waight of glory in you, who care not for the viſible but for inuiſible thinges; for thoſe thinges which are viſible are teporall, but thoſe which are inuiſible are eternall.* And that the time wil not be long (though our impatience may thinke it ſo) but quickle they ſhall ſee the help of God, ſaying to them. *I haue heard you in a fit tyme, and I haue ſuccoured you in the day of ſaluation;* and that crafty lips and wicked tongues were not to be feared, but that we muſt reioyce in our Lord and helper; and that we muſt heare him admoniſhing vs thus by his Prophet:

Feare

Feare not the flaunders of men & be not troubled at their blasphemies; for the worme shall consume them as it would doe a garment, and the moath shall deuoure them, as if they were wooll. And by your patience you shall posseffe your foules; And *The fufferinges of this life, are not worthy of that future glory which shall be reuealed in vs.* And in another place; *VVe must suffer tribulation vpon tribulation, that we may proceed with patience, in all those thinges which happen to vs. For the patient man is full of wifedome; but he who is pufill animous, is extremely a foole withall.*

In her frequent infirmities, and fickeneffes, fhe would fay: *VVhen I am weake, then am I strongest; and we keep a treafure in brickle veffells, till this mortality of ours put on immortality, and this corruption be apparelled with incorruption.* And againe: *As the fufferinges of Chrift haue fuperabounded in vs, fo alfo hath confolation aboũded in vs, through Chrift.* And then againe: *As you are companions in fuffering, fo shall you alfo be in receauing comfort.*

In her forrowes fhe would fay thus: *VVhy, O my foule, art thou fad and why art thou troubled within me? Put thy truft in God, for ftill I will confeffe to him, who is the health of my countenance, and my God.* In her dangers fhe would fay: *He that will come after me, muft deny himfelfe, and take vp his Croffe and follow me.* And againe: *He that will faue his life shall loofe it; and he that for my fake, will be content to loofe his life, shall faue it.* When fhe fuffered loffes in her fortunes, and when the ouerthrow of all her patrimony was declared to her, she fayd: *But what doth it profit a man, if he gaine the whole world, and hurt his owne foule withal? VVhat exchãge shall a man giue for his foule?* And; *Naked I came out of my Mothers wombe, and naked I shall returne; As it pleafed our Lord, fo is it done, bleffed be the name of our Lord.* And that other: *Do not loue the world, nor thofe things which are in the world, for whatfoeuer is the world is the defire of the flesh, the concupifcence of the eyes, and the pride of this life, which is not of the father, but of the world; and the world paffes with the concupifcence therof.* For I know when her friends wrote to her of the dãgerous infirmities of her children, & efpecially of her Toxotius, whome fhe did moft dearely loue, & when fhe had effectually fulfilled that faying, *I am troubled, & haue not fpoken*, she broke forth with thefe wordes: *He who loues his fonne, or his daughter more then me, is not worthy of me.* And praying to our

Lord

Lord ſhe ſayd : *Poſſeſſe thou, O Lord, the children of them who are mortifyed, and who mortify themſelues daily for thy ſake.*

I know a certaine Whiſperer (and this is a moſt peſtilent race of people) who could her vnder the colour of good will, and care of her, that through the exceſſiue feruour of her vertue, ſhe ſeemed mad to ſome ; and that ſhe were beſt looke to her head ; to whome ſhe anſwered thus ; *VVe are made a ſpectacle to the world, to Angells, and to men ; and we are fooles for Chriſt, but the folly of God, is wiſer then men .* Whereupon our Sauiour ſayth to his Father : *Thou knoweſt my ſimplicity .* And againe : *I am made like a kind of Monſter to many , but thou art my ſtrong helper , I am made as a beaſt before thee, and I am euer with thee .* He, whom in the Ghoſpell euen his neere friendes ſought to bind, like a mad Man, and his aduerſaries did bitterly taxe him , and ſay : *He hath a Diuell , and is a Samaritan ; He caſts out Diuels in Belzebub who is the prince of Diuells .* But let vs heare how the Apoſtle exhorts vs, ſaying : *This is our glory , the teſtimony of our conſcience, becauſe we haue conuerſed in the world with ſanctity and ſincerity , & in the grace of God .* And let vs heare our Lord ſaying to the Apoſtles : *Therefore doth the world hate you, becauſe you are not of the world, for if you were, the world would loue that which is his owne .* And to our Lord himſelfe ſhe would be turning her wordes, and ſaying : *Thou knoweſt the hidden thoughtes of the hart .* And : *All theſe thinges are come vpon vs , neither yet haue we forgotten thee, nor haue we done wickedly againſt thy will, nor is our hart turned backe frō thee .* And : *For thee are we mortifyed all the day long, and we are reputed as ſheep , fit for ſlaughter .* But *Our Lord is my helper, and I will not feare what man can do to me.* For I haue read , *My ſonne honour thou our Lord, and thou ſhalt be comforted, and beſides our Lord , thou ſhalt feare none .*

By theſe and the like teſtimonies of Scripture (as if it had beene with ſome armour of God) did ſhe defend her ſelfe againſt all ill oppoſition ; but eſpecially againſt cruell enuy ; & by ſuffering iniuries, ſhe would mitigate the fury of their enraged minds . In a word , her patience did appeare in al things euen to the day of her death : and ſo did the enuy of others , which euer gnawes vpon the harbourer thereof ; and whileſt it ſtriues to hurt the contrary party it growes mad and moſt furious

rious

rious vpon himſelfe.

I will now ſpeake of the order of her Monaſtery, & how ſhe conuerted the pouerty of the Saints, into her owne gaine ; *Shee ſowed carnall thinges, that she might reap ſpirituall.* She gaue earthly things, that ſhe might obtaine heauenly ; ſhe gaue temporall thinges, that ſhe might exchange them for eternall. Beſides a Monaſtery of men, which ſhe aſſigned to be gouerned by men, ſhe gathered many Virgins together out of diuers Prouinces; ſuch as were very noble, ſuch as were of midle ranke ; and ſuch as were of the meaneſt condition; and theſe, ſhe diuided into three troupes of Monaſteries; but yet ſo, as that being ſeparated in their worke, and in their food, yet in their Pſalmes and prayers they were ioyned. As ſoone as the *Alleluia* was ſung, which was the ſigne whereby they were called together, it was lawfull for none to forbeare coming. But *Paula* being either the very firſt, or at leaſt one of the firſt, would expect the arriuall of the reſt ; prouoking them ſo by her example to be diligent; and working vpon them, rather by the way of ſhame, then terrour. In the morning early, at the third houre, at the ſixt, at the nynth, and at midnight, they ſung the Pſaltery in order. Neither was it lawful for any of the Siſters, to be ignorant of the Pſalmes, and not to learne ſomewhat daily of the holy Scriptures. vpon the Sundaies only, they went forth to Church, at the ſide whereof they dwelt. And euery troupe followed their peculiar Mother, and from thence returning together, they attended to the worke which was appoynted, and made cloathes either for themſelues, or others. Such a one as were of the nobler ſort, was not permitted to haue any companion of her owne family, leaſt being mindefull of former thinges they might refreſh the auntient errours of their idle youthe, and renew them by often ſpeech.

They went all in one habit or attire. They vſed no linnē at all, but onely for the wiping of their hands. They were ſo perfeﬅly ſeperated from men, as that ſhe ſeuered them euen from Eunuches alſo, leaſt otherwiſe occaſion might haue bene giuen to ill tongued men, who are apt to carpe at Saints, for their owne greater priuiledge to ſinne. If any of them came later to the Quier, or were more ſlacke in working thē the reſt,

ſhe

she would let vpon her seueral wayes. If she were cholericke, by faire language; if she were patient, by reprehension, imitating that of the Apostle, *what will you haue me do, shall I come to you with the rod, or in the spirit of lenity and meekenes?* Excepting food and cloathes, she suffered no one of them to haue any thing, according to S. Paul; *Hauing food and cloaths, be contented therewith*, least by the custome of hauing more, she should minister occasion to auarice, which is satisfyed with no wealth; and how much the more it hath, so much the more doth it require; and it is not lessened either by plenty, or pouerty Such as were fallen out amongst themselues, she would vnite, by her most milde manner of speech.

As for the vnbridlednes of the younger sort, she would tame their flesh, with frequent and double fasts, choosing rather to let their stomacks ake, then their minds. If she saw some one of them any thing curious or choyse, she would reproue that errour, by a contracted brow, and sad face, saying, That the affected cleanlines of the body and of cloathing, is vncleanes to the soule, and that an vndecent or immodest word, was neuer to proceed out of a virgins mouth; for by those signes, a lustfull mind is shewed, and by the outward man, the vices of the inward are declared. Whomsoeuer she obserued to be tatling, full of tongue, or forward, and delighted with brawles, and that being often admonished, she did not mend, she would make her pray in the hindermost rancke and sometimes out of the community of the *Sisters*; and againe at the doores of the *Refectory*; and to eat alone: To the end that whome chiding could not mend, shame might. She detested theft, like sacriledge. And whatsoeuer was accounted either little, or nothing amongst secular people, that did she esteem to be a most grieuous crime in Monasteries.

What shall I say of her pitty, & diligence about sicke persons, whome she cherished with strange obsequ ousnes and seruice. And she who liberally affoarded all thinges to sicke folkes, and would also giue them flesh to eat; whensoeuer her selfe was sicke, she gaue her selfe no such liberties; and in that, seemed vniust, that being so full of pitty to others, she exercised so much seuerity vpon her selfe. There was none of the

younger

younger ſort healthfull and ſtrong, who gaue her ſelfe to ſo
much abſtinence, as *Paula* did with that broken and aged and
weake body of hers. I confeſſe that in this poynt,ſhe was ſomewhat too peremptory ; for ſhe would not ſpare her ſelfe, nor
hearken to any admonition. I will tell you what I know by
experience. In *Iuly*, when the heates were at the higheſt, ſhe
fell into a burning feauer, and when by the mercy of God ſhe
was recouering, after ſhe had bene deſpaired of ; and the Phyſi-
tians were perſwading her,that for the getting of ſome ſtrēgth,
ſhe would vſe a little wine, which was very ſmall, leaſt continuing to drinke water, ſhe might grow hydropicke; & when
I had priuately deſired the bleſſed Pope *Epiphanius* to aduiſe, or
rather to compell her to drinke wine, ſhe as ſhe was diſcret, &c
of a quicke piercing wit, did preſently find that ſhe was as it
were betrayed ; and ſmiling, declared that that was my doing,
which was his ſaying. To be ſhort, when the bleſſed Biſhop,
after hauing vſed much perſwaſion, was gone forth, & I was
asking her, what he had done, ſhe anſwered, *I haue gone ſo farre*
as that almoſt I haue perſwaded the old man, that I might drinke no
wine. I haue related this particular, not that I allow of thoſe
burdens which are vndertaken inconſideratly, & aboue ones
ſtrength; for the ſcripture fayth, *Take not a burdem vpon thee*;but
only to the end that I may proue euen hereby, the ardour of
her mind, and the deſires of her faithfull ſoule. And ſhe ſaid,
My ſoule thirſt towards thee ; and how plentifully doth my fleſh alſo
thirſt A hard thing it is, to keep the meane in all things. And
indeed, according to that ſentence of the Philoſopher, *vertue is*
in the meane, and exceſſe is reputed vitious; which we expreſſe
by one ſhort little ſentence, *Take not too much of any thing.*

She,who was ſo peremptory, and ſtriĉt in the contempt
of food; was tender in the occaſions of her greif ; and was euen
defeated by the death of her friends, and eſpecially of her children For in the death both of her husband, & of her daugters,
ſhe was euer in danger of her owne life. And though ſhe would
Signe both her mouth, and her breſt, and procure to molliſy a
mothers grief by the impreſſion of the Croſſe,yet ſhe was ouercome by her affeĉtion ; and thoſe bowels of a mother did euen
aſtoniſh her tender hart : and though ſhe were a conquerour in

her mind; yet she was conquered, by the frailty of her body
And once, vpon such an occasion, a sicknesse taking hold of
her, did possesse her for so long a time, that it gaue care to vs, &
daunger to her. But she reioyced, & said, *Miserable creature that
I am, who shall free me from the body of this death?*

But here the discreet Reader will say, that I writ matter
of reproofe, rather then praise. I take *Iesus* to witnes, whom
she serued in deed, and whom I serue in desire, that I fayne
nothing on either side; but that I deliuer truthes, as one Christian should do of another; and that I writ no *panegyricke*, but a
story of her, and that those thinges which go for vices in her,
would be vertues in an other. I call them vices according to
the mind whereof I was, and to the desire of all the sisters, and
brothers who loued her, and are looking for her now she is
gone. But she *hath fulfilled her course, she hath kept the faith, & now
enioyes the crowne of iustice and followes the lambe wheresoeuer he goes.*
She is now satisfyed to the full, because she was hungry; & she
sings thus with ioy; *As we haue heard, so haue we seen it, in the Citty
of the Lord of power, in the Citty of our God.*

O blessed change of things! she wept that she might for
euer reioyce; she despised these leaking cesternes, that she might
find the fountayne which is our Lord. She wore a haircloath,
that now she might be apparelled in white roabes, & say, *Thou
hast torne my sackloath, and hast apparelled me with ioy.* She fed vpon
ashes like bread, and she mingled her drinke with teares, saying, *My
teares were bread to me, day and night,* that she might feed for e-
uer vpon the bread of Angels, & sing, *Taste & see how sweet our
Lord is.* And *My hart hath earnestly vttered a good word; I consecrat
my workes to the King.* And she saw those words of *Esay,* or rather
the words of our Lord by *Esay,* fulfilled in her selfe, *Behold
they who serue me, shall eat; but you shall be hungry: Behold they who
serue me, shall drinke; but you shall be thirsty: Behold they who serue
me shall reioyce; but you shall be shamefully afflicted: Behold they who
serue me shall exult; but yon shal cry out in the sorrow of your harts, &
shall howle through the contrition of your spirit.*

I was saying that she euer fled from those leaking Cesternes,
that she might find the fountayne which is our Lord, & might
sing with ioy, *As the hart desires the fountaynes of water, so doth
my*

my ſoule aſpire to thee , O my God: when ſhal I come & appeare before the face of God ? I will therfore briefly touch, how ſhe auoyded thoſe durty lakes of the heretikes ; and eſteemed them to be no better, ther Pagans. A certaine crafty old companion , and who in his owne opinion was a ſhrewd kind of ſchollar, begā, without my knowledge , to propound certaine queſtiōs to her, and ſay , *VVhat ſinne hath an Infant committed, that he ſhould be poſſeſſed by a Diuell ?* It *what age ſhall we be when we are to riſe from the dead ? If in the age when we dye ſome of vs will need nurſes after the reſurrection : If otherwiſe , it will not be a reſurrection of the dead, but a transformation of them , into others . Beſides , there will either be a diuerſity of the Sexes of man and woman, or there will be none. If there be, it will follow that there will be marriage , and carnall knowledge , yea and generation . If there be not, then, taking away the difference of Sex , they will not be the ſame bodies , which riſe againe : for an earthly habitation doth aggrauate and oppreſſe the vnderſtanding , which hath many thinges to thinke of ; but they ſhall be ſpirituall and ſubtill, according to the Apoſtle , The body is ſowed carnall , and it ſhall riſe ſpirituall.* By all which he deſired to proue that reaſonable ſoules, for certaine vices & auntient ſinnes, were ſlipped downe into bodies, and according to the diuerſity , and demerit of the ſame ſinnes were to be ſubiect to ſuch, or ſuch a condition; ſo that either he ſhould enioy health of body , or riches, and nobility of parents, or els ſhould fall into ſicke fleſh ; or els by coming into poore houſes , might pay the puniſhment of thoſe antient ſinnes, & be ſhut vp in this preſent life , and in their bodies as in a priſon.

Which as ſoon as ſhe had heard, and related to me, letting me know who the man was , and that a neceſſity lay vpon me, of reſiſting this moſt wicked viper, & deſtroying the beaſt, who the Pſalmiſt mentions ſaying , *Do not deliuer vp to beaſts, the ſoules of ſuch as confeſſe to the;* And *Rebuke O Lord , theſe beaſts of the reed, who writing iniquity , do ſpeake a ly againſt our Lord ; and exalt their mouths againſt the moſt high.* I met with the man (& by his owne diſcourſe , whereby he procured to deceiue her, I ſhut him vp, by asking him this ſhort queſtion . *VVhether or no he belieued the future reſurrection of the dead.* When he had anſwered that he did, I purſued him thus ; Shall the ſame bodies riſe? or ſhall they be other ? When he had ſaid the ſame ; I asked him , whether in

the felfe fame fexe, or in another? Vpon which queſtion holding his peace (and toſſing his head too & fro, like fome ſnake
leaſt he ſhould be hurt) becauſe ſaid I, you hold your peace, I
will anſwere my felfe for you, and inferre the confequences.
If a woman ſhall not rife as a woman, nor a man as a man,
there will be no refurrection of the dead. For the fex implyes
diſtinct parts, and the parts make vp a whole body; but if there
be no fex, and parts; what will become of the refurrection of
bodies, which conſiſt not without parts, and fex? And then, if
there be no refurrection of bodies, there can be no refurrection
of the dead. But as for that alfo, which you obiect towching
marriage, *If they shall be the same parts, it muſt follow that there will
be marriage*, it is anſwered by our Sauiour ſaying, *You erre, not
knowing the Scripture, not the vertue of God. For in the Reſurrection
of the dead, they shall neither marry, nor be marryed but shall be like
the Angels of God.* In that he ſaith, they ſhall neither marry nor
be marryed, the diuerſity of fex is ſhewed; for no man ſaith of
wood, or ſtone, that they shall neither marry, nor be marryed, which are not capable of marriage; but of them who may
marry, & yet forbeare to do it by the power & grace of Chriſt.
If you reply and aske, *How then shall we be like to Angells, ſince
among the Angells there is no difference of male and female?* I will
anſwere you in few words. Our Lord doth not repromife to
vs the ſubſtance, but the conuerſation and felicity of Angells.
As *Iohn Baptiſt*, euen before he was beheaded, was called an
Angell; and all the Saints and Virgins of God, do expreſſe in
themſelues, the life of Angells, euen in this world. For when
it is ſayd: *You shall be like to Angels*, a refemblance is promiſed,
but the nature is not changed. And anſwere me befides, how
you interprete, *that Thomas touched the handes of our Lord, after
the Reſurrection, and ſaw his ſide boared through with a Lance?* And
*That Peter ſaw our Lord, ſtanding vpon the shoare, and eating part of
a broyled fish, and a hony combe?* Certainly, he who ſtood, had
feet; he who ſhewed a wounded fide, had doubtles a belly, &
breſt, without which he could not haue ſides, which muſt be
contiguous to them both. He who ſpake, did ſpeake with a
tongue, a pallat, and with teeth. For as the quill hath relation
to the ſtringes, ſo the tongue preſſes towards the teeth, and

makes

makes a vocall found. He whofe handes were felt, muft by cō-
fequence, haue armes . Since therefore he was fayd to haue all
the parts, he muft neceffarily haue had the whole body, which
is framed of the partes, and that no feminine, but mafculine,
that is, of the fexe wherein he dyed . If now you shall reply,
that by the fame reafon we muft eate after the Refurrection;
and that our Lord entred in, when the doores were shut, -a-
gainft the nature of true, aud folid bodies: giue eare a while .
Do not draw our Fayth into reproach, by fpeaking of meat after the Refurrection. For our Lord bad them giue meat to
the Daughter of the *Archifynagogue*, when she was raifed again
to life . And *Lazarus*, who had been dead foure dayes, is written to haue fed with him at the fame table, leaft his Refurrection should be thought to be but a conceit . But if becaufe he entred in while the dores were shut, you would therefore ftriue
to proue, that his body was but aeriall and fpirituall; by the
fame reafon it muft alfo haue beene but fpiritual, before he fuffered, becaufe he walked then vpon the Sea, which is contrary
to the nature of waighty bodyes. And the Apoftle *Peter*, who
alfo walked vpon the waters with a wauering pace, muft be
belieued to haue had but a fpirituall body, wheras the ftrength
& power of God, is shewed more, when any thing is done a-
gainft nature. And to the end that you may know, that by the
greatnes of wonders, not the change of nature, but the omnipotency of God is shewed; he who walked by fayth, began by in
fidelity to finke downe, vnles the hand of our Lord had kept
him vp, when he fayd : *VVhy doft thou doubt, O thou of little fayth?*
But I marueile that you will haue fo obftinate a mind when
our Lord himfelfe did fay : *Bring in thy finger hither, and touch
my handes; and reach forth thy hand, and put it into my fide, and be not
incredulous, but belieue*. And els where : *See my handes and my feet,
for it is I . Feele and fee, for a fpirit hath no flesh and bones, as you fee I
haue*. And when he had fayd fo, he shewed them his hands &
his feet . I tell you of bones, and flesh, and handes, and feet; &
you come talking to me of *Globes of the Stoickes*, and certaine do-
ting fancies of the ayer . But if now you aske me, *VVhy an infant
who neuer finned, is poffeft by a Diuell? or of what age we shall be, whē
we rife againe ; fince we dye of feuerall ages?* I shall anfwere you

good

good cheape with this; *The iudgments of God are a great abysse.* And *O the altitude of the riches of the wisedome, and knowledge of God how inscrutable are his iudgments, and how vnsearchable his wayes? For who hath knowne the sense of our Lord, or who hath beene called by him to counselle.*

But the diuersity of ages, doth not change the truth of bodies. For since our bodies doe continually change, and either encreafe, or decreafe, we shoud, by that reafon, be euery one of vs, many men, as we daily vndergo changes; & I was an other being ten yeares old, an other at thirty, an other at fifty, an other now that I haue my whole head ful of hoary haires. Therfore according to the traditions of the Churches, and of the Apoftle *Paul*, we muft anfwere thus. *That we shall rife in perfeft man, in the meafure of the age of the fulnes of Chrift*; in which age the Iewes conceiue *Adam* was created, and when we read that our Lord and Sauiour rofe againe; befides many other proofes, which I brought out of both Teftaméts, wherewith to ftrágle the hereticke. And from that time *Paula* did fo beginne to deteft the man, and all them, who were of his doctrine, that fhe proclamed them with a loud voice, to be the enemyes of our Lord Now thefe thinges I haue mentioned, not that I would briefly confute the herefy, which is to be anfwered in many volumes, but to the end I might fhew the faith of fo great a woman, as fhe was, who chofe rather to vndergo the continuall emnities of men, then to pronoke the wrath of God, by entertayning fuch friendships as were faulty.

I will therefore fay as I began, there was nothing more docile then her wit. She was flow to fpeake, & fwift to heare, as being mindefull of this precept, *Hearken, O Ifrael, and hold thy peace.* She had the holy Scriptures without booke. And though she loued the hiftoricall part thereof, and faid *that it was the foundation, and the ground of truth*; yet she did much more affect the fpirituall meaning of it and by that high fence she fecured the edificatió of her foule. In fine she compelled me, that together with her daughter, she might read ouer both the old Teftament, and the new, whileft I expounded it. Which I denying at the firft for modefties fake, yet at laft, in regard of her frequent defires, I was content to teach that, which I had

learnt

learnt of my selfe ; that is to say I learnt it not of presumptiō, which is the worst Master of all others, but of the most illustrious men of the Church. If at any time I were at a stand, & did ingenuously confesse myne owne ignorance, she would neuer leaue me in peace, but by a perpetuall kind of demaund, compel me to declare, out of many various opinions which seemed the most probable to me.

I will also speake of another particular which in the eye of enuious persons will seeme to haue somewhat of the incredible. She had a mind to learne the *Hebrew tongue*, which I had gotten in some measure with much labour and sweat, from my very youth ; and euen yet I do not forsake the study, with a kind of indefatigable meditation thereof, least I should grow to be forsaken by it. And she also hath so obtayned this tongue, as that she can read the psalmes in *Hebrew*, and pronounce the language, without any accent of the *Latin tongue*, which we also see euen to this day in her holy daughter *Eustochium*, who euer so adhered to her mother, and so liued vnder her comādments, that she neuer lodged, nor fed, nor went without her, nor had one penny in her power, but did reioyce to see that little fortune which was left of her Fathers and Mothers patrimony, to be bestowed by her Mother, vpon poore folkes; and she esteemed the duty she ought her parent, to be her greatest inheritance and riches.

I must not passe ouer in silence with how great ioy she did euē exult, when she heard that her grādchild the young *Paula*, who was begotten and borne of *Leta*, and *Toxotius*, yea & conceiued with a desire, and promise from them both, of future chastity, did sing forth *Alleluia* with her stammering tongue, in her cradle, in the middest of other childish toyes; & did breake forth the names of her grandmother, and her aunt, by halfe words. In this alone, she had still a desire concerning her coūtry, to know that her sonne, her daughter in law, & her grandchild, had renounced the world, and serued Christ our Lord: which in part she hath obtayned; for her grand-child is reserued to weare the vayle of Christ. Her daughter in law, deliuered her selfe ouer to eternall chastity; her sonne in law followes on in faith, almes, and other good workes ; and endeauoureth to

expresse

expreſſe that at *Rome*, which ſhe hath accompliſhed at *Ieruſalem.*
But what do we, O my ſoule? why feareſt thou to come
ſo farre as her end? Already the booke is growne big, whileſt
we feare to come to this laſt caſt; as if whileſt we conceale it, &
employ our ſelues vpon her praiſes, we were able to put off
her death. Hitherto we haue ſayled with a fore-wind, & our
ſliding ſhip hath plowed vp the criſping waues of the Sea at
eaſe. But now my diſcourſe is falling vpon rockes, and I am
in ſuch daũger of preſent ſhipwracke, as makes me ſay, *Saue vs,*
Maſter, for we periſh; And againe, *Riſe vp O Lord, why doeſt thou*
ſleep. For who can with dry eyes ſpeake of *Paula* dying? She fel
into extreame indiſpoſitiõ, or rather ſhe found what ſhe ſought
in leauing vs, and in being more fully ioyned to our Lord. In
which ſickneſſe, the approued dear affection of the daughter
Euſtochium to her mother, was more confirmed in the eyes of al
Sſ e would be ſitting vpon the beds ſide, ſhe would hold the
fanne, to moue the ayre; ſhe would beare vp her head, apply
the pillow, rubbe her feet, cheriſh her ſtomacke with her hand,
compoſe her bed, warme water for her, bring the baſon, and
preuent all the maydes in thoſe ſeruices; and whatſoeuer any
other had done, to hold that ſhe her ſelfe had loſt ſo much of
her own reward. With what kind of prayers, with what kind
of lamentations and groanes, would ſhe be ſhooting her ſelfe
ſwiftly vp and downe, betweene that caue where our Lord
had bene layd, & her mother lying in her bed? that ſhe might
not be depriued of ſuch an ineſtimable conuerſation, that ſhe
might not liue an houre after her; & that the ſame Bier might
deliuer them both vp to one buriall. But O frayle and caduke
nature of mortall men! for vnleſſe the faith of Chriſt raiſed vp
to heauen, and that the eternity of the ſoule were promiſed,
our bodies would be ſubiect to as meane condition, as beaſts, &
they of the baſeſt kind. The ſame death ſeiſes vpon the iuſt, and
wicked man; vpon the good and bad; the cleane and the vncleane; him who ſacrifices, and him who ſacrifices not: as the
good man, ſo him who ſins; as him who ſweares, ſo him who
feares to ſweare an oath. Both men & beaſts are diſſolued into
duſt, and aſhes, after the ſame manner.
    Why do I make any further pauſe, and encreaſe my ſor-
                                                                    row

row by prolonging it? This moft wife of woemen found, that death was at hand; and that fome part of her body, and of her limmes being already cold, there was onely a little warmth of life, which weakely breathed in her holy breft; & yet neuertheles, as if fhe had bene but going to vifit her friends, & take her leaue o f ftrangers, fhe would be whifpering out thofe verfes; *O Lord, I haue loued the beautifull order of thy houfe, & the place of the habitation of thy glory.* And; *How beloued are thy tabernacles, O God of power; my foule hath euen faynted, with an amorous kind of defire of entring into the Court of thy houfe.* And *I haue chofen to be an abiect in the houfe of my God, rather then to dwell in the tabernacles of finners.* And when, vpon occafion, I would be asking her why she was filent, and would not anfwere? & whither fhe were in any payne or no? fhe anfwered me in *Greeke, That she had no trouble, but that she faw all things before her, in tranquility & peace.* After this, fhe was filent and fhutting her eyes, as one who, by this time, defpifed mortall thinges, fhe repeated thofe verfes aforefaid, but yet fo, that it was as much as we could do to heare her: and then applying her finger to her mouth, fhe made the figne of a Croffe, vpon her lippes. Her fpirit fainted, and panted apace towards death; and her foule euen earneft to breake out, fhe conuerted the very ratling of her throate, wherewith mortall creatures vfe to end their life, into the praifes of our Lord. There were prefent, the Bifhops of *Ierufalem,* and of other Citties, and an innumerable multitude of Priefts, and Leuites of inferiour rancke. All the Monaftery was filled with whole Quiers of virgins, and Monks. And as foon as fhe heard the *Spoufe* calling thus, *Rife vp aud come, O thou my neighbour, my beautifull creature, and my doue; for behold the winter is fpent, and paft and the rayne is gone,* fhe anfwered thus with ioy, *The flowers haue bene feen in our land, the time of pruning is come, and I belieue that I fhall fee the good thinges of my Lord, in the land of the liuing.*

From that time forward, there was no lamentation, nor dolefull crye, as is wont to be vpon the death of men of this world; but there were whole fwarmes of people, who chated out the *Pfalmes* in different tongues. And *Paulas* body, being tranflated by the hands of Bifhops, & they bending their necks

N   vnder

vnder the Bier, whileſt ſome other Biſhops carryed lampes, &
tapers before the body, and others led on the Quiers of them
who ſung, ſhe was layd in the midle of her Church of the Na-
tiuity of our B. Sauiour. The whole troope of the Citties of
Palaſtine came in, to her funerall. Which of the moſt hidden
Moncks of the wildernes, was kept in by his Cell? which of
the virgins, was then hidden vp by the moſt ſecret roome ſhe
had? He thought himſelf to comit ſacriledge, who performed
not that laſt Office, to ſuch a creature. The widowes and the
poore, after the example of *Dorcas*, ſhewed the cloathes which
ſhe had giuen them. The whole multitude of needy people
cryed out, that they had loſt their mother and their nurſe. And
which is ſtrange, the palenes of death had not changed her
face at all; but a certaine dignity and decency, did ſo poſſeſſe
her countenance, that you would not haue thought her dead,
but ſleeping. The *Pſalmes* were ſounded forth in order, in the
Hebrew, and Greeke, and Latin, & in the Syrian tongue; not
onely for thoſe three dayes, till her body was interred, vnder
the Church, and neer the caue of our Lord; but during the
whole weeke all they who came in, did the like belieuing beſt
in thoſe funerals which themſelues made, and in their owne
teares. The venerable virgin, her daughter *Euſtochium*, like an
infant weaned from her nurſe, could ſcarce be drawen from her
mother. She kiſſed her eyes, and euen adhered to her face, and
embraced her whole body, and euen would haue bene buryed
with her mother. I take Ieſus to witnes, that there remayned
not one penny to her daughter; but as I ſaid before, ſhe left her
deeply in debt; and (which yet is matter of more difficulty) an
immenſe multitude of brothers and ſiſters, whom it was hard
to feed, and impious to put away.

What is more admirable then this vertue, that a woman
of a moſt noble family, endued once with a huge eſtat, ſhould
haue giuen away all ſhe had, with ſo great faith, as to become
almoſt to the very extremity of pouerty? Let others brag of
their moneyes, and of almes caſt into the poore mans boxe; &
of the Preſents which they haue hung vp, in ropes of gold. No
one hath giuen more to the poore, then ſhe who reſerued nothing to her ſelfe. Now, ſhe enioyes riches, and thoſe good
thinges,

thinges, which *neither the eye hath ſeen, nor the eare hath heard, nor bath it aſcended into the hart of man.* We lament our owne caſe, & we shall ſeem but to enuy her glory, if we lament her longer, who is raigning. Be you ſecure, O *Euſtochium,* that you are enriched with a great inheritance. Our Lord is your part; and to the end that your ioy may be the more complet, your mother is crowned with a long martyrdome. For not only is the effuſion of blood reputed for ſuch a confeſſion, but the vnſpotted ſeruice of a deuout mind, is a daily martyrdome. The former crowne is wreathed, & made of roſes, and violets, the later of lillies. Wherupon it is written in the, *Canticle of Canticles, My beloued is white and red;* beſtowing the ſame rewardes vpon ſuch as ouercome, whether it be in peace, or warre. Your mother heard theſe words with *Abraham; Go forth of thy country ; & of thy kinred, and come into the land, which I will shew the ;* and ſhe heard our Lord commanding thus by *Ieremy, Fly you out of the middle of Babylon and ſaue your ſoules.* And till the very day of her death, ſhe returned not into *Chaldea,* nor did ſhe couet the pots of *Egypt,* nor that ſtincking fleſh; but being accōpanyed with quiers of Virgins, is made a fellow-Citizen of our Sauiour ; & aſcending vp to thoſe heauély kingdomes from the litle *Bethleem,* ſhe ſaith to that true *Noemi, Thy People is my people, & thy God my God.*

I haue dictated this booke for you, at two ſittings vp, with the ſame grief which you ſelfe ſuſteynes. For as often as I put my ſelfe to writ, and to performe the worke which I had promiſed, ſo often did my fingars growe numme, my had faynted, my wit fayled, and euen my vnpoliſhed ſpeech, ſo farre from any elegancy or conceit of words, doth witnes well in what caſe the writer was. *Farewel O Paula,* & helpe thou by thy prayers, this laſt part of his ould age, who beares thee a religious reuerence. Thy faith and workes, haue ioyned thee in ſociety to Chriſt ; and now being preſent, thou wilt more eaſily obtayne what thou deſireſt. I haue finiſhed thy monnment , which no age will be able to deſtroy. I haue cut thy *Elogium* vpon thy ſepulcher : and I haue placed it at the foot of this volume, that whereſoeuer our worke ſhal arriue, the Reader may vnderſtand, that thou wert praiſed, and that thou art buryed in *Bethleem .*

The Title written on the Tombe.

She, whom the Paulo's got, the Scipio's bore,
The Graccho's, and great Agamemnons race,
Lyes here interr'd, cal'd Paula heretofore,
Eustochiums mother, Court of Romes chief grace.
Seekes for Christ poore, and Bethlems rurall face.

Written vpon the Front of the Grot.

Seest thou cut out of rocke, this narrow tombe?
T'is Paulas house, who now in heauen raynes;
And leauing brother, kinred, country, Rome,
Children, and wealth, in Bethlems grot remaynes.
Here is thy crib, O Christ, here vnprofand
The Magi Presents brought, to God human'd.

The holy and blessed *Paula*, departed this life vpon the seauenth of the Kalends of *February*, on the Tuesday after Sunset. She was buryed on the fifth of the Kalends, of the same moneth, *Honorius Augustus* being the sixt time Consull, and fellow Consull with *Aristenius*. She liued in her holy *purpose* fiue yeares at *Rome*, and twenty yeares at *Bethleem*. She had in all, fifty six yeares of age, eight moneths, and one and twenty daies.

S. Hierome to Nepotianus of the life which a Priest ought to lead. VVhereof I haue omitted the former part or rather Preface, which is both very long, and but personal, and not belonging at all to the chiefe matter in hand, which is; what liues Priests ar to lead.

HEARKEN, as the Blessed *Cyprian* aduises, not to such thinges as are eloquently deliuered; but to such as haue strength and truth in them: Hearken to him, who in function is your brother, in age your father, who brings you from the
swathing

fwathing cloutes of faith, to a perfect age, and who fetting downe rules throughout all the steps of your life, may inftruct others alſo, by your meanes. I well know, that both already you haue learned ſuch thinges as are holy, & that you are dayly learning them, of the Bleſſed man *Heliodorus*, your vncle, who is now a Bishop of Chriſt; and the example of whoſe vertue, may be the very rule of a mans life. But yet accept of theſe our endeauours how poore foeuer they may be, & ioyne you this booke to 'his; that as he inſtructed you how you might be a Monke, this may teach you how to be a perfect Prieſt.

A Prieſt therfore, who ſerues the Church of Chriſt, let him firſt interpret that word; and when he hath defined the ſame, let him ſtriue to be that very thing, which the word ſignifyes For if the word κλῆρ⊕ in greeke, do ſignify *portion* in Latin, then it will follow, that Prieſts are called ſo, either becauſe they are of the *portion* of our Lord, or els becauſe our Lord is the *portion* or part of Prieſts. But he who either is the *part* of our Lord, or who hath our Lord for his *part*, ought to ſhew himſelfe to be ſuch an one, as that he poſſeſſes our Lord, & is poſſeſſed of our Lord. He who poſſeſſes our Lord; & faith with the Prophet, Our Lord is my *part*, can poſſeſſe nothing but our Lord; and if he will haue any thing beſides him, our Lord wil not be his part. As for example, if he will haue gold, ſiluer, or choice of coſtly houſhould ſtuffe, our Lord with theſe *Partes*, will not voutchaſe to be his *Parte*. And if I be the parte of our Lord, and the bounder wherby his inheritance is meaſured and do not take a *Parte* amongſt the reſt of the Tribes, but as a Leuit and Preiſt, do liue of the Tenthes, and ſeruing the Altar do liue vpon the oblations of the Altar, if I may haue *food, and cloathing, I will be content therewith*, and being naked I will follow the naked Croſſe, I beſeech you therefore, and repeating my ſuit to you againe and againe; I will admoniſh you, that you thinke not the Office of Prieſthood, to be a kind of warefare, after the old faſhion; that is to ſay that you ſeeke not the commodities of the world in the warfare of Chriſt, & that you procure not to be richer, then when you began to be a Prieſt, & that it be not ſaid of you, Their *Prieſtes haue not bene of profit to them.* For many haue bene richer being Monkes, then when they were secular persons and Priests. There are some who possesse more riches now in the seruice of Christ being poore, then formerly they possessed by their seruice vnder the rich and false diuell: and the Church doth euen groane with their being rich, whom before, the world knew for beggers.

Let your table be frequented by poore people, and Pilgrimes; & let Christ be a guest with them. See you fly as you would do the plague, any Priest who is a negociator of affaires, and who growes rich of poore, and glorious insteed of base. *Ill speech corrupts good manners.* You contemne gold, an other mã loues it; you tread riches vnder your feet, an other man hunts after it; you cordially loue silence, meekenes, recollection, but another likes prating, and bouldnes, and takes no pleasure but in streetes, market-places, fayres, and to be sitting in Apothecaryes shoppes. In such a difference of manners, what agreement can there be?

Let your house either seldome or neuer be troden ypon by woemens feet; and be you either equally ignorant, or doe you equally like, all the maydes and virgins of Christ. Doe not dwell with them vnder the same roofe, and presume not vpon your former chastity. You are not holyer then *Dauid,* nor can you be wiser then *Salomon.* Be euer remembring, how a woman cast the inhabitant of Paradise out of his possession. When you are sicke, let some deuout brother of yours assist you and some sister, or your mother, or some other woman, who is of vntouched fame, with the world. If you haue not perhapes of your consaguinity, who are withal of piety, the Church entertaines many old widowes, who may performe that duty, and receiue some benefit by their seruice; that so your sicknes may also inable you to gather their fruit of almes. I know of some, who haue recouered in body, and begun to fall sicke in mind. She affoardes you a dangerous kind of seruice, vpon whose countenance, you are often looking with attention. If in regard you are a Priest, some Virgin or widow must needes be visited by you, yet neuer goe into their house alone. Take such company with you, as may not defame you by their society. If some *Lector,* or some *Acolytus* or some other who hath the Office of singing in the Church follow you, let them not

be

be adorned with cloathes, but good conditions; nor haue they haire curled with irons, but promise vertue by the very apparance of their persons. Sit neuer with any woman alone in secret, and without some witnes or looker on. If you be to say any thing in familiar manner, the woman hath some auntient person belonging to the house, or some Virgin, or wife, or widow, she is not so inhumane, as that she hath none besides you with whome she dares trust her selfe. See you be carefull of giuing no ground to suspicions, and procure to preuent whatsoeuer may probably be deuised against you. A holy affection doth not admit the vse of frequent Presents & handkerchiues, and scarfes, and garments which haue bene kissed, and meat which hath beene tasted to your hand, nor the changing of certaine deare delightfull letters. These wordes, *My light, my hony, my desire*, and all those delicacies, and conceits and certaine ciuilities, which deserue to be derided, and the rest of those toyes of louers we blush at euen in Comedies, we detest euen in secular men; and therefore how much more are we to doe it in the case of Monkes, & Priests, whose Priesthood is adorned by their Chastity, and their Chastity by their Priesthood. Neither do I say thus much, as fearing these thinges in you, or in holy men, but becausethere are found good, and bad, in euery course, in euery degree, and sexe, and the condemnation of the wicked serues for the comendation of the good. I am ashamed to speake of these men, who might better be the Priests of Idolls.

Iesters, carters, and queanes may inherit landes; only Priestes, and Monkes may not : and this is prohibited, not by persecutours, but by Christian Princes. Nor doe I complaine against the law, but I am sorry we haue deserued, that such a law should be made. A cautery is a good remedy, but why should I haue a wound, which must stand in need of such a cure. The caution of the law is not only prouident but seuere; yet couetousnes is not bridled euen thereby. We ouerreach the lawes by certaine deeds made in trust; and as if the Ordinatious of Emperours were of more authority then they of Christ : we feare their lawes, & we contemne his Ghospels.

Let there be an heire, but withal let there be the mother of the chil-

children ; that is to fay , the Church of the flocke, which hath bred, nourifhed, and fed them . Why do we interpofe our felues between the mother and the children? It is the glory of a Bifhop, to prouid for the comodities of poore people, and it is the ignominy of Priefts to attéd to acquire riches . I who was borne in a poore houfe, or rather in a country cottage , who fcarce had meanes to fill my windy ftomacke with the bafeft grayne, and rye bread, can now fcarce thinke of the fineft flower, & hony, with contentment . I am alfo come to know the names, and kindes of fifhes ; yea and vpon what part of the coaft, fuch a fhell fifh was taken; and in the tafte of foule I de-cerne the difference of countryes; & the rarity of thofe meates, yea and euen the very hurt they do men by dearly buying thé, delights me .

I vnderftand befides , that fome Prieftes, performe certen bafe feruices to old men and woemen , who haue no children. They hold the fpitting bafon , they befeige the bed round a-bout, and they take fometimes , the fleame of the lungs, & the rotten filth of the ftomacke , in their very hands . They trem-ble when the Phyfitian comes to make his vifit , and their lips fhake with feare, when they aske him, if the ficke man be men-ded ; & if the old man , chance to be grown better or ftronger, themfelues are indangered by it . For taking a face of ioy vpon them , their couetous mind is rackt within; as fearing leaft they may loofe their hope of gayne, but then agayne they will needes compare the liuely old man , to *Mathufalem* , O how great would their reward be, at the hand of God , if they ex-pected no reward in this life ! What fweating doth the getting of fuch a poore inheritance coft ! the pearle of Chrift, might be fought at an eafyer rate .

Be diligent in reading the holy Scriptures, or rather, let that diuine booke be neuer layd out of your handes . Learne that which you are to teach . Procure to be able to vfe that faythfull fpeech, which is according to knowledge, that you may be able to exhort men, with found doctrine, and fo con-fute fuch as contradict you . Stand faft in thofe things which you haue learned, and which are committed to you in truft , as knowing of whome you learned them; and be euer ready to

giue

giue fatisfaction to all fuch as demand a reafon at your handes, of that fayth and hope which is in you. Let not your ill deeds put your wordes out of countenance ; leaft fome body who heares you fpeake at Church, make this anfwere to you within himfelfe ; *VVhy do you not practife what you fay?* He is a delicate inftructer, who difcourfes of fafting, when his belly is full. Euen a murdering theefe may be able to cry out againft couetoufnes. Let the mind and the handes of the Prieft of Chrift keep correfpondence with his mouth.

Be fubiect to your Bifhop, and reuere him as the Father of your foule. It is for a fonne to loue, and for a flaue to feare. *If I be thy Father*, fayth he, *where is myne honour; if I be thy Lord, where is that feare which is due to me?* In his perfon which is but one, there are many feuerall titles to be confidered by you: a Monke, a Bifhop, an Vncle of your owne, who already hath inftructed you, concerning all good thinges. You shall alfo know, that Bifhops muft vnderftand themfelues to be Priefts, and not Lordes ; let them honour Priefts, as Priefts, that Priefts may deferre all due honour to them, as to Bifhops. That of the Oratour *Demitius* is vulgarly knowne ; *VVhy should I carry my felfe towardes you, as towardes a Prince, when you regard not me as a Senatour?* That which *Aaron* and his fonnes were, in relation to one an other, that muft the Bifhop, and the Priefts be. *There is one Lord, and one Temple*, and the myftery alfo muft be one. Let vs euer remember what the Apoftle *Peter* enioyneth Priefts ; *Feed that flocke of our Lord, which is among you, prouiding for it according to God, not after a compulfiue, but free and chearefull manner, not for filthy lucres fake, but willingly; nor as exercifing dominion ouer the Clergy, but after the forme of a shepheard ouer his flocke, to the end that when the Prince of Paftours shall appeare, you may receiue an immarcefsible crowne of glory.*

It is an extreame ill cuftome in fome Churches, that Priefts are filent, and refufe to fpeake in the prefence of Bifhops, as if Bifhops enuyed them fo much honour, or would not voutchfafe to heare them. But *S. Paul* fayth, *If a thing be reuealed to any man who fits by, let the former hold his peace.* For you may prophecy by turnes, that all may learne, and all may be comforted, and the fpirit of Prophets, is fubiect to Pro-

phets; for God is not a God of diſſention, but of peace. It is a
glory to the Father, when he hath a wiſe ſonne , and let a Biſhop take comfort in his owne iudgement, when he hath choſen ſuch Prieſts, for the ſeruice of Chriſt. When you are preaching in the Church, let not the people make a noyſe , but let
them profoundly ſigh. Let the teares of yours Auditours, be
your prayſe. Let the diſcourſe of a Prieſt, be ſeaſoned by reading holy Scripture. I will not haue you a declamer, nor a
iangler, nor to be full of talke without reaſon; but skillfull in
the myſteries, & moſt excellently inſtructed in the Sacraments
of your God. It is the vſe of vnlearned men, to toſſe wordes vp
and downe, and by a ſwift kind of ſpeech, in the eares of an
vnskillfull Auditory, to hunt after admiration. A bold man
will interpret many tymes he knowes not what, and in the
perſwaſion which he vſes to others, he arrogates the reputation of knowledge to himſelfe. *Gregory Nazianzen* myne old
Maſter, being deſired by me to expound what that *Sabboth*, called δευτερόπρωτος, meant in *Luke*, he did elegantly allude thus ; *I
will inſtruct you about this buſines, when we are at Church , where the
whole people applauding me, you ſhall be forced whether you will or no,
to know that , whereof you are ignorant now .* There is nothing ſo
eaſy, as to deceiue a poore baſe people, and an vnlearned aſ-
ſembly, by volubility of ſpeech, which admires whatſoeuer it
vnderſtands not. *Marcus Tullius* (of whome this excellent *Elogium* was vſed, *Demoſthenes depriued you of being the firſt Oratour, &
you him of being the only Oratour*) ſayth that in his Oration for
Quintus Gallus, concerning the fauour of the people, and ſuch as
ſpeake abſurdly before them, which I would fayne haue you
marke, leaſt you ſhould be abuſed by theſe errours. I ſpeake of
that, whereof my ſelfe haue lately had experience. A certaine
Poet, a man of name and learned (who made certaine Dialogues
of Poets and Philoſophers) when in one and the ſame place, he
bringes in *Euripides*, and *Menander* , and *Socrates*, and *Epicurus* ,
diſcourſing altogether one with another, whom yet we know
to haue liued, not only at different tymes, but in different a-
ges, what applauſes and acclamations did he moue ? For in the
Theatre , he had many condiſciples who performed not their
ſtudies together.

Be

Be as carefull to auoid blacke courfe cloathes as white . Fly from affected ornaments, at as full fpeed , as you would do from affected vncleanes ; for the one of them fauours of delica-cy , the other hath a tafte of vaine glory . It is a commendable thing , I fay not , to vfe no linnen , but not be worth any : for otherwife it is a ridiculous thing , and full of infamy to haue the purfe well filled, & then to bragge , that you are not worth fo much as a handkerchiue . There are fome who giue fome little thing to the poore, to the end that they may receiue more , and fome man feekes after wealth , vnder the pretence of vfing Charity ; which is rather to be accounted a kind of hū-ting then almes-giuing . So are beafts and birds , and fo are fi-shes taken . Some little bayte is layd vpon the hooke , that the money bagge of the Matrons, may be brought forth vpon that hooke .

Let the Bishop, to whome the care of the Church is com-mitted, confider whome he appointes to ouerfee the difpenfa-tion of goodes , to the poore . For it is better for a man not to haue any thing to giue away , then impudently to begge fom-what , for himfelfe to hide . Nay it is a kind of arrogancy , for one to feeme more meeke , and mercifull then the Prieft of Chrift is . We cannot all do all thinges ; fome one is an eye in the Church, an other is a tongue, an other a hand, an other is a foot, an eare, or a belly, and fo forth . Read the Epiftle of *Paul* to the *Corinthians* , *How diuers members ferue to conftitute one body* . But yet let not the rufticke, and fimple man , thinke himfelfe to be holy , becaufe he knowes nothing ; nor if a man be elo-quent and skillfull, muft he efteeme that he hath as much fan-ctity, as he hath tongue; and of the two defects, it is much bet-ter that he haue a holy rudenes , then a finfull eloquence .

Many build vp wals , and raife pillars in Churches , the marbles fhine , the roofes glifter with gold , the Altar is fet with pretious ftones; and the while , no care is taken, to chofe fit Minifters for Chrift. Let no man obiect to me, that rich tem-ple of the Iewes , the Table , the Lampes, the Incenfories, the Bafons, the Cuppes, the Morters , and other thinges, made of gold . Then were thefe thinges approued by our Lord, when the Prieft did immolat facrifices , and when the blood of beafts

was

was the redemption of finnes . Though all thefe things did go
before in figure , yet *they were written for our inſtruction, vpon whō*
the ends of the world are come . But now , when our Lord , by being poore, hath dedicated the pouerty of his houſe, let vs thinke
vpon his Croſſe , and eſteem of riches , as of durt . What marueile is it , that Chriſt called riches by the name of *vniuſt Mam-*
mon? Why ſhould we admire and loue that , which *Peter* doth
euen after a kind of glorious manner profeſſe himſelfe not to
haue ? For other wiſe , if we onely follow the letter , and that
yet the apparance of the hiſtory , ſpeaking of gold and riches,
delight vs ; then together with the gold let vs take vp other
thinges too ; and let the Biſhop of Chriſt , marry virgins , and
make them their wiues . If that argumēt, I ſay, be to hold, then
let him who hath any skarre , or other corporall deformity be
depriued of his Prieſthood , though he haue a vertuous minde,
& let the leproſy of the body be accounted a worſe thing then
the vices of the ſoule Let vs encteaſe, and multiply, and fil the
earth, and let vs not ſacrifice the lambe, nor celebrat the myſti-
call Paſcha, becauſe theſe thinges are forbidden by the law , to
be done any other where , then in the *Temple* . *Let vs faſten the*
tabernacle in the ſeauenth moneth, and let vs chant out the ſolemne faſt,
with the ſound of the cornet. But now if comparing all theſe to ſpirituall thinges and knowing with *Paul* ; *that the law is ſpirituall* ;
and that the words of *Dauid* are true, who ſings thus ; *Open thou*
myne eyes , and I will conſider the wonderfull thinges of thy law ; we
vnderſtand them as our Lord alſo vnderſtood them , and as he
interpreted the Sabboth ; either let vs deſpiſe gold with the
reſt of the ſuperſtitions of the Iewes ; or elſe if we ſhall like
gold , let vs alſo like the Iewes , whom of neceſſity we muſt
either like , or diſlike ; together with the gold .

The Feaſting of ſecular perſons , and eſpecially of ſuch as
ſwell vp in high place of honour , muſt be auoyded by you . It
is an vgly thing , that before the doores of a Prieſt of Chriſt
crucifyed , (who was ſo poore , and had no meat of his owne)
the Officers of Coſuls, & bands of ſouldiers ſhould ſtand way-
ting; and that the gouernour of the Prouince ſhould dine better at your houſe, then at the Court . And if you ſhall pretend ,
that you do ſuch thinges as theſe , to the end that you may obtaine

tayne fauour for inferiour and miferable people; know that a temporall Iudge will deferre more to a mortifyed Prieſt, then to a rich one; & will carry more veneratiō to your vertue, thē to your wealth. Or if he be ſuch a one, as that he will not fauour Prieſts ſpeaking for afflicted perſons, but whē he is in the middeſt of his cups, I ſhall be well content to want the obtayning of ſuch a ſuit;and will pray to Chriſt in ſteed of the Iudge, who can helpe me better, and ſooner then he. *It is better to confide in our Lord, then to confide in man. It is better to hope in our Lord, then to hope in Princes.* Se that your breath do not ſo much as ſmel of wine, leaſt you deſerue to heare that ſaying of the Philoſopher, *This is not to giue me a kiſſe, but to drinke to me in wine.* As for Prieſts, who are winebibbers, both the Apoſtle condemnes them, and the old Lawe forbids them, ſaying, *They who ſerue at the Altar, muſt drinke no wine,or Sicera* ; by which word *Sicera*; in the hebrew tongue, al ſuch drinkes are meant, wherby any man may be inebriated ; whether they be made of wheat, or of the ioyce of fruit, or when together with fruit they take hony, and make a ſweet and barbarous potion thereof, or els ſtrayne the fruit of palmes till they yeeld liquore; or by the boyling vp of corne, giue a different colour and ſtrength to water. Whatſoeuer may inebriat,and ouerthrowe the ſtate of the mind,you muſt auoid,with as much care,as you would do wine.Neither yet do I ſay this, as condemning the creature of God, ſince our Lord himſelfe was called a drinker of wine; and the taking of a little wine was permitted to the weake ſtomacke of *Timothy*; but we require a moderation in the vſe thereof, according to the quality of conſtitutions, and to the proportion of age , and health . But yet, if without wine I burne with youth, and am inflamed by the heat of my blood, and am indued with a young & a ſtrong body, I will gladly ſpare that cuppe, wherin there is ſuſpicion of poyſon. It ſounds elegantly in Greeke , but I know not whether it will carry the ſame grace with vs, *A fat full belly, doth not beget a ſlender and well proportioned mind .*

Impoſe as great a meaſure of faſting vpon your ſelfe; as you are able to beare . Let you Faſts be pure, chaſt, ſimple, moderat, and not ſuperſtitious . To what purpoſe is it, that a man will needes forbeare the vſe of Oyle; & then vndergo certaine

vexations

vexations, and difficulties, how to get and make meat, which he may eat ; as dryed figs, pepper, nuts, the fruit of palmes, hony, and piftacho's? The whole bufbandry of the kitchin gardens is vexed from one end to the other, that forfooth we may be able to abfteyne from fo much as rye bread ; and whileft we hunt after delicacies, we are drawen backe from the kingdome of heauen. I heare befides, that there are certaine perfons, who contrary to the nature of men and other creatures , will drinke no water, & eate no bread; but they muft haue certaine delicat little drinkes, and fhred herbes, and the ioyce of beetes; and that forfooth, they will not drinke in a cup, but needes in the fhell of fome fifh . Fy vpon this fhamefull abfurdity, and that we blufh not at thefe follies ; & are not weary with feorne of thefe fuperftitions, befides that we feeke for a fame of abftinence, euen in the vfe of delicacy . The moft ftrong faft of all others, is of bread and water. But becaufe it carryes not fuch honour with it, becaufe we all liue with the vfe of water and bread, it is fcarce thought to be a faft, in regard that it is fo vfuall and common . Take heed you hunt not after certaine little eftimations of men, leaft you make purchafe of the people praife with the offence of God . If yet (faith the Apoftle) *I fhould pleafe men , I fhould not be the feruant of Chrift .* He ceafed from pleafing men, & became the feruant of Chrift. The fouldier of Chrift marches on, both through good fame and bad, both by the right hand and by the left ; & is nether extolled by praife, nor is he beaten downe by difpraife. He doth not fwell vp with riches, nor is he extenuated by pouerty; & he contemnes both thofe thinges , which might gaine him ioy, and thofe alfo which may afflict, *The fonne burnes him not by day, nor the Moone by night .*

I will not haue you pray in the cornes of ftreetes, leaft the ayre of a popular fame fhould diuert you prayers , from the right way to their Iournyes end. I will not haue you inlarge the borders, nor make oftentatiō of the skirtes of you garmēts, and againft your confcience to be enuironed by a Pharifaicall kind of ambition. How much better were it, not to carry thefe things in the exteriour, but at the hart; and to obtayne fauour in the fight of God, rather then in the eyes of men? Hereupon

                                                              hange

hange the Gho∫pell, hereupon the law and the **Prophets**, and the holy and Apo∫tolicall do∂rine ; for it is better to carry all the∫e thinges in the mind, then in the body . You who reade this faithfully with me according to a faithfull and right intention, do vnder∫tand euen that which I conceale; & which I ∫peake ∫o much the louder, euen becau∫e I am ∫ilent. You mu∫t haue an eye to as many rules, as you may be tempted with kindes of glory.

    Will you know what kind of ornaments our Lord de∫ires to ∫e in you ? Procure to haue Prudence, Iu∫tice, Temperance, and Fortitude . Be you enclo∫ed by the∫e coa∫ts of the sky . Let this charriot of foure hor∫es carry you on with ∫peed, to the end of the race, & let the charriot driuenes by Chri∫t. There is nothing more pretious then this Iewell, nothing more beautifull then the variety of the∫e pretious ∫tones . You ∫hall be beautifyed on euery ∫ide; you ∫hall be compa∫∫ed in, and prote∂ed ; they will both defend you, and adorne you, & the∫e gemmes will become bucklers to you .

    Take you al∫o heed, that you neither haue an itching tongue, nor ears ; that is to ∫ay, that neither your ∫elfe detra∂ from others, nor that you endure to heare detra∂ers . *Sitting (* ∫aith *he) thou ∫pake∫t again∫t thy brother, and thou layd∫t ∫candall before the ∫onne of thy mother ; the∫e thinges dide∫t thou, & I held my peace. Thou dide∫t wickedly think, that I would be like thee: but I will reproue thee before thy face.* Take care that you haue not a detra∂ing tongue, and be watchfull ouer your wordes ; and know that you are iudged by your owne con∫cience, in all tho∫e thinges which you ∫peake of others, and of tho∫e things, which you condemned in other folkes, your ∫elfe is found guilty. Nor is that a iu∫t excu∫e, when you ∫ay that you do no wrong, when you do but heare the report of others . No man reports thinges to an other, who hears them vnwillingly. An arrow enters not into a ∫tone ; but ∫tarting backe, ∫ometimes it hurts him who ∫hot it . Let the detra∂er learne, that he is not to detra∂ in your hearing, whome he findes to heare him ∫o vnwillingly. *Doe not mingle your ∫elfe,* ∫aith Salomon, *with detra∂ours, becau∫e his de∫tru∂ion ∫hall come ∫uddenly, and who knowes how ∫oone they ∫hall both be ruined,* that is to ∫ay, he who detra∂s, and he who
giues

giues audience to detracters. It is your duty ro visit the sicke, to
be well acquainted with the houses of Matrons and their children, & to keep safe the secret of great persons. It is your duty
not onely to haue chast eyes, but a chast tongue also.

You must neuer dispute nor argue of the beauties of woemen; nor euer let any house vnderstand by you, what hath passed in any other house. *Hippocrates* adiured his disciple before he
taught them, and made them sweare to follow his directions,
and commanded them religiously to promise silence; and prescribed the speech, the gate, the habit, and the conuersation,
which they were to vse. How much more must we, to whom
the charge of soules is comitted; loue the houses of all Christians, as our owne. Let them know vs to be rather comforters
of them in their aflictions, then companions and feasters with
them in their prosperity. That Priest is ordinarily contemned, who being often inuited to dinner, doth not refuse to go.
Let vs neuer desire to be inuited, and euen when we are inuited, let vs go seldome, *It is a more blessed thing to giue, them to
receiue*. And it is strange, but so it is, that euen he who desires
you to receiue a curtesy at his handes, thinkes the meanlier of
you, when you haue accepted thereof; and doth strangely honour you afterward if you chance to lay aside that request of
his.

You who are a preacher of chastity, must not meddle with
making of marriages. He who reades the Apostle saying thus,
It remaynes that they who haue wiues, be so as if they had them not,
Why should he compell a virgin to marry? He who is a Priest
after hauing bene marryed but once, why should he exhort a
widow to marry againe? The stewards and ouerseers of other
mens houses, & possessions, how can they be Priests, who are
comaunded to contemne their owne fortunes? To take any
thing violently from a mans friend, is theft; to deceiue the
Church, is sacriledge. To take away that which were to be
distributed vpon the poore, and when there are many hungry
people, to be reserued or wary, or (which is a most abhomi-
nable crime) to take their due from them, doth exceed the cruelty of any robber by the high way. I am tormented with hũ-
ger, and you will be measuring out, how much I may haue an
                                                    appetite

appetite to eat. Either diftribut that prefently, whith you haue receiued ; or els if you be a timorous difpencer, turne is backe vpon the proprietary, that he may beftow his owne. I will not haue your purfe to be filled, by occafion of difpenfing my goods. No man can better difpofe of my things, then my felfe. He is the beft difpencer, who referues nothing for his owne vfe.

Youe haue compelled me, moft deare *Nepotianus* (after thee booke which I wrote to holy *Euftichium* at *Rome* concerning the cuftody of virginity, which hath bene ftoned to death) that now againe I haue vnfealed my mouth in *Bethleem* , and haue laid my felfe open, to be ftabbed by the tongues of al men. For either I muft writ nothing, leaft I fhould become fubiect to mens cenfure (which you forbad me to regard;) or els I muft know when I wrot that the dartes of all ill fpeaking tongues would be turned againft me. But I befeech them to be quiet, & that they will giue ouer to backbite. For we haue not written this, as to aduerfaries, but as to friendes; nor haue we made any inuectiue againft them who finne ; but only aduifed them not to do fo. Nor haue we only bene feuere iudges againft fuch as do ill , but againft our felues alfo : and being defirous to picke the moat out of anothers eye , I haue firft caft the beame out of myne owne. I haue done no man wrong , nor poynted at any mans name in my writing. My fpeech hath not applyed it felfe to particulars , but hath difcourfed onely in generall againft vice. He who fhall be angry with me , will thereby confeffe himfelfe to be in fault.

Saint Hierome to Læta about the inftruction of her daughter .

THE Apoftle *Paul*, writing to the *Corinthians*, & inftructing the Church of Chrift , which was then but yong or rude, with holy directions, did propound this commaundment amongft the reft , *If any woeman haue an vnbelieuing husband , and if he confent to liue with her , let her not feperate her felf from him for the vnbelieuing husband is fanctifyed by the belieuing wife, and the vnbe-*

P

lieuing

lieuing *wife is fanctifyed by the belieuing hubands* ; *for otherwife your children would be vncleane, but now they are cleane,* If perhaps it may haue feemed to any hitherto , that the bonds of difcipline were too much relaxed , & that the indulgéce of the Mafter was too forward , let him confider the houfe of you father, (a man , I confeffe , moft illuftrious , and moft learned ; but yet walking hitherto in darkenes) , and he will perceiue that the counfelle of the Apoftle hath produced this effect ; that the fweetnes of the fruit might make a recompence for the bitternes of the root; & that bafe twigs, might fweat forth pretious *balfamū* . You are borne of an vnequall marriage , & *Paula* is begotten & brought forth, by my *Toxotius,* & you. Who would euer belieue that the grand-child of *Albinus* the pagan high Prieft, fhould be borne vpon the fore promife of a Martyr ; that the ftámering tongue of the little one, fhould found forth the *Alleluia* of Chrift ; that the old man fhould cherifh the virgin of God , in his bofome . And we haue wel & happily expected, *that the holy, & belieuing houfe may fanctify the vnbelieuing husband .* He is now, in a kind of ambition, & expectation to become a Chriftian, whom a troupe of belieuing fons, & grand children doth already enuiron. For my part, I think that *Iupiter* himfelf might haue come to belieue in Chrift, if he had had fuch a kinred . Let him derid & fpit at my Epiftle, & and cry out that I am either fond, or mad. His fonne in law did alfo this, before he belieued. Men are not born Chriftians, but they are made fo. The golden Capitoll is out of cofitenáce now , for lacke of looking to & al the heathen Temples of *Rome,* are ouer growne with cobwebs. The very citty is now fleeting from it felfe, and the people runnes downe, like a flood towards the Martyrs Tombes , whileft the Heathen Temples are not yet halfe pulled downe . If wifedome will not oblige them to embrace the faith , me thinkes they fhould do it now euen for fhame . This (O *Læta* my moft deuout daughter in Chrift) is faid to you , to the end that you defpaire not of the conuerfation of your Father; and that by the fame faith, wherby you haue deferued to obtayne you daughter, you may alfo gaine your father ; and fo the whole houfe may be happy , by knowing this which was promifed by our Lord , *Thofe thinges which are impoßible with men , are poßible with God.* A mans conuerfion

sion neuer comes too late. The *theefe* passed on from the *Crosse*
to *Paradice*. *Nabuchodonozor* the King of *Babylon*, after he had
growne wild both in body and disposition, and had fed in the
wildernes like a beast, was restored to the reason of a man. And
(that I may passe ouer autient stories least they might seem fa-
bulous to incredulous persons) did not your kinsman *Gracchus*,
(whose name doth sufficiently shew the antiquity of his nobility, some few yeares since (when he had the prefecture of the
Citty) ouerthrowe, breake downe, burne that denne of *Mi-
thra*, and all those prodigious Idols wherby *Corax*, *Niphus*, *Nilon*,
Leo, *Perses*, *Helios*, and father *Bromius* or *Bacchus* are dedicated
to those vses? and hauing sent these hostages before him, did he
not obtayne the Baptisme of Christ? *Gentility* suffers a kind of
desolation of a wildernes euen in the Citty. The Gods which
heretofore we adored by the Nations of the world, are now
onely remayning in the tops of houses, with skrich Owles.
The Ensignes of the Crosse, are now become the standars of the
campe. The healthful picture of the same Crosse, serues to beau-
tify the Purple Robes of Kings, & the bright burning gemmes
of their diademes. Now the *Egyptian Serapis* is turned Christian; *Marnas* who is shut vp in *Gaza*, mournes, and perpetually trembles for feare of the euersion of that Temple. Out of
India, *Persia*, and *Ethiopia*, we daily enterteyne whole troopes
of Monckes. The *Armenian* hath layd his quiuers aside; the
Huns learne the Psalter; the frozen *Scythia* doth euen boyle vp
through the heat of faith The red and yellow Army of the
Getes carry Churches like Tents round about; and therefore is
it perhaps, that they make their part good against vs by way of
Armes, because they embrace our Religion.

I am almost fallen away into an other matter, & the wheele
running round, whilest I was thinking vpon a little pitcher,
my hand hath made a great tankerd. For my purpose was, to direct my speech (vpon the request of holy *Marcella*, and you) to
a Mother, that is to your selfe; and to teach you how you are to
instruct our *Paula*, who was consecrated to Christ before she
was borne; and whome you conceiued in your vowes, before
you did it in your wombe. Somewhat we haue seene in our
tyme, of the propheticall Bookes. *Anna* exchanged barrennes

for

for fruitfullnes; and you haue now changed your said fruitfullnes, for hopefull children. I speake it confidently, you shall
haue more children, you who haue payd the first borne to God.
These are those first borne, which were offered in the law. So
was Samuel borne, and so was Sampson; and so did Iohn Baptist
reioyce and exult, vpon the arriuall of Mary. For he heard the
words of our Lord thũdering in his eares, by the mouth of the
virgin, and he stroue to breake forth of his Mothers wombe,
that he might haue met him. So that she who was borne by
repromission, must obtaine such instruction from her parentes,
as may be worthy of her birth. Samuel was brought vp in the
Temple. Iohn was prepared in the desert. The former was venerable by his sacred haire, and druncke neither wine, nor any
other thing which could inebriate; and whilest he was yet but
a little one, he had conuersation with our Lord. The later
flyes from Citties, he was bound in by a girdle of haire, he
was fed with locusts and wild hony; and (in type of the pennance which he was to preach) he was apparelled with the
spoile, or skine, of the Camel, that most crooked beast. So must
that soule be instructed, which is to become the Temple of
God. Let her learne to heare, and speake nothing, but that
which belongs to the feare of God. Let her not vnderstand a
fowle word, and let her be ignorant of the songes which the
world is wont to sing. Let her tongue be enured to sweet
Psalmes, whilest it is young.

Away with the vsuall wantonnes of children, and let the
girles, and waiting maides be remoued from secular conuersation, least what they haue learned ill, they teach worse. Let
some Alphabet of letters be made for her, either of Boxe or I-
uory; & let them be called by their names. Let her play with
them, that so her very playing, may be learning; and let her
not only learne the order of the letters, that the memory of
names may passe into the tune of some songe; but let euen that
very order be inuerted, and let the last letters be mingled with
them of the middest, and they of the middest with the foremost
that she may not only know them by roat, but by vse. But
when she beginnes with a weake shaking hand, to draw her
stile vpon waxe, let either the tender ioyntes of her fingers be
ruled

ruled by the cafting of fome hand ouer hers, or els let the letters be grauen vpon fome little table; that the lines may be drawne & ftill fhut vp in margens by the fame hollowes, & fo they may not wander abroad. Let fome reward be propounded to her, when fhe beginnes to ioyne the fillables; and let her be animated, by fuch kind of Prefents, as are wont to take the moft flattering hold, vpon that tender age, Let her alfo haue companious in learning, whom fhe may enuy, and by whofe prayfes fhe may be ftung. If fhe be at all flowe of wit, let her not be chidden; but you muft raife it with comendation of her, that fhe may be glad when fhe hath conquered, and be forry when fhe is ouercome. You muft chiefly take care, that fhe be not brought to miflike learning, and that the bitter way of teaching her, in her infancy, may not be remembred by her, whē fhe fhall haue paffed beyond thofe tender yeares. Thofe names whereby fhe fhall accuftome her felfe by little and little to knit words together, muft not be cafuall, but appointed, and induftrioufly compiled; namely of the Prophets, & the Apoftles; & let the whole feries of the Patriarkes from *Adam*, be brought downe, as it is deliuered in *Matthew*, and *Luke*. That fo whileft fhe is about this other bufineffe, a preparation of matter may be made for her memory, to be layd vp thereby for after tymes. Some Mafter muft be chofen of fit yeares for her, and of good life & knowledge. And I hope a learned man will not thinke much, to do that in the behalfe of a noble virgin, which *Arifto-tle* did for the fonne of *Phillip*, who tooke the office of clarckes or booke wrighters away, by teaching him firft to reade. Thofe thinges are not to be contemned as little, without which great thinges cannot ftand. The very ayre or manner of the letters, and the firft teaching of Rules, doth found after one fafhion out of a learned mouth, and after another, if the man be ignorant and rude. And therefore you muft prouide, that through the foolifh dandlings of woemen, your daughter get not a cuftome of pronouncing certaine halfe wordes. Nor to play with gold, or gay cloathes, though it be but in ieft; for the former of thefe two things hurts the tongue, & the latter hurts the mind; and fhe may chance learne that, when fhe is young, which afterward fhe muft be fayne to vnlearne. The maner of *Horten-*

fius

fius his speech was gotten by him in his fathers armes. That is hardly scraped out , which young vnfashioned mindes haue drunke in. Who shall be able to reduce purple wooll , to the former whitenes? A new vessell long retaynes both that odour and taste, whereof it receiued the first impression. The *Grecian* history relates , how *Alexander*, that most powerfull King and conquerour of the world , had not power to want the defect of his Tutour *Leonides* , both in his gate , and behauiour other-wise , wherewith he was infected being a little one. For it is a matter of much ease, to grow like an other in any thing which is ill ; and you may readily imitate their vices, to whose ver-tues you cannot ariue. Let not euen her nurse be giuen to wine, nor be wanton or tatling . Let her be carryed by some modest creature , & let the man who ouerlookes her , be a graue per-son. When she sees her grandfather , make her skippe into his bosome , and hang about his necke ; and sing *Alleluia* to him , whether he will or no . Let her grand mother snatch her to her selfe , and acknowledge that she smyles like her father . Let her be amiable to all , and let the whole kinred reioyce , that such a rose is sprung from thence . Let her quickly be told , what her other grand mother , and aunt she hath ; and for the seruice of what Emperour , and for what Army she is brought vp , though yet she be but a green souldier. Let her desire to be with them ; and let her threaten you , that she will be gone to them from you .

   Her very habite , and cloathing , must tell her to whom she is promised . Take heed you bore not through her eares , & that you paynt not that face , which is consecrated to Christ , either with white or red , nor oppresse her necke with gold, & pearle , nor load her head with gemmes ; nor make her haire yellow , and bespeake not by that meanes, a part of hell-fyer for her. Let her haue an other kind of pearles , by the selling whereof afterward , she may purchace that one great Pearle , which is the most pretious of all . A certaine noble woman of the higest rancke , vpon the comaundment of *Hymetius* her hus-band, who was vncle to the virgin *Eustochium* did once change the manner of her habit , and dressing ; and knit vp her negle-cted haire after a secular fashion, desiring thereby to ouercome
                                               both

both the purpofe of the virgin her felfé, and the defire of her
mother. But behould the very felfe fame night, fhe fees (when
fhe was at reft) that an angell was already come towards her,
threating punifhment with a terrible voice, and ftorming out
thefe words, *Haſt thou prefumed to preferre the comaundment of thy*
hufband, before Chriſt? Haſt thou prefumed to touch the head of the
virgin of God, with thy facrilegious handes? which euen at this inſtant,
ſhall wither vp; that thou mayeſt feele with tormentes, what thou haſt
done; and at the end of the fifth moneth from hence, thou ſhalt be lead
downe to hell. All thefe thinges were fulfilled in the felfe fame
order as they were foretold; and the fwift deftruction of that
miferable creature, declared the latenes of her penance. So
doth Chrift reuenge himfelfe vpon the violater of his temples;
and fo doth he defend his owne iewels, and moft pretious ornaments.

I haue related this particular, not that I would infult vpõ
the calamities of vnfortunat creatures, but that I may admonifh
you, with how great feare and caution you muft preferue
that which you haue promifed to God. *Heli* the Prieft offended
God by the finnes of his fonnes. He muft not be made a Bifhop, who hath luxurious and difobedient children. But on
the other fide, it is written of woman, that fhe fhall be faued
by the bringing forth of children; if they remayne in faith, and
charity, and fanctification, with chaftity. But now if a fonne
of perfect age, and who hath difcretion to guide himfelfe be
put vpon the account of his parents when he doth il; how much
more fhall it be fo, in the cafe of fucking and weake children;
who, according to the iudgment of our Lord, *know not their right*
hand from the left; that is to fay, the differéce between good & ill.
If you will prouide with extraordinary care that you daughter
be not bitten by a viper; why will you not prouide with the
like care, that fhe may not be ftroken by that beetle, which
beates vpon the whole earth; that fhe may not drinke of the
golden cup of *Babylon*; that fhe go not forth with *Dina*, to fe the
daughter of a ftraung nation; that fhe dance not, and weare
not curious cloathes? Poyfon is not offered, vnles it be ouerfpred with hony; and vice deceiues not, but vnder the fhadow
and fhew of vertue. But how, will you fay; The finnes of
fathers

fathers are not punished vpon the children , nor of the children vpon the parents ; but *that foule which sinnes shall dye.*

This is said of them who haue discretion , and of whom it is written in the Ghospell, *He is of age, let him speake for himselfe;* But he who is a little one , and who iudges of thinges like a little one , till he come to the yeares of discretion , and till the letter of *Pythagoras* , the Y bring him to the parting of the two wayes , both the good , and ill ; of such a one is imputed to the parents . Vnles you will perhaps conceiue , that the children of Christians , if they receiue not Baptisme , are onely guilty of that sinne; and that the wickednes hath no relation to them, who would not giue the *Baptisme* ; especially if it be at such tyme, as when they who are to receiue *Baptisme* , haue no power to refuse it . But so on the other side , the good of those Infants , is also the gayne of their parents . It was in your power, whether or no you would offer vp your daughter, though yet your case be different , who made a *vow* of her , before you conceiued; but that now you should neglect her breeding, whē you haue offered her , will touch you selfe in point of danger . He who makes oblation of a Sacrifice , which is lame or maymed or defiled with any spot, is guilty of sacriledge; and how much more will she be punished , who is negligent in preparing a part of her owne body , and the purity of an vntouched mind , *for the embracements of the King* ?

When she beginnes to be a little growne , and *to encrease in wisedome , age , and grace , both with God and man ,* after the example of her spowse , let her go to the Temple of her true father , with her parents ; but let her not depart with them out of the Temple . Let the seeke her in the iourney of this world, and amongst the troupes of her kinred , but let them find her no where els, but in the secret retiring place of holy scriptures, asking questions of the Prophets , and Apostles , couering her spirituell mariage. Let her imitatat *Mary* , whome *Gabriel* found aboue in her chamber; and who was therefore stroken with feare , because she saw a man, as she was not wont to do . Let her imitate her , of whom it is said , *All the glory of that daughter of the King* , *is from within* Let her also say to her elect , being wounded by the dart of his charity , *The King hath led me into his chamber.*

chamber. Let her neuer go forth, leaſt they meet with her, who walke round about the citty, and leaſt they ſtrike and wound her, and take the pure veile of chaſtity from her, & leaue her ſtarke naked in her owne blood; but rather when any body knockes at the doore, let her ſay : *I am a wall, and my breaſts are a tower, I haue waſhed my feet, and I cannot find in my hart to fowle them.*

Let her not feed in publike, that is to ſay, at her parents table, that ſo ſhe may ſee no meat which ſhe may affect. And though ſome thinke, that it is an act of higher vertue to con-temne pleaſure, when it is at hand; yet for my part, I hold it to be the ſafer way towardes abſtinence, to be ignorant of that, which you muſt not ſeeke. I read this of old, when I was a boye at ſchoole ; *You haue no good title to reprehend that, which you ſuffer to take roote by cuſtome.* Let her beginne to learne, euen al-ready, not to drinke wine, *wherein is Luxury.* Before one come to be of ſtrong age, abſtinence is both grieuous and dangerous. Till that tyme ſhe may (if need require) both bath, and vſe a little wine, for the help of her ſtomake, and be ſuſtayned by the eating of ſome fleſh, leaſt her feet fayle her, beorſe ſhe can begin to runne. And this I ſay, according to indulgence, but not according to commaundment; fearing weaknes, but not teaching the way to luſt. For otherwiſe, that which is partly done by the ſuperſtition of the Iewes, in reiecting ſome beaſts, and other food ; and which the *Brachmanni* of the *Indians,* and the *Gymnoſophiſts* of the *Egyptians* do alſo vſe, euen in excluding the vſe of ſo much, as flower, or barly, and only to feed vpon rootes ; Why ſhould not the Virgin of Chriſt obſerue wholy? If glaſſe be ſo much worth, why ſhould not pearle be worth more? She who is borne vpon a fore-promiſe, let her liue ſo, as they liued who were borne vpon ſuch a kind of fore-pro-miſe. A like grace ought to be obtained by a like labour.

Let her be deafe to muſicall inſtruments, and not know why the *Pipe,* the *Lyra,* and the *Harpe* were made. Let her dai-ly giue account of the taske of thoſe flowers, which ſhe daily is to gather out of Scripture. Let her learne from thence a cer-taine number of Greeke verſes. Then preſently let the tea-ching of the Latin tongue follow after, which if it caſt not her

Q   *young*

young mouth into a frame from the beginning, her tongue wil
be peruerted towardes some strange accent ; and her naturall
language will be abased with forraine errours . Let her haue
you for her Mistres, & let her téder youth admire you. Let her
see nothing in you, or in her Father , which if she doe, she may
sinne . Remember you who are the parents of a Virgin, that
you are to teach her more by your deeds, then by your words.
Flowers quickly fad, and an vnwholsome ayre doth soone
corrupt the Saffran, the violet, and the lilly . Let her neuer
goe into publike , but with you . Let her not goe euen to the
tombes of Martyrs, or to Churches, without her mother . Let
no youth, let no dapper fellow smile vpon her. Let our young
virgin so celebrate the dayes of Vigills, and solemne pernocta-
tions, that she may not depart from her mother , euen for one
haires breadth .

I will not haue her loue any one of her maides, more then
another; nor that she be euer whispering in her eare . Whatsoeuer she sayth to one of them, let them all know . Let that cō-
panion please her, who is not tricked vp, nor fayer, & wantō ,
and who singes not a sweet song with a clear voyce; but who
is graue, pale, neglecting her selfe, and inclining to sadnes. Let
her gouernesse be some auntient virgin of approued trust, modesty and couuersation ; who may instruct her, and accustome
her by her owne example, to rise by night to prayers & *Psalmes*
to sing hymnes in the morning, and at the *third* , the *sixth* , and
ninth houre ; to stand in the skirmish, & like a warryer of Christ
to offer the *euening sacrifice* with her lampe lighted. Let the day
passe in this manner, and so let the night find her labouring .
Let reading come after prayer, and then prayer after reading .
That tyme will seeme short, which is imployed vpon such variety of workes . Let her learne also to make yarne, to hold
the distaffe, to lay the basket in her lap , to turne the spindle ,
& to draw downe the threed with her fingars . Let her despise
silke, and the wooll of the *Sereans*, and gold which is wrought
into fine thred . Let her get such garments, as wherby the cold
may be driuen away, and not whereby the body which is pretended to be clad, may be discouered . Let her food be some
little pot of herbes, and flower , and little fishes for some sel-

dome tymes . And (that I may not draw on thefe rules againſt gluttony into length, whereof I haue alfo fpoken more at large elfwhere) let her fo eate, that ſhe may be euer hungry, and may be able to read,& ſing pſalmes prefently after meat. Thofe long and immoderate faſts are not allowed by me (efpecially when the party is very young)wherin they go empty from one weeke to another, and when it is forbidden to eat fruites, and to vſe oyle in the dreſſing of meat. I haue learned by experience, that an aſſe when he is weary, feeks places into which he may diuert . This do thofe worſhippers of *Iſis,* and *Cybeles,*who with a gluttonous kind of abſtinence, deuour pheaſants & turtles, when they are brought fmoaking in, leaſt otherwiſe forfooth, they ſhould defile the gifts of *Ceres* . This is the precept, which I giue for that kind of faſt, which is to be continuall, that our ſtrength may laſt for a long iourney, leaſt being able to runne in the firſt part of therace,whē we come to the fecond we fal downe. But (as I haue writen hertofore) in *Lent* the fails of abſtinence are to be hoifed vp, and all the raines of the charriot-driuer, are to be layd in the horfes neckes, as when they are in great haſt . Though yet, there be ſtill a difference betweene the condition of fecular perfons, and that of Virgins and Monkes . A fecular man concoĉtes the former rauin of his appetite, and liuing vpon his owne iuyce (after the manner of fnailes) he prepares his panch for future food,and fat prouiſion: but a Virgin, and a Monke, muſt fo loofe the raines to their horfes, as to remember that they muſt euer runne. That labour which endes not, muſt be moderate; but that which is to haue an end, may for the tyme be more intenfe. For there we are euer going, and here we pawfe fometimes. If euer you goe to the houfes of recreation neere the Citty, doe not leaue your daughter at home. Let her not know how , nor let her be able to liue without you; and when ſhe is alone, let her be affraid, let her not haue conuerfation with fecular perfons, nor cohabite with ill bred Virgins . Let her not be prefent at the marriage of your feruants, nor mingle her felfe with the fports of the vnquiet family .

I know fome who haue aduifed, that the virgin of Chriſt maynot bath her felfe, with fo much as Eunches,nor with mar-

Q 2   ryed

ryed woemen; for the former lay not downe the mindes of mē; and the later, by their great bellyes ſhew about what buſines they haue bene . For my part, I am vtterly againſt liking, that a virgin of ripe yeares ſhould vſe bathes at all; who ought to be aſhamed, and euen not to ſee her ſelfe naked. For if ſhe macerate her body, and reduce it to ſeruitude by watching, and faſting, if ſhe deſire to extinguiſh the incentiues, and flame of luſt of her boyling youth by the cooleues of abſtinance, if by the deſire of neglecting her ſelfe ſhe make haſt to put her natural beauty in diſorder ; why ſhould ſhe on the other ſide ſtirre vp couered fyer, by the entertainment and incouragement of *Bathes* ?

Inſteed of ſilke and gemmes, let her loue the diuine bookes; wherein not the picture which is limmed with gold vpon *Babylonian* parchment, but an exact and learned edition or coppy may giue delight . Let her firſt learne the *Pſalter*, let her diuert her ſelfe from vanity, by thoſe ſonges; and let her life be inſtructed by the Prouerbs of Salomon . In *Eccleſiaſtes*, let her learne to deſpiſe worldly thinges. In *Iob* let her follow the examples of vertue and patience. Let her paſſe from thence to the Ghoſpels , and neuer lay them out of her hands. Let her ſucke in, the Acts of the Apoſtles, and the Epiſtles, with the whole affection of her hart . And when ſhe hath enriched the ſtorehouſe of her breſt with thoſe goods, let her commit the Prophets to memory, the fiue bookes of *Moyſes*, the bookes of *Kinges* the *Cronicles*, and the volumes alſo of *Eſdras* , and *Heſter* . At the laſt, ſhe may without danger , learne the *Canticle of Canticles*, which if ſhe had red in the beginning , ſhe might perhaps haue been wounded; through want of vnderſtanding that nuptiall ſonge of ſpirituall Marriage , which is expreſſed vnder corporall wordes . Let her take heed of all Apocriphall bookes. And if at any time ſhe will read them , not for the truth of doctrine, but for the reuerence which is due to Miracles; let her know that they are not theirs, vnder whoſe names they goe; and that many vitious thinges be mingled, therewith; and that the man had need of much prudence , who is to ſeeke gold in duſt . Let her euer haue the workes of *Cyprian* in her hand, and ſhe may with a ſecure foot runne ouer the Epiſtles of *Athanaſius* , and the

the bookes of *Hilarius*. Let her be delighted with their tracts and wits, in whoʃe bookes the piety of faith wauers not. And as for other Authours, let her read them ʃo, as that ʃhe may rather iudge of them, then be ruled by them,

But you will ʃay, how can I, being a ʃecular woman, obʃerue all theʃe things at *Rome*, in ʃuch a great crowd of people? Do not vndergo that burden, which you are not able to beare; but when you ʃhall haue wenaed her, with *Iʃaac*, and ʃhall haue clad her with *Samuell*; ʃend her to her grandmother, and her aunt. Reʃtore that moʃt pretious gemme to the chamber of *Mary*; and let it be ʃet vpon the cradle of *Ieʃus*, who is crying out there, like an infant. *Let her be brought vp in the Monaʃtery, let her life be ʃpent among thoʃe quiers of virgins; let her not learne to ʃweare; let her hold a lye to be a ʃacriledge; let her be ignorant of the world; let her liue angelically; let her conuerʃe in fleʃh without fleʃh; & let her hold all others to be like her ʃelfe*. And that I may paʃʃe ouer the reʃt with ʃilence, let her free you from the difficulty, & danger of côʃeruing her. It is better for you to wiʃh for her, when ʃhe is abʃent; then to be frighted concerning her vpon al occaʃions, when ʃhe is preʃent, about what ʃhe is ʃaying, with whome ʃhe is ʃpeaking, towardes whome ʃhe makes a ʃigne, and vpon whome ʃhe lookes with a good will. Deliuer this little one ouer to *Euʃtochium*; the childes very crying, now like an infant is a kind of prayer for you. Deliuer to *Euʃtochium* this companion of ʃanctity, whome hereafter ʃhe may leaue her heire thereof, Let her looke vpon her Aunt, loue her, and admire her euen from her infancy, whoʃe ʃpeech, whoʃe gate, and whoʃe conuerʃation, is the very doctrine it ʃelfe of vertue. Let her be in the lappe of her grandmother, who may hereafter reap in her grand-child, whatʃoeuer ʃhe ʃowed in her daughter; who hath learned by long experience to bring vp, to conʃerue, to inʃtruct virgins; whoʃe crowne is wouen with chaʃtity, and it hath the increaʃe of a hundred fould.

O happy virgin! O happy *Paula*, the daughter of *Toxotius*, who through the vertue of her grandmother, and of her aût, is more honourable by ʃanctity, then by nobility of ʃtock! O that you might happé to ʃee that mother and ʃiʃter in law of yours, and behold thoʃe great mindes in little bodies! I doubt not

but

but according to that modesty, wherwith you are naturaly indued, you would outstrip your daughter, and change that first sentence of God, for that second law of the Ghospel; nor would you only contemne the desire of hauing more posterity, but would rather offer your selfe to God. But because *there is a time for embracing, and a time for abstayning ; and the wife hath not power ouer her body*. And *; Let euery one who is called , continue in the same vocation, in our Lord*. And since he, who is vnder the yoke with another, must so runne, as not to leaue his companion in the durt, doe you restore that wholly in your offspring, which you defer in the meane time, concerning your selfe. *Anna* did neuer receaue her sonne againe, whom she vowed to God, when once she had offered him in the Tabernacle; esteeming it to be an indecent thing, that he who was to be a Prophet, should grow vp in her house, who had still a desire of more children. In fine after she had conceiued , and brought him forth, she durst not approach to the Temple, nor appeare empty handed before our Lord, till first she had payd what she ought ; and hauing made an immolation of that sacrifice , and returning home , she brought fiue children for her selfe : for her first borne was brought forth by her for our Lord . Admire you the fidelity of this holy woman ? Imitate also her fayth . If you will send *Paula* hither , my selfe make you a promise, that I will be both her teacher, and her foster-father . I will carry her vpon my shoulders; and though I be an old man, I will by imitation of stammering frame wordes fit for her , and will esteeme my self much more glorious , then that Philosopher of the world ; I , who shall not be instructing that Macedonian King, who was to be destroyed by poison ; but a hand-maid and spouse of Christ our Lord, to be prepared for his celestiall kingdome.

Saint Hierome to Furia ; about keeping her selfe in State of widdowhood .

YOV desire me by your letters, and you entreat me in a lowly kind of manner to answere you : and I will write, how you ought to liue , and conserue the crowne of widowhood,

hood, without touch to the reputation of your chaſtity. My mind reioyces, my hart exults, and the affection of my ſoule doth euen earne with gladnes, to ſee you deſire that, after your husbands life, which your mother *Titiana* of holy memory did mainteyne and performe a long time, whileſt her huſband liued. Her petition, and prayers are heard. She obtayned that her only daughter ſhould arriue to that, which her ſelfe when ſhe was aliue, did poſſeſſe. You haue beſides a great priuiledge, from the houſe whereof you came, in that, ſince *Camillus* his dayes, it is hardly writen, that any woman of your family was euer marryed a ſecond tyme. So that you are not ſo prayſe-worthy if you cōtinue a widdow, as you will deſerue, to be deteſted if you keep not that being a Chriſtiā, which Pagā woemen haue kept for ſo many ages. I ſay nothing of *Paula* & *Euſtochium*, who are the flowers of your ſtocke; leaſt by occaſion of exhorting you, I may ſeeme to prayſe them. I alſo paſſe by *Bleſilla*, who following your husband, and your brother, ran through much tyme (after the account of vertue) in a ſhort ſpace of her life. And I wiſh that men would imitate that, for which woemen may be prayſed, and that wriņkled old age, would reſtore, what youth doth offer of his owne accord.

I do wittingly, & willingly thruſt my hand into the fyre. The browes will be knit, the arme will be ſtretched out & angry *Chremes* rage, till his face ſwell. The great Lords will ſtād vp againſt this letter, the nobility of lower ranke wil thunder, crying out, *that I am a witch, I, a ſeducer, and fit to be carryed away into the furtheſt part of the world.* Let them add if they will, *that I am alſo a Samaritan,* to the end that I may acknowledge the title of my Lord. But the truth is, I deuide not the daughter frō the mother, nor doe I bring that of the Ghoſpell, *let the dead bury the dead.* For he liues whoſoeuer he be, that belieues in Chriſt But he that belieues in him, muſt alſo walke as he walked. A way with that enuy, & malignitity, which the ſharpe tooth of ill tongued men would euer be faſting vpon Chriſtians; that whileſt they feare reproach, they may be vrged to forſake the loue of vertue. Except it be by letters, we know not one another; and then piety is the onely cauſe, where there is no notice of fleſh and blood. Honour you father, if he ſeperate you not

from

from the true Father. So long you mult acknowledge the tye
of blood, as he fhall know his Creatour. For otherwife, *Dauid*
will fpeake thus to you in playne termes; *Hearken, O daughter, &*
fee, and incline thyne eare, and forget thy people, and thy fathers houfe
and the King will earneftly defire thy beauty; for he is thy Lord. A great
reward, for hauing forgoten a father; *The King will earneftly de-*
fire thy beauty. Becaufe you fawe, becaufe you inclined your eare, and
haue forgotten your people, & your fathers houfe, therfore the King will
earneftly defire your beauty, and will fay to you; Thou art all fayre, my
friend, and there is no fpot in thee. What is more beautifull then a
foule, which is called the daughter of God, and cares for noe
exterior ornaments? She belieues in Chrift, and being aduanced to this high honour, fhe paffes on to her fpoufe, hauing
him for her Lord, who is her hufband.

What troubles are found in thefe other marriages, you
haue found in the marriages themfelues; and being fatisfyed e-
uen to a glut with the flefh of quailes, your iawes haue bene
filled with extreme bitternes. You haue caft vp thofe fharpe
and vnwholofome meates, you haue rendred that boyling &
vnquiet ftomacke. Why will you cramme you felfe againe
with that, which did yea hurt, *like a Dog returning to his vomit,*
and a Sow made cleane in a wallowing place of durt? Euen bruit
beaftes, and wild birdes, are not apt to fall againe, into
the fame ginnes and nets. Are you perhaps affrayd, that the
family of your *Furia's* fhould faile, and that your father fhould
not haue fome little child fprunge from your body, who may
craule vp and downe his breft, and bedaube his necke with
filth? As if all they who were marryed had borne children; or
they who haue had children, had them euer anfwerable to the
ftocke whereof they came. Belike *Cicero'es* fonne, did refem-
ble his father in eloquence; and your aunceftour *Cornelia* who
was indeed the example both of chaftity and fecundity, was
glad belike, that fhe brought the *Gracchi* into the world. It is a
ridiculous thing to hope for that, as a thing certaine, which
you fee, that many haue not, & others haue loft when they had
it. But to whom fhal you refigne fo great riches? to Chrift, who
cannot dye. Whom fhall you haue for your heire? him, who
is alfo your Lord. Your father will be troubled at it; but Chrift
will

Will be glad your family will mourne , but the angels will reioyce . Let your father do what he will with his eftate ; you
belong not to him of whom you were borne ; but to him by
whom you were regenerated, & who redeemed you with that
great price of his owne blood . Take heed of thofe nurfes , and
thofe woemen who are wont to carry the children in their armes ; and fuch venemous creatures as they , who defire to feed
their bellyes , euen out of your very skinne . They perfwade
you not to that which is good for you , but for themfelues . And
they are often giuing out thofe verfes :

VVilt thou alone confume thy youth in vayne ,
And children fweet , and loues rewards disdayne ?

But men will fay, that where the fanctity of chaftity is, there
is frugality , where frugality is , there are the feruants put to
loffe . They thinke themfelues robbed , of whatfoeuer they
carry not away ; and they confider but how much , and not of
how much , they receiue it. Wherefoeuer they fee a Chriftian,
they encounter him with that common fcorne of being an Im-
poftor . Thefe people fow moft fhamefull rumours ; and that
which came firft from themfelues , they giue out , to haue had
from others ; being both the authors , and exaggerators of the
report. A publique fame grows out of a meere lye which being
once come to the Matrons eares , and hauing bene canuafed by
their tongues , paffes on , and penetrates euen through whole
Prouinces . You fhall fee many of them , fall into the very rage
of mad people , and with a fpotted face , and vipers eyes , and
woorm-eaten teeth , raile at Chriftians .

Heere one, who in fome ftately purple mantle goes ,
And mumbling out fome filthy thing , through her fowle nofe ,
Trippes vp her wordes , and doth her toothles mouth difclofe .

And then forfooth all the company , makes a buz on her
fide ; and the audience barkes out againft vs ; yea and fome of
our owne inftitute ioyne with them, being both the detractors
and the detracted . Againft vs they haue tongue inough , but
they are dumbe in finding fault with themfelues, as if euen they,
were alfo any other thing , then Monkes ; and that whatfoeuer is fpoken againft Monkes , did not redound vpon Priefts ,
who are the fathers of Monks . The loffe of the fheep , is a re-

R   proach

proach to the fhepheard, as on the other fide ; the life of that Monke deferues praife, who reuerences the Priefts of Chrift; and detracts not from that order, whereby he is made a Chriftian.

I haue faid thus much to you, O daughter in Chrift, not doubting of your purpofe, for you wolud neuer haue defired my letters of exhortation, if you had made any queftion of the good of fingle marriage; but to the end, that you might vnderftand the wickednes of feruants, who fet a price vpon you; and the fleights of kinfmen, and the pious errour of your father, to whō though I will eafily allow that he loues you, yet I cannot grant, that it is a loue according to knowledge. But I fay with the Apoftle, *I confeffe they haue zeale, but not according to knowledge.* Do you rather imitate (for this I muft often repeat) that holy mother of yours; whom as often as I remember, it occurres to me to thinke of her ardent loue towards Chrift, her palenes through fafting, her almes to the poore, her obfequioufnes to the feruants of God; the humility both of her exteriour, and of her hart; and her fpeech which was fo moderate vpon all occafions. Let your father (whom I name with honour and all due refpect; not becaufe he is of Confular authority and a Seuator, but becaufe he is a Chriftian) fulfil the effect of his name. Let him reioyce that he begat a daughter, not for the world, but for Chrift; or rather let him grieue that you haue loft your virginity in vayne; and with all, haue not gathered the fruit of marriage. Where is the husbād which he gaue you? Though he had bene amiable; though he had bene good, death would haue fnatched all away; and his departure would haue vntyed the knot of flefh and blood. I befeech you take fpeedy hold of the occafion, and make a vertue of neceffity. The beginning of Chriftians, doth not fo much import, as the end. *Paul* began ill, but ended well; and the beginnings of *Iudas* are praifed, but his end was made dānable by his trechery. *Read Ezechiel. VVhāfoeuer the iuſt man shall finne, his iuſtice shall not deliuer him; and the impiety of the wicked, shall not hurt him whenfoeuer he shall be conuerted from his impiety.* This is *Iacobs* ladder, by which the Angels afcend, and defcend; from the top whereof our Lord leaning downeward reaches out his hand, to fuch as are weary, fufteyning

ning the weake steps of them who climbe, by the contemplatiõ
of himselfe. But as *he desires not the death of a sinner, but that he may
be conuerted and liue*; so he hates such as are tepid, & they quickly make him ready euen to cast the gorge. *She to whome more is
forgiuen, loueth more.* That vncleane woman, who was bapti-
sed in the Ghospell in her teares; and she who had formerly deceiued many with the haire of her head, was saued by wiping
the feet of our Lord. She brought not frizled dressings with her,
nor crackling shooes, nor eyes which were smoaked ouer with
Antimony. So much the fowler she was, so much was she the
fayrer. What should painting white or red, doe vpon the face
of a Christian? whereof the one tels a lye in making red the
lips and cheeks; the other doth as much, in making white the
forehead and necks; They are fyer to enflame young people;
they are the entertainments and encouragements of lust; and
they are testimonyes of an vnchast mind. How will such a one
weepe for her sinnes, whose teares shew her skine, and do e-
uen make furrowes in the face? This is not an ornament according to our Lord, but it is a couering of Antichrist. With what
confidence can a woman lift vp that faceto heauen, which the
Creator of all thinges, knowes not? It is impertinent for any
to alledge her youth, or tender yeares. The widow who hath
left to please her husband, & who (according to the Apostle)
is a widow indeed, hath need of nothing but perseuerance. It
is true. that she remembers her former pleasure; she knowes
what she hath lost; and wherin she tooke delight; but these
burning arrowes of the diuell, are to be quenched by the rigour
of watching, and fasting. Either let vs frame our discourse according to that kind of life which we seem to lead otherwise,
or els let vs seem to liue according to the discourse we hold.
Why do we professe one thing & practise another? The tongue
talkes of chastity, and the exteriour of the whole body iust the
contrary. And this I haue thought good to say, of the dressing
and habit of the body.

But the *widow who liues in delights, is dead, euen whilest she is
aliue*; and this is not my saying, but the Apostles. What is the
meaning of this, *She is dead, euen whilest she is aliue?* She seemes
indeed to liue, in the eyes of ignorant people, and not to be

dead in Chrift, from whome no fecret is concealed : *The foule which finnes, the fame shall dye* . Some mens finnes are manifeft, & precede their iudgment ; but fome other mens finnes follow it. And fo alfo good deedes are manifeft , and fuch as are not good cannot lye hid . He fpeakes therefore to this effect . There are fome who finne publikely , and fo freely, that fo foone as you fee them, you prefently vnderftand them to be finners ; but others who hide their finnes with craft, are knowne afterward by their conuerfation ; and in like manner, the good deedes of fome are very publike, and they of others are not knowne to vs , but only by long experience afterward . To what purpofe is it therefore, that we ftand bragging of chaftity, which is not able to wine credit for it felfe, without her companions, and acceffaries, which are Abftinence & Thirft? The Apoftle macerates his body, & bringes it vnder the fubiection of his foule, for feare leaft otherwife he fhould not find that to be in himfelf which he had inioyned to others. And fhall a young woman, whofe blood is boyling vp with meat , be fecure concerning her chaftity ? Neither yet whileft I am faying this, do I condemne thofe meates which God hath created to be vfed by vs , with thankefgiuing ; but I take from young people & maides, the motiues and intertainments of pleafure ? They are not the fire of *Ætna*, nor that land of *Vulcan*, nor eyther *Vefuuius*, or *Olimpus*, which boyle vp in fo huge a heat, as do the moft inward veines of young people, when they are full of wine, and inflamed with curious fare .

There are many , who tread vpon couetoufnes ; and it is layd afide by them as eafily as their purfe. A reproachfull tongue, is mended by impofing filence vpon it. To reforme the habite and order of our cloathing, doth but coft an houres work. All other finnes are without the man , and that which is without, is foone caft away . Only luft , to which we are enable by God, for the procreation of children, if it paffe beyond the due boundes , proues vicious , & by a kind of courfe of nature, it ftriues to breake out into copulation . It is therefore a point of great vertue, and requires a carefull diligence to ouercome that, to which you are borne, and not to liue in flefh, after a flefhly manner; to fight daily with your felfe, and to haue the

hundred

hundred eyes of *Argus* (which the Poets faigne) vpon that enemy who is shut vp within our selues. This is that which the
Apostle deliuers to vs in other words: *All sinne which a man com-*
mits is without the body, but he who commits fornication, sinnes against
his owne body. The Phisitians, who writ of the nature of mans
body, and especially *Galen* sayth in those bookes which are in-
tituled *Of preseruing bodily health,* that the bodies of youthes, and
young men, and of men and woemen of perfect age, boyle vp
through their inuate heate, and that such food is hurtfull to
them, at those yeats, as doth increase their heat; & that on the
other side it conduces to their health, to take such other meate
and drinke, as cooles the blood. And so also old wine, and
warmer food, is good for old men who are subiect to crudities and fleame. Whereupon our Sauiour also sayth; *Looke to*
your selues, that your hartes be not oppressed, through gluttony & drun-
kennes, and with the cares of this life. And the Apostle speakes of
wine, *wherein there is luxury.* Neither is it any marueile, that the
Potter framed this iudgment of the poore little pot which himselfe had made, when the Comedian, whose end was no more
then to describe the conditiō of mankind, sayd, that *Venus* grew
could without *Ceres* and *Bacchus.*

First therefore (if yet the strength of your stomacke will
endure it) let water be your drinke, till you shall haue passed
ouer the heat of your youth. Or if your weakenes will not admit of this, hearken to *Timothy; Vse a little wine for your stomacke,*
and for your frequent infirmities. In the next place, you must in
your food, auoyd all kind of thinges which are hot. And here
I speake not only of flesh, vpon which the vessell of election
pronounces this sentence; *It is good for a man not to drinke wine,*
nor to eate flesh; but also euen in *Pulse,* to auoyd all those things,
which are windy, and heauy; and know you that nothing is
so good for Christians, as the feeding vpon kitchin herbes.
Whereupon he saith also in another place? *He that is infirme, let*
him eat herbes; and so the heat of our bodies, is to be tempered
with this cooler kind of cates.

Daniel, & the three children were fed with *Pulse.* They
were but young, & were not yet come to the fiery paine wherin that Babylonian King fryed those old iudges. By vs, that

good & fayre ſtate of body which (euen beſides the priuiledge of Gods grace) appeared in them, by theyr feeding vpon ſuch-meates, is not eſteemed; but the ſtrength of the ſoule is ſought by vs; which is ſo much the ſtronger, by how much the fleſh is weaker . From hence it is, that many who deſire to lead a chaſt life, fall groueling downe in the mideſt of their iourney, whileſt they attend only to abſtayne from fleſh; and load the ſtomacke with pulſe, which being taken moderately and ſpa-ringly, is not hurtfull . But if I ſhall ſay what I thinke, there is nothing which doth ſo much inflame a body, and prouoke the partes of generation, as meate when it is not wel digeſted, but makes a kind of conuulſion in the body through windynes.

I had rather O daughter, ſpeake a little too plainly, then that the matter we ſpeake of, ſhould be in danger . You muſt thinke all that to be poyſon, which makes a ſeminary of plea-ſure. A ſparing diet, & a ſtomacke which is euer in appetite, I preferre before a faſt of three daies; and it is much better to take ſome little thing euery day, then to feed full, at ſome few ti-mes . That rayne is the moſt profitable, which deſcends into the earth, by little and little . A ſudden and exceſſiue ſhower, which fals impetuouſly, turnes the field vp ſide downe. When you eat, conſider that inſtantly after, you muſt pray and read . Rate your ſelf to a certaine number of verſes of holy Scripture, and performe this taske to our Lord; and allow not your body to take reſt, till you ſhall haue filled the basket of your breaſt with that kind of worke. Next after holy ſcriptures, read the writings of learned men; of the I meane whoſe faith is known. There is no cauſe, why you ſhold ſeeke gold in durt, but you muſt ſell pearles, to buy that one . Stand according to the ad-uiſe of *Ieremy*, neer many wayes, that you may meet with that one which leades to our country Transferre your loue of ie-wels, and gemmes, and ſilken cloathes, to the knowledge of holy ſcripture . Enter into that land of promiſe flowing with milke and hony. Eate flower, and oyle, and apparayle your ſelfe with the variouſly coloured garments of *Ioſeph* . Let your eares be boared through with *Ieruſalem*, that is to ſay, by the word of God, that the pretious grayne of new corne, may bow downe from thence. You haue holy *Exuperius*, a man of fit age
and

& approued faith, who will often inftruct you with his good aduice. *Make friendes for your felfe of the vniuſt Mammon, who may receiue you into thoſe eternal Tabernacles:* beſtow your riches vpon them, who eat not pheaſants, but browne bread, who driue hunger away, and who do not call luſt home. *Haue vnderſtanding of the poore, and needy*; giue to euery one that askes of you, but eſpecially to the houſhould of faith. Cloath the naked, & the hungry, & viſit the ſicke. As often as you ſtretch forth your hand, thinke of Chriſt. Take heed, that when your Lord God is begging of you, you increaſe not the riches of other folkes.

Fly from the conuerſation of young men, and let not any roof in your houſe be able to ſee theſe dapper, curious, and loofe fellowes there. Let the muſitian be ſent away like a malefactour, and thruſt you rudely out of your houſe, all Fidlers, and minſtrells, and ſuch quiers of the Diuell, as you would auoyd thofe *Syren* ſonges, which bring deſtruction. Goe not forth in publicke, & be not carryed vp and downe (according to the liberty which widowes takes) with that army of Eunuches going before you. It is a moſt wicked cuſtome, that a frail ſexe, and a weake age ſhould abuſe power, and ſhould thinke that all is lawfull, which they liſt. Though all thinges were lawful, al things are not expedict. Let not any follicitour who is curled vp, nor any fine ſoſter-brother, nor any dainty fairefaced page, be neere you. Sometymes the Ladyes mind, is vnderſtood by the habit of her maides. Procure the ſociety of holy Virgins, and widowes; and if there be neceſſity that you muſt ſpeake with men, doe not auoyd by-ſtanders; and let your confidence in ſpeach be ſuch, as that you neither tremble, nor bluſh, when any other body comes in. Let your face be the glaſſe, wherein your mind may be ſeene; and let your ſilent eyes confeſſe the inward thoughtes of your hart. We find, that lately, a certaine ignominious rumour did flutter throughout all theſe Eſterne partes. Both the age, the faſhion, the habite, the pace, the indiſcreet conuerſation, the exquiſite Feaſts, the princely prouiſion of *Nero*, and *Sardanapalus* ſpake of nothing but marriage. By the correction of the wicked, the wiſe man will grow ſo much the wiſer. A loue which is holy, is not ſubiect to impatience. A falſe report is

ſoone

foone repreft, the the later part of a mans dayes, is made the iudge of the former. I confeffe indeed, that no man can paffe the courfe of this life, without being bitten by ill report; and wicked men make it their comfort, to caft reproach vpon the good, as conceuing that their finnes are made leffe faulty by it. But yet a fyer made of ftraw goes out quickly, and the raging flame is content to dy by little and little, if it be noe longer fed. If fame belyed you the laft yeare, yea or euen if it fayd true, let the fault ceafe now, & the rumour will alfo be at an end. I fay not this, as if I doubted any ill of you; but becaufe I loue you fo much, that I feare euen fuch thinges as are fafe. O that you might but fee your fifter, and that you might chance to heare the wife difcourfe of that holy mouth; you would difcerne ftrange power in that little body. You would perceiue that whole fuite of ftuffe, both of the old & new Teftament, euen boyle out of her holy mouth. She makes a paftime of fafting, and her delight is her prayer. She holds the Timbrell in her hand, after the example of *Maria*; and *Pharao* being drowned, fhe inuites the quier of virgins by faying thus, *Let vs fing vnto our Lord, for he is magnifyed, after a glorious manner ; he hath caft downe both horfe, and Rider into the fea*. She addreffes this kind of fingers to Chrift, and fhe inftructes this kind of mufique for our Sauiour. So paffes the day, and fo the night, and the oyle being prepared for the lampes, the cōming of the fpoufe is expected. Doe you therefore imitate her. Let *Rome* haue fuch a one in it, as *Bethleem* poffeffes which is leffe then *Rome*. You are rich, & it is eafy for you to minifter the help of food to fuch as are poore. Let vertue fpend that which was prouided by you as the matter of luxe, and let no woman feare pouerty, who defpifes matrimony. Help to make fuch virgins, as you may bring into the Kings chamber. Relieue widowes whome you may mingle as fo many violets, betweene Virgins lillyes, and Martyrs rofes; & make your felfe a coronet of fuch flowers as thofe, infteed of that crown of thornes in which Chrift carryed the fins of the world.

Let your moft noble Father, both be glad, and be affifted by this example. Now let him learne that of his daughter which he learned before of his wife. Now the hayre is growne white, the knees tremble, the teeth fall, and the forehead being plowed with wrinkles by his great years, death muſt needes be euen at the gates, and the funerall fire is there at hand. We grow old whether we will or no. Let him make that prouiſion for himſelfe, which is neceſſary for a long iour-ney. Would he carry that with him, from which he muſt part againſt his will? Nay rather let him ſend it to heauen before him; which if he refuſe to do, the earth will take it.

Theſe younger widowes, *wherof many going backe after Sa-than, when they haue beene luxurious againſt Chriſt,* are wont to ſay when they are about to marry a ſecond tyme : *My litle fortune is dayly periſhing ; the inheritance of my auuceſtours is deſtroyed, My ſer-uant hath ſpoken ſaucily to me ; my may'd neglects my commandement; who ſhall ſhew himſelfe againſt theſe thinges? VVho ſhall anſwere the charges which are layd vpon my landes? VVho ſhall inſtruct my children? who ſhall bring vp my young ſhe ſlaues ?* And, O vnſpeakable wic-kednes, they bring that as a cauſe of marriage, which euen a-lone were a ſufficient reaſon to haue hindred it. The Mother bringes not a foſter-father, but an enemy vpon her children; not a Father, I ſay, but a tyrant. Being inflamed by luſt, ſhe forgets the children of her owne wombe ; and, in the middeſt of her little ones, who are not capable yet to vnderſtand their miſery, ſhe, who heereafter will lament it, is now tricking her ſelfe vp, like a new bride. Why doe you pretend the care of your patrimony? Why the vnruly pride of your ſeruants? Con-feſſe your filthines. No woman marryes a husband, to the end that ſhe may not lye with a man. Or yet if it be true, that you are not vrged by luſt, what kind of madnes is it, that you ſhould proſtitute your chaſtity, after the manner of harlots, to the end of augmenting your eſtate; and that for the obtayning of a baſe and tranſitory end, your chaſtity which is precious, and eternall, ſhould be defiled.

If you haue children already; why deſire you a ſecond marriage? If you haue none; why feare you not that barrenes, whereof already you haue ſome proofe? And why preferre you a thing vncertaine, before purity which is certaine? The con-tractes of marriage are now written out for you to ſigne, that ſhortly you may be compelled to make your will. Your huſ-

band

band will counterfeit himselfe to be sicke; and that which he
defires you fhould do, when you are about to dy, he will doe
now, when he meanes to liue. Or if it happen, that you haue
children by the fecond husband, there is already a quarell, and
a ciuill warre within doores. It shall be no longer lawfull for
you, to loue your former children, nor fo much as to looke vp
on them with indifferent eyes. If you feed them by ftealth,
he will enuy the dead man, and vnleffe you hate your childrē,
you will feeme to be ftill in loue with their Father. But then,
if he hauing children by a former wife, fhall lead you home to
his houfe, all the Comedians, and Verfifyers, and the commō-
plea-bookes of the towne, will declame againft you, as a moft
cruell ftep-mother, though indeed you fhould be moft benigne
towardes them. If your fonne in-law be ficke, or if he haue
but euen an aking head, you fhall be defamed for a Witch. If
your felfe giue him not meat, you will be accounted cruell; if
you feed him, you will be fayd to poyfon him. I befeech you
tell me, what good do thefe fecond marriages produce, which
may ferue to counteruaile fo great miferyes.

Would we know what kind of thinges widdowes ought
to be? Let vs read the Ghofpell according to *Luke*. *And Anna
the Propheteffe* (fayth he) *was the daughter of Phanuel of the tribe of
Affer. Phanuel*, in our tongue fignifyes *the face of God; Afer*, is
tranflated to fignify, both *riches* & *felicity*. Becaufe therfore fhe
had endured the burden of widowhood, from her youth til fhe
came to be fourefcore and foure yeares old, and departed not
from the Temple of God, infifting day and night by fafting &
prayer, therefore did fhe deferue fpirituall grace, and to be fti-
led, *the daughter of the face of God*, and to be endowed with the
riches, and felicity of her anceftours. Let vs remember the widow of *Sarepta*, who preferred the hunger of *Elias* before her
owne, or her childrens health. So that fhe being to dye with
her fonne that night, refolued to leaue her gueft fafe behinde
her; and choofing rather to loofe her life, then her giuing of
almes, did in that handfull of floure, prepare for her felfe the
feminary of a harueft, from our Lord. The floure is fowed, &
the veffels of oyle fpringes out. In *Iury* there was fcarcity of
wheat, for the graine of corne was dead there; & there flowed

great

great fountains from the widowes oyle. We read in *Iudith* (if men be yet difpofed to receaue that booke) of a widow, who was defeated by fafting, and defaced by mourning weedes, who lamented not her dead husband, but fought the coming of a new fpoufe, by the extreme neglect of her owne perfon. I fee that fhe appeares with a warlike fword, and with a bloody right hand. I perceaue fhe hath the head of *Holophernes*, which fhe hath brought, euen from the middeft of her enemies. A woman ouercomes men, and chaftity cuts off the head of luft; and changing fuddenly her habit, fhe comes backe to that conquering neglect of her felfe, more glorious then all the ornaments of this world could giue her. Some there are, who ignorantly reckon *Deborah* among the widowes, & thinke that *Barach* the Captaine, was the fonne of *Deborah*, though the fcripture fpeake otherwife. By vs, fhe fhall be named in regard that fhe was a Prophetefle, and is reckened among the number of the Iudges. And becaufe fhe could fay, *How fweet are thy wordes to my throat, more then hony or the hony combe to my mouth;* fhe tooke the name of a *Bee*, being fed by the flowers of holy Scripture, and being imbrued by the odour of the Holy Ghoft, and compofing the fweet iuyce of *Ambrofia*, with her Propheticall mouth. *Noemi* (which fignifyes παρακεκλημένη, and which we may interpret *The comforted*) her husband and children being dead in foraigne parts brought bake her chaftity into her country, and being fuftained by that prouifion, fhe had a *Moabite* for her fonnes wife, that this prophecy of *Ifay* might be fulfilled: *Send forth, O Lord, the Lambe, the fubduer of the earth, from the rocke of the defert, to the mountaine of the daughter of Sion.* I com now to the widow of the Ghofpell (that poore widow, more rich then all the people of *Ifraell*) who taking a grayne of Muftard-feed, and putting leuen into three cakes of flower, did by the grace of the holy Ghoft, temper a confeffion of the *Father*, and the Sonne, and did caft two mytes into the Treafury. Whatfoeuer fhe could be worth in all the world, and all her riches without exception, fhe offered, in both the Teftaments of her fayth. Thefe are the two *Seraphims*, who thrice did glorify the Trinity, and are layd vp for a treafure to the Church, whereupon a burning coale being by the tonges of both thofe

·Tefta-

Teſtaments, doth purify the lippes of a ſinner .

Why ſhould I repeat theſe auncient particulars , and produce the vertues of woemen out of books, when you may propoſe many to your ſelfe in the Citty , where you liue, whoſe example you ought to imitate . And that I may not ſeeme to ſpeake of them in particular by the way of flattery ; the holy *Marſella* will ſerue your turne , who correſponding with the ſtocke wherof ſhe came, hath preſented vs with ſomewhat our of the Ghoſpel . *Anna* liued ſeauen years with her husband, frō the tyme of her virginity; *Marſella* ſeauen moneths. The former expected the coming of Chriſt ; this later holdes him faſt, whome that other receaued . The former , ſaw him crying, the later preaches him triumphing . The former ſpoke of him , *to all ſuch as expected the redemption of Iſrael,* the later cryes out thus with the nations, which are now redeemed : *A brother doth not redeeme , a man ſhall redeeme.* And out of another Pſalme: *A man is born in her , and the moſt high hath founded her .* I remember that almoſt two yeares ſince, I wrote ſome bookes againſt *Iouinian,* wherein by the authority of Scriptures I fully ſatisfyed the queſtions, which came againſt me ; where the Apoſtle grants liberty of ſecond mariages . And there is no neceſſity to repete them here at full length, ſince you may haue what I haue writ ten there . And now that I may not exceed the meaſure of an Epiſtle , I will only giue you this leſſon : *Remember daily that you muſt dye, for then you will not be thinking of a ſecond mariage .*

Saint Hierome to Paulinus, about the inſtitution of a Monke .

A Good man bringeth forth good thinges, out of the good treaſure of his hart ; and the Tree is knowne by his fruit-You meaſure vs by your owne vertue , and being great , you extoll vs who are little ; and you fill the loweſt roome ar the banket, that you may be aduanced , by his direction who makes the Feaſt. For what is there in vs, or how little is there that we ſhould deſerue to be prayſed, by learned wordes ? that we, who are poore and meane, ſhould be commended by that
mouth,

mouth, wherby that most religious Prince is defended? But do not, my deare brother, esteeme of me according to the number of my yeares, & value not my wisedome by my age; but my age by my wisedome, according to that of *Salomon: A mans wisedome is his grey haires*. For *Moyses* was commaunded to choose seuenty six such Priestes, as he knew to be Priestes, that is to say, such as were to be esteemed according to their wisedome, not according to their age. And *Daniel*, whilest he was yet a youth, gaue iudgment vpon aged men; and their lasciuiousnes condemned them of vnchastity. I say, you must not iudge of a mans sufficiency, after the rate of his age, nor must you therefore thinke me to be more vertuous, because I began to serue in the campe of Christ before you. *Paul* the Apostle, was changed from being a persecuter, to be a vessell of election, and being last in order, he became first in merits; because though he were the last, *he laboured more then they all : Iudas* (of whome it was sayd, *But thou O man, who diddest eate familiarly with me, and wast my captaine, and we walked togeather in the house of God*) was the betrayer of his friend, and of his Master, and was reproued by our Sauiours wordes, and tyed the knot of his owne vgly death, vpon a high tree. On the other side, the theefe exchanged the Crosse for Paradice, and made that punishment of his murders, to stand for Martyrdome.

How many do at this day, euen by liuing long carry themselues (as it were) dead to Church, and being whited sepulchres without, are full of dead mens bones within. A sudden lusty heat is better then a long tepidity. In fine you hearing those words of our Sauiour (*If thou wilt be perfect go, and sell all though hast, and giue it to the poore, and follow me*) do turne those wordes into deeds; & being naked do follow the naked Crosse, and so doe more lightly and nimbly clime vp *Iacobs* ladder you haue changed you mind with your habite, and do not, with a full purse, affect any glorious kind of filth, but with cleane hand and a pure hart, you prize your selfe to be poore in deed, and in spirit. For there is no great matter, in counterfetting or making ostentation of fasting, by carrying a pale and wanne face about; and for a man to bragge of carrying a poore cloake vpon his backe, when he is rich in reuenues; That Crates of *Thebes*; y. no formerly had bene extremely rich, when he came to be a Philosopher at *Athens* , cast away a great somme of gold, nor did he thinke that a man could possesse vertue and riches, both together. But we, being all stuffed with gold, will needs follow Christ, who was so poore ; and attending to our former rich estates, vnder the pretence of enabling our selues to giue almes, how shall we distribut the goods of other men faithfully to others, when we do so fearfully reserue our owne ? It is an easy matter for a full belly to dispute of fasting .

It deserues no comendation to haue liued at *Ierusalem*; but to haue liued there wel . *That Citty is to be desired, that to be praised, not which kils the Prophets , and which hath spilt the blood of Christ; but which the impetuousnes of the riuer doth make glad ; which placed vpon the hill,cannot be concealed ;* which the Apostle cals *the mother of Saints ; of which Citty he reioyces , that he is made a free-denison.*Neither yet by saying this, do I taxe my selfe of inconstancy , or condemne that, which I do ; that so I should in vayne seem to haue left my friends, and country , after the example of *Abraham* : but I dare not circumscribe the omnipotency of God to so narrow as compasse ; and to confine him to a small place of the earth, whom heauen is not able to contayne. The faithfull are not waighed by the diuersity of places, but by the merit of their faith . And they who are true adorers, adore not the father either in *Ierusalem*, or in *Mount Gasarim* : for God is a spirit, and they *must do it in spirit, and truth* . *The spirit breaths where it will* . *The earth & the fulnes therof, is our Lords.* Since the whole world was bathed with that celestial dew,the fleece of *Iury* being dry , *and many coming from the East and VVest , haue reposed in the bosome of Abraham, God hath giuen ouer to be only knowne in Iury, and to haue his name great in Israell ; but the sound of the Apostles , is now gone ouer the whole earth, and their wordes euen to the ends of the world*. Our Sauiour speaking to his Disciples when he was in the Temple, sayd thus; *Ryse vp,let vs goe hence.*And to the Iews; *Your house shall be left desert to you* . If heauen & earth shall passe, certainly all thinges which are earthly, shall passe . And therfore the places of the Crosse, and Resurrection, shall profit thē, who carry their Crosse; who ryse daily with Christ, and who make themselues worthy of such an excellent habitation . But
they

they who fay, *The temple of the Lord, the temple of the Lord;* Let them heare the Apostle fay, *You are the temple of our Lord, and the holy Ghost dwells in you.* And that heauenly Court is open a-like, both towardes *Hierusalem*, and towardes *Britanny*. For the kingdome *of God is within you*. *Anthony*, and all thofe fwarmes of Monkes of *Egypt*, and *Mefopotamia*, *Pontus*, *Capadocia*, and *Armenia* neuer faw *Hierufalem*, and heauen is open to them without any relation to this Citty. Blefsed *Hilarion*, who was of *Palestine*, and liued there, did neuer fpend but one day in the feeing of *Hierufalem*, to the end, that being fo neere hand, he might neither feeme to contemne thofe holy places, nor yet on the other fide, might feeme to fhut vp our Lord in any one place. From the tymes of *Adrian*, to the empire of *Constantine* (which imported about the tyme of a hundred and foure fcore yeares) in the place of the Refurrection, there was an Idoll of *Iupiter*. In the rocke of the Crofse, there was placed a marble ftatue of *Venus* to be worfhipped. The perfecutours who were authours therof, conceiuing that they might abolifh our Fayth of the Refurrection, and of the Crofse, when they had polluted the holy places by their Idols. That wood which is called *Thamus*, that is to fay, of *Adonis*, did ouerfhaddow the moft imperiall place of the whole world, namely this *Bethleem* of ours, whereof the *Pfalmift* fayth : *Truth is fprung out of the earth*, and in that hollow place where Chrift being an Infant did once cry, the paramour of *Venus* was lamented. But you will afke me to what end I am fo large in this particular? To the end that you may not thinke, that any thing is wanting to your fayth, becaufe you haue not beene at *Hierufalem*; and that you may not efteeme vs to be the better men, becaufe we enioy this habitation. But whether you liue here or there, you fhall obtaine of our Lord, a reward which fhall be equall to your workes.

But yet that I may plainely confefse what the pulfe of my hart is in this bufinefse, confidering both your purpofe, & that ardour of mind wherewith you haue difclaimed the world, I do really belieue, that you will then find difference in places, if forfaking Cittyes & the concourfe of people which is found therein, you will dwell in fome little retyred corner, & feeke Chrift in the defert, and pray alone in the mountaine with

Iefus,

Iesus, & enioy the neighbour-hood of thefe holy places. That is to fay, that both you may eftrange your felfe from the Citty, and not loofe the purpofe of being a Monke. I fpeake not this for Bifhops, or Priefts, who haue other imployments; but I fpeake of it for a Monke, and fuch a one as formerly was noble in the world, who layd the price of his pofseffions at the feet of the Apoftles; thereby teaching, that money was to be troden vnder foot, that fo liuing in humility and fecrecy, he might continue to defpife that, which he had once defpifed. If the places of the Crofse, and of the Refurrection were not exceedingly frequented in this Citty, where there is a Court, where there is a guarde of fouldiers, where there are lafciuious people iefters, mimickes, and all other things which were wont to be in other Citties; or if it were only frequented by troopes of Monkes; all Monkes indeed might well defire fuch an habitation as this. But now it is extreme folly, for a man to renounce the world, to forgoe his country, to forfake his Cittyes, to profefse Monafticall life; and then to liue in greater concourfe of men abroad, then he was to haue liued in his owne country. Men flocke hither from all the partes of the world; the City is full of all kind of people, and there is fuch a crowding here of folkes of both fexes; that here you are to endure that whole incouenience, whereof you auoyded but a part, by going from any other place.

Since therefore you doe fo confidently aske me by what way you are to goe. I will vnmaske my felfe, and tell you clearely what I thinke. If you will exercife the office of a Prieft, if you be delighted in the imployment of Epifcopal dignity, liue in Citties and Townes, and procure that the faluation of others foules may be profitable to yours. But if you defire to be that, which now you are called, that is to fay, a Monke, which fignifyes to be a folitary perfon; what make you in Citties, which are not the habitations of feuerall fingle perfons, but of many, who liue togeather? Euery profeffion hath his chiefes. Let Captaines of Roman armyes, imitate the *Camillo's*, the *Fabricia's*, the *Regulo's*, and the *Scipio's*. Let Philofophers propound to themfelues *Pythagoras*, *Socrates*, *Plato*, *Ariftatle*. Let Poets imitate *Homer*, *Virgil*, *Menander*, and *Terence*.

Hiftorians

Hiftorians, *Thucydides, Saluft, Herodotus, Liuy*; Orators, *Lyfias* the *Gracchi, Demofthenes,* & *Tully.* And(that we may come neerer to our felues,)let Bifhops and Priefts haue the Apoftles and Apoftolicall perfons for their patternes, & let them endeauour to haue their merit, fince they haue their honour. But let vs haue for the prime men of our inftitute, the *Paulo's*, the *Anthonies,* the *Iulians, Hilarions*, and the *Macario's.* And (that I may returne to the authority of fcriptures) our Generall is *Elias*, and *Elizeus*; and our Captaines are the fonnes of the Prophets, who dwelt in folitary places and deferts, and who made Tabernacles for themfelues, neer the waters of *Iordan*. The children of *Rechab,* are of this kind, *who drunke no wine, nor other thing that could inebriat*; *who dwelt in Tents,* who were praifed in *Ieremy,* by the voice of God; and it was promifed to them, that fome one of their ftocke, fhould not be wanting, who might ftand before our Lord. This I thinke is fignifyed by the title of the 70. Pfalme, fpeaking of the fonnes of *Ionadab*, and of them, who were led into captiuity. This is *Ionadab* the fonne of *Rechab*, who is affirmed in the booke of Kinges, to haue mounted the chariot of *Hieu,* and his fonnes they are, who (euer dwelling in Tents, and being at laft compelled vpon the breaking in of the Army of *Chaldea*; to enter into *Hierufalem*) are faid to haue bene the firft, who were led into captiuity; becaufe after hauing enioyed the large liberty of a defert, they were fhut vp in that Citty, as if it had bene a prifon. I befeech you therefore, becaufe that holy Sifter of yours hath a kind of tye vpon you, and for that you paffe not on as yet, with a pace which is wholly free, yet whether you be here or there, fly from complements, and vifits, and feafts, as from certaine chaines which will tye you to pleafure. Let your food be meane, as herbes, and pulfe; and take it not till night; and little fifhes fometimes, which you muft hold for a great delicacy. He who defires Chrift, and feeds vpon that bread, muft not greatly care of how pretious meates his excrement be made: whatfoeuer delicate thing you eat is all one with bread and pulfe, when once it is paffed downe below the throat. You haue two bookes of myne againft *Iouinian,* of the contempt of delight in eating. Let your hand euer haue in it fome holy booke.

T   You

You muſt often pray with your knees bent, & your mind muſt
be raiſed vp to our Lord. You muſt watch often, and often
ſleepe with an empty ſtomacke. Theſe carryers of tales, and
theſe prety little vanities, and ſmoothing flatterers, you muſt
fly like ſo many enemyes. Diſpence your almes with your
owne hand, for the eaſe of the charge of poore and vertuous
people. Honeſty is growne rare amongſt men. Doe you not
belieue what I ſay? Thinke of *Iudas* his purſe.

Do not affect poore cloathes, with a prowd mind. What
need haue you to ſee thoſe thinges often, for the contempt whereof you became a Monke. Eſpecially let your ſiſter decline
the conuerſation of theſe Matrons, and let her haue no cauſe,
either to be ſorry for her ſelfe, or to admire her ſelfe, when ſhe
ſees her ſelfe all neglected and ill clad, amongſt the ſilkes and
iewels of other woemen, who ſit about her. For one of theſe
two will bring you to repent your good purpoſe, & the other
is a Seminary of vainglory. Take heed that you, who haue
formerly bene a faithfull & excellent diſpencer of your owne
goods, take not vpon you to diſtribute the money of other
folkes. You conceaue well what I ſay : for our Lord hath
giuen you a very vniuerſall vnderſtanding. Carry the ſimplicity of a doue, that you procure not to deceiue any man; and
the ſubtility of a ſerpent, that you be not ſupplanted by the
ſleights of others. It is not much leſſe vitious for a Chriſtian,
to be deceiued then to deceaue. Whom you ſhal find to be euer,
or often ſpeaking of money (except it be in the way of almes,
which muſt be open to all) hold him rather to be, a mer-
chaunt, then a Monke. Beſides that which muſt ſerue for
food, and cloathing, and other manifeſt neceſſities, doe not
giue to any, *leaſt the dogs, eate vp the childrens bread*. The belieuing ſoule is a true temple of Chriſt. Apparel that, adorne that,
offer preſents to that, and receiue Chriſt in that. For what
ſerues it, that the wals ſhould gliſter with pretious ſtones, and
that Chriſt ſhould be in danger to dy of hunger, in the perſon
of a poore man? They are no goods of yours, which you poſſeſſe, but you are only truſted with diſpenſing them. Remember *Ananias*, and *Saphira*. They did too miſerably keepe their
owne; and take you heed, that imprudently you ſcatter not
the

the fubftance of Chrift; that is to fay , that by indifcretion or affection , you beftowe not the goods of the poore, vpon fuch as are not poore; and that (according to the faying of that moft wife man) *Liberality be not deftroyed by liberality* . Do not looke backe vpon the martiall ornaments, and the vayne title of the Cato's . I know you within , euen to the very rootes . It is a high poynt , to be indeed & not only to feem a Chriftian; And I know not how , but fo it is, that *they , who pleafe the world, difpleafe Chrift* .

I fpeake not thefe thinges, as if according to the Prouerbe, *The fowe were reading a leffon to Minerua* , but now that you are fetting to Sea, I haue admonifhed you as one friend fhould do another: choofing, that you fhould rather obferue my skill to be little, then my good will; and defiryng that wherein I haue flipt, you may paffe on with a firme pace .

I haue gladly read that booke , which you compofed for the Emperour *Theodofius,* with much prudence and eloquence; and efpecially I liked the fubdiuifion thereof. And as in the firft parts, you ouercome others, fo in the later you outftrip your felfe . The very manner of difcourfe is clofe, and cleane, and together with the purity of *Tully* it is full of fentences . For that kind of eloquence (as one faith) is but cold and weake , when onely the words deferue praife . Befides, you make your confequences of thinges very well, & one thing hangs handfomly vpon another . Whatfoeuer you affume, is either an end of that which goes before, or a begining of that which followes . *Theodofius* is happy , in being defended by fuch an Orator of Chrift . You haue giuen luftre to his princely roabes , and you haue confecrated the profitablenes of his lawes, to fuccee- ding ages . Proceed on in vertue you, who haue layd fo good foundations . What kind of fouldier will you proue when you haue experience ? O that I were fo happy , as to haue the leading of fuch a wit as yours, not through the *Aonian* moun- taynes and thofe tops of the hill of *Helicon* , (whereof the Poets fpeake) but by the tops of *Sion* , and *Itabirium* , and *Sina* . If I might but teach you, what I haue learned , and deliuer the myfteries of Scriptures, as it were into your hands, fome fuch thing would grow vp to vs, as the learned *Greece* neuer had .

Hearken

Hearken therefore my fellow feruant, my freiend,my brother; obferue a little, by what path you are to walke , in the holy Scripture. All that which we read in thofe diuine bookes,doth fhine indeed, and that brightly , euen in the barke, but it is much fweeter in the fubftance and depth thereof. He who wil eat the kernell , muft breake the nut : *Reueal myne eyes* (faith *Da-uid*) *and I will confider the wonderfull thinges of thy law* . If fo great a Prophet confeffe fo great darkenes of ignorance ; with what a night of ftupidity may we conceiue our felues to be enuironed, who are but little ones , and as it were but fucking babes? But this veyle was not onely put vpon the face of *Moyfes,* but vpon that alfo of the Euangelifts and Apoftles . Our Sauiour fpake to the people in parables ; & auowing that that which he deli-uered had fomewhat in it of the *Myfticall,* he faid , *He who hath eares to heare, let him heare* . Vnles all things which are written of him be opened by him, who hath the keye of Dauid, *which shuts and no man opens , and which opens and no man shuts,* they will neuer be difclofed by any other . If you had this ground,and if your worke were perfected by this laft hand , we fhould haue nothing more gracefull, nothing more learned, nothing more delightfull , nothing more Latin then your bookes . *Tertullian* is frequent in fentences , but of no very delightfull fpeech. *Blef-fed Cyprian* walkes on , all fweet and fmooth , like a moft pure fountayne, but (employing himfelfe wholy vpon the exercife of vertue , and taken vp by the troubles of perfeeution) he dif-courfed not at all of holy Scriptures . *Victorinus,* who was after crowned with an illuftrious marytrdome, is not able to ex-preffe what he vnderftands . *Lactantius,* who was a very flood of *Ciceronian* eloquence, I would to God he could as well haue confirmed our doctrine, as he did eafily confute that of others . *Arnobius* was vnequall, and fubiect to exceffe , and with al con-fufed , without diuiding his worke . Saint *Hilary* is aloft in his french ftile , and hauing the ornament of thofe flowers of *Gra-cian eloquence* , he is iuuolued fometimes in long periods; and is farre out of the reach of ordinary men . I paffe ouer the reft in filence , whether they be dead , or ftill aliue , of whom others may iudge either way , after our time .

  And noW I come to you, who are my fellow in profef-
                                                           fion

sion, my companion, and my friend, (I say my friend, though
you be not yet of my acquaintance) and I will pray you, not
to suspect my friendship of flattery, but rather conceiue, that I
am in errour, or that I slip through the loue I beare you; then
that I would deceiue a friend, by speaking him fayre. You haue
a great wit, and an vnspeakeable store and copie of speech; and
you expresse your selfe purely, and with ease, and the same facility and purity is seasoned with prudence; for the head being sound, all the sences are in vigour. If labour and the vnderstanding of Scripture were added to this prudence, & eloquence, we should see you in a short time to hold the very
highest place amongst our men; and (ascending vp to the house
of *Sion*, with *Iacob*) to sing vpon the house tops, that which
you had learned and knowne in the priuate roomes of the
house. Gird your selfe vp, I beseech you, gird your selfe vp.
Nothing of this world is giuen to mortall men, but vpon the
price of great labour. Let the Church haue you noble, as the
Senate had you in former time; and now prepare riches for
your selfe, which you may daily bestowe, and yet will neuer
fayle, as long as the world lasts. Doe it whilest yet your head
is not sprinkled with grey haires; before you be ouergrowne
with diseases, and melancholy, and old age, and payne, and before sad death carryes vs vnmercifully away. I cannot be content with any mediocrity in you; but I desire that all may be
eminent, all excellent. With what greedy gladnes I haue receaued the holy Bishop *Vigilantius*, it is fitter that you learne by
his wordes, then by my letters. Vpon what ground he went
hence, and left vs so soon, I must not say, least I may seem to
offend some. I haue entertayned him a while as he was passing
by in hast; and I haue giuen him a taste of our friendship to the
end that you may learne by him, that which you desire to know
of me. I entreat that by your meanes, I may salute your fellow
seruant, who labours with you in our Lord.

FINIS.

THE LIVES OF
SAINT PAVL
THE FIRST HERMITE,
OF SAINT
HILARION
THE FIRST MONKE OF STRIA,
AND OF
SAINT MALCHVS,

Written by Saint Hierome.

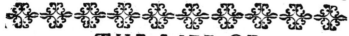

THE LIFE OF
SAINT PAVL
THE HERMITE,
WRITTEN BY S. HIEROME.

THE ARGVMENT.

PAVL *of* Thebais *hauing about the age of* 15 *yeares, being instructed in the literature as* well of the Græcians, *as of the* Ægyptians, *both his Parents being dead, and he accused by his Sisters husband, for being a* Christian, *and flying from* Decius *and* Valerianus *the persecutors, betooke himselfe to the* wildernes. *There did he lead his life, by the space of ninety foure yeares, in admirable abstinence and sanctity till such tyme as being* visited *by that great* Anthony (who was directed so to do by a diuine reuelation) *he sleptin our* Lord. *The life of this* Paul, *is elegantly described by* Saint Hierome.

THE LIFE.

IT hath beene often doubted among many, by what Monke the Desart was first inhabited. Some haue reached at it so high, as to ascribe the first beginning to B. *Elias,* & then to *Iohn.* But *Elias* seemes to vs, to haue rather beene a Prophet, then a Monke; and *Iohn* to haue begun to be a kind of a Prophet, before he was borne. But some others

A   affirme

affirme (and they haue brought the whole vulgar to be of
their opinion) that *Anthony* was the firſt in vndertaking this
kind of life, which yet is but partly true . For it is not ſo properly to be ſayd, that he was the firſt of all the Eremites,
as that he gaue ſpirit to the endeauours, and deſignes of them
all . But *Amathas* and *Macharius*, who were the diſciples of
this *Anthony* (and whereof the former buryed the body of his
Maiſter) affirme euen to this day, that a certaine *Paul* of *Thebais*, was the chiefe, and prime man of this Inſtitute , which
opinion we alſo approue, though not ſo much, becauſe he
carries the name of it, as vpon other reaſons. Many there are
who ſpread abroad both theſe, and other thinges at their
pleaſure, as namely that there was a certaine man all hairy
to his very feet, who hid himſelfe in a hoale vnder ground,
and they deuiſe many incredible thinges, not worth the relating ; and ſince their affirmation is ſo voyd of ſhame , their
opinion ſeemes not worthy of confutation . But now for as
much as a diligent account hath beene giuen vs of this *Anthony*, both in the Greeke and Latin tongue, I haue diſpoſed
my ſelfe to write ſome few thinges of the beginning, & end
of *Paul* ; rather becauſe it hath beene omitted by others, then
that I preſume vpon my ſelfe . For as for the manner of his
life, in the middle part of his age, and what ſubtil ſly temptations of Sathan he ſuſtayned, there is no mortall man, who
can tell vs any newes thereof.

Vnder *Decius* and *Valerianus* the perſecutors, at ſuch time
as *Cornelius* at *Rome*, & *Cyprian* at *Carthage*, were condened to
the felicity of ſhedding their blood, many Churches in *Aegipt*
& *Thebais*, were blaſted by a bitter ſtorme of perſecution. The
Chriſtians of that time , deſired no better then to giue their
liues for the name of Chriſt , by the compendious ſtroke of
the ſword ; but the crafty aduerſary going in ſearch after ſlo-
wer puniſhments, for the deliuery of men ouer to death , did
more deſire to cut the throates of ſoules, then of bodies ; and
(as was ſaid by *Cyprian*, who himſelfe ſuffered Martirdome)
he would not permit them to be killed , who were euen de-
ſirous to dye. And now to the end that his cruelty may be the
more

more notorious, we haue heere committed two examples to memory.

When a certaine Martyr was perseuering in his faith, and continued to be conquerors in the middest both of rackes, & burning plates, the persecutor commanded that he should be anoynted all ouer with hony and so (with his handes bound behind him) be extended vnder a scorching Sunne with his face vpward; to the end that he might yeild himselfe, vpon the sting of flyes, who before, had bene victorious ouer the torments of fyer. He commanded another Martyr, who was flourishing in the very prime of his youth to be led aside into a most delicious garden & there in the middest of pure lyllies, and blushing roses, (where also a streame of water was creeping on with a soft bubling noise, and the wind gently whisling checkt the leaues of the trees) to be spred with his face vpward vpon a bed stuffed with downe, and to be left tyed there with silken bandes, to the end that so he might not be able to deliuer himselfe from thence. Now vpon the retiring of all them who were present, a beautifull Curtisan came to make her approach, and began with her delicate armes, to embrace his necke; and (which cannot be modestly related) did also impurely touch him otherwise, to the end that his body being altered, and inflamed by lust the lasciuious conquerors might ouerspred him. This souldier of the band of Christ, knew not what to do, nor which way to turne himselfe, whome torments had not subdued, delight was beginning to ouercome, when at length (inspired from heauen) he bit of his owne tongue, & spitting it into the face of her, who kissed him, the sense of lust, was subdued, by the sharpenes of that payne which succeeded.

At that time therefore, when such thinges as these were acted, in the inferiour *Thebais*, (when the Sister of *Paul* was then already bestowed by him in marriage, (himselfe hauing a rich inheritance descended to him by the death of both his Parents; whilest then he was of the age of about fifteene years) and hauing beene eminently instructed in the literature both of the *Gracians* and *Ægyptians*, & indued with a meeke fpirit, & which greatly loued God, and finding that the ftorme of perfecutions brought fuch thunder with it), he tooke a refolution of retiring into a remote, and priuate villa of his owne.

But, O thou vaſt defire of gould;
How hugely doeſtthou make men bould?

His Sifters husband grew to betray him, whome he ought to haue concealed; nor could the teares of the wife nor the refpects of common blood, nor the confideration of God behoulding all thinges from on high, diffwade him from that wickednes. But ciuelty vrged him to do thofe thinges, though the pretext which it tooke was from piety. Now as foone as this moft difcreet young man grew to vnderftand thus much, he fled towardes the defart Moun-taynes, where he might expect the end of this perfecution, and fo voluntarily he made a vertue of neceffity. And pro-ceeding on by little and little, and then pawfing, and often doing the fame thing; at laft he met with a great rocky hill, neer the bottome whereof there was a large kind of caue fhut vp by a ftone. Vpon the remouing of which ftone he being more earneft in making new difcoueries (according to the nature of man which loues the knowledge of hidden thinges) he perceaued a great entry there within, which being open to the sky aboue, was ouerfpred by the wide braunches of an ould Palme tree, poynting out a moft cleare fountayne, the ftreame whereof breaking onely out of the ground, the fame earth which had brought it forth did inftantly fucke it vp againe, through a little hole. There were moreouer, throughout that worne mountayne not a few old roomes, wherein there might be feene certaine an-uiles, & hammers, which by that tyme were growen rough with ruft, and formerly had beene imployed vpon ftamping coyne. And it is related by the Ægyptiars, that this place had beene vfed as a fecret mint-houfe of money, at fuch tyme as *Cleopatra* kept that clofe intelligence with *Antonius*. But *Paul* growing now to carry a particular kind of loue to this Caue, as if it had beene expreffely defigned to him by Al-mighty God, did there imploy his whole life in folitude & pryaprayer. The Palme tree ferued his turne, both to affoard him food, and cloathes. Which, that no man may thinke impoſſible,I take Iefus, and his holy Angels to witnes,how, in that part of the defart, which ioynes *Syria* and *Sarazens* to-geather, I haue feene certaine Monkes, whereof one being a recluſe, had liued during thirty yeares, vpon barly bread, and puddle water ; and another who continuing in an old Celterne, which the *Syrians* in their language call *Caba*, was ſultayned by the only eating of fiue dryed Figs euery day. Theſe thinges will feeme incredible to them who are of vn-belieuing minds, for to others, all thinges are poſſible.

But to returne to that from which I had digreſſed,when now the B . *Paul* had lead a celeſtiall life on earth, being by that tyme, a hundred and thirteen yeares ould, and when *Anthony* hauing ninety yeares of age, had remayned alone in another Defart, as himfelfe was wont to relate ; a thought ſlipt once into the fayd *Anthonyes* mind, as if no perfect Monke remayned in that wildernes, befides himfelfe. But whileſt he was at reſt by night, it was reuealed to him, that there was another much more excellent then he, whome he was appointed to find out, and vifit. Therefore inſtant-ly vpon breake of day, the venerable ould má, vphoulding his weake limmes by the fupport of a ſtaffe difpofed himſelf to be going, though he knew not directly whether. But ſhortly then the high noone began to inflame the world vn der a fcorching Sunne, and yet he was not difcouraged from his new iourney, but fayd: *I confide that my God will shew me that feruant of his, whome he hath promifed*. Not a word more then this, when behould he fees a creature made of horfe & man, fuch as Poets are wont to call *Hippocentaures*. Vpon which fight, he armes his forehead with the impreſſion of that falutiferous figne,and fayth: *Tell me, O thou, where dwells that feruant of God?* But he gnafhing out I know not what kind of barbarous found, and rather breaking then pronoun-cing his wordes, did yet by meanes of that horrid fpeach,de-fire to entertaine fome pleafing difcourfe, with the old man; and by extending his right hand, made difcouery of the way which was fought, and fo ſtriking through thofe open

plaines,

plaines, with a fwift flight, he vanifhed out of the wódring
eyes of the behoulder. Now whether the Diueil did contriue thefe thinges to fright the man, or els whether the wildernes, which is wont to be fruitful of monftruous creaturs,
did alfo bring forth this beaft, or no, is vncertaine to vs But
Anthony the while, being all amazed, and reuoluing within
himfelfe what he had feene, proceeded on. And behould he
perceaues in a certaine ftony defcent, which lay betweene
two hilles, a kind of little man, with a crooked nofe, and a
rugged brow with hornes, the lower parte of whofe body
was made vp into the feet of a Goat. And *Anthony* being alfo
ftroken by this fpectacle, tooke inftantly to himfelfe the buc-
kler of fayth, and the breft-plate of hope, like a good warryer, but yet the aforefayd *Animal*, brought him the fruit of
Palmes, for his prouifion, as pledges of peace. Vpon the vnderftanding of this, *Anthony* made a paufe, and demanding of
the other who he was, receaued this anfwere: *A mortall crea-*
ture I am, and one of the inhabitants of the defart, whome the Pa-
gans, being deluded with variety of errour are wont to worship, by
the name of Fawnes, Satyres, *and* Incubo's, *I performe the of-*
fice of an Embaffadour for the reft of the flocke whereof I am. And our
fuit is, that thou wilt pray for vs to our cõmon God, whome we know
to be come for the faluation of the world, & the found of him is exten-
ded ouer all the earth. Whileft he was deliuering thefe words,
our aged trauayler did abundantly bedew his face with tears
which the greatnes of his ioy fent forth, as the interpretors of
his hart; for he reioyced in the glory of Chrift, and the deftruction of Sathan. And wondring withall, that he was
able to vnderftand the others fpeach, and ftricking vpon
the ground with his ftaffe, he fayd: *VVe be to thee, O Alexan-*
dria, who worshipeft Monfters infteed of God. VVoe be to thee, O thou
adulterous Citty, to which the Diuells of the whole world refort.
VVhat remaines for thee now to fay? Beafts publish Chrift, and
thou worshipeft Monfters, infteed of God. Nor had he yet ended
fpeaking, when behould the clouen footed creature flead a-
way, as if it had beene borne by winges. That this may not
moue fcruple, through the mind, which men haue, not to
belieue; it was made good vnder King *Conftantine*, by the

te ftiteſtimony of all the world, that ſuch a kind of man as this being brought aliue to *Alexandria*, became a ſpectacle to the whole people, and when the body was once without life, it was ſalted for feare of corrupting through the heat of the ſeaſon, and brought to *Antioch*, that the Emperour might alſo ſee it.

But, to proceed in my purpoſe. *Anthony* went on in his way, as he had begun, diſcerning no other thing, then the footſteps of Bufaloes,& wiid beaſtes, and the vnlimited vaſtity of a *deſart*. He knew not what to do, nor which way to direct his courſe. Already the ſecond day was ſpent, and there remayned now but one, wherein he hoped that he ſhould not be forſaken by Chriſt. He ſpent that whole ſecond night in prayer, and while yet it was no more then twylight, he diſcerned a ſhe Wolfe farre off, who panting through the heat of thirſt, crept neer to the foot of a mountayne. He followed her with his eyes, and drawing neer (when the beaſt was gone) to a certaine caue thereby, he was beginning to looke in ; his curioſity not ſeruing his turne, becauſe the darkenes droue backe his ſight. But as the ſcripture ſaith, *Perfect loue diſpatches feare away* ; and ſo moderating his pace,and houlding his breath,the cuning ſpy went in ; and ſometimes going on, and then often ſtaying againe, he ſucked vp euery little noiſe into his eare. At laſt,through the horrour of that deepe darkenes , he diſcerned light farre off, and going on with a kind of greedy haſt, his foot gaue a-gainſt a ſtone, and made a noyſe. Vpon the ſound whereof, the bleſſed *Paul* ſhut, and locked the doore, which had bene open before. But *Anthony* then caſt himſelfe outright before the gates, and was begging entrance, till it had growen to be the ſixth houre of the day & more , ſaying: *You know who I am ; from whence, and for what cauſe I come, I confeſſe that I de-ſerue not to appeare in your preſence ; but yet vnles I ſee you, I will not retire. You who receaue beaſtes, how can you reiect a man? I haue ſought now, and I haue found now ; and now I knocke, that it may be opened to me. If I obtaine not thus much, I will dye heer at your gates; at leaſt you will not refuſe to bury me, when I ſhall be dead.*

Such

Such thinges as this he speake ; and fixed stayed ;
To whom the Heroe, this short answere made .

No man doth so desire , as that he wil threaten withall . No man
accompanies his teares with iniury or reproach . And can you mer-
uayle if I receaue you not , when your errand is but to dye at the
gate . Then did *Paul* smile , and open the doore ; which was
no sooner done , but they did euen incorporate themselues
by mutuall embracements , and saluting one another by
their proper names , did ioyne in giuing thākes to our Lord .
Now *Paul* sitting downe with *Anthony* , after he had giuen
him a holy kisse , began thus to speake ; *Behould how he ,*
whom you haue sought with so great labour , is all couered with rude
gray haires . and hath his body euen rotten already with ould age. Be-
hould yow see a man , who is shortly to become dust . But yet becaufe
charity endures all thinges, tell me , I befeech yow , how fares it with
the race of mankind ? Are new houfes erected,in thofe ould Citties. To
what Empire is the world subiect now ;whether yet remayne there any
who are transported by the sinne of worshipping diuels? As they were
in speech of thefe thinges , they looked vp , and saw a Crow
sitting vpon the braunch of a tree, who flying gently downe
layed a whole loaf of bread before their wondring eyes. Whē
the Crow was gone , *Behould* (saith *Paul*) *our Lord who is*
truly full of pitty and mercy , hath sent vs our dinner. They are alrea-
dy threefcore yeares , fince I haue dayly receiued halfe a loaf; but now
vpon your arriuall,Christ hath doubled the prouifion of his souldiers .
When therefore they had performed the action of thankes giuing to our Lord , they both sat downe vpon the brimme of
a cleare fountayne. But heer the question growing between
them vpon the poynt of who should breake the bread , did
almost draw downe the day to Euening. *Paul* vrged *Anthony*
to do it,vpon the right of hofpitality which *Paul* was to pay;
but *Antony* excufed himfelf,vpon the refpects which he ought
to the antiquity of the other. At length this refolution was
takē that both of them should take hould of the bread, which
each of them , pulling by contrary wayes towards himfelfe,
might find his part in his owne handes. After this,they stoo-
ped to the fountayne , and tooke a taft of the water , and offering vp the Sacrifice of praife to God , they passed through
that

that night in watching. And as soone as the world saw day agayne, the B. *Paul* spake to *Anthony* after this manner. *It is long O brother, since I knew you were an Inhabitant of these parts, it is long since God made me a promise, that I should haue you as a fellow seruant of myne. But now because the time of my long repose is at hand, and for (that according to my desire of being dissolued & being with Chrift,) there remaynes a crowne of Iustice for me, vpon the finishing of my course; you are sent by our Lord, to couer this poore body with earth, or rather to restore one earth to another.* Vpon the hearing of these wordes, *Anthony* (all in teares and sighes,) besought him not to forsake him so, but to accept him for a companion in that Iourney. But then *Paul* replyed thus: *You must not desire thinges for your selfe, but condescend to the conueniencies of others. It were good indeed for you, if laying downe the burde of flesh and blood, you might follow the lambe; but it is also expedient for the rest of your brethren, that they may be more instructed by your example. I beseeh you therefore returne, (vnles my suit be of too much trouble to you) and bring that Cloake for the wrapping vp of this poore body, which Athanasius the Bishop bestowed vpon you.* This request was made by the blessed *Paul*, not becanse he greatly cared, whether his corps were to putrify naked, or coured (he who had liued so many yeares, without any other garment then of the woeuen leaues of palmes,) but to the end that the grief for his death, might be asswaged in the mind of *Anthony*, by his departing away. But *Anthony* being amazed at that which had bene sayd to him, cocerning *Athanasius* & his cloak, as if he had seen Christ in *Paul*, did worship God in his person, and presumed not to make him any answere, but shedding teares in silence, & kissing both his hands and eyes, he returned to his Monastery, which was afterward take by the *Saracens*. Neither did his feet suffer his hart to out strippe them; for though his body, being extenuated by fasting, were then also defeated by his many yeares, yet with his mind he ouercame his age. At length, all weary & panting, he ended his iorney, and got home. And when two of his disciples, who had beene wont to serue him a long time before, came running towards him with these words; *Where, O Father, haue you been, and stayed so long?* He answered: *Woe be to me sinfull man, who carry but the false name of a* Monke*, I haue seen* Elias*, I haue seen a* Iohn *in the desart, and I haue truly seen* Paul *in a paradise.* And so holding his peace, and beating his breast with his hand, he fetch the cloake out of his little *Cell.* And his disciples beseeching him that he would declare more fully what the matter was, he answered thus: *There is a tyme for silence, and a tyme for speech.* Then going forth, and taking not so much as a bit of food, he returned by the same way he came, thirsting after him, desiring to behould him, and contemplating him, both with eyes, and hart. For he was full of feare least (as indeed it came to passe) the other should in his absence, render vp that spirit of his, which was due to Christ. And when the next day was come, & he had iornyed some three houres, he saw *Paul*, brightly shyning, in pure whitenes, & ascending vp on high, in the middest of troupes of *Angels*, and of the quiers of *Prophets*, and *Apostles*. Then *Anthony* casting himselfe headlong downe vpon his face, drew his hood ouer his head, and weeping, yea and euen roaring out, he sayd: *VVhy, O* Paul*, dost thou forsake me? VVhy art thou gone without letting me so much as take my leaue? Thou, whome I came to know so late, why art thou departed so soon?* it was afterward related by *Anthony*, that he dispatched that rest of the way, with so great speed, as that he flew like a very bird. And he had reason to make hast, for being entered into the caue, he saw the body without life, his knees doubled vnder him, his necke erected, and his hands extended abroad on high. And conceauing at the first that he had been yet aliue, he ioyned with him in prayer; but afterwards, when he heard him not send forth any such sighes, as he was wont to vse in prayer, he rushed vpon him, with a dolefull kisse; and then grew to vnderstand, that euen the dead corps of the Saint, did pray after a fort, to God (to whome all things liue) by that posture of reuerence. *Anthony* therefore hauing shrouded the body, & brought it forth; and singing hymnes and psalmes, according to the tradition of the Christian Church, was troubled that he had not there some spade, wherewith he might dig, and make a graue. And wauing betweene the variety of seuerall passions, and casting with his thoughtes many wayes, he sayd

thus

thus within himfelfe : *If I returne to the Monaſtery, it is a iour-ney of no leſſe then three dayes ; if I ſtay heere, I ſhall looſe my tyme & labour ; my beſt way would be euen to dye, and by caſting my ſelfe headlong againſt this warryer of thyne , O Chriſt , to deliuer vp my laſt breath.* Whilſt he was reuoluing theſe things in his mind, behould, from the more inward part of the deſart, two Ly-ons bore themſelues with ſpeed towardes him, their manes al wauing about their neckes. At the firſt, vpon this fight, he was much frighted ; yet then inſtantly caſting vp his mind to God, he remayned as void of feare, as if he had but ſeene ſome paire of Doues. But the Lyons, hauing directed their courſe to the corps of that other bleſſed ould man, made a ſtand, and fawning with their tailes, they lay downe at his feet, roaring out with a huge noyſe, ſo as a man might plainely vnderſtād, that they bewayled the death of *Paul* after the beſt manner they could. Soone after, they alſo began to ſcrape the ground with their pawes, caſting out ſand (as if it had beene with a kind of ſtrife who ſhould do it faſteſt) they digged a place, which might be able to containe a man ; and then inſtantly caſting downe their necks, and wagging their eares, they went towardes *Anthony*; and as if they had demanded ſome wages for their paynes, they licked both his handes, and feet. But he vnderſtood it, as if they had deſired a bleſſing from him, and therefore inſtantly inlarging his hart towardes the prayſe of Chriſt, for that euen theſe dumme Beaſts, did alſo vnderſtand that there was a God, he expreſſed himſelfe thus, *O Lord, without whoſe becke, neither doth any leaſe fall from a Tree, nor any Sparrow light vpon the ground, be good to theſe creatures, as thou knoweſt.* And ſo making a ſigne with his hand, he gaue them a commandement to be gone. As ſoone as they were departed, he ſubmitted his old ſhoulders to the waight of that holy corps ; and laying it downe in the graue, and then caſting earth vpon it, he made a kind of tombe, according to the manner. But then , vpon the next day (leaſt this pious heyre ſhould not become the owner of ſome of the inteſtates goods) he tooke the coat, which *Paul* had wouen for himſelfe after the manner of Baskets, of Palme leaues. And ſo retur-ning to his Monaſtery, he made relation of al to his Diſciples,

in

in order as it had paſſed; and vpon the ſolemnities of Eaſter, & Pentecoſt, he euer vſed to weare the coat of *Paul*.

And now vpon the end of this little worke, I will take the liberty, to aske thoſe men, who haue ſuch ſtore of Lands, as that they hardly know the names therof; they who apparell their houſes in marble, & thread the price of whole Manours, vpon roapes of pearle; what thing was euer wanting to this halfe naked man? You drinke in cupps made of precious ſtone; this man ſatisfyed Nature, by the vſe of a paire of hollow handes. You imbroder your garments with gold, but he had not ſo much as the meaneſt cloath, which belonged to any drudge of yours. But then, Heauen on the other ſide will be open to that poore man; and you with your guilt, will go downe to Hell. He was ſtill cloathed with Chriſt, though he were naked; you, being clad with ſilke, haue loſt the garment of Chriſt. *Paul* lyes couered vnder poore light duſt, and he ſhall riſe vp againe into glory; wheras you are preſſed downe by thoſe weighty and coſtly Tombes of ſtone, and are to burne in hell fire with your wealth. I beſeech you be good to your ſelues, or els at leaſt, be good to your riches, which you loue ſo well. Why wrappe you vp the bodyes of your dead friendes, in goulden cloathes? Why do you not permit, that Ambition and Pride may ceaſe at leaſt in the mideſt of your ſorrowes and teares? Are not perhaps the Carkaſes of rich men able to rot, vnles they be layd vp in ſilke? I beſeech you, whoſoeuer you be, that read this, be mindfull of *Hierome*, that ſinnefull man; to whome yet, if our Lord ſhould graunt his wiſh, he would much rather chooſe the coat of *Paul* with his merits, then the purple of Kinges with their paynes.

FINIS.

THE

THE LIFE OF
S. HILARION
THE HERMITE,
WRITTEN BY S. HIEROME.

THE ARGVMENT.

HILARION *was a Monke, borne at* Thabatha *a little towne of Palestine, a disciple of that great* Anthony ; *with how singular abstinence and sanctity he lead his life, and with how great Miracles it was continually illustrated, euen when he procured to lye most concealed* S. Hicrome *doth largely and learnedly expresse ; and so, as that a man may cleerely see, the true patterne of a perfect Monke in his personne .*

THE LIFE.

EING to write the life of S . *Hilarion* , I inuoke the holy Ghoſt, who inhabited his ſoule; that ſo he, who gaue power to him , may giue ſpeech to me , wherwith to manifeſt the ſame ; and ſo my wordes, may grow to equall his deedes . For (as *Criſpus* ſayth) their merites who haue wrought wonders , haue beene held iuſt as great by men , as the more excellent kind of wits haue beene able to magnify them by wordes . *Alexander* the Great , the *Mace-*

donian

donian (whome *Daniel* calls the *Ramme*, or *Leopard*, or *Goat*,)
when he came to *Achilles* his tombe ; *Happy* (fayth the young
man) *art thou, who enioyest such a mighty publisher of thy merits* ;
reflecting thereby vpon *Homer*. But as for me, I am to relate
the conuerfation, and life of a perfon fo great, and fo qualify-
ed, as that *Homer* himfelfe, if he were prefent, would either
enuy the excellency of the fubiect, or els would finke vnder
the burden. For though S. *Epiphanius* the Bifhop of *Salamina*
in *Cyprus*, who conuerfed much with *Hilarion*, wrote his prayfes in a fhort Epiftle, which is vfually read, yet one thing is
to prayfe a dead man, according to the nature of a common
place ; and another, to relate the vertues, which were proper to that dead man. Whereupon we alfo, rather vnder his
fauour, then with meaning to fhew him any difrefpect, will
fet vpon the worke, which was begun by him; refoluing to
contemne the exceptions of ill tongued men, who formerly
detracting from the life, which I wrote of *Paul*, will now
perhaps doe as much, for this of *Hilarion* ; taxing the former of
exceffe in folitude, and chalenging the later, for expofing
himfelfe ouermuch to publicke view ; that fo he, who lay e-
uer hid, might be thought as good, as not to haue beene at al;
and this other, who was feene by fo many, might be held
thereby in leffe high account. Their Predeceffors the Pha-
rifies did the felfe fame thing heeretofore, when neither the
defart, and fafts of *Iohn*, nor the couerfation or fociety, in eating and drinking, which was vfed by our Lord & Sauiour,
knew how to pleafe. But I will begin the worke which I
haue in hand, and paffe by thofe barking Dogs, with a deafe
eare.

Hilarion was borne in a little towne called *Thabatha*, which
is fituated towardes the South, about fiue miles from *Gaza*,
a Citty of Paleftine ; and he fprung (as men are wont to fay)
like a Rofe out of thornes, for he had Idolaters to his Parets.
He was fent by them to *Alexandria*, and applyed to the ftudy
of Grammar ; and there (for as much as might be expected
from one of his tender yeares,) he gaue great teftimony in a
fhort tyme, both of his wit, and good conuerfation. He was
deere to all them who knew him, and he was a Maifter of
speech

ſpeech; and (which paſſes theſe prayſes) he was a belieuer in our Lord Ieſus, and did not delight in thoſe mad ſportes, which were exhibited in the *Circus*, nor in the luxurious entertainements of the Theatre, where ſo great effuſiō of blood was made. His whole comfort was to be at Church, when Chriſtians were aſſembled there. Being then growen to heare the famous name of *Anthony*, which was celebrated through all the parts of Ægypt, he went on towards the deſart, through a deſire he had to ſee him. This he no ſooner did, but inſtantly he changed his former habit, and remayned with him, vpon the point of two Months, contemplating the order of his life, and the grauity of his conuerſation, how frequent he was in prayer, how humble in receauing bis brethren, how ſeuere in reprehending them, how cheerefull in exhorting them; and how no corporall indiſpoſition did at any time interrupt the abſtinent & rigid dyet, which he kept. But then *Hilarion* being no longer able to endure the frequēt concourſe of them who reſorted to *Antony*, by occaſion either of being poſſeſſed by Diuels, or of ſeuerall other infirmityes; and not houlding it to be conuenient for him to endure ſuch troupes of inhabitants of Cittjes, in ſuch a wildernes as that, and conceauing that he was rather to begin as *Anthony* had done; and that *Anthony* was then enioying the fruites of his victory, like an ould ſouldier, but that himſelfe had ſcarce begun to carry armes; he returned with ſome Monkes into his owne countrey. And his Parents, by that tyme being dead, he diſtributed part of his ſubſtance to his Brothers, and part to the poore, reſeruing nothing at all to himſelfe, as fearing both the example, and puniſhment of *Ananias* and *Saphyra* in the Acts of the Apoſtles, and remembring this ſaying of our Lord; *He, who renounces not all that which he poſſeſſes, can be no diſciple of myne.* He was then about fifteene yeares of age, and thus being naked, but yet armed with Chriſt, he entred into that Deſart, which is diſtant ſeauen mile from *Maioma*, the ſtaple of *Gaza*, which lyes vpon the Sea coaſt, on the left hād of them, who go towards Ægypt. And although thoſe places were all ſtained with the bloud of many murthers, and his friendes and kindred did declare the imminent danger to

which

which he expofed himfelfe;yet he defpifed one kind of death,
that he might efcape another . All men wondred at his courage , and they wondred alfo at his tender yeares, fauing that
the flame of his hart, and certaine fparkes of fayth, did euen
fhine out by his eyes . His face was but thinne , his body was
delicate and leane, and fenfible of any iniury of weather , &
of the trouble of any little either heat or could. Hauing therfore all couered himfelfe with facke- cloath, and befides wearing a fhirt of haire, which the B . *Anthony* had giuen him, togeather with a country Caffocke at his departure, he betooke
himfelfe to a vaft and terrible kind of wildernes, betweene
the Sea fhore on the one fide, & certaine fenns on the other,
eating only fifteene dryed Figs euery day after Sunne fet.
And becaufe thofe parts were growen infamous by the multitude of cruell robberies which were comitted there abouts,
he neuer vfed to ftay long in the felfe fame place . What had
the Diuell now to do ? Which way fhould he turne himfelfe?
He who once had vaunted and fayd : *I will plant my throne vp-*
on the ftarres of Heauen, and I will be like the moft High, perceaued himfelfe now to be ouercome by a child, and to be fooner
troden vpon by him, then he was able in effect , through his
tender yeares, to tread at all. The Diuell did therefore then
begin to moue the fence of *Hilarion*, and to fuggeft fuch motiues of luft, as be vfuale when bodies are budding firft;in the
fpring of youth. This young fouldier of Chrift was euen conftrayned to thinke vpon obiects, whereof he was ignorant ;
& to looke with the eye of his phanfy, vpon the whole ftory
of that bufineffe,wherof he had neuer taken any experience .
Vpon this, being angry with himfelfe, and beating his breaft
with his fift, (as if he had beene able to deftroy his thoughts ,
with his handes : *I will take order* (fayth he) *thou little Affe, that*
thou fhalt not kicke, nor will I feed thee with corne, but with ftraw ; *I*
will ftarue thee , and I will lay heauy load vpon thee, I will exercife ,
and tyre thee out, both by heates and coldes , that fo thou mayft haue
more care , how to get a bit of meat , then how to fatisfy thy luft . So
that whe his very life would be fayling, after the faft of three
or foure dayes, he would fuftaine it with the iuyce of herbes ,
and a few dryed Figs ; praying & finging often, & he would
                                                    alfo

alſo be breaking the ground with a rake; that ſo the labour of his working, might ad to the trouble of his faſting. And wea-uing ſmall twigs together with great ruſhes, he imitated the diſcipline of the *Ægiptian Moncks*, & remembred the ſentenceof the Apoſtle,ſaying: *He,who doth not worke, muſt not eat.* Being thus extenuated, and hauing his body ſo farre exhauſted, as that it would ſcarce hang together, he began one night, to heare the crying of Infants, the bleating of Sheep, the bel-lowing of Oxen,the lamentation as if it had been of Woemē, the roaring of Lyons,the claſhing noyſe of an Army; and ſuch a confuſion of prodigious ſounds, that being frighted with the noyſe of them; before he perçeaued any ſight,his hart be-gan to faynt. But he ſoone found them to be ſcornes & plots of the Diuell; and ſo caſting himſelfe then vpon his knees, he ſigned his forhead with the Croſſe of Chriſt. Being defended with ſuch a helmet as that, and compaſſed in by the coat ar-mour of fayth, he fought more valiantly, as he was layd downe, then before; already then deſiring toſee them,whom formerly he had euen trembled to heare; and looking for thē round about, with earneſt eyes. When behould, vpon the ſodayne, he perçeaued by the ſhining of the Moone, that a charriot drawen by burning horſes came ruſhing on towards him, and as ſoon as he had called vpon Ieſus, all that buſi-neſſe was ſwallowed vp before his eyes, by a ſudden ga-ping of the earth. Vpon this, he ſayd; *He hath caſt the horſe and the horſeman into the ſea; and ſome truſt in their chariots, and ſome in their horſes, but we will be magnifyed in the name of the Lord our God.* Many were his temptations, and many ſnares were ſet by the Diuels for him, day & night;all which if I would vndertake to relate, I ſhould exceed the meaſure of one vo-lume. How often would naked Woemen appeare to him, as he was reſting? How often would moſt ſumptuous dyet be ſet before him, when he was faſting? Sometimes the yelling wolfe,and the grinning fox,would be leaping ouer him, when he was praying;and when he was ſinging,ſome fight of *Gladiators*, would preſent it ſelfe; and one, as if he had bene killed, did once fall downe before his feet,deſiring buriall at his hands. He was praying, with his head bowed
C   downe

downe to the ground, and his mind being once diftracted
(according to humane fraylty) he had I know not what o-
ther thought ; when inftantly a nimble rider, got vpon his
backe, beating his fides with his heeles, and his necke with
his whippe, and fayd; *why fleepeft thou ?* & fcornfully laughing
at him as he fat, did aske him, when he was faynting, whether he would eat any prouender, or no ?

Now from the fixteenth years of his age, til the twentyth,
he declyned the heates, and raynes, in a poore fhort little
Houel, which he had woeuen of reeds, and boughes. Afterwards he built a little poore Cell for himfelfe, which is extant to this day. It had but the breadth of foure foot, and the
height of fiue; 'fo that it was lower then he; in length it
was a little longer then the extent of his body ; fo that you
would rather haue efteemed it to be a graue, then a houfe.
He cut his haire once euery yeare, and it was at *Eafter*. He
lay perpetually till his death, vpon the bare ground, with a
matte. He neuer wafhed that facke-cloath, which he had oce
put on ; affirming *that it was idle, to looke for neatnes in hair-
cloathes*; nor did he euer change any coat, till it were vtterly
worne out. The holy fcriptures, he had without booke; and
after his prayers, and the pfalmes, he would recite them, as in
the prefence of God. And becaufe it would be a long bufineffe to difcouer, ftep by ftep, how he rofe vp towards perfection in the feuerall ages of his life, I will briefly firft com-
prehend the hiftory thereof in groffe, and fo lay it before the
eyes of the Reader; and then I will in order, deliuer a more
particular Relation.

Between the one and twentyth, & the feauen & twentyth yeare of his age, he daily tooke for three yeares, a little
more then half a pint of pulfe, fteeped in cold water; and during the other three, he tooke dry bread with water, and falt.
From the feauen & twentyth, to the thirtyth, he was fuftay-
ned by wild herbes, and by the rootes of certaine plantes
taken rawe. From the one & thirtyth to the fiue & thirtyth,
he tooke for his dayly food, fix ounces of barly bread, and
fome kitchin herbes, but halfe boyled, and without oyle. But
obferuing that his eyes began already to dazle, and that his
whole

whole body grew to haue a kind of itch vpon it , and to be
ſubiect to an vnnaturall kind of roughnes ; he added oyle to
his former dyet ; and till the ſixtyth yeare of his age he ranne
on in this degree of abſtinence , not once ſo much as taſting,
either pulſe , or fruit or any other thing : At laſt , when he
found his body to be euen all ouerwrought , and conceiued
that his death was very neer at hand; from the ſixty fourth,
till the eightyth yeare of his age , he abſtayned euen from
bread alſo with incredible feruour of mind ; proceeding as if
he were but then newly entring into the ſeruice of God;
whereas others at that time , are wont to be more remiſſe in
their manner of life. But hauing foureſcore years of age there
were made for him , certaine little poore broths of flower
and herbs , which were broken or cut; the whole proportion
both of meat , and drinke , ſcarce arriuing to the waight of
foure ounces; & thus he wēt through the whole order of his
life ; & neuer broke his faſt till Sun ſet , though it were vpon
the higheſt feaſts, or in his greateſt ſicknes. But now it is time
that I returne to ſpeake particularly of thinges in order .

When he was yet dwelling in his houel, hauing eighteen
yeares of age, there came vpon him , certaine murthering
theeues, either as thinking , that he had ſomewhat, which
was worth the carrying away; or els , as houlding that it a-
mounted to be a kind of contempt of them, that a ſolitary
youth ſhould preſume not to be affrayd of theyr force . So as,
ſcouring that quarter , between the ſea and the Fens , from
the euening to Sūne riſing, & neuer being able to meet with
his lodging; but once hauing found him in broad day light,
what wouldeſt thou do (ſayd they) *if now the murthering theeues
ſhould come?* To whom he anſwered . *That the naked man feares
no theeues .* Whereupon they ſayd , *yet there is no doubt but thou
mayeſt be killed . I may* (ſaith he) *and therefore do I feare no murthering theeues , becauſe I am ready to dy.* But they, admiring his
conſtancy , and ſtrong faith, & confeſſing how they had been
wandring by night; and that theyr eyes had been blinded
from finding him, did make him a promiſe to lead a better life
from that tyme forward.

By this time , he had been two and twenty yeares in

that

that defart, and was generally knowne by fame, and publifhed ouer all the cittyes of *Paleſtine*; when in the meane while
a certaine woman of *Eleutheropolis*, who perceaued her felfe to
be neglected by her husband by reafon of her barrennes (for
already fhe had paffed fifteene yeares without yeelding any
fruit of mariage.) was the firft, who prefumed to breake in ,
vpon the Bleffed *Hilarion*. And he fufpecting no fuch matter,
fhe caft her felfe fodainly downe at his knees, and fayd : *Par-*
don this bouldnes, pardon this necefsity of myne. VVhy doe you turne
away your eyes? VVhy fly you from your ſuiter? Looke not on me as
a woman, but as a miſerable creature. Yet, this ſexe brought forth
the Sauiour of the world : not the whole, but the ſicke, need the
Phyſitian. At length he ſtayed, and looking after fo long time
vpon her, he demanded the reafon, both of her comming &
of her weeping, which as foone as he had vnderftood, he caft
vp his eyes to heauen, bidding her haue fayth ; and following her with teares, he faw her with a fonne at the yeares
end. This firft miracle of his, was illuftrated by another, &
greater.

　　Ariſtæne (the wife of *Elpidius* who afterward was Captaine of the Guarde) a woman of great nobility in her Country, and yet more noble among Chriftians, returning from
Bleffed *Anthony* with her husband and three children, made
ftay at *Gaza*, by reafon of her ficknes. For there, whether it
were by corruption of the ayre, or as it appeared afterward ,
for the glory of *Hilarion* the feruant of God, they were fur-
prifed all togeather, with a dangerous double Tertian, and
the Phyfitians defpayred of them all. The mother lay lamé-
ting loudly, and ſtill was running to and fro betweene her
three children, as if already, they had beene three coarfes;
not knowing which of them fhe was to bewaile firſt. But
vnderftanding that there was a certaine Moncke in the wildernes neere at hand, fhe forgot the trayne fit for a Matrone,
and only knew her felfe to be a Mother, and went attended
but by her maydes and Eunuches, and would fcarce be per-
fuaded by her husband, to eafe her felfe by ryding thither v-
pon a poore little Affe. When fhe arriued with him, fhe fayd:
I befeech you for the loue of Iefus, our moſt mercifull God, and by his
Croſſe,

Croße, and bloud, that you will reſtore me my three ſonnes; and that the name of our Lord, and Sauiour may be glorifyed in this Citty of the Gentils . But he refuſing, and ſaying that he would neuer go out of his cell, and being wont not only not to paſſe into any Citty, but not ſo much as into any little houſe, ſhe caſt her ſelfe proſtrate vpon the ground, crying often after this manner : *Hilarion thou ſeruant of Chriſt, reſtore me my children, let them, who were cheriſhed by* Anthony *in Ægypt, be preſerued in Syria by thee .* All they who were preſent wept, yea and euen he wept who denyed her ſuite . Why ſhould I vſe many wordes ? The woman would not away, till firſt he had promiſed her, that he would go to *Gaza* after Sunne ſet. As ſoone as he came thither, and had conſidered how they lay, & ſeen the dryed limmes of all the ſicke, he inuoked Ieſus. And (o admirable power) the ſweate broke out from them all, as if it had beene out of three fountaines . At the ſame tyme they tooke meat, and recouering the knowledge of their ſad Mother, and bleſſing God, they kiſſed the handes of the Saint . When this was knowne, and had beene ſpread farre & wide, men came crowding in vpon him, both out of *Syria* & *Ægypt,* ſo that many by occaſion thereof, grew to belieue in Chriſt, and profeſſed that they would be Monckes, for as yet there were no Monaſteries in *Paleſtine*; neither did men know of any Moncks in *Syria,* before *S . Hilarion*: he was the founder, he the inſtructer of men in this kind of life, and Inſtitute in this Prouince. Our Lord Ieſus had the old *Anthony* in *Ægypt* and *Hilarion* a younger man in *Paleſtine .*

    Facidia is a little towne of *Rinocorura* a Citty of *Ægypt ,* and ſome ten yeares ſince, a blind woman was brought from thence to the Bleſſed *Hilarion,* and being preſented to him, by ſome of his brethren (for by that tyme he had there many Moncks) ſhe related how ſhe had ſpent her whole fortune vpon Phyſitians . To whome he ſpake thus : *If you had giuen that to the poore, which you haue caſt away vpon Phyſitians, Ieſus , the true Phiſition would haue cured you .* But ſhe crying out, and begging mercy, he ſpit into her eyes, and inſtantly according to the exáple of our Sauiour, the like miracle was wrought .

    Moreouer a certaine Carter of *Gaza,* being poſſeſſed by a

D iuell,

Diuell, as he was in his Carte, grew all fo ftiffe, as that he could neither ftirre a hand, nor turne his head. Being therefore brought in his bed, and being only able to moue his tongue for help; he was tould, that he could not be cured, till he would belieue in Iefus, and renounce his old courfes. He belieued, he promifed, he was cured, and did more exult for the recouery of the health of his foule, then of his body.

There was befides, a mighty ftrong young man called *Marfitas*, of the territory of Hierufalem, who did fo glory in his corporall force, as that he would carry about feauen buſhells of corne a great way, and a long tyme, and he vaunted himfelfe to exceed euen big Affes in ftrength. This man was afflicted by a moft wicked Diuell, nor did he permit, that chaines, or fetters, or euen the barres of doores, fhould remaine whole. He had bitten off the nofes, and eares of many, he had broken the feet of fome, and the neckes of others; and had ftrocken all men with fuch terrour, that being loaden with chaines, and roapes, he was drawne like fome fierce Bull, towardes the Monaftery, by men who kept him in fit diftance, by ftrayning feuerall way. When the Brothers of the Monaftery faw him, they being all in a fright (for the man was of a wonderfull huge bulke) made it known to their Father. Now he, as he was fitting, required that the man fhould be brought before him, and let loofe; which being done, he fayd: *Bow downe thy head, and come hither*. He trembled, and turned his necke, nor prefumed he to looke him in the face, but laying downe all his fiercenes, he began to licke the feet of *Hilariõ* as he was fitting. And fo the Diuel, who had poffeffed the young man, being adiured and tormented, departed out of his body, on the feauenth day.

Neither is it to be concealed, how *Orionus*, a principall & very rich man of the Citty of *Aila*, which lyes clofe vpon the red fea, was poffeffed by a legion of Diuels, and brought to *Hilariõ*. His hands, his necke, his waft, his feet, were al loadē with yron; and his fierce gloomy eyes, did threaten men with extreme cruelty. Now when the Saint was walking with thofe Brothers, and was declaring fomewhat to them of holy fcriptures, the poffeffed man broke forth of theyr handes.

handes, who had held him ; and clafping-in the Saint behind
his backe, and lifting him vp on high, they all cryed out who
were prefent ; for they feared, leaft he fhould euen breake
that body in peeces, which was fo defeated otherwife with
fafting. But the Saint fmiling, fayd; *Neuer trouble your felues,*
but let me alone with my wraftler. And fo cafting backe his hand
ouer the others fhoulder, he touched his head, and laying
hould vpon his haire, he brought the man before him, and
held faft both his hands ; and treading with his feet vpon the
feet of the poffeft perfon, he often repeated thefes wordes :
Be tormented, o you troupe of Diuells, be tormented. And when
the party roaring out, and wreathing backe his necke, did
euen touch the ground with the crowne of his head. *Hilariō*
fayd : *O Lord Iefus, free this captiue, free this miferable creature; it*
is in thy power, as eafily to conquere many, as one. I fhall tell you a
ftrange thing. There were heard diuers voices, yea the con-
fufed clamour of whole people, proceeding out of the mouth
of that one man at once. This man being cured, came alfo,
not long after, with his wife and children to the Monaftery,
bringing many prefents with him in the way of gratitude.
Of whome the Saint asked this queftion : *Haue you not read,*
what Giefi, *and what* Simon Magus *fuffered, whereof the one*
tooke a reward that he might fell, and the other offered one, that he
might buy the guift of the holy Ghoft? And when *Orionus* had fayd
with teares, *Receaue my prefent, and do you beftow it vpon the*
poore. He anfwered : *Your felfe can beft tell, how to diftribute*
your owne goodes, you who walke vp and downe the world, & know
the perfons of poore people: but I, who haue giuen away, that which is
myne owne, why should I meddle with that of others? The name of
diftributing to the poore giues occafion of coueteoufnes to many ; but
true mercy hath no trickes. No man beftoweth goodes better then
he, who referues nothing to himfelfe. But the party being ftill in
griefe, and lying vpon the ground, *Hilarion* fayd : *Be not af-*
flicted, o my fonne, at this which I do, both for my good and for thyne
owne ; for if I take thy prefent, both I shall offend God, and the legi-
on of Diuells, will returne to thee.

But who can paffe ouer in filence, how one of *Maioma*,
the Staple of *Gaza*, who fquared ftones for building, vpon

the

the Sea coſt, not farre from his Monaſtery, being all defeated
by a Palſy, and brought by his fellow-labourers to the Saint,
did inſtantly returne againe to his worke. For that coaſt,
which ſpreades is ſelfe both before Paleſtine and Ægypt, being ſoft by nature, becomes rough, by reaſon that the ſand
growes by degrees into the nature of ſtone; and ſo grauell
ſticking to it by little and little, it becomes other to the hand,
though it become not other to the eye . There was alſo another called *Italicus*, a free man of the ſame towne, & a Chriſtian, who kept horſes for the *Circus*, which vſed to runne a-
gainſt other horſes of an Officer of *Gaza* who was a worſhip-
per of the Idoll *Marnas* . For it hath beene maintained in the
Citties ſubiect to the Roman Empire, euer ſince *Romulus* his
tyme, that in memory of that fortunate rape of the *Sabines*, &
in honour of *Conſus* the God of Counſaile, certaine charriots
ſhould runne ſeauen tymes round about the place, and the
victory ſhould be his, whoſe horſes could outſtrip and ouercome the reſt . This *Italicus* therefore, finding that his con-
current vſed the help of a Witch, who by the meanes of certaine diabolicall imprecations, did giue impediment to his
horſes, and add ſpeed to his owne, came to the Bleſſed *Hilarion* & begged of him, not ſo much that his aduerſary might
be diſaduantaged, as that himſelfe might be aſſiſted. It ſeemed an improper thing to the venerable old man, to imploy his prayers vpon ſuch toyes . And when he ſmiled, and
ſayd : *Why rather do you not beſtow the price of your horſes, vpon the
poore, for the ſaluation of your ſoule* ? He anſwered, That the
profeſſion, which he followed, was allowed, and that the
thing which he then deſired, was rather vpon conſtraint,
then choice; That a Chriſtian man might not indeed haue
recourſe to Magick-Arts, but rather deſire help from a ſeruāt
of Chriſt, eſpecially againſt them of *Gaza*, who were the aduerſaries of God, and inſulted, not ſo much ouer him, as o-
uer the Church of Chriſt. The Saint being therefore entreated by the Monckes, who were preſent, required that a cup
of earth, wherein he vſed to drinke, ſhould be filled with water, and deliuered to *Italicus*, which as ſoone as he had receaued, he ſprinkled the ſtable with that water, and the horſes,

and

and their riders, and the charriot, & the bars of the race. The people was in a wonderfull expectation of the euent : for the aduerſaries of *Italicus* had publiſhed all this buſineſſe with ſcorne ; and his fauourers did exult out of the certaine pro-miſe of victory, which they made to themſelues. But the ſigne being giuen, the horſes of *Italicus* fly away, and thoſe others were able to make no haſt ; the wheeles of *Italicus* charriots grew hot with ſpeed, but thoſe others were ſcarce able to keep ſight of the former. There was an exceſſiue noiſe made by the people, in ſo much as that euen the Pagans themſelues cryed out, that, *Marnas was ouercome by Chriſt*. But then the ad-uerſaries being mad with rage, made inſtance that *Hilarion* might haue had his proces framed, as being a Witch in fauour of Chriſtians. But in the meane tyme, that vndoubted victo-ry, both in thoſe preſent ſports of the *Circus*, and in many o-thers afterward, was the occaſion that very many were con-uerted to the Fayth of Chriſt.

There was a Virgin conſecrated to God, belonging to the ſame ſtaple towne of *Gaza*, to whome a young man dwelling neere her did make loue. Not preuailing in his enterpriſe, though he had beene frequent in touching, in ieſting, in ma-king ſignes, and whiſling, with the like, (which are wont to be a kind of preface, to the deſtruction of virginity) he made a iourney to *Memphis*, that vpon manifeſtation of the wound, which he had receaued, he might by meanes of Magicke arts, returne ſtrong enough to ſubdue the Virgin. So that after a yeare, being inſtructed how to proceed by the Prieſts of *Æſcu-lapius*, who was not wont to cure, but to deſtroy mens ſoules, he came with a mind full of preſumption, that he ſhould pre-uaile in his wickednes, and he cauſed certaine coniuring wordes, and prodigious figures, to be grauen in a plate of *Cyprian* braſſe, & to be conueyed by digging, vnder the threſ-hold of the virgins houſe. Inſtantly vpon this ſhe began euen to runne mad with loue, and caſting away the dreſſing of her head, ſhe fell to ſhake and toſſe her haire, to gnaſh with her teeth, and to cry out after the name of the young man. For the exceſſe of loue, had exalted it ſelfe euen into a meere rage. She therfore, being brought by her Parents to the Monaſtery,

was

was deliuered to the old man ; the Diuel beginning to howle
and confeſſing himſelfe in this manner : *I was remoued by force,
I was brought from thence againſt my will ; with what eaſe did I de-
lude men with dreames, when I was at* Memphis! *o the torments that
I endure* ! *Thou compelleſt me to go forth ; but I am tyed faſt vnder the
threshold* . *I departe not therefore , vnles the young man diſmiſſe me,
who detaines me* . To this , our old man ſayd : *Doubtleſſe thy
ſtrength is great , who art held ſo faſt by a little thread, and a plate of
braſſe* . *Declare how thou couldeſt preſume to poſſeſſe the virgin of God.
That I might keep her* (ſayd he)*a virgin* . *Thou keep her ſo , o thou
traytor of chaſtity* ? *VVhy dideſt thou not rather enter into him who
ſent thee* ? *To what end* (ſayd the Diuell) *should I enter into him ,
who already was poſſeſſed by a colleague of myne, the Diuell of loue* ?
But the Saint reſolued not to require , that either the young
man, or thoſe ſignes of Witchcraft ſhould be produced, till firſt
the virgin were free, leaſt either the Diuell might ſeeme to
haue departed vpon any other vſuall inchantments , or els
leaſt he ſhould be thought to haue giuen credit to the Diuels
ſpeach. And vpon this occaſion he tould them, how crafty
and deceitfull theſe Diuells are in their deuiſes. But he rather
reſolued, as ſoone as the Virgin was reſtored to health, to reproue her for doing theſe other thinges, whereby the Diuell
entred to take poſſeſſion of her .

His fame grew not only ouer *Paleſtine* , and in the neighbouring Cittyes of *Ægypt* and *Syria,* but throughout other
Prouinces moſt remote . For a neere ſeruant of the Emperour
Conſtantius, ſhewing well of what country he was by the
whitenes of his kinne and the brightnes of his haire (whoſe
nation lying betweene the *Saxons* and the *Allmans,* was not ſo
largely ſpread as ſtout, and among hiſtorians hath been called
Germany, but now enioies the name of *Franconia*)was poſſeſſed
anciently , that is to ſay , from his very infancy by a Diuell ,
who conſtrained him mightly to roare out, to fetch deep
groanes , and to gnaſh with his teeth . This man did ſecretly
deſire comodity of paſſage from the Emperour, but declaring
ingenuouſly the true cauſe to him . He carryed alſo letters of
fauour to the perſons, who had Cōſular authority in *Paleſtine,*
and ſo he was conducted to *Gaza* with mighty honour , and
atten-

attendance. And demanding of the Officers of that place, where *Hilarion* the Moncke remayned; they of *Gaza* being frighted, & withall conceauing, that he was fent by the Emperour, thought good to attend him to the Monaftery, both that they might exhibite due honour to the perfon recommē-ded, as alfo, that if there fhould be any memory of former wronges done to *Hilarion*, it might be defaced by this new act of obferuance. The old man was then walking in the deep fand, and was foftly repeating fomewhat to himfelfe of the Pfalmes; but feeing fuch a troupe approaching, he ftayed him felfe; and refaluting all the company, & giuing them a bene-diction with his hand, he required the reft to depart from thence within an houre; but that the party indifpofed, with his feruants and officers fhould remaine there; for he knew by his eyes and countenance, why he was come thither. The man therefore who was pofsefsed being in fufpenfe vpon the queftion, which was asked him, & fcarce touching the groūd with his feet, and roaring after a moft hideous manner, made his anfwere in the *Syrian* language, wherein *Hilarion* fpoke. And there you might haue feene the mouth of a Barbarian, which was only acquainted with the *Franconian* and *Latin* tongue, fpeake fo perfect *Syrian*, as that neither the hiffing part, nor the afpiration, nor any *Ideome* of the fpeach of *Pale-ftine* was wanting to him. He confeffed therefore, after what forte he had entred into that body. And to the end that his In-terpreters might alfo know what paffed (who vnderftood no other tongues but *Greeke* and *Latin*) *Hilarion* asked him fome queftions in *Greeke*. Who anfwering him alfo in the fame lā-guage, and difcourfing about many occafions of inchantmēts, and the great force of Magicke artes: *I care not* (fayth Hilari-on) *how thou entredft in; but I commaund thee, in the name of our Lord Iefus Chrift, that thou go out*. And when the party was cu-red, & was prefenting him with ten pound weight in gould, he on the other fide was cōtent to accept a barly loafe, which the old man offered him, with a plaine country kind of fim-plicity, and he was made to vnderftand thereby; that they, who liue vpon fuch food as that, value gold no more then durt.

But it is no great matter to tell of ſtrange thinges concerning men ; for brut beaſtes were daily brought to him ſtarcke
mad , among which there was a Bactrean Camell of hideous
bignes, who had euen ground many men to death, like duſt;
and there were aboue thirty perſons , who brought him thither at that tyme, with great noiſe , and all fettered with extreame ſtrõg ropes. His eyes looked red like blood, his mouth
foamed, his rowling tongue ſwelled ; but the noiſe of his hideous roaring went beyond al the other terrour that he ſtrok.
The old man therefore, commaunded him to be let looſe ; &
inſtantly, both they who brought him, and they who were
with the old man, did euery one of them fly away . Only he
went on alone to meet him, and ſayd thus in the *Syrian* language : *Thou doſt not fright me, a Diuell, by that ſo great bulke of thy
body ; for whether thou be in the little* Foxe *, or in the large Camell ,
thou art ſtill the ſame* . In the meane tyme, he ſtood ſtill with
one of his handes extended forth . And as ſoone as the Beaſt
was coming, all furious towards him, he ſuddenly fell down
and layd his head low and leuell with the ground ; all they ,
who were preſent, being in a wonder, that ſo great benignity
could ſo inſtantly follow vpon ſo great fury . But the old man
taught them, how the Diuell is wont to enter into Cattell,
for their ſakes who are the owners ; and that he hates men ſo
highly, that he deſires not only the deſtruction of themſelues,
but of whatſoeuer is theirs . Of this he propounded an example, how the Diuell before he was permitted to tempt the B .
Iob , killed all the goodes he had . And how it ought not to
make any man wonder, that vpon the commandement of our
Lord, two thouſand ſwine were caſt away by Diuels ; for that
was done, becauſe they who ſaw it, would neuer haue belieued that ſo great a multitude of Diuels was departed out of
one man, vnleſſe a mighty heard of ſwyne had periſhed al-
togeather ; and ſo, as if it had beene driuen by a multitude of
Diuells .

The tyme will fayle me, if I ſhall pretend to ſpeake of all
the wonderful thinges which were wrought by *Hilarion* . For
he was rayſed by our Lord to ſo great glory, as that the Bleſſed *Anthony* vnderſtanding of his manner of life, did willingly
write

write to him, & receaue letters from him. And if at any time there came ficke perfons towardes *Anthony* out of *Syria*, he would fay thus to them: *VVhy would you needs vexe your felues by vndertaking fo long a iourney., when you haue my fonne Hilarion at hand?* By his example therefore, there grew to be innumerable Monafteryes ouer all *Paleſtine*; & all thofe Monkes would come flocking towordes him with a kind of ftrife. When he faw this, he prayfed our Lord for his grace, and exhorted euery one of them to profit in the way of fpirit, faying: *That the figure of the world paſſeth, and that the other future life is the true life, which is obtayned by ſuffering incommodities in this preſent life*.

Being defirous to fhew them an example both of humility, and curtefy, he vfed vpon certaine dayes, before the tymes of vintage, to vifite the Cels of the Monckes. As foone as this was knowne by thofe Brothers, they all flocked to him, and being accompanied by fuch a guide as that, they went in circuit to the Monafteries, carrying their prouifiō with them; for fometymes they would arriue to the number of two thoufand perfons. But in proceſſe of tyme, euery little Towne growing glad of the intertainement which was to be giuen to the Saint, would bring in fome of their commodityes, to their next neighbouring Monckes. Now how great care he had, not to paſſe ouer any one brother vnuifited how meane foeuer or poore he were, this one thing may ferue to demonftrate, that he went into the defart of *Cades*, to vifit one fingle difciple of his with a huge troupe of Monckes. He came then to *Eluſa*, and it was by accident, vpon that day, when by reafon of an Anniuerfary folemnity, the whole people of the Towne was affembled in the Temple of *Venus*; for they worfhip her as *Lucifer*, to whofe veneration the Nation of the *Saracens* is addicted. Moreouer the Towne it felfe, for the moft part is halfe barbarous, by reafon of the fituation of the place. They hauing therefore vnderftood, that S. *Hilarion* paffed by that way (for he had often cured many of the *Saracens*, who had beene poſſeſſed by the Diuell) they came forth to meet him, by whole troupes, with their wiues and children, bowing downe their heades, and crying out to him in that *Syrian* word, *Barac*, that is, *Giue vs thy bleſsing*. Thefe men did he receaue with all humility and benignity , and befought them to worfhip God rather then ftockes and ftones; and withall he would abundantly weep, looking vp to heauen , and promifing them, that if they would beliaue in Chrift, he would come often to them . And a wonderfull grace of our Lord it was , that they fuffered him not to depart, till he fhould make a defigne, and draw the firft lines of that Church , which futurely was to be built in that place; and till their Prieft, as he was then already crowned for the offering of fome idolatrous Sacrifice, might be marked with the figne of Chrift.

In another yeare alfo, when he was going forth to vifite the Monafteries, and did fet downe in a lift by whome he would only paffe, and with which others he would ftay , the Monckes obferuing, that one of the company was fomewhat neer and fparing , and being defirous to cure that fault of his , they wifhed the Saint to ftay fome tyme with him. But why, fayth *Hilarion*, will you wrong your felues, and vexe him? Which as foone as that fparing Brother vnderftood, he was out of countenance, and they all drawing one way. had yet much a do to obtaine of him who was vnwilling, that his Monaftery might be in the nuber of them, where the Saint fhould lodge . Yet at length after ten dayes, they went to him; but in the meane tyme certaine Guards or Keepers were placed by him in the vinyard, where the Moncks were to paffe, & frighting fuch as came towardes them , by throwing ftones and clods of earth, and by vfing alfo the fling, all thofe guefts departed the next day , without eating fo much as one grape; the old man laughing at it, but yet not taking knowledge of what had paffed .

But being receaued by another Moncke, called *Sabas* (for it is fit that we name this liberall-hearted man, as we concealed that other, who was a mifer) they were all inuited by him into his vinyard, to the end that by eating grapes before dinner (for it was on Sunday) they might be refrefhed from their labour . The Saint then fayd : *Curfed be he who preferres the refe- ction of his body before that of his foule : let vs pray, let vs fing , let vs perforume our duty to God ; and then you may make haft to the vinyard.* Hauing performed this Office, and being afcended vp to a

higher

higher place , he bleſſed the vinyard , and ſo gaue his ſheep
leaue to feed vpon it. Now they were not fewer then three
thouſand eaters . And whereas the vinyard when it was yet
vntouched, was eſteemed likely to bring forth, but a hundred
veſſells of Wine, within twenty dayes after the owner made
three hundred . And that other ſparing Brother, making leſſe
wine then he was wont , did lament too late, that euen what
he had , was turned into veriuyce; which the old man had
foretould to many of the Brethren. He did in particular maner deteſt thoſe Monckes, who through a kind of infidelity ,
did hord vp any thing for the future , and did vſe either diligence, or coſt about their cloathing; or any other of theſe
thinges , which were tranſitory . And obſeruing that one of
the Brothers, who dwelt almoſt fiue miles from him, was too
carefull and curious in keeping his garden, and withall had
layd vp a little money , he droue him out of his ſight. And the
party deſiring to be reconciled, came to ſome of the Brothers,
and particulerly to *Heſychius,* in whome the old man tooke very much contentment . When therefore vpon a certaine day ,
the ſame party had brought a bundell of greene peaſe, as they
were in the cod , and *Heſychius* had ſerued it that euening vpō
the table , the old man cryed out and ſayd : *That he was not able
to endure the ſtincke thereof ; and withall demanded whence it came?*
Heſychius anſwering that a certaine Brother had preſented it ,
as the firſt fruites of his field : *Doſt thou not feele* (ſayth he) *a moſt
abominable ill ſauour, and that couetouſnes ſtinkes in the very peaſe ;
caſt them out to the Oxen, and ſuch brute beaſtes as thoſe , and ſee if
they will eate thereof?* Now he hauing layd them in the manger
(as he was bidden) the Oxen fell into a fright, and lowing
after an extraordinary manner , brake their teathers , and ran
euery one by a ſeuerall way . For the old man had this guift ,
that by the ſmell of bodyes , or garments , or other thinges
which any man had touched, he would know to what vice ,
or Diuell he was ſubiect .

But in the threeſcore and third yeare of his age , obſeruing
how great the Monaſtery was then growne to be , as alſo the
multitude of the Brothers who liued with him , & the troups
of other men who brought ſuch perſons thither , as were
taken

taken by feuerall difeafes, and poffeffed by vncleane fpirits, in
fuch fort as that the wildernes was ftuffed round about him
with all kind of people; he daily wept, and remembred his
former kind of life, with an incredible defire to recontinue it.
And being demaunded by thofe Brothers what he ayled, and
why he afflicted himfelfe, he fayd: *I am returned againe to the
world, and haue receaued my reward in this life* . *Behould the men
of Paleſtine, and the neighbour Prouinces, eſteeme me to be fome body ;
and vnder the pretext of gouerning a Monaſtery for the vfe and conue-
niency of the brothers, I find my felfe poſſeſſed of fome poore little ſtuffe
of my own* . This was kept by the Brothers, and efpecially by
Hefychius, who with an admirable kind of loue, was addicted
to the veneration of the old man. But when he had lamented
in this fort, for the fpace of two yeares, that fame *Ariſtane* (of
whom we fpake before) being the wife of the Captaine of the
Guard, but hauing no part of his afpiring condition, came to
Hilarion with intention alfo afterwards to go on towards *Anthony* . To her he fayd weeping: *And I alfo would be glad to go, if
I were not kept prifonner in this Monaſtery, & if indeed it were to any
purpofe; now it is two dayes, fince the whole world is depriued of fuch
a Father.* Shee belieued it, and forbore her iourney: & within few dayes after, a meffenger came, by whome fhe heard
the newes, that *Anthony* was dead.

Let others wounder at the Miracles, which *Hilarion*
wrought, let them wounder at his incredible abftinence, his
knowledge, and his pouerty. For my part I am not fo much
amazed at any thing in him, as that he could fo tread honour
and glory vnder his feet. There came to him Bifhops, Priefts,
whole flockes of Religious perfons, and Moncks, and Matro-
nes alfo, which is a great temptation; and from all fides,
both out of the Citties, and Fieldes, there came multitudes of
common people, yea and Iudges alfo, and great perfons, that
they might be able to get fome bread or oyle, which had
beene bleffed by him. But he on the other fide, had his mind
fixed vpon nothing but fome wildernes: fo that one day, he
he refolued to be gone, and hauing procured a little Affe (for
he was then fo confumed with fafting, that he was fcarce a-
ble to go) he meant to vndertake his iourney with all fpeed.

Now

Now as foone as this was knowne, it wrought vpon the world there about, as if fome defolation had been at hand, & as if the Courts of Iuftice were to haue been fhut vp in *Paleftine* for fome extreme calamity which had happened . And there grew to be affembled, aboue ten thoufand perfons, of both fexes, and feuerall ages, for the ftaying of him. Whereas he inflexible to their prayers, and fcattering the fand with the end of his ftaffe fayd thus to them : [*I will not make my Lord a lyer, nor can I endure to fee Churches ouerturned, nor the Altars of Chrift troden vpon, nor the blood of my children fpilt.* All they who were prefent, vnderftood that fome fecret had beene reuealed to him, which he would not confeffe; but yet howfeuer, they watched him, that he might not get away. He therefore refolued, and he tooke them all to witneffe, that he would not taft either meat or drinke, till he were difmiffed; & fo after feauen days of his rigorous fafting, he was at length releafed. And bidding very many of them farewell, there came yet to *Betilium,* a huge troupe of followers; but yet perfwading thofe multitudes, to returne, he chofe out forty Monckes, who might make and take prouifion, and were able to goe fafting, that is to fay, not to eat till Sunfet. The fifth day therefore he came to *Pelufium,* and hauing vifited thofe brothers, who were in the *defart* neer at hand, and who remayned in that place which is called *Lychnos,* he went forward after three dayes, to the fort of the *Theubatians,* to vifit *Dracontius* the Bifhop and Confeffor, who liued there in banifhment. The Bifhop being incredibly comforted by the prefence of fo great a perfon, after three dayes more, & with much a do, our old man went to *Babylon,* that he might vifit *Philo* the Bifhop, who was alfo a Confeffor. For *Conftantius* the King, who fauoured the herefy of the *Arrians,* had fent them both out of the way into thofe feuerall places. But *Hilarion* going from thence, after three other dayes, came to the towne called *Aphroditos,* where meeting with *Bayfanes* the Deacon, (who by reafon of the vfuall great want of water in that defart was wont to hire out Camels and dromedaries, to fuch as went to vifit *Anthony,* and fo conduct them to him) he confeffed to thofe Brothers, that the Anniuerfary of *Anthonyes*

E   death

death was at hand, & that he was then to celebrate the same
to him by watching all that night, in that very place where
he dyed. After three dayes therefore of trauaile, through that
vaft and horrible defart, at length they came to a huge high
mountaine, where they found two Monckes, *Isaac* and *Pelu-
fianus*; which *Isaac* had beene *Anthonyes* interpreter. And becaufe occafion is heere fo fairely offered, and that already we
are vpon the place, I will in few wordes defcribe the habitation of fo great a perfon, as *Anthony* was.

There is a high and ftony mountaine, of a mile in circuit,
which hath aboundance of fpringing water at the roote therof. The fand drinketh vp part, and the reft fliding downeward
grows by little and little to make a brooke; vpon the banks
wherof, on both fides, the innumerable Palme-trees, which
grow there, giue both great comodity & beauty to the place.
There you might haue feene our old man paffe nimbly vp &
downe with the difciples of Bleffed *Anthony*; heere they fayd
he fung; heere he prayed; heere he wrought; heere when he
was weary he vfed to reft. Thefe vines, and thefe little trees
did he plant himfelfe: this little bed of earth did he compofe
with his owne hands: this poole did he contriue with much
labour, for the watering of his garden: with this Rake, did he
vfe to breake vp the earth many yeares. He lay in the lodging of *Anthony*, and kiffed that place of his repofe, which as a
man may fay, was yet warme; his Cell was of no larger meafure, then fuch a fquare wherein a fleeping man might extend himfelfe. Befides this, in the very higheft top of the
mountaine, which was very fteep, and could not be afcended
but by circling, there were two other Cells of the fame proportion, wherein he would ftay fometymes, when he had a
mind to fly from the frequent recourfe of comers, and the couerfation of his Difciples. Now thefe two were hewen out
of free ftone, and had no addition but of doores. But when
they were come to his garden; do you fee fayd *Isaac*, that part
thereof, which is the orchard, fet with young trees, and fo
greene with herbes? Almoft three yeares fince, when a heard
of wild Affes came to deftroy it, he willed one of the leading
Affes to ftay, and beating the fides of it with his ftaffe: *How
chaunceth*

chaunceth (fayth he) *that you eat of that which you did not fow?* And from thence forth, when they had druncke their water, for which they came, they would neuer touch tree, or fruit any more. Our old man defired befides, that they would fhew him the place of *Anthonyes* tombe: but they leading him apart, we are yet vncertaine, whether they fhewed it or not. They fay, that the reafon why *Anthony* commanded it to be concealed, was for feare leaft one *Pergamus*, who was a very rich man in thofe partes, fhould carry the Saints body to his village, & fo there erect a fhryne.

But now *Hilarion* returning to *Aphrodites*, (and adioyning oly two of his Brothers to himfelfe) remayned in the defart, which is next that place, in the practife of fo great abftinence and filence, as that he fayd, he began to ferue Chrift but then. Now then it had beene about three yeares, when the heaué̃s feemed to be fhut, and had dryed vp the earth; fo that they vfed to fay, that euen the Elements did lament the death of *Anthony*. Neither did the fame of *Hilarion* ly hidden from the inhabitants alfo of that place; but the men & woemen there, hauing their faces all growen wanne and worne with hunger, came crowding to defire fome fhowres of rayne of the feruant of Chrift, that is, of the fucceffour of the Bleffed *Anthony*. As foone as he beheld them, he was ftricken with ftrange griefe, and cafting his eyes vp to heauen, and rayfing both his handes on high, he inftantly obtayned what they defired. But behould that dry and fandy country, as foone as it was wel watered with raine, budded forth vpon the fudden fuch a multitude of Serpents, and other venemous creatures, that innumerable perfons had inftantly perifhed, if they had not made recourfe to *Hilarion*. But all thofe Sheepheards, & Country people, applying certaine Oyle which he had bleffed, did affuredly recouer their health. Yet perceauing himfelfe to be alfo obferued there with ftrange kindes of honour, he went on to *Alexandria*, & refolued to proceed from thence to that defart of the more remote *Oafa*: and becaufe from the firft tyme that he had beene a Moncke, he had neuer remayned in any Citty, he turned a while to certaine Brothers wel knowne to him in *Brutium* not farre from *Alexandria*, who

when

when they had receaued the old man with an admirable kind
of ioy, they fuddenly heard (the night being then at hand) that
his difciples were making ready his Affe, and that he was prouiding to be gone. And therfore cafting themfelues at his feet
they defired him to change his mind, and then lying alfo proftrate before the threfhold of the doore, they profeffed that
they would rather dy, then loofe fuch a gueft. He anfwered
them after this manner: *I make haft to be gone, for the preuenting
of your trouble; and you shall be fure to know heereafter, that I went
not hence fo fuddenly without caufe.* The next day therefore they
of *Gaza* went forth with their officers (for they knew that *Hilarion* was come thither the day before) and they entred into
the Monaftery; and when they found him not there, they
fayd thus to one another: *Are not thofe thinges true, which we haue
fayd of this man? A Magitian he is, and knowes future thinges.* But
the Citty of *Gaza* (when once *Hilarion* was gone out of Paleftine, and *Iulianus* had fucceeded in the Empire, (hauing already deftroyed the Monaftery) made a petition to the Emperour for the death of *Hilarion* and *Hefychius,* and they obtayned
it, and warrants were fent out through the whole world, that
they fhould be fought. *Hilarion* therfore being gone from *Brutium,* entred into *Oafa* by an impenetrable kind of defart, and
there hauing fpent little more or leffe then a yeare, he could
only thinke of fayling ouer to fome Ilandes; that whome the
earth had publifhed, at leaft the Sea might conceale: for the
fame of him had alfo arriued, as farre as that place, where the
he was, and now he could no longer hide himfelfe in the Ea-
fterne partes of the world, where he was knowne to fo many
both by reputation, and perfon. About that very tyme *Adrianus* a difciple of his, came fuddenly to him out of Paleftine,
bringing newes that *Iulian* was flaine, and that a Chriftian
Emperour began to raigne, and that it became him to returne
ro the Relickes of his Monaftery. He heard, but detefted that
motiõ, & hauing procured a Camell, he came through a vaft
folitude to *Paretonium,* a Sea-towne of *Libya*: but the vnfortunate *Adrian,* being willing to returne to Paleftine, and feeking
to enioy his former glory vnder the title of his Mafter, did
him many wronges, and at laft hauing truffed vp thofe things
togeather

togeather, which had beene sent to *Hilarion* by certaine Brothers, he went away without his priuity. Vpon this occasiõ
(because we are not likely to haue any other) I will only tell
you, for the terrour of such as despise their Maisters and teachers, that shortly after, this man did rot of the Kings euill .

The old man therefore, hauing one of *Gaza* with him,
did embarke himselfe vpon a ship, which was bound for *Sicily*,
and when by the sale of a booke contayning the Ghospell
(which himselfe being young had written with his owne hã-
des) he meant to haue payd for his passage; the Masters sonne
was suddenly possessed by a Diuell, about the middest of the
Adriatike sea, and began to cry out, and say : *Hilarion, thou seruant of God, why dost thou not permit vs to be in safety, euen at Sea* ?
*Giue me day till I may come to land, least being cast out heere, I be
precipitated into the Abysse.* He made answere to him thus : *Stay,
if my God will let thee stay ; but if he will cast thee out, why dost thou
lay it to my charge, who am a sinnefull man, and a beggar* ? This he
sayd, least the Marriners, and Marchants, who were in the
ship should publish him, when they came to land . But soone
after this, the boy was freedy both his father and the rest, who
were present giuing their wordes, that they would not name
him at all . Being entred within *Pachinum*, which is a Promõ-
tory of *Sicily*, he offered the Maister his booke of the Ghospels
for the passage of himselfe and the man of *Gaza*, which Maister euen from the first had no mind to receaue it, especially
when he saw that they had nothing but that booke, and their
cloaths, and so at last he swore he would not take it. But the
old man being inflammed through the experimentall comfort
he had in being poore, did reioyce so much the more, both
because in very deed he had nothing of this world, and for
that he was also esteemed a beggar by the Inhabitants of
that place . And yet doubting least some Marchants, who v-
sed to come out of the Easterne parts, might detect him, he
fled towardes the In-land, that is, some twenty miles from
the Sea, and there in a kind of wild little Country, making
daily vp some fagot of wood, he would lay it vpon the backe
of his disciple ; and that being sold in the next Towne did
help them to some very little bread, which might serue by

way of reliefe, both to themſelues, and ſuch others as by
chaunce vſed to paſſe that way.

But indeed according to that which is written, *The Citty
placed vpon a hill cannot be concealed* . For when a certaine Buckler-maker was tormented in S . *Peters* Church at Rome, the
vncleane ſpirit cryed out in him after this manner : *Some few
dayes ſince Hilarion the ſeruant of Chriſt came into Sicily, and no mā
knowes him, and he thinkes he lyes ſecret there; but I will go, and reueale him* . Soone after this, the ſame man ſhipping himſelfe at
Porto with his ſeruants, arriued at *Pachinum*, & the Diuel conducting him, till he might proſtrate himſelfe before the little
poore cottage of the old man, he was immediatly cured. This
ſirſt miracle of his in *Sicily*, drew an innumerable multitude
of ſicke men, as alſo of deuout perſons to him; ſo farre forth,
that a certaine man of much quality being ſicke of a Dropſy,
was cured by him the ſame day he came thither : who afterwardes being willing to make him many preſents, heard the
Saint vſe this ſaying of our Sauiour to his Diſciples, *Freely you
haue receaued, freely giue* .

Whileſt theſe thinges were doing in *Sicily*, *Heſychius* his
diſciple went looking the old man ouer the whole world, making diſcouery vpon the Sea-coſts, and penetrating euen into
the deſarts, & hauing in fine this only confidence, that wher
ſoeuer he ſhould be, it was not poſſible for him to be long concealed. When therefore three yeares were ſpent, he vnder
ſtood at *Methona* by a certaine Iew (who was ſelling certaine
traſh to the people) that a Chriſtian Prophet had appeared in
Sicily, working ſo many miracles and wonderfull things, that
he might be held for one of the auncient Saints . Being asked
concerning his habit, his gate, his language, & eſpecially his
age, he could make no anſwere; for he affirmed that he knew
not the man, but by report . Entring therefore into the *Adriaticke*, he came with a proſperous wind to *Pachinum*, & enquiring after the fame of our old man, in a certaine little towne
which was ſeated vpon that crooked ſhoare, he found by the
vniforme relation of them all, where he was, and what he
he did : all they wondring at nothing ſo much in him as that,
after ſo many ſignes, and miracles, he had not taken ſo much
as

as a bit of bread, of any man in thofe partes . And to make fhort, the holy man *Hefychius,* coming at length to caft himfelf at his Maifters feet, and to water them with his teares, was rayfed vp by him, & after the difcourfe of two or three dayes, he vnderftood by him of *Gaza,* that the old man would now no longer remaine in thofe partes, but that he would go on, to certaine Barbarous nations, where his name and language might be vnknowne. He lead him therefore to *Epidaurus,* a Towne of *Dalmatia,* and remayning a few dayes in certaine partes neere by, he yet could not ly concealed. For a Dragon of wonderfull bignes, whome in their tongue they call *Boas,* in regard they are fo great as to fwallow vp whole Oxen, wafted all that Prouince farre and neere, and drawing to him-felfe with the force of his breath, not only heards of Cattel, & flockes of fheep, but Country people alfo and Shepheards, he would fucke and fwallow them vp. When therefore he had firft fent vp his prayer to Chrift, & had appointed a great pile of wode to be prepared, he called the monfter, & com-maunded him to clime vp that maffe of wood, and he put fire to it vnderneath: and fo (the whole people looking on) he burnt vp that vaft and moft cruell beaft. But he being in great difficulty, what he were then beft to doe, and which way to turne himfelfe, was preparing to make another flight. And reuoluing the moft folitary countryes in his mind, he grieued, that whileft his tongue was filent, his Miracles would not hould their peace.

At that tyme, the Seas tranfgreffed their boundes, vpon that earthquake of the whole world, which happened after the death of *Iulian.* And as if God would threaten men with fome new deluge, or els that all thinges were to returne into their firft *Chaos,* fo hung the fhips, being ho yfed vp to the ftee-py tops of thofe mountaines. Which as foone as they of *Epidaurus* faw, namely thofe roaring and raging waues, and that maffe of waters ; and that whole mountaines were brought in vpon the fhoares, by thofe rapid floods, (being in feare of that which already in effect they found to be come to paffe, that the Towne would vtterly be ouerwhelmed) they went on to the old man, and as if they had beene going to a battell, they

they placed him for their Captaine vpon the fhoare. But as foone as he had made three fignes of the Croffe vpõ the fand, and held vp his handes againft the Sea, it is incredible to be tould into what a huge height it fwelled, & ftood vp before him, and raging fo, a long tyme, and being as it were in a kind of indignation, at the impediment which it found; it did yet by little & little flide backe againe into it felfe. And this doth *Epidaurus*, and all that Region proclaime euen to this day, & mothers teach it to their children, that fo the memory thereof may be deliuered ouer to pofterity. That which, was fayd to the Apoftles, *If you haue fayth, and shall fay to this mountaine,. tranfport thy felfe into the fea, and it shall be done*, may truely and euen litterally be fullfilled now, if any man haue the fayth of an Apoftle, or fuch fayth as our Lord commanded them to haue. For wherin doth it differ, whether a mountaine defcend into the Sea, or els whether huge mountaines of water, grow fuddenly hard, being as if they were of ftone, iuft befor the feet of the old man, and that yet on the other fide, they fhould runne fluid and foft. The whole Citty was in a wonder, and the greatnes of the miracle was publickly knowne as farre as *Salon*. But as foone as the old man vnderftood thereof, he ftole away by night in a little boate, & within two dayes after, finding a Marchants fhip, he went on towards *Cyprus*. But the Pirates then, betweene *Malea* and *Cythera*, hauing left their fleet vpon the fhoare (which was not gouerned by way of mafts, and fayles, but by longes pooles) were coming towardes our Paffingers, in two large Brigantines, with the waues beating vpon them on euery fide. All the Marriners who were in his fhip, began to quake, to weep, to runne vp and downe, to make their long poles ready; and (as if one meffenger were not fufficient) to crow'd in vpon the old mã, and to tell him that the Pirates were at hand. Whome behoulding, before they were yet come necre, he fmiled, and turning towardes his difciples fayd: *Why are you frighted, O yee of little fayth? Are thefe men more in number, then Pharaos army? yet all that was drowned by the will of God*. Whileft he was yet fpeaking, that multitude of enemies came on with the ftemme of their boates all in a foame, and were then clofe vpon him,

within

within a ftones caft. He therefore went to ftand in the prow of his fhip, and ftretching forth his hand againft the affailáts, he fayd: *Let it fuffice that you are come fo farre*. O wondrous ftrãge thing to be belieued! The Boates did inftantly fly of, & the men were ftill ftriuing the cõtrary way with their oares, but yet the boates ftill gaue backe towardes their Pup. The Pirates were amazed at it, ftill refoluing not to retire: but yet though they laboured with the imploiment of their whole ftrength, that they might reach the fhip, they were ftill borne away towardes the fhoare, with farre greater fpeed, then they came from thence.

I forbeare to fpeake of the reft, leaft I fhould feeme to extend my felfe too farre in the relation of this miracles. This only I will fay, that whileft he was fayling among thy *Cyclads* the noyfe of impure fpirits was heard to be crying out from the Citties and Townes there abouts, as if they were approaching towardes the fhoare. He therefore being come to *Paphos*, that Citty of *Cyprus* (which hath beene fo ennobled by the inuention of Poets, and which being fallen by frequent earthquaks, doth now by the only appearance of the ruines, fhew what formerly it had beene) liued obfcurely within two miles of that place, & was glad that he might fpend thofe few dayes in peace. But twenty dayes more were not fully paffed, when throughout that whole Iland, all thofe perfons who were poffeffed with vncleane fpirits, began to cry out, that *Hilarion* the feruant of Chrift was come, & they muft haften towards him. This did *Salamina*, this did *Curium* and *Lapetha*, and this did all thofe other Cittyes proclaime, moft of them affirming, that indeed they knew *Hilarion*, and that he was the true feruant of God, but that they knew not where he kept. So that within thirty or few dayes more, there came to him two hundred poffeffed perfons, as well men, as woemen. As foone as he faw them, he did fo grieue, that they would not giue him leaue to be quiet; and (being cruell after a fort, in the way of reuenge vpon himfelfe) he did fo whip vp thofe fpirits by the extreame inftance of his prayers, that fome of the poffeffed were prefently deliuered, others after two or three dayes, and all within the compaffe of a weeke. Staying therfore

F

fore

fore there two yeares, and euer being in thought how to fly
away, he fent *Hefychius* into Paleftine to falute his Brethren,
and to vifit the afhes or ruines of his Monaftery, with order,
that he fhould returne the next fpring after. Now though v-
pon the former returne of *Hefychius* thither, *Hilarion* refolued
to haue gone againe into *Ægypt*, and namely to certaine places which are called *Bucolia*, becaufe no Chriftiãs were there,
but it was a fierce and barbarous nation: *Hefychius* did yet per-
fuade him that he fhould rather procure to find out fome more
retired place in that very Iland where he was. And when after long fearch in all thofe partes, *Hefychius* had found one, he
conducted him twelue miles of from the Sea into the middle
of certaine feeret & craggy mountaines, to which a man was
hardly able to afcend, euen by creeping vpon his handes and
knees. He entred then, and contemplated that fo retyred and
terrible place, enuironed on all fides with trees, and hauing
ftore of water defcending from the brow of the hill, and a
little kind of very delightfull garden, and great ftore of fruit-
trees, the fruit wherof he yet did neuer tafte. There were alfo
the ruines of a moft ancient Temple, from whence (as himfelf
related, and his difciples teftify to this prefent day) there was
heard the noyfe of fuch an innumerable multitude of Diuels,
as that a man would euen conceaue it to haue beene fome Army. He was much delighted with this, as finding that he had
Antagonifts at hand; and there he dwelt fifteen yeares, and in
that laft part of his life, he was much comforted by the often
vifits of *Hefychius*. For otherwife by reafon of the great difficulty and cragginee of the place, and the multitude of Ghofts
which were vulgarly fayd to be walking there, either very
few or none, had both the power and the courage to go vp
thither. But yet vpon a certaine day, going out of his little
gardẽ, he faw a man, who had the Palfy in all his limes, lying
before his dore, and he asked *Hefychius*, who that was, and
how he had beene brought thither? The ficke man anfwered
and fayd that formerly he had beene the Steward of a little village, to the confines whereof that very garden belonged,
wherein they were. But the old man weeping, & ftretching
forth his hand to the ficke perfon, who lay before him, fayd:

I require thee in the name of our Lord Iesus Christ, that thou ryse and walke. An admirable haſt was made, for the wordes were yet but tumbling out of the ſpeakers mouth, and euen very then, his limmes being growne ſtrong, were able to ſupport him. Now as ſoone as this was heard, the difficulty of the place and of the way, which was euen almoſt impenetrable, was yet ouercome by the neceſſityes of men; the people round a-bout hauing no care more at heart then to watch, that by no meanes he might get away. For already there was a rumour ſpread of him, that he could not ſtay long in a place; which yet he was not ſubiect to, as being obnoxious to any leuity, or childiſh humour; but to the end that he might fly from ſo-nour, & importunity by that meanes: for the thing to which he euer aſpired, was a remote and poore priuate life. But in the eightyth yeare of his age, whileſt *Heſychius* was abſent, he wrote him a ſhort letter with his owne hand, in the nature of a kind of *VVill*, bequeathing al his riches to him; that is to ſay, his booke of the Ghoſpels, his coate of ſacke-cloath, his hood, and his little cloake; for his ſeruant dyed ſome few dayes be-fore. Now whileſt himſelfe was ſicke, there came many de-uout perſons to him from *Paphos*, and eſpecially, becauſe they had heard, he ſayd, that he was to depart to our Lord, and to be freed from the chaines of this body. With them, there came a certaine *Conſtantia* a holy woman, whoſe ſonne in law and daughter, he had freed from death by anoynting thē with oyle. He adiured them all, that they would not reſerue his body any one minut of an houre, after he ſhould be dead, but that inſtantly, they ſhould couer him with earth in the ſame garden, all apparelled as he was, in a haire-cloath, a hood, and a country caſſocke. By that tyme, he had but a very little heat, which kept his breaſt luke-warme, nor did any thing ſeeme to remaine in him of a liuing man, beſides his vn-derſtanding; only his eyes, being ſtill open, he ſpake thus: *Go forth, what doſt thou feare? Go forth, O my ſoule: what doſt thou doubt? It is now vpon the point of threeſcore and ten yeares ſince thou ſerueſt Chriſt, and doſt thou now feare death?* As he was ſpeaking theſe wordes, he rendred vp his ſpirit, and inſtantly being al couered with earth, the newes of his buriall was more ſpee-

dily

dily carryed to the Citty, then of his death. But as foone as the holy man *Hefychius* had vnderftood thus much in Paleftine, he went towardes *Cyprus* and (pretending that he had a mind to take vp his dwelling in the fame garden (that fo he might free the Inhabitants of the Country from the opinion, that they had need to keep fome ftrict guard vpon the body) he grew able to fteale it away, after the end of ten moneths, with extreame hazard of his life. He brought it to *Maioma*, whole troupes of Monckes, and euen whole Townes attending it; and he buryed it in his ancient Monaftery; his hairecloath, his hood, and his little cloake, being vntouched, and his whole body was alfo as entire as if he had beene the aliue, and it yeilded and odour fo very fragrant, as if he had beene pretioufly imbalmed.

And now me thinkes, that in the laft period of this booke I may not conceale the deuotion of that moft holy woman *Conftantia*, who vpon receauing the newes, that the dear body of *Hilarion* was now carryed away into Paleftine, did inftantly giue vp the ghoft, approuing euen by death her true loue to that feruant of God. For fhe had beene wont to fpend whole nights in watching at his fepulcher; and for her better help in prayer, to fpeake to him as with one who were ftill prefent with her. To this very day you may difcerne a wonderfull contention betweene them of *Paleftine*, and them of *Cyprus*; the former challenging his body, and the later his fpirit, and yet in both thefe places, great wonders are daily wrought; though more in the garden of *Cyprus*, perhaps becaufe his heart was more fet vpon that place.

FINIS.

THE

THE LIFE OF
S. MALCHVS

WRITTEN BY S. HIEROME.

THE ARGVMENT.

THE *life & captiuity of* MALCHVS, *who was borne in* Maronia *a towne of* Syria, *is described by* S. Hierome; *and in the perſon of* MALCHVS *he expoſes firſt to the Readers eye a ſolitary and famous Moncke; and then the ſame, as he was vexed and afflicted with temptations.*

THE LIFE.

THEY who are to fight ſome ſea battell, diſ-poſe themſelues firſt to ſtirre their ſhips in the hauen, or at leaſt in a ſtill Sea; they ſtretch their Oares; they prepare their iron handes & hookes, and they frame the ſouldiers, who are ranged out vpon the deckes, to ſtand faſt with vſe, though at the firſt their paces were vnequall, and their ſteps ſliding: that ſo what they haue learned in this picture of fight, may make them feare the leſſe, when they come to a true Sea battell. After this very ſort I, who haue long held my peace (for he hath made me ſilent, to whome my ſpeach is a torment) deſire firſt to exerciſe my ſelfe in ſome little work,

F3

and

and, as it were to rub off a kind of ruft from my tongue, that I
may come afterwardes to write a more ample hiftory . For. I
haue refolued if our Lord giue me life , & if my calumniators
will leaue perfecuting me (at leaft now that I am fled & fhut
vp from them) to write from the coming of our Sauiour till
this age; that is to fay, from the Apoftles, till the dregges of
thefe our prefent dayes; in what manner , and by the meanes
of what men the Church of Chrift was inftituted; and how it
came to growth; how it increafed by perfecution, and was
crowned by Martyrdomes; & how afterward when the Empire was put into the hand of Chriftian Princes, it grew greater in wealth , and power , but leffe in vertue . But of thefe
things at fome other tyme : now let vs declare what we haue
in hand.

There is a little Towne lying towardes the Eaft of *Ma-*
ronia , a Citty of *Syria*, vpon the point of thirty miles from *An-*
tioch . This towne after hauing beene in the handes of many ,
either abfolute Lords or Poffeffours of it otherwife, came at
laft (when I being a young man remained in *Syria*) into the
hands of Pope *Euagrius* a neere friend of myne; whome therefore I haue named now , to fhew by what meanes I might
come to know that, whereof I am about to write. In that
Towne therefore there was a certaine old man called *Malchus,*
whome we in Latin may call *King* . A *Syrian* he was by natiõ,
and by language, and indeed *Autochthon*. There was alfo in his
fociety a very aged decrepit woman, who feemed to be come
to the very dores of death . They were both fo diligently deuout, and fo did they weare the very threfhold of the Church
away, that you might haue taken them for the *Zachary* and *E-*
lizabeth of the Ghofpell , faue only that they had no *Iohn* betweene them . Concerning thefe two, I made diligent inqui-
ry of the dwellers there about , by what tye of coniunction
they were knit? of mariage? of confanguinity ? or of fpirit? Al
men made but this one anfweare, that they were Saints, and
perfons very pleafing to God ; and they tould I know not
what ftrange thinges of them : and fo being drawne on with
this delight, my felfe did fet vpon the man, and curioufly af-
king him the truth of things , he made me this account of himfelfe.

felfe . I am (fayth he,) my fonne, a husband-man of that tract which belonges to *Maronia,* and I was the only child of my Parents, who being willing to make me marry , as being the only fpring of their ſtocke, and the heire of their family; I an-fweared that I rather chofe to be a Moncke . By how great threates of my Father , and by how faire allurements of my Mother, I was perfecuted, to the end that I might be content to loofe my chaſtity; this only confideration may ferue to ſhew, that I forfooke my home, & fled from my Parents. And becaufe I could not goe Eaſtward (for that *Perfia* was fo neer at hand, where there was a guard of Roman fouldiers) I tur-ned my courfe toward the Weſt, carrying I know not 'what little thing with me, by way of prouiſion, which might only fecure me frō the extreamity of want. Why ſhould I vfe many wordes? At length I came to the defart of *Chalcis* , which lyes fomewhat Southward of *Imma* , and *Eſſa* , and meeting there with certaine Monckes, I deliuered my felfe ouer to their dif-cipline; getting my liuing by the labour of my handes, and reſtraining the luſtfullnes of fleſh and blood, by faſting. After many yeares , a defire came into. my mind of returning into my country ; & whileſt my Mother was yet aliue (for by that tyme I had heard of my Fathers death) to become a comfort of her widdowhood, and that then after this, hauing fould the little poſſeſſion which I was to enioy, I might beſtow a part vpon the poore, a part vpon erecting a Monaſtery, and a part (for why ſhould I bluſh to confeſſe my little confidence in the prouidēce of God ?) vpon the fupply of myne owne expence & charge. My Abbot began to tell me alowd , that it was but a temptation of the Diuell,and that the fubtile fnare of the old enemy, did but lurke vnder a fpecious pretext . That this was but to returne, as a dogge would do to his vomite : that many Monckes had beene thus deceaued : that the Diuell is neuer wont to ſhew his face without a maske . He propounded ma-ny examples to me out of Scripture, and that among the reſt, how in the beginning of the world *Adam* and *Eue* were fup-planted by a hope of diuinity . And when he could not per-fuade with me, he befought me euen vpon his knees, that I would not forfake him, nor deſtroy my felfe, nor looke backe

ouer

ouer the shoulder, when I had the plowgh in my hand. But woe be to me wretched man, I ouercame this Counsellour of myne by a most wicked kinde of victory conceauing indeed that he sought not my good, but his owne comfort. He went following me therefore out of the Monastery, as if he had beene carrying me to a graue, and giuing me at last a long farewell: *I shall see thee* (sayth he) *o my sonne, marked out by the burning iron of Sathan; I inquire not after thy reasons, nor do I admit of thy excuses; the Sheep which goes out of the fould, doth instantly lye open to the wolues mouth.*

Vpon the passage from *Beria* to *Eßa*, there is a desert neer the high way, where the *Saracens* are euer wandring vp and downe in their inconstant kind of habitations, the feare wherof make trauaillers resolue not to passe that way but in great troupes; that so their eminent danger may be auoyded by the mutuall help of one another. There were in my company men and woemen, old men, young men, and children to the number of seauenty in the whole; and behould those *Ismaeliticall* riders of their horses and Camels, rushed in vpon vs with their heades full of haire tyed vp with ribandes, their bodyes halfe naked, wearing but mantles, and large hose: at their shoulders hung their quiuers, and shaking their vnbent bows, they carryed also long dartes; for they came not with a mind to fight but to driue a prey. We were taken, we were scattered, and all distracted into seuerall wayes. As for me, who had beene the naturall owner of my selfe for a long tyme before, by lot I fel vnder the seruitude of the same Maister with a certaine woman. We were lead, or rather we were carryed loftily away vpon Camels, and being alwayes in feare of ruine through out all that vast desert, we did rather hang, then sit. Flesh halfe raw was our meat, and the blood of Camels our drinke. At length hauing passed ouer a large riuer, we came to a more inward desert, where being commanded (according to the manner of that nation) to adore the Lady, and her children whose slaues we were, we bowed downe our necks. But heere being as good as shut in prison, and hauing our attyre changed, I begun to learne to go naked; for the intemperatenes of that ayer permits not any thing to be couered,
but

but the fecret parts . The care of feeding the fheep was turned ouer to me; & in comparifon of a greater mifery, I might
account my felfe to enioy a kind of comfort , in that by this
meanes I feldom faw either my Lords, or my fellow-feruāts:
me thought I had fomewhat in my condition, like that of
holy *Iacob* ; I alfo remébred *Moyfes* : for both they had fometymes beene fhepheardes in the defert. I fed vpon greene
cheefe and milke ; I prayed continually, and fung thofe pfalmes which I had learned in the Monaftery . I tooke delight
in my captiuity , I gaue thankes to the iudgments of God for
my hauing found that Moncke in the wildernes , whome
I had loft in myne owne country . But, o how farre is any
thing from being fafe from the Diuell ! O how manifould,
and vnfpeakeable are his fnares! For euen when I fo lay hid,
his enuy made a fhift to find me out . My Lord therefore obferuing, that his flocke profpered in my hand, and not finding any falfhoud in me (for I knew the Apoftle to haue
commaunded, that we fhould faythfully ferue our Lords , as
we would do God) and he being willing to reward me ,
that thereby he might oblige me to be yet more faythfull to
him, gaue me that fhe-fellow-flaue, who had formerly been
taken captiue with me . And when I refufed to accept her,
affirming that I was a Chriftian, and that it was not lawfull
for me to take her for a wife, who had a husband yet aliue
(for that husband of hers had alfo beene taken togeather
with vs, and carryed away as the flaue of another Lord) he
grew all fierce and implacable towardes me , and euen like
a mad man began to runne at me with his naked fword, and
if inftantly I had not ftretched forth myne armes, and taken
hould of the woman, he had not fayled to take my life. And
now, that night arriued, which came too foone for me, and
was the darkeft that euer I faw . I lead this new halfe defiled wife, into a caue ; hauing taken bitter forrow for the y-
fher, who was to lead vs home from the wedding ; and both
of vs abhorred one another, though neither of vs confeft fo
much . Then had I indeed a liuely feeling of my bondage ,
and laying my felfe proftrate vpon the ground , I began to

bewayle the Moncke whome I had loft, faying: *Wretched creature that I am, haue I beene kept all this while aliue for this? Haue my grieuous finnes beene able to bring me to fo great mifery, as that hitherto being a Virgin, yet when now I find my head full of hoary haires, I should become a marryed man? VVhat auayles it me to haue contemned my Parents, my Country, and my goodes for the loue of our Lord, if now I doe that thing, for the auoyding whereof, I contemned all the reft? vnleffe perhaps all thefe miferies are come iuftly vpon me, becaufe I would needes returne to my Country? But tel me, o my foule, what are we doing? Shall I perish, or shall I ouercom? Shall I expect the hand of God, or shall I runne my felfe vpon the point of my owne fword? Turne thy fword vpon thy felfe: the death of thy foule is more to be feared, then that of thy body. It is a kind of Martyrdome for a man rather to haue fuffered death, then to haue loft his virginity. Let this witnes of Chrift remaine vnburyed in the wildernes; my felfe will be both the perfecutour & the martyr.* Hauing fpoken thus, I vnfheathed my fhining fword, in that darke place, and turning the point againft my felfe, I fayd: *Farewell vnfortunate woman, and take me rather as a Martyr, then as a marryed man.* But fhe cafting her felfe downe at my feet, fpake to me in thefe wordes: *I befeech you for the loue of Iefus Chrift, and I adiure you by the ftraightes, wherein we find our felues in this fad houre, do not caft the guilt of shedding your blood vpon me; or if there be no remedy, but that you will needs dye, turne firft your fword vpon me, and let vs rather be married thus in death, then otherwife. Although myne owne husband should returne to me, I would obferue chaftity, which I haue beene taught by my captiuity; yea I would keep it fo, as that I would rather wish that I might perish, then it. VVhy should you dy, rather then be marryed to me, who would refolue to dy, if you should refolue to marry? Take me to you, as the wife of chaftity, and efteeme more the coniunction of the foule, then of the body. Let our Lords conceaue vs to be man and wife; but let Chrift know vs to be as Brother and Sifter. VVe shall eafily perfwade men that we are marryed, when they fee that we do fo entirely loue one another.*

I confeffe I was amazed, and admiring the vertue of the woman, I loued her the better for that kind of wife:

but

but yet did I neuer fo much as behould her naked body; I neuer touched her flesh, for feare least I might loose
that in peace, which I had preserued in warre. Many dayes
passed on betweene vs in this kind of matrimony; this mariage making vs more acceptable to our Lords and Maisters,
as freeing them from all suspition of our running away: yea
fometymes it would fall out, that I might be absent in that
defert for a whole moneth togeather, like a Shepheard well
trusted with his flocke. After a long space of tyme, whilest
I was fitting alone in the wildernes, feeing nothing but
heauen and earth before me, I began to confider with my
felfe in filence, and to reuolue many thinges in my heart,
which I had knowne, when I conuerfed with the Moncks;
and especially I called to mind the countenance of that Father of myne, who had instructed, who had cherished, and
who had lost me. And whilest I was beating vpon thefe
thoughtes, I behould a flocke of Antes, to fwarme in a certaine straight passage, who carryed burdens euen greater the
their own bodyes; some of them had taken vp certaine feeds
of herbes with their mouthes, as if it had been with pincers;
others were carrying earth out of ditches, and would make
certaine fences against the entry in of water; some, remembring that there was a winter to come, tooke of graines of
corne, & brought the in, least the earth when it should grow
wet, might conuert the corne already gathered into new
corne for the next yeare; others carryed the bodyes of their
dead with a fad kind of folemnity; and (which yet is more
to be wondered at) there was none going forth, of all that
troupe, who would hinder any one that entred in, but rather if they difcouered any, who were in danger of falling
vnder their waight or burden, they would lend him their
fhoulders to keep him vp. What fhall I fay more? That day
fhewed me a pleafant obiect. Whereupon, remembring *Sa-*
lomon, who fendes vs to imitate the fharp fighted prouidence
of Antes, and stirring vp our floathfull mindes by their example; I began to be weary of my captiuity, and to afpire
towardes the Cels of Monkes againe, and to loue the refem-

blance

blance of thofe Antes, in that they labour in common, where nothing is proper to any one, but all thinges belong to all. When I went backe to my lodging, I fee the woman coming towardes me, nor was I able to diffemble the forrow of my heart. She asked me, why I was fo troubled? I tell her my reafons, and fhe exhorted that we might take our flight. I coniure her to promife filence; fhe giues me affurance, and fo continually whifpering about this bufines, we were layd and toffed betweene hope and feare.

I had in that heard two Goates of a huge bignes; which being killed, I make veffells of their skinnes, and I prepare their flefh, for our prouifion. And the firft euening when our Lords might conceaue that we were layd to reft, we fet vpon our iourney, carrying the skinnes and the meat. When we were come to a riuer, which was fome ten miles of, we commit our felues to the waters, hauing firft layd our felues vpon thefe skines, which were ftuffed out; and we holpe our felues with our feet, as it might haue beene with oares, that fo the riuer carrying vs downeward, and landing vs much lower on the other fide of the bancke, then where we put our felues into the water, they who followed vs might loofe the trace of our feet. But in the meane tyme our flefh being wet, and part of it alfo being loft, it did hardly promife vs food for three dayes. We drunke euen to fatiety, by way of prouifion againft the thirft which we were to haue afterward. We ranne, and yet euer looking behind our backes; & made more way by night then by day, partly by reafon of the danger, which might haue growne to vs by the *Saracens,* and partly through the exceffiue heate of the Sunne. Wretch that I am; I tremble euen whileft I am but telling it: and though indeed I be wholy now fecure, yet all my body quakes to thinke thereof. For after the third day, we faw a farre of in a doubtfull kind of fight, two men fitting vpon Camells, who were coming towardes vs at full fpeed: and prefently our mind, which was apt to foretel mifchiefe to vs, began to thinke that our Lord and Maifter had refolued our death; and that we euen faw the Sunne grow blacke to-

wardes

wardes vs . Whileſt we were thus in feare, & conceaued our ſelues to be betrayed by our footeſteps printed vpon the ſand; we founda Caue vpon our right hand, which pierced farre vnder ground . But fearing leaſt we might fall vpon ſome venemous beaſtes (for Vipers and Baſiliskes and Scorpions, & ſuch other creaturs, declining that great heat of the Sunne, are wont to betake themſelues to the ſhad)we entred indeed into the Caue ; but inſtantly at that very entráce, we committed our ſelues to a hollow, which was within vpon the right hãd, not daring to proceed any further on , leaſt by flying one kind of death, we might haue fallē vpon another: conceauing this within our ſelues, that if God will help vs as being miſerable, we ſhall be ſafe ; but if he deſpiſe vs, as being ſinnefull, we ſhall fall into the handes of death . What kind of heart do you think we had?What kind of fright were we in, when our Lord, & a fellow ſlaue of ours were ſtanding neere the Caue, and by the print of our feet were already arriued as farre, as that darknes would giue them leaue ? O death how much more grieuous art thou in expectation , then in effect! Euen againe my tongue growes to falter with feare and care, and as if my Lord were but now crying out vpõ me , I haue not the heart to whiſper out a word. He ſent his ſlaue to fetch vs out of the Caue ; himſelfe houldes the Camells, and hauing drawne his ſword , he expects our coming forth. In the meane tyme, that ſeruant being gone three or foure cubites on, we ſeeing him with his backe towardes vs, (for the nature of our ſight is ſuch, as that all things are darke to thoſe who enter into any obſcure place, after they haue beene in the Sunne) we heard his voice ſound through the denne: *Come forth you villaines.out, you who are deſigned for death . VVhat do you expect ? VVhy do you ſtay? get you out our Lord calls you, he expects you with patience* . Whileſt he was yet ſpeaking, behould we ſaw , euen in that darknes, that a Lyoneſſe already ruſhed vpõ that man,& hauing ſtrangled him, drew him all bloody in . Deare Ieſus , how full were we of terrour, and of ioy withall ! We perceaued our enemy deſtroyed , though our Lord and Maiſter knew it not . For

G3

when

when he faw the delay, he fufpeſted that we two had refifted one, and fo not being able to differ his wrath, he came
forward to the Caue with his fword in his hand, and reproa-
ching his flaue of cowardife, with a furious kind of rage, he
was firft feifed vpon by the Beaſt, before he came to our
retreate . Who are they, which can belieue, that the Beaſt
fhould fight for vs, in our owne prefence ? But being freed
from that feare, the like deftruſtion prefented it felfe before
our imaginations ; fauing that it was fafer to endure the rage
of a Lyoneffe, then the wrath of a man . We were afflicted
with feare, euen to the very heartes, and not venturing fo
much as once to ftirre, we expeſted the euent of the bufines,
in the middeſt of fo many dangers, being only defended, as
with a wal, by the confcience which we had of our chaftity.
The Lyoneffe being wary, leaſt fhe might chance to fall into fome fnare ; and finding that fhe was feene, takes faft
hould of her whelpes, and carryes them forth, and leaues the
lodging to our vfe . Neither yet were we fo credulous as to
breake out in haft ; but expeſting long, and fometimes thinking to go out, we neuer had a fancy, as if we were to fall v-
pon wild beafts . But at length, after the end of the next day,
the horrour in which we were being remoued, out we went
in the euening, and we faw fome kind of Camels, whome
for the exceffiuenes of their fpeed they call *Dromedaries*, rumi-
nating vpon thofe meates which they had eaten before, and
then drawing them downe againe into their ftomackes .
And we mounting on them, and being refrefhed with new
prouifion, arriued by that defert to the Roman Garrifons, v-
pon the tenth day after, & there being prefented to the Tri-
bune, we gaue him an orderly account of what had paffed .
From thence we were fent ouer to *Sabinus* the Gouernour of
Mefopotamia, where we receaued a iuft price for our Camels.
And becanfe that Abbot of myne, did now reft in our Lord,
when I was brought to that place, I reftored my felfe to the
Monckes, and I deliuered her ouer to the Virgins ; louing
her as my Sifter, but not trufting my felfe with her, as with
my Sifter . This ftory did *Malchus* being ould relate to me,
                                                when

when I was young: and now my felfe being ould, I haue deliuered it to you, and I prefent a hiftory of Chaftity to chaft perfons, aduifing fuch as are virgins to keep their chaftity with care. Tell you it ouer to pofterity, to the end that they may know, that in the mideft of fwordes, deferts and wild beafts, Chaftity can neuer be captiued ; and that a man who is confecrated to Chrift, may well be killed, but not conquered.

FINIS